Hollywood
behind the Wall

MANCHESTER
1824

Manchester University Press

For Chris, Hannah and Zoë

Hollywood behind the Wall

The cinema of East Germany

Daniela Berghahn

Manchester University Press
Manchester and New York
distributed exclusively in the USA by Palgrave

Published by Manchester University Press
Oxford Road, Manchester M13 9NR, UK
and Room 400, 175 Fifth Avenue, New York, NY 10010, USA
www.manchesteruniversitypress.co.uk

Distributed exclusively in the USA by
Palgrave, 175 Fifth Avenue, New York,
NY 10010, USA

Distributed exclusively in Canada by
UBC Press, University of British Columbia, 2029 West Mall,
Vancouver, BC, Canada V6T 1Z2

British Library Cataloguing-in-Publication Data
A catalogue record for this book is available from the British Library

Library of Congress Cataloging-in-Publication Data applied for

ISBN   0 7190 6171 7   *hardback*
EAN   978 0 7190 6171 4
ISBN   0 7190 6172 5   *paperback*
EAN   978 0 7190 6172 1

First published 2005

13 12 11 10 09 08 07 06 05   10 9 8 7 6 5 4 3 2 1

Typeset in 10/12pt Minion
by Graphicraft Limited, Hong Kong
Printed in Great Britain
by Bell & Bain, Glasgow

Contents

List of figures

Acknowledgements

The impetus to write this book came from three people in particular: when John Sandford and Seán Allan invited me to contribute to the first British conference on East German cinema, I discovered a research area that was – if not exactly uncharted territory – then at least a terrain that was beckoning to be explored further. Though I was enthused by this discovery, I might not have embarked on a project of such daunting dimensions, had it not been for the encouragement of my friend Britta Baron, who firmly believed in me and in the book that I wanted to write.

Researching DEFA has been an engrossing experience, not least because all those individuals and institutions concerned with the legacy of East Germany's erstwhile film culture have been so ready to share their invaluable insights with me in long conversations and extensive email correspondence. I should like to express my sincere gratitude to Ralf Schenk, Hiltrud Schulz, Erika Richter, Elke Schieber, Horst Pehnert, Egon Günther, Andreas Dresen, Helmut Diller and Hans-Rainer Otto for finding the time to answer my countless questions and for making the interviews the most fascinating and most memorable part of my research. Many thanks also to Wolfgang Klaue at the DEFA-Stiftung, Ines Pengel-Schönfelder at Progress Film-Verleih, Angelika Müller at Studio Babelsberg, Klaus Eder of FIPRESCI and Andy Engel at Artificial Eye for providing essential information or for helping me establish useful contacts.

I am equally indebted to everyone who helped me to access DEFA feature films at a time when only a few were as easily available as they are now through ICESTORM and the DEFA Film Library. Though I still cannot lay claim to having seen all of DEFA's 750 feature films, thanks to Kerstin Lommatzsch, Peter Franzke and Anne Harrap, who supplied me with hundreds of videos, I have managed to study a representative cross-section and, indeed, many more than I could possibly discuss in a book of this length.

Throughout my research in Berlin I benefited from the expert help of Herr Müller at the Stiftung Archiv der Parteien und Massenorganisationen der ehemaligen DDR im Bundesarchiv and Frau Kiel at the Bundesarchiv Filmarchiv who retrieved countless files of hard-to-find documents for me as well as archival treasures I did not even know existed. The library staff at the Filmhochschule für Film und Fernsehen Konrad Wolf in Babelsberg kindly permitted me to use their extensive collection of DEFA materials. Renate Göthe, in particular, has made my numerous visits to the press archive of the HFF productive and pleasurable. I also received a warm welcome at the Filmmuseum Potsdam where both Heidrun Schmutzer and Elke Schieber assisted me in finding stills and posters of DEFA films and in identifying the copyright holders. Many thanks to everyone who gave me permission to reproduce the enclosed illustrations.

The completion of this book would not have been possible without the kindness and encouragement of colleagues who vetted the project in its initial stages and provided critical feedback on draft chapters. My heartfelt thanks go to John Sandford, Richard Taylor, Barton Byg, Dina Iordanova, Paul Cooke and my friend Petra Pinger. The manuscript benefited greatly from their critical comments and intellectual guidance. However, I alone take full responsibility for any errors and oversights. I should also like to thank Matthew Frost and Kate Fox at Manchester University Press for their assistance and patience.

I gratefully acknowledge the generous research grants awarded to me by the Arts and Humanities Research Board and the German Academic Exchange Service, which provided the financial support for a sabbatical and a final research visit to Berlin. The School of Arts and Humanities at Oxford Brookes University granted me research leave when it mattered most. I am also indebted to my colleagues in the Department of Modern Languages, in particular to Seán Hand and Valerie Worth-Stylianou, for their help and encouragement. My sincere thanks go to my former colleague, Anna Richards, for her fabulous editorial work and, more importantly, for her friendship and moral support.

And finally, my deepest gratitude to my family, who have kept reminding me that there is life beyond *Hollywood behind the Wall* and who have filled my life with love and happiness over the past few years. Thank you, Chris, for giving me the time I needed to complete this book by being such a wonderful father to the girls.

Introduction

'Due to public demand, we're keeping *Goodbye Lenin!* for another fortnight', read the notice at my local cinema in Oxford where the film had been showing three times a day for three weeks already. At last, thirteen years after German unification, the popular imagination in the West was captured by a narrative about the East. The film marks a watershed in the cinematic discourse on the GDR and German unification. Whilst in the early to mid-1990s collective memories of the GDR revisited the trauma of living under a totalitarian regime, *Good Bye Lenin!* (*Goodbye Lenin!*, 2003) constructs a simulated memory of the GDR's erstwhile everyday culture that primarily reflects how West Germans imagined life on the other side of the Berlin Wall. Made by the West German director-scriptwriter team Wolfgang Becker and Bernd Lichtenberg the film consciously eschews the darker side of East Germany's past, suggesting instead that the limitations and restrictions which state socialism imposed upon the citizens of the 'workers' and peasants' state' were so bizarre that they were, in fact, immensely funny. Simulated and nostalgically embellished memories of the GDR take the shape of a media-collage, consisting of televised news programmes (authentic and forged), documentary and home-movie footage. *Good Bye Lenin!* is an ironic, thoughtful and humorous reflection on the missed opportunity to create a socialist utopia. In Germany, the film was seen by over six million viewers within the first six months of its release in 2003. Even more remarkably for a German film with a theme very specific to Germany, *Good Bye Lenin!* has been sold to more than sixty other countries (Osang 2003: 222).

Since the box-office success of *Good Bye Lenin!* the German media have been seized by an *Ostalgie-Welle* (a wave of nostalgia for the former East) that nobody would have imagined possible only a few years ago. The ex-GDR has become trendy. Its hammer-and-sickle ensign now features on fashionable clothes; books like Thomas Brussig's *Helden wie wir* (Heroes Like Us, 1995) and Jana Hensel's *Zonenkinder* (Children from the Eastern Zone, 2002) rank high in the German best-seller lists. Televised game shows that feature East German sports and media celebrities, celebrating the fun side of life under communism, achieve top ratings in both the old and the new federal states.

The *Ostalgie* phenomenon and the spectacular international success of *Good Bye Lenin!*, hailed as the most popular German film ever, mark an auspicious moment for anyone with a scholarly interest in the German Democratic Republic and, in particular, its film culture. Scholarly interest in 'Hollywood behind the Wall',[1] as East Germany's film industry has sometimes been referred to, has only really evolved in the West since the fall of the Berlin Wall and the demise of the socialist German state. Even so, an authoritative film history of German cinema that was published in the early 1990s privileges the cinema of the Federal Republic, relegating four decades of East German film culture to just forty pages, compared with 150 pages on post-war West German cinema (Jacobson, Kaes and Prinzler 1993). Likewise, the *BFI Companion to German Cinema* (Elsaesser and Wedel 1999) is very selective in referencing East German cinema. Only Sabine Hake's concise yet comprehensive survey on *German National Cinema* (2002) redresses this imbalance by examining the cross-border dynamics of image-making in the divided nation. Especially in view of the vast amount of scholarship that has been undertaken on post-war West German cinema, notably New German Cinema, much still needs to be done to compensate for the relative paucity of academic research on East German cinema.[2]

This book aims to shift the focus eastwards by providing a representative survey of feature films made by DEFA (Deutsche Film-Aktiengesellschaft), as the GDR's state-owned film studios were called, between 1946 and 1990, as well as those made by East German filmmakers after German unification.[3] By situating East German cinema in the broader contexts of international cinema and cultural history, I aim to make East Germany's still largely unknown film culture accessible to scholars of European Film Studies, German Studies and historians. Given the increasing prominence of East German cinema on university curricula in North America and Great Britain, this monograph provides a much-needed general survey which aims to complement the growing number of publications focusing on specific aspects or periods of East German cinema.[4]

Through this book I also hope to broaden interest in a part of German film history that has until recently been sorely neglected, not just because DEFA films have been much more difficult to access than West German films, but more importantly because scholars and audiences have been biased against films made in the GDR and in other Soviet bloc countries. With the exception of some internationally acclaimed masterpieces of East European New Wave cinema, the majority of films made behind the Iron Curtain have remained unknown in the West or have been summarily dismissed either as political propaganda or as depictions of drab socialist life, devoid of glamour or entertainment value. Mostly, their aesthetic qualities have been denied outright. Even in 1992, two eminent West German film scholars sarcastically commented that the only difference between DEFA's first film and its last was the addition of colour (Pflaum and Prinzler 1992: 178).

The films best suited to invalidate the prejudices commonly held against socialist film art – while admittedly conjuring up other ones instead – are those which transgress the boundaries of aesthetic and political orthodoxy and which, consequently, fell victim to state censorship. When, in 1990, a number of films that had been banned and shelved in the mid-1960s were released, they succeeded in attracting audiences to the cinema and scholars to take a fresh look at DEFA, primarily on account of the notoriety of their censorship histories. These conveniently confirmed the persistent and much-publicised Cold War stereotype of the repression of artistic freedom under state socialism. While the allure of the forbidden and the subversive was initially useful to awaken interest in Hollywood behind the Wall, fourteen years after the end of state socialism in the GDR and in Eastern Europe this line of enquiry is no longer productive. Therefore, this study endeavours to move beyond the still prevalent ideologically charged assessment of East Germany's cinematic legacy and its film industry, by re-evaluating the advantages and disadvantages of film production and circulation under state socialism and by providing a more balanced account of the rationale behind this system of cultural production (see Chapters 1 and 6).

I further propose to expand the range of discursive frameworks in which DEFA has to be considered and, thereby, shift the academic discourse on DEFA beyond the isolationist approach that was appropriate when DEFA was – at least for scholars in the West – a still largely uncharted terrain. On an imaginary map of national cinemas, German cinema is at the epicentre of the ideological divide between communism and capitalism. The cinema of the divided Germany, therefore, emerges as a microcosm which throws the fault lines of Cold War tensions and ideological contests into stark relief. In particular East German cinema is ambiguous in terms of its ideological and political allegiances within the Soviet bloc on the one hand, and its historical, political and cultural affiliations with West Germany on the other. In exploring DEFA's feature films it is, therefore, instructive to look eastwards and westwards in order to fully understand the ambivalent position which East German cinema assumes in the discursive frameworks of East European and Soviet cinema on the one hand and German national cinema on the other.

There are several good reasons to explore East German cinema in the context of East European cinema (see Trumpener 2002; Iordanova 2003: 15), not least because the disintegration of the so-called Eastern bloc post-1989 has given rise to a reassessment of its boundaries, as the former geopolitical division between Eastern and Western Europe has become invalidated. This has also resulted in a re-mapping of East European film history in the post-communist era, which now distinguishes between East Central European cinema (Hungary, Poland, the Czech Republic and Slovakia) and Balkan cinema (the former Yugoslavia, Bulgaria, Romania and Albania, as well as Greece and sometimes Turkey), including countries on the Southern periphery that previously would never have been included for political reasons (Iordanova 2003: 13–16). Paradoxically, the cinema of the former German Democratic Republic, which in the past was considered to be an integral part of East European film culture and which traditionally featured in studies on East European cinema (see Liehm and Liehm 1977; Goulding 1989), has in the wake of German unification been claimed as the new research domain of German film scholars, but has 'vanished from all East European conceptual contexts' (Iordanova 2003: 15).

Only as a result of the re-configuration of this research context has it become necessary to stress the need to continue appraising East German film culture in its previous context, which prioritised the GDR's position within the Soviet empire over its position within a German national context. After the Second World War the Soviet-occupied zone, and subsequently the GDR, became a constituent part of the Soviet hegemony alongside many other Eastern bloc countries. In terms of economy, politics and culture these Soviet satellite states followed the example, if not the command, of the USSR. Thus major political events – such as the Thaw that followed de-Stalinisation during the late 1950s, or the reform movements of *glasnost* (literally 'giving voice') and *perestroika* (literally 'restructuring'), which were initiated by Gorbachev after his accession in 1985 and which ultimately led to the end of communism – originated in the USSR before their repercussions were felt across the Soviet sphere of influence.

With respect to the film industries of these Soviet bloc countries, the powerful and homogenous influence of the Soviet Union is reflected in the imposition of the ideological and aesthetic doctrine of Socialist Realism, the overt politicisation of film culture and a centralised system of state-funded and controlled film production and distribution. Moreover, there was a lively cultural exchange between these so-called socialist brother states. In terms of film imports and circulation (though not necessarily in terms of market share) films from the Soviet Union, Czechoslovakia, Poland and other East European countries played a far more dominant role in the GDR than imports from West Germany, other West European countries and America (see Chapter 1 of this volume). This exposure to the cinematic traditions of Eastern Europe has, according to filmmakers' own testimonies, been a strong formative influence on their own work. These cross-cultural connections were further enforced by the fact that, in particular before the establishment of the GDR's own Babelsberg film academy, many of DEFA's filmmakers studied at the Prague Film School FAMU (e.g. Frank Beyer, Ralf Kirsten, Frank Vogel) or VGIK (the All-Union State Cinema Institute) in Moscow (e.g. Konrad Wolf, Helmut Dziuaba, Iris Gusner). Moreover, DEFA engaged in several co-productions with studios in Eastern Europe and the Soviet Union, while stars such as the Russian Donatas Banionis, the Czech actor Vlastimil Brodský, and the Polish actress Krystyana Stypulkowska played leading roles in some of DEFA's most acclaimed films.[5]

Conversely, the case for including East German cinema in the study of German national cinema is so obvious that it requires no further justification, except for the fact that a case has to be made in favour of examining DEFA against the background of an all-German cinema rather than in isolation. Naturally, and in particular in the wake of the *Ostpolitik* (policies regarding East Germany) during the 1970s, which led to a rapprochement of the two German states, a considerable amount of cultural exchange – both official and unofficial – was taking place. While West German films were by no means as heavily promoted in the GDR as those from its socialist neighbours, and the number of imports was restricted chiefly due to economic factors, West German films met with widespread public interest. And even films that were not officially imported could be accessed in the East once they were released on West

German television, which was widely received in the GDR, providing the proverbial 'hole in the Wall'. With regard to film production, there was a certain amount of East–West cross-fertilisation, but co-productions were a relatively rare occurrence. Until the erection of the Berlin Wall in 1961, a considerable number of artistic staff based in the West were involved in DEFA productions. Not to be overlooked in this context is the impact which actors such as Manfred Krug, Angelica Domröse, Katharina Thalbach and Armin Mueller-Stahl had on film culture in the West after they left the GDR.

However, the reasons for studying East German cinema against the comparative background of West German cinema go far beyond issues of film production, circulation and reception. What is at stake is, of course, the fundamental question as to what degree German cinema can be called a national cinema given that for more than forty years Germany was a nation with a split identity. The overarching concern of this book is, therefore, to examine what contributions East and West German cinema have made to the multiple narrative discourses surrounding the construction of Germany's post-war history and its national identity.

Indebted to certain premises of cultural studies, I conceive of history not as ontology (truth about events of the past), and of nation not as an enduring, primordial entity but both of these as constructs and signifying practices that are constituted by ever-shifting discourses. The signifying practices and narrative strategies of cinema make a specific contribution to those discourses. While concepts of history and national identity must always be seen as shifting, this is particularly valid for Germany, a nation that for more than forty years experienced a split identity that now merits re-examination.

In this book I propose to examine East German cinema through its feature films, by addressing issues that have proved central to critical debates on national cincma,[6] but that take a rather specific inflection in the context of Germany's split screen. To what extent does the cinema of the divided Germany enunciate a shared sense of nationhood and a common core of cultural heritage? What parts of a common history and tradition are appropriated by East and West German cinema? More revealing, where do screen memories of a collective past reflect national amnesia and thus get history 'wrong' (see Hayward 2000: 90)? What are the myths which East and West German cinema articulate in order to legitimise the foundation and the co-existence of two separate German states? To what extent are these nation-building myths shared? To what extent are they competing and conflicting? And how do East and West

German cinema invest the nation and its history with meaning in the ideologically polarised context of Cold War division? What role does post-unification German cinema assume in the construction of a new German identity? In addressing these questions I shall explore how East and West German feature films evoke what Mettje Hjort (2000) refers to as 'themes of nation'. Hjort, and others before her, argue that national cinemas are to an important extent defined by their thematic focus. As opposed to 'perennial themes' – which revolve around concepts such as human nature, pride or sexual passion – themes of nation are 'topical', which means that they 'involve only concepts that arise within, and re-main relevant to, a highly specific historical and cultural formation' (Hjort 2000: 106). Topical themes – and the theme of nation is a topical theme par excellence – are often politically motivated and arise from specific cultural and social contexts. This would explain why national cinemas, as opposed to Hollywood cinema that favours perennial themes, rarely successfully traverse national boundaries: the culturally and socially specific themes which they address frequently lack relevance beyond national boundaries.

The selection of films discussed in this book is thus based on their thematics or, more specifically, to what extent they engage with themes of the German nation. The most prominent ones are the theme of *Vergangenheitsbewältigung* (coming to terms with the past, i.e. the Third Reich); the appropriation of Germany's cultural tradition and heritage; the critical examination of contemporary German society; and German re-unification. As one would expect, these thematisations of nation are much more consistently flagged and foregrounded in what has become recognised as the established canon of DEFA films (of which more later) than in DEFA's genre cinema. Therefore, and in contrast to the general trend to include popular cinema in studies of national cinema, I have chosen to limit the discussion of East and West German popular cinema, as well as the discussion of DEFA's much acclaimed fairy-tale films, to just a brief survey in Chapter 1. Though I do not deny, and actually demon-strate with reference to DEFA's *Indianerfilme* (the East German variant of the Western), sci-fi and fairy-tale films, that genre cinema also nar-rates themes of nation, albeit in a more oblique way, I would argue that these films focus primarily on perennial themes. Faced with the usual dilemma of insufficient space in a book of this length, it seemed appropriate to dedicate more attention and space to those films that make themes of nation their main concern.

In examining how DEFA's feature films narrate these themes of nation, I construct discursive frameworks within which representative films are placed and analysed. Chapter 1 sets the scene by outlining the institutional framework of East Germany's film industry in relation to other film industries of highly politicised cultures and that of post-war West Germany. Chapter 2 links DEFA's anti-fascist films to the discourses of *Vergangenheitsbewältigung*, East–West-German memory contests and the GDR's anti-fascist myth of origin. Chapter 3 explores what role the appropriation of the pre-socialist cultural heritage played in the cultural legitimisation of the two German states, focusing on cinematic adaptations of literature and artist biopics. Additional discursive contexts include the so-called *Erbedebatte* (debate concerning the reception of the traditional literary canon), European heritage cinema and the unifying role that was ascribed to Germany's shared cultural heritage in the formation of a new German identity post 1989. Chapter 4 examines DEFA's forbidden films in the wider context of film censorship on either side of the ideological divide. In particular, this chapter is concerned with tracing the strategies which filmmakers employed to reconcile the inherent tensions and contradictions between film's officially assigned mission as a purveyor of socialist values, and its so-called *Stellvertreterfunktion* (replacement function), which enabled filmmakers to obliquely articulate issues which could not be publicly voiced. Focusing on aesthetically unorthodox and ideologically subversive practices of filmmaking during the mid-1960s, I also try to answer the question why DEFA, unlike other East European cinemas, never experienced a New Wave. Chapter 5 analyses East German films depicting women in contemporary society against the comparative background of West German feminist filmmaking on the one hand, and Soviet films about women on the other. It also looks at the ideological discourses surrounding women's emancipation in the East and the West and asks why, despite the fact that women feature so prominently in East German and Soviet cinema since the mid-1960s, the 'feminist cause' always remained a minor concern. Chapter 6 links the cinematic representation of re-unified Germany to the continuing debate about Germany's new identity and asks what impact unification has had on Germany's divided film culture: has the split in the screen been sutured?

I propose to address these issues in close readings of twenty films chosen for their paradigmatic significance. These holistic case studies investigate the films' narrational strategies and enlist generic, authorial and institutional perspectives in the reconstruction of the films' changing meanings. Where appropriate, examples are chosen from different decades in order to trace the diachronic development of themes and modes of representation. Several of the selected films have achieved canonical status and are generally regarded as milestones in German film history. When in 1995, on the one-hundredth anniversary of cinema, German film critics and producers were asked to compile a list of the one hundred most important German films of all time, there were fourteen DEFA films on that list (Byg 2002: 6–8). My choice of films reflects the now-established canon insofar as seven of the twenty films are part of that canon, whilst no less than 170 of DEFA's features are discussed or mentioned since they provide important reference points for the contexualisation of the chosen twenty. I decided against centring this study exclusively on DEFA's acclaimed masterpieces because revisiting only such films that have already attracted a considerable amount of scholarly attention would have involved the risk of setting the established canon in stone instead of taking the opportunity to encourage a more inclusive approach to East German cinema past and present. All but three of the twenty films are currently available on video or DVD, and all but seven with English subtitles.[7] This ease of access will hopefully entice some readers of this book – to cite the famous slogan of DEFA's first weekly newsreel *Der Augenzeuge* (The Eyewitness) – 'to see for themselves, to hear for themselves, to judge for themselves', and to assign East German cinema a more prominent position in their research and teaching.

Notes

1 The catchphrase 'Hollywood behind the Wall' was originally coined by ICESTORM International, the company that distributes DEFA films on DVD and video worldwide. Being used on the company's website www.icestorm-video.com, it has become a commonly used reference to DEFA.

2 To date, the number of monographs on DEFA is still limited: Schenk (1994b), written exclusively by prominent film historians of the former GDR, is considered to be the most authoritative and comprehensive study of DEFA's feature films, whilst Jordan and Schenk (2000) is the standard text on DEFA's documentaries. Other comprehensive German-language accounts of DEFA include Jansen and Schütte (1977); an essay collection based on a retrospective organised by Filmarchiv Austria (Pflügel and Fritz 2001); and the yearbook of the DEFA Foundation, edited by Schenk and Richter (2000, 2001, 2002). The most comprehensive English-language anthologies on East German cinema to date are Allan and Sandford (1999) and Byg and Moore (2002).

3 DEFA's 750 feature films are only one, albeit a very important, aspect of East German cinema. In addition, the DEFA studios produced 750 animated films, 2,250 documentaries and shorts and over 2,000 episodes of the news weekly *Der Augenzeuge* (The Eyewitness). Given the scope of this book I have, however, chosen to limit the focus of this study to DEFA's feature films.

4 The focus of these studies is as follows: DEFA's early period (Heimann 1994; Mückenberger 1994); anti-fascist films (Kannapin 1997); issues relating to the representation of contemporary society (Blunk 1984; Feinstein 2002); fairy tale films (König, Wiedemann, and Wolf, 1996); and issues of state control and film censorship (Geiss 1997; Schittly 2002). While many of the earlier studies examine the cinema of East Germany in isolation, there are now a number of books available that take a comparative approach to East and West German cinema, notably König, Wiedemann and Wolf's (1995) exploration of Eastern and Western versions of youth films; Shandley's (2001) study on rubble films; Meurer's monograph (2000) on East and West German cinema during the 1980s; and Naughton's (2002) account of post-unification cinema.

5 For example, Banionis played the lead in the co-production with Lenfilm, *Goya* (Konrad Wolf, 1971) and in *Beethoven – Tage aus einem Leben* (Beethoven – Days from a Life, Horst Seemann, 1976); Brodský played Jakob in *Jakob der Lügner* (Jacob the Liar, Frank Beyer, 1975); and Stypulkowska appeared alongside Manfred Krug in the forbidden film *Spur der Steine* (Trace of Stones, Frank Beyer, 1966/90).

6 Surveying the vast amount of literature on national cinema, I have found the following texts particularly useful: Anderson (1983); Rosen (1984); Higson (1989, 2000); Hayward (1993, 2000); Silberman (1996); Walsh (1996); Hall (1997); and Hjort (2000).

7 ICESTORM International, based in Northampton, Massachusetts, and ICESTORM Entertainment, based in Berlin, are independent video and DVD distributors for DEFA's film stock. English-subtitled videos or DVDs are available from www.icestorm-video.com and the DEFA Film Library www.umass.edu/defa/ while an even wider range of German-language DEFA films can be purchased from www.icestorm.de. Some of the post-unification films discussed in this book are available from www.goethe.de ('GI Spielfilmkatalog') or from www.amazon.de. 16mm and 35mm prints of DEFA feature films, documentaries, newsreels, archival footage and German-dubbed film imports into the former GDR can be obtained via Progress Film-Verleih GmbH (www.progress-film.de). The DEFA Film Library and Research Centre, set up by Professor Barton Byg at the University of Massachusetts, Amherst, has substantial holdings of film material and publications relating to DEFA and handles the non-commercial circulation of DEFA prints in North America (www.umass.edu/defa). Finally, the DEFA-Stiftung (DEFA Foundation) aims to preserve the DEFA heritage by providing financial aid and assistance for projects relating to DEFA (www.defa-stiftung.de).

1

The East German film industry and the state

The beginnings

East Germany's state-owned film production company, DEFA, was re-built on what was left of the once-powerful Nazi dream factory, which was dismantled by the Allies several months before Germany's unconditional surrender on 8 May 1945. In fact, DEFA's feature film studios at Potsdam-Babelsberg, on the western outskirts of Berlin, were based on the very same site where, during the 1920s, UFA (Universum Film AG) produced such internationally acclaimed masterpieces as Friedrich Wilhelm Murnau's *Nosferatu* (1922); Fritz Lang's *Metropolis* (1927); Joseph von Sternberg's *Der blaue Engel* (The Blue Angel, 1930) starring Marlene Dietrich and Emil Jannings; and later, under the strict supervision of Hitler's *Reichspropaganda* minister, Joseph Goebbels, such seductive propaganda devices as *Hitlerjunge Quex* (Hilter Youth Quex, Hans Steinhoff, 1933); *Triumph des Willens* (Triumph of the Will, Leni Riefenstahl, 1935); and seemingly apolitical entertainment films like *Wunschkonzert* (Request Concert, Eduard von Borsody, 1940). The Nazi film industry had been a huge success in terms of both its ideological impact on the German public and its economic power. In particular the war effort had resulted in a rapid expansion of the market for German films across Europe while the ban on Hollywood imports gave domestic production unrivalled dominance in the home market. During the twelve years of Nazi dictatorship, the four main studios (UFA, Bavaria, Tobis and Terra), which in 1942 were subsumed under the UFI holding company into which the entire Nazi film industry was organised, produced more than one thousand feature films.

The confiscation and dismantling of the Nazi film industry by the triumphant Allies required little justification. The victors were entitled to use the Reich's assets as reparation payments. Moreover, given that the film industry had been such a powerful weapon of mass manipulation, they could rightly argue that this weapon had to be destroyed or, at the very least, put under the control of the Allies.

On 24 November 1944 the Allied Military Command, which assumed supreme power in invaded Germany, passed Law 191 which in effect banned the Germans from any access to the mass media and performing arts. All cinemas which had not yet been destroyed were closed; film studios were used as barracks and for storage; technical equipment and raw film stock were confiscated; and distribution companies had to relinquish all film stock. Through such measures 'the Allies transformed the German film industry from an industrial superpower to a cottage industry in a matter of weeks [. . .] By the time of surrender . . . the once powerful German film industry had ceased to exist' (Shandley 2001: 10–11).

Soon after Germany's unconditional surrender, the four Allies divided the German territory into four occupation zones, each with its own military government. Although they agreed on the principal goals of their joint military rule, namely demilitarisation, de-Nazification and democratisation, the actual policies which they devised differed significantly, reflecting the Allies' ideologically divergent interpretations of fascism. The Western Allies interpreted fascism as a corrupt manifestation of political will that had resulted in a 'distortion of the German collective and individual consciousness' (Carter 1997: 436). De-Nazification tribunals that aimed to assess the complicity of individual Germans in the Nazi atrocities became a key instrument of rehabilitation, while various re-education initiatives were to instil the spirit of democracy in a people who had been exposed to twelve years of NS-propaganda. De-Nazification in the Soviet zone, by contrast, was underpinned by the Marxist interpretation of fascism, which ascribes the rise of fascism to the contradictory nature of modern industrial capitalism. Consequently, the Soviet Military Administration considered the fundamental transformation of the economic system from capitalism to state-socialism, coupled with the purging of Nazis from the public sphere, to be the most effective means of de-Nazification.

All Allies, irrespective of their ideological leanings, agreed that the cultural sphere was to play a central role in the process of German democratisation and reconstruction. In particular the mass media, which had been so effectively used by the Nazis for their propaganda purposes, were tightly controlled. When Law 191 was amended on 12 May 1945 and the Germans were gradually given access to the media again, a licensing system was set up that gave the Allies complete control of the public sphere and enabled them to determine which cultural products were appropriate for the process of re-education. While in the Western occupied zones print media were assigned a leading role in the process of political enlightenment, the Soviets put their faith in the medium of film: 'zuviele Menschen würden keine Zeitung lesen, geschweige denn ein Buch, aber auf alle Fälle ins Kino gehen' (too many people would not read newspapers, never mind books, but would certainly go to the cinema) (cited in Heimann 1994: 26), speculated Hans Rodenberg, later to become the director of the DEFA feature film studio, in 1944 while he was still in Moscow exile. He was right, for cinema offered a welcome diversion from the miserable struggle for survival in Germany's bombed-out cities. Moreover, tickets were cheap – just one Reichsmark, compared with 250 Reichsmark for a pound of butter on the black market.

The Germans, keen cinema-goers who bought more than one billion tickets in 1943, did not have to wait long to fall back into old habits. The first cinemas in Berlin re-opened as early as 28 April 1945, that is, even before Germany's unconditional surrender. Initially they showed films made by the Allies. Thus audiences in the Soviet zone were acquainted with the achievements of Soviet culture in the shape of dubbed Soviet film classics, alongside musicals and entertainment films made in the Soviet Union, Hollywood, Britain and France. But it did not take long before light entertainment films from the Third Reich, which were deemed ideologically inoffensive, made their re-entry into German cinemas. By 1948 more than four hundred films made under NS rule had been cleared for distribution by the Allies (Bathrick 1998: 174).

The resumption of German film production was, by comparison, a more complex matter. The first step was the de-Nazification of the German film industry. But film personnel with the relevant expertise were hard to come by. Those who had emigrated from Germany after Hitler's rise to power in 1933 because of political oppression or to avoid persecution and who had established their careers in Hollywood or elsewhere had little reason to return, whereas the majority of those who had stayed had worked for the Nazi dream factory in some form or another. The seamless continuities of personnel were more common in the Western occupation zones than in the Soviet zone. According to Klaus Kreimeier's calculations, 'the twenty-eight West German films of the years 1946–48 were almost without exception produced and directed by former employees of the National Socialist Ufa or of other Ufi companies' (Kreimeier 1999: 376). Even though the Soviet occupation powers were more rigorous in their efforts to de-Nazify the industry and tried hard to recruit emigrants including Slatan Dudow, Wilhelm Dieterle and Gustav von Wangenheim, some conspicuous continuities in personnel existed here too. Among DEFA's employees during the early post-war years were Arthur Maria Rabenalt, Günther Rittau and Gerhard Lamprecht. Even Wolfgang Staudte, the director of DEFA's first feature film *Die Mörder sind unter uns* (The Murderers Are among Us, 1946) had taken small roles in a number of films during the Third Reich, including Veit Harlan's infamous anti-Semitic *Jud Süß* (Jew Süss, 1940) and Arthur Maria Rabenalt's . . . *reitet für Deutschland* (. . . Riding for Germany, 1941), before directing the comedy *Akrobat Schö-ö-ö-n* (Acrobat Schö-ö-ö-n, 1942). Former UFA cameramen Friedl Behn-Grund and Bruno Mondi were in great demand because of their excellent technical skills. Wolfgang Zeller not only composed the music for Kurt Maetzig's *Ehe im Schatten* (*Marriage in the Shadows*, 1947), a film portraying the suffering of Jews under Hitler, but had been a leading film composer during the Third Reich and had, rather ironically, also written the score for *Jud Süß*.

Several months would pass before the Germans were given licences to shoot their own films again. Initially, the Allies themselves made and exhibited a number of explicit re-educational documentaries and newsreels in order to acquaint the Germans with the principles of democracy and to impress upon them that they were collectively to blame for the rise of Nazism, the war and even the atrocities of the death camps. Despite the fact that, for some films, attendance was mandatory, Germans stayed away in droves. Taking a lighter touch, the Americans also imported Hollywood films which had not been shown in Germany during the war, arguing that these would 'acquaint German audiences with "American ideals and the American way of life"' (Pommer cited in Fehrenbach 1995: 64). Rebuilding the German film industry was considered to be untimely, since films made by Germans themselves would neither 'counteract the long years of Nazi propaganda' nor stimulate 'the necessary mental catharsis' (Pommer cited in Fehrenbach 1995: 64). Undeniably, economic considerations played an even more prominent role in the Americans' film policy than educational ones.

However, the Americans' commerce-driven approach to democratic re-education was by no means unique. Allies in all four zones readily responded to the significant potential of the untapped German market by importing their own films and achieving market shares of between 70 and 90 per cent (Greffrath 1995: 118; Heimann 1994: 64). The official rationale for these imports was that exposure to films from

France, Britain, America and the Soviet Union would facilitate the defeated nation's identification with their erstwhile enemies.

The Allied Control Commission, which was in charge of all supra-zonal questions concerning the occupied territory, discouraged the establishment of a centralised film industry since it could easily once again become a state-controlled monopoly like the film industry during the Third Reich. Instead, each occupation zone was free to develop its own policy of film production, distribution and exhibition. Notwithstanding initial reservations of the British military government, the Western Allies eventually agreed upon a decartelisation of the film industry in their territories. What this meant in practice was that in the Western zones the centralised and vertically integrated film industry which the Allies inherited from the Nazis was dismantled and split up into numerous small companies. Disentangling and re-privatising the Reich's film assets ultimately resulted in a loss of efficiency and competitiveness of the indigenous German film industry, exposing it to foreign, in particular American, domination.

The Soviets, by contrast, decided to convert the legacy of UFI's numerous companies in and around Berlin into a centralised film company with monopoly status. Despite the fact that the Soviets had ruthlessly dismantled whatever was left of the Reich's film industry, leaving major gaps in the technical infrastructure and in film stock, conditions for the resumption of film production in the Soviet-occupied zone were generally much more favourable than in the Western zones. The heart of the Reich's film industry had been located in what was now the Soviet-occupied zone and the Soviet sector of Berlin. Because the most important film studios, including the legendary UFA studio in Potsdam-Babelsberg, alongside production and copying facilities, as well as distribution organisations, were situated in the Soviet zone, the lion's share of the Nazi film industry, namely 70 per cent of the entire capital of the NS-holding UFI and 75 per cent of the entire film studio capacities automatically fell into the hands of the Soviets (Heimann 1994: 39–40; Kreimeier 1999: 57–8). Agfa Wolfen, the main supplier of raw film stock, was also based on Soviet-occupied territory. Moreover, at a time when forty small film production companies in the Western zones competed for private funding, film production in the Soviet zone benefited from a centralised system of cultural administration and financial support.

Nevertheless, economic advantages alone cannot explain why film production was resumed earlier in the Soviet occupied zone. The Soviets, experienced in the use of film as an instrument of mass education since the Bolshevik revolution, were convinced of its effectiveness as an ideological weapon. Moreover, being more interested in ideological than economic control, their prime objective was to win over 'the former foes to a Soviet-style political culture' (Shandley 2001: 17). Consequently, they had to acknowledge that the process of anti-fascist, democratic re-education could only be successful if the Germans themselves became involved in expressing the ideals and values which the Allies tried to implant in them.

At a time when the military governments in the Western zones still held reservations about the re-establishment of a German film industry, the Soviet Military Administration (SMAD) was already taking steps to help domestic film production back onto its feet.[1] Colonel Sergej Tulpanov and Major Alexander Dymschitz, in charge of the political and cultural divisions of the SMAD's *Verwaltung für Information* (Administration of Information), assumed a leading role in creating an administrative infrastructure in which film would be assigned a central role in the process of anti-fascist re-education. On 25 August 1945 the SMAD set up the *Zentralverwaltung für Volksbildung* (Central Administration for People's Education) headed by the communist Paul Wandel. In October 1945 Herbert Volkmann, head of the section responsible for literature and the arts, set up an action committee, the *Filmaktiv*, to devise proposals for the revival of German cinema in the Soviet-occupied zone. The *Filmaktiv*, the precursor of DEFA, consisted of six men, all of whom had relevant experience in the film industry or cultural sector and who had the right political credentials: all were members of the KPD (German Communist Party) and several had been active in the anti-fascist resistance. Among them were assistant director Kurt Maetzig who, being half-Jewish, had been excluded from working in the film industry after 1933; Adolf Fischer and Alfred Lindemann, both of whom had worked for the proletarian film company Prometheus-Film during the Weimar Republic; set designers Karl Hans Bergmann and Willi Schiller; and Hans Klering, who had worked as an actor while exiled in Moscow and who was familiar with the structure of the Soviet film industry. He was appointed head of the *Filmaktiv* and would assume a crucial role as a mediator between the SMAD and the Central Administration for People's Education (Heimann 1994: 49).

On 22 November 1945 the *Filmaktiv*, members of the communist party, the SMAD, the Central Administration for People's Education and a number of writers and film directors met at the famous Hotel Adlon in Berlin to discuss the future of the German film industry in the Soviet zone.[2] There was general agreement that the new German cinema would break with UFA tradition in terms of aesthetics, themes and personnel. It was to promote a new anti-fascist and democratic culture that would be based on humanistic ideals.

After the *Filmaktiv*'s proposals had been officially approved by the SMAD, the shooting of the first two films began as early as January 1946. Highest priority was given to the production of the first edition of the newsreel *Der Augenzeuge* (The Eyewitness), directed by Kurt Maetzig. The first feature film to be completed was Staudte's *Die Mörder sind unter uns*, which went into production on 4 May 1946 and which premiered on 15 October 1946. It was the first post-war German feature film.

The official production licence was handed over to Hans Klering, DEFA's artistic director, on 17 May 1946. The occasion was marked by a festive ceremony at the Althoff Studio in Potsdam-Babelsberg, where Colonel Sergei Tulpanov, head of the political section of the SMAD, outlined the ideological aims of Germany's first post-war film production company as follows:

> Die Filmgesellschaft DEFA hat wichtige Aufgaben zu lösen. Die größte von ihnen ist der Kampf um den demokratischen Aufbau Deutschlands und die Ausrottung der Reste des Nazismus und des Militarismus aus dem Gewissen eines jeden Deutschen, das Ringen um die Erziehung eines jeden Deutschen, das Ringen um die Erziehung des deutschen Volkes, insbesondere der Jugend im Sinne der echten Demokratie und Humanität und damit Achtung zu erwecken für andere Völker und Länder. (cited in Mückenberger 1994: 38)

> (DEFA faces a number of important tasks. Of these, the most crucial is the struggle to restore democracy in Germany and to remove all traces of fascist and militaristic ideology from the mind of every German, the struggle to re-educate the German people – especially the young – to achieve an understanding of genuine democracy and humanism, and in so doing, to promote a sense of respect for other people and other nations.)

On 13 August 1946 DEFA was officially registered as a joint stock company based in Berlin, adopting the now famous black-and-white filmstrip with the letters DEFA on it as its company logo.

Although DEFA had been founded as a private company, film production actually depended entirely on state sponsorship. The 'starting capital of 20,000 marks [had been] supplied by *Zentrag*, a subsidiary organisation of the recently constituted Socialist Unity Party (SED)' (Allan

1999: 5). Moreover, ownership of the film production facilities and studios in Berlin (the former Tobis studios) and in Potsdam-Babelsberg (the former Althoff studios) remained with the Soviet company Linsa and were only leased by DEFA, while film distribution rights remained with the Soviet company Sojusintorgkino (later Sovexport). Hence the newly founded company was in no position to generate any money.

The wide-ranging transformation of the entire economic structure in the Soviet zone over the next few years had significant implications for the ownership of DEFA. Like all industrial plants in the Soviet zone, insofar as they had not been dismantled and moved to the USSR as part of the reparation agreements, all film production facilities and studios were transformed into *Sowjetische Aktiengesellschaften* (SAGs, Soviet Joint Stock Companies). In July 1947 DEFA's headquarters were moved from Berlin to Potsdam-Babelsberg. On 3 November 1947 the company was converted into a Soviet–German joint stock company, with the Soviets holding a 55 per cent majority interest and the Germans a minority stake of 45 per cent. While nominally the increase in the company's capital was provided by the Soviet company Linsa (5.5 million Mark) and the German Central Administration for People's Education (4.5 million Mark), the actual German investor was once again the Socialist Unity Party. In this way the Party contractually ensured its influence upon future film production in the Soviet zone and later in East Germany. An official body charged with overseeing DEFA's film production and staffing, the *Filmkommission* (film commission or 'DEFA commission') within the Central Committee of the SED was set up on 10 November.[3]

The actual structure of control and ownership – in particular, the majority interest held by the Soviets – was skilfully hidden from the public. Such camouflage was necessary in order not to alienate artists, many of whom lived in West Berlin and would have shied away from working for a film company with a strong allegiance to the SED and strong ties with Moscow. Especially as Cold War tensions were beginning to rise, a further concern was that the American military government might boycott the inter-zonal film agreement, which provided for an exchange of films between all four zones. From 1948 onwards, DEFA was granted a licence to distribute its own films, while Sovexport continued to hold the distribution monopoly for all other films in the Soviet zone.

The *Erste Film-Autoren Kongreß* (First Conference of Filmmakers), held at Postdam-Babelsberg in June 1947, was attended by filmmakers from all four zones and devised policies for cooperation that were based on the assumption of a unitary German state. Yet soon thereafter, global

political developments superseded the decisions reached at the conference. In 1948 tensions between East and West rose and the beginning
of the Cold War led to a re-definition of former friends and foes. The
SED chose to strengthen its allegiance to the big socialist brother by
opting against 'a German path to socialism', instead modelling 'itself on
Stalin's Communist Party in the Soviet Union' (Allan 1999: 6). When
on 23 May 1949 the Federal Republic of Germany was founded on the
territory of the Western occupation zones, and on 7 October 1949 the
German Democratic Republic was founded on the territory of the Soviet-
occupied zone, hopes for an all-German film culture, or any common
culture for that matter, were quickly dispelled.

These developments had significant repercussions for DEFA: the
Soviets relinquished their ownership and control of the studio and subsequently of film distribution. Following the model of other film industries
in the Soviet bloc, on 1 January 1953 DEFA was nationalised. VEB DEFA
– short for *Volkseigener Betrieb* (people's owned company or collective
corporation) – comprising production centres specialising in feature films,
educational films, newsreels and documentaries, children's films, animation
and dubbing, was now under the firm control of the East German state,
its new patron and censor. While the Soviet film officers, notably such
educated men as Dymschitz and Tulpanov, had promoted relatively
liberal film policies, the Germans who took over tended to be SED
hardliners, and thus typically more interested in the political correctness
than in the artistic merits of films. In any event, the Soviet sphere of
influence was maintained even after the Soviets officially relinquished
their control since all senior management positions were filled with loyal
SED Party members who would issue discreet reports to Moscow via
the appropriate information channels. The multi-layered structure of
supervision and control which existed between the film industry, the Party
apparatus, the leaders of the state and the government in Moscow was
replicated across all Eastern bloc states. It was instrumental in ensuring
the Soviet hegemony over the film industry – indeed the entire cultural
sphere – across the Eastern bloc.

The East German film industry and its models

The similarity between the two acronyms DEFA and UFA is suggestive
of the affinities between these two German film companies at the service of two totalitarian regimes. Both were, at least in part, based on the
same site at Potsdam-Babelsberg and both were powerful constituents

of German media dictatorships which operated along similar structural principles, albeit under different ideological premises. Both film industries were centralised, nationalised and controlled by a state apparatus that determined the entire film production process from the initial idea to the finished film, as well as the film's distribution and exhibition and its official reception in the public sphere. Under both regimes film was utilised as a device for ideological indoctrination, yet the ways in which this was achieved differed significantly.

As Eric Rentschler has so aptly put it, Hitler and his Propaganda Minister, Goebbels, relied on 'film's ability to mobilize emotions and immobilize minds' (Rentschler 1996: 1). To this end, overt propaganda was largely eschewed, at least in feature films. The overwhelming majority of narrative films offer seemingly politically innocuous entertainment. Feature films typically avoid Nazi emblems or Hitler salutes, in fact glimpses of everyday life in Nazi Germany are rare. Instead audiences are invited to take refuge from their burdensome daily lives in the utopian realms created by the Nazi dream factory. 'Ideology more often than not came sugar-coated, in gripping, engaging, and pleasant packages of entertainment' (Rentschler 1996: 217). In a carefully orchestrated division of labour between the various constituents of Goebbels' propaganda machine, overt propaganda was relegated to newsreels and *Kulturfilme* (culture films or documentary short subjects), whereas feature films were assigned the role of subliminal mass seduction, creating the illusion that they offered pure entertainment and recreation, a space beyond the reach of state control.

In the GDR, by contrast, ideological indoctrination through film was far less skilfully camouflaged and arguably less effective, not least because, according to the self-understanding of the state's political leaders, film, alongside the other arts, was used as an instrument of enlightenment and education, not as a device for mass manipulation. East Germany's political leaders, cultural functionaries, artists and intellectuals all considered themselves as perpetuating the tradition of the Enlightenment in assigning art a genuinely emancipatory role. Such good intentions did not have to be hidden. Consequently, the intersection of art and politics was handled in a much more transparent way than Nazi cultural administrators would ever have considered to be opportune. Thus major film conferences, where the GDR's *Verband der Film und Fernsehschaffenden* (Association of Film and Television Workers) publicly discussed and presented their new film policies, were usually preceded by meetings of the Central Committee of the SED where these policies and resolutions were formulated in advance. The resultant didacticism of many DEFA features makes them in many respects the very antithesis of the products of the Nazi dream factory. Whereas the Nazis had used entertainment for political purposes and camouflaged it as sheer fantasy, DEFA's founders and their successors denounced escapist entertainment as a manifestation of decadent bourgeois culture. This attitude explains also the dearth of popular genre cinema amongst DEFA productions, of which more below.

What the East German film industry shares with that of the Third Reich – and that of all highly politicised societies for that matter – is the all-encompassing supervision and control through the state, which is an indispensable prerequisite if film is to be utilised as an instrument of political indoctrination. That such structural correspondences can exist in the absence of ideological correspondences has been convincingly demonstrated by Richard Taylor in his comparative analysis of film propaganda in Soviet Russia and Nazi Germany (Taylor 1998). Given the ideological affinities between the GDR and the Soviet Union and the Soviet cultural hegemony over Eastern Europe after 1945, it comes as no surprise that in many respects the organisational structure of East Germany's film industry mirrors that of the Soviet Union.

Since the days of the revolution the Bolsheviks had assigned film a key role in instructing people in the spirit of socialism. Yet while Lenin had conceived of film primarily as an educational instrument that would raise the cultural level of the people and thus create the necessary precondition for the development of a socialist society, Stalin envisaged a cultural revolution that would destroy the last vestiges of artistic autonomy in a bid to harness all aspects of culture and, most importantly, film culture to the purposes of political propaganda. To this end in 1930 all Soviet film studios were incorporated into a single state bureaucracy, which under the leadership of Boris Shumyatsky – and arguably Stalin, who was fanatical about film himself – exercised complete control over film production in all Soviet republics. Their output was determined by centrally devised production plans, which not only specified the number of films to be made by each studio but also their themes. To put a definitive end to the cultural pluralism which had prevailed during the 'golden age' of the 1920s, the aesthetic doctrine of Socialist Realism was uniformly imposed on all arts, including film. Censorship was severe and, during the 'age of terror', artists who displeased the state did not just fear for their jobs but for their lives. After Stalin's death in 1953 restrictions loosened and greater artistic diversity began to prevail.

While East Germany's film industry followed similar structural and ideological principles, the extent of state intervention was far more moderate. Moreoever, although a fair share of DEFA's feature films can be described as overtly didactic, only a few could be classified as propagandistic in the sense of consciously attempting 'to control or change the attitudes and behaviour of a group, through manipulation of communication' (Edgar and Sedgwick 1999: 313).

What the highly politicised film industries discussed here have in common is their more or less subtly disguised admiration for Hollywood, an industry that is associated with light, apolitical entertainment and which guaranteed a mass appeal that Goebbels, Stalin and Honecker could only dream of. Goebbels encouraged filmmakers to emulate the masterful illusionism of Hollywood cinema and modelled the vertically integrated, centralised structure of the National Socialist film industry on the Hollywood studio system. Shumyatsky, who was appointed head of the centralised state Soyuzkino organisation in 1930, even travelled to America in 1935 to study the American film industry and uncover the secrets of its success because he was planning to build 'a Soviet Hollywood in Crimea', yet 'the projected Soviet Hollywood never materialised' (Kenez 2001: 118).

Likewise the GDR's leaders aspired to create a 'Hollywood behind the Wall' or 'Honecker's Hollywood' – as DEFA has been referred to retrospectively (www.icestorm-video.com; Mattusek 1990). However, this metaphor is more an indication of the Party's grand aspirations for its national film industry than a reflection of DEFA's real stature. Nationally, only a handful of DEFA productions were a cinema for the millions, and internationally DEFA was never more than a 'minor cinema' (Byg 1995). Undeniably, certain structural similarities between DEFA and Hollywood do exist, but this is not surprising given that Hollywood's formula for success has been widely copied the world over. DEFA, like UFA under the Nazis, modelled itself on the traditional studio structure of the Hollywood of the 1930s and adopted the principle of vertical integration, whereby the cycle of production, distribution and exhibition of films was centrally managed by the major studios themselves, which all had their own distribution and export arms and owned a number of cinemas. In the case of DEFA, the cycle of production, distribution and exhibition was centrally managed by a government agency in the Ministry of Culture. Whilst in Hollywood there were several studios competing for market shares, profit and prestige, in the GDR there was only the one. And this difference is crucial. When salaried film directors employed by Hollywood studios were fired, they could seek employment in another studio. When DEFA directors were banned from filmmaking, either by being dismissed or by being assigned projects that would never come to fruition, they had no alternatives.[4]

What is of greater significance in the analysis of DEFA's models is that the fascination with and emulation of certain aspects of the Hollywood film industry point towards an inherent dilemma of the highly politicised film industries discussed here, in particular the Soviet and East German variety. The state urged its filmmakers to make films that would be as popular as Hollywood productions, but that would at the same time support the state's political agenda and be of considerable artistic merit. To square this circle was impossible and hence Hollywood always remained the audience's first choice, unless access to it was denied (see Stott 2000, 2002).

The institutional structure of East Germany's film industry

All aspects of the GDR's film industry, including production and distribution, import and export, the manufacturing of film and equipment, and the state film archive were centrally controlled by the *Hauptverwaltung Film* (Central Film Administration). Such government agencies in charge of managing and supervising the national film industries existed in all Soviet bloc countries. One of their key functions was to ensure that the national film culture reflected the grand master narrative of socialism, to which all Soviet satellite states subscribed. The *Hauptverwaltung Film*, a department in the Ministry of Culture, was established in 1954, replacing the *Staatliche Komitee für Filmwesen* (State Committee for Film Issues). It was headed by the Deputy Minister of Culture, colloquially referred to as the 'film minister', and was home of the *Staatliche Filmabnahme* (State Certification Board), which had to authorise the theatrical release of all DEFA productions as well as all film imports and exports.

DEFA was a vertically integrated film production and distribution company, consisting of several studios to which different aspects of national film production were assigned. While the configuration and remit of the various DEFA film production centres underwent a number of changes during the period between 1946 and 1992, by the time of its privatisation in 1992 the DEFA complex consisted of the feature film studio at Potsdam-Babelsberg, the documentary film studios in Berlin and Potsdam, the Dresden-based animation studio and the dubbing

studio in Berlin-Johannisthal.[5] DEFA also had its own import and export
division, DEFA-Außenhandel, and a distribution company, Progress-Film-
Verleih, which circulated domestic and imported films within a system
of state-controlled film exhibition.

Since the establishment of East Germany's own film academy in
1954, (later to be named *Hochschule für Film und Fernsehen Konrad Wolf*
in honour of one of East Germany's most highly acclaimed film directors), aspiring film professionals no longer needed to go abroad to
VGIK in Moscow or FAMU in Prague, but could do their entire training under the tutelage of experienced DEFA filmmakers. Just like writers,
filmmakers in the GDR had their own professional association, the
Verband der Film und Fernsehschaffenden (Association of Film and
Television Workers), which provided a forum for discussion and exchange
of ideas while, at the same time, being an important mediating body which
ensured that the Party's cultural policies would be implemented in the
film industry. The Association's official film journal, *Film und Fernsehen*,
provided an important discursive framework for East German film culture. Other titles included *Deutsche Filmkunst* (1953–62), *Neue Film-Welt*
(renamed *Film-Spiegel* in 1954), and *Film heute und morgen* (renamed
Treffpunkt Kino in 1969).[6]

National film culture played an important role in the GDR's legitimisation. That is why the Party did not stint when it came to supporting
this important art form and weapon of class struggle. During the 1980s,
for example, the state invested approximately 120 million Marks per year
in the industry as a whole, of which 35 million alone were allocated to
film production (Pehnert and Berghahn 2002). Budgets were controlled
by the department of *Filmökonomie* (film economy) within the HV
Film: it financed the production of films, each of which cost on average
between two million and four million East German Marks; it subsidised
film distribution and exhibition; it paid the salaries of DEFA's permanently employed staff as well as fees to freelance writers, composers, actors
and actresses, who were generally not on permanent contracts. In addition, all sorts of bonus payments and prize moneys were paid on successful completion of a film which boosted the basic and, by Western
standards, modest salaries of directors and other artistic staff. These payments not only rewarded the creation of films deemed of considerable
artistic and/or ideological merit, but also credited a film's box-office
success or the efficiency of an artistic team that managed to complete
a project on schedule or without exceeding the projected amount of
material.[7]

The fixed costs alone for the running of the DEFA feature film studio, the biggest of all DEFA studios, were considerable. The studio occupied the historic 43-hectare site at Babelsberg, which was in effect a self-sufficient film city, as it had been in the days of UFA. In addition to a vast studio complex with twelve sound stages with a total capacity of 10,000 square metres and dubbing and post-production facilities, the DEFA feature film studio had an enormous props and costume department with over a million props and 200,000 costumes and uniforms at its disposal. Over 2,400 employees were permanently employed, but only a small fraction were directly involved in film production. This large number of employees on the studio's payroll is explained by the fact that in addition to artistic and technical staff, a whole range of other staff, including carpenters, builders, plasterers, tailors, musicians belonging to DEFA's own symphony orchestra, firemen, archivists and nursery teachers were employed by the studio, providing DEFA staff with all the facilities and services they required to produce films and manage their daily lives.

Though the rate of productivity fluctuated over the years, on average DEFA produced between fifteen and eighteen feature films per year and twice as many for television. Compared with other East European film industries DEFA's output was small: Czechoslovakia produced between forty and seventy films annually from the early 1960s onwards; even Poland and Hungary's annual feature film production averaged around twenty and thirty-five respectively. In the Federal Republic of Germany figures for the corresponding decades were significantly higher, ranging between fifty and one hundred per year (Vincendeau 1995: 464–5), though not all of these productions were distributed.[8]

Film production and the mechanisms of state control

The HV Film, with its combined roles of patron and censor, was the chief agent to safeguard a representative socialist film culture. Additional monitoring of the film industry was provided by the Central Committee's culture unit, *Abteilung Kultur: Sektor Film* (Department of Culture: Film Section), which was more powerful than the HV Film in passing a definitive verdict on a film. In other words, the HV Film held a somewhat equivocal position in the complex process of film regulation, as became particularly evident in the context of the Eleventh Plenum, when its officials acted less as censors than as mediators between the film-makers on the one hand and the Party on the other. As a result, they

were reprimanded or dismissed from their positions alongside the filmmakers (see Chapter 4).

In fact, mediation and negotiation were key aspects of film regulation,
which generally ensured that the banning of completed or nearly completed films could be prevented. Since the HV Film officials closely monitored all of the studio's activities, there were hardly ever any surprises
at the final certification stage (*Filmabnahme*). The first monitoring stage
consisted in the HV Film approving DEFA's annual production plans,
which would specify how many films would have to represent a certain
genre or theme, such as anti-fascist films, children's films, or films
about contemporary society, so-called *Gegenwartsfilme*. The HV Film
would then draft a master plan for the entire film industry and submit
this to the culture minister, who in turn would incorporate it into a
master plan for the entire cultural sector. This needed to be approved by
the GDR's highest executive body, the Council of Ministers (*Ministerrat*).
Such was the procedure in theory at least. In practice, controversial projects were immediately referred to the Central Committee's Cultural Section
(*Kulturabteilung*), which possessed far greater authority, since its staff
worked under the direct supervision of the Politburo. While the proce-
dural details of film control and censorship underwent subtle changes
over the years, the overall goal was always the same, namely to ensure
that East Germany's film production would reflect what David Bathrick
calls the 'foundational narratives about the genesis of the German socialist state' (Bathrick 1995: 16) and the ever-changing priorities of the cultural agenda.

During the early 1960s the feature film studio enjoyed considerable
artistic autonomy. Following the example of the Polish and Czech film
industries, in the late 1950s the DEFA studio management introduced
Künstlerische Arbeitsgruppen or KAGs (Artistic Working Groups).[9] Consisting of several directors, cameramen, dramaturges and production man-
agers, each of these groups were relatively autonomous units, in charge
of their own production budgets and empowered to make major decisions without having to fear direct political supervision from above. Thus
the introduction of KAGs heralded a significant form of decentralisation
in the process of film production and regulation. Consistent with this
increased democratisation, more power was given to the studio directorate when, from 1957 onwards, scripts no longer had to be submitted
to the HV Film but could be approved by the studio directorate itself.
This meant that all stages of film production from script development
through to the rough cut were entirely self-regulated by the DEFA studio.

In the aftermath of the Eleventh Plenum, however, this high degree of artistic autonomy was significantly curtailed again (see Chapter 4).

At any time, the demarcation line between the studio's self-regulatory mechanisms and state control was fluid because the studio's management and the agents of state control sought frequent consultation with each other as well as with the Central Committee. For example, even after the decentralisation of the studio's management structure it was still customary for the DEFA studio director to send a script together with an official studio assessment (*Einschätzung* or *Stellungnahme*) to the HV Film even though this was no longer mandatory. Similarly, it was not uncommon to invite the film minister to a preview of the rough cut at the studio prior to the official certification meeting which took place at the HV Film (Pehnert and Berghahn 2002).

Once the studio directorate had approved of a film and submitted an official report to the HV Film,[10] a meeting would be convened at the HV Film which would typically be attended by the film minister, the head of DEFA's distribution arm, Progress Film-Verleih, the head of DEFA-Außenhandel, a representative from the HV Film section film economy, the DEFA studio director and chief dramaturge, as well as the film director, script writer and several other members of the artistic work unit that made the film. This certification board at the HV Film would then either license the film's theatrical release, demand certain alterations, or ban it. Separate licences were issued for the film's release in GDR cinemas and abroad. Likewise, all imported films had to be certified prior to their theatrical release in the GDR. Following the studio's recommendation, the certification board would also issue an official quality rating, which usually had repercussions for the film's distribution and was likely to be reflected in film reviews in the national press. A good quality rating such as 'Prädikat besonders wertvoll' (predicate: particularly valuable) also resulted in bonus payments to the artistic production group.[11] For example, the quality rating 'Prädikat besonders wertvoll' resulted in a bonus payment of 45,000 Marks to the KAG that had produced the film, while the rating 'valuable' was rewarded with a payment of 20,000 Marks.

In order for a film to successfully pass the final certification stage, it was subjected to complex mechanisms of internal studio control. At the heart of self-regulation at the DEFA studio were its twenty-seven full time *Dramaturgen* (dramaturges or script editors). They fulfilled a crucial role in the studio's organisational hierarchy and their status was often comparable to that of the director. Each year they had to vet around two hundred proposals and treatments for films, supervise the development of screenplays and, being something of an 'ideological midwife' (Bathrick 1995: 37) to each film, ensure that a film project would successfully pass all the various stages of censorship. A good dramaturge was above all a good negotiator, someone who was capable of defending a potentially controversial film against any objections from above. Dramaturges were assigned to the studio's different artistic production groups and often forged long-standing partnerships with directors and other artistic staff in these groups. The studio's chief dramaturge (*Chefdramaturg*) provided an additional level of mediation and control.[12]

Further supervision by the state in the studio was provided by the presence of *informelle Mitarbeiter* (unofficial informants) and other agents of the Stasi (the popular name for the *Staatssicherheitsdienst* or State Security Service).[13] In particular after the Eleventh Plenum, the Stasi's presence in the studio was significantly increased, presumably to prevent a future recurrence of such ferocious and highly visible censorship as had been inflicted upon the film industry at the Eleventh Plenum in 1965 (see Chapter 4). It has been suggested that during the 1970s and 1980s there were around sixty unofficial informants in the feature film studio alone (Geiss 1997: 58). One of DEFA's most popular actors, Erwin Geschonneck, was one of many unofficial informants, working between 1958 and 1982 for the Stasi under the code names 'Richter' and 'Erwin' (Schittly 2002: 298–303). Numerous filmmakers who were presumed to represent 'feindlich-negative Kräfte' (hostile-negative forces) were subjected to various processes of observation, control and discrediting. The Stasi kept files on several such 'operative Vorgänge' (OV or operative processes) or 'operative Personenkontrolle' (OPK, operative control of an individual) which were, like the informants, referred to with code names in order to disguise their real identities. Amongst others, files were kept on Frank Beyer (OPK 'Karbid', the code name 'carbide' being a reference to his film *Karbid und Sauerampfer* (Carbide and Sorrell, 1963); Ulrich Weiß (OPK 'Bruder' (brother)); the director and scriptwriter couple Egon Günther and Helga Schütz (OPK 'Ehepaar' (couple)); and the director couple Sybille and Hannes Schönemann (OV 'Zweifler' (doubter)).

The repercussions which these surveillance operations had for the filmmakers' careers varied from case to case. The Schönemanns ended up in prison; the director Ulrich Weiß was effectively barred from filmmaking; others were luckier. Usually attempts were made to channel the filmmakers' creative energies in a direction that benefited the socialist national film industry. After making two 'subversive' films in succession, the forbidden film *Wenn du groß bist, lieber Adam* (When You Are Grown Up, Dear Adam, 1966/90) and *Abschied* (Farewell, 1968), Günther and Schütz were given another chance. The respective entry in the file OV 'Ehepaar' reads:

> Um zu verhindern, dass G. eine Entwicklung nimmt, die ihn mehr und mehr von unserer Partei entfernt, organisierten IM in Schlüsselpositionen, dass er einen Gegenwartsfilm macht, in dem er sich für alle sichtbar eindeutig für den real existierenden Sozialismus in der DDR festlegt. Durch das Spielfilmstudio wurde eine Arbeitsbezichung zwischen Günther Rücker und G. sowie Sch. organisiert In einer für dieses Projekt relativ kurzen Arbeitsphase entstand 1972 der Spielfilm 'Der Dritte', dessen Gegenstand die Entwicklung einer Arbeiterin in einem volkseigenen Betrieb der DDR ist. [. . .] Durch Organisierung einer straffen Anleitung und Kontrolle bei der Entstehung dieses Projektes von Anfang an, schafften Vertreter der damaligen Studioleitung günstige Voraussetzungen dafür, dass G. nur bedingt seinen individualistischen Auffassungen folgen konnte und sich konsequent an die politischen Vorgaben halten musste. (OPK 'Ehepaar', cited in Schittly 2002: 305)

> (In order to prevent G.'s further alienation from the Party, unofficial informers in key positions assigned him to a film project on contemporary social issues, in which he would have to make a clear commitment to the real existing socialism of the GDR. The feature film studio organised a close working relationship between Günther Rücker, G. and Sch. In 1972, following a relatively short development phase, *Der Dritte* (Her Third), a film about the development of a female worker in a socialist co-operative in the GDR, was completed. [. . .] From the beginning of the project's development, the then representatives of the studio management had implemented a system of strict supervision and control that made it difficult for G. to follow his individualistic tendencies and encouraged him instead to comply with the political requirements.)

But ultimately Günther did not conform to the Party's expectations. One of his next films, *Die Schlüssel* (The Keys, 1972/74) runs counter to many of the officially held views, depicts the taboo topic of death, and employs semi-documentary aesthetics. When Günther's 'individualism' could not even be contained through assigning him to politically innocuous heritage films (see Chapter 3), he was granted permission to work in the West.

The infiltration of DEFA through the Stasi provided the state with a useful channel for gathering information about all creative and organisational processes in the studio, thus constituting an effective form of pre-censorship and indirect control which aimed to secure and stabilise the state's authority in this important sector of the cultural sphere. Moreover, the presence of informants instilled a sense of caution and fear amongst DEFA staff and thus effectively inhibited free expression and promoted self-censorship.

However, what looks like a rather rigid system of state control from 'the outside', from 'the inside' looks like an efficient and even democratic form of film production. According to Horst Pehnert, the GDR's last film minister (1976–89), the notion of a dichotomy between film-makers on the one hand and cultural functionaries on the other is misleading. The HV Film was not an institution outside the film industry that intervened as a censor, Pehnert explained in an interview, but rather a collective producer, comparable to public service broadcasting corporations in the West. Like a producer in a capitalist film industry, who also vets projects at various stages of their genesis in order to maximise profits, the HV Film exercised a similar form of quality control (Pehnert and Berghahn 2002). From a Western perspective such interference is entirely legitimate, whereas ideologically motivated interference is viewed with mistrust. Why is one form of intervention acceptable but not the other, Pehnert asks:

> Es hat Fälle gegeben, wo wir dann schon am Drehbuch erkannt haben, daß uns irgendwas nicht paßt, daß uns irgendwas wider die öffentliche Meinung, wie sie geprägt war von der SED, dem Staat, unserer Ideologie, geht. Wir waren ein Staat, der geprägt war von der SED, nicht von der englischen Labour Partei, sondern von der SED und die hatte ihre spezifischen gesellschaftlichen Optionen. Und das glaube ich auch sagen zu können, es war doch relativ selten. Meistens haben wir solche Dinge im Gespräch geklärt . . . Es herrschte eine gewisse Produktionsdemokratie. Aber wenn gar nichts mehr half, dann wurde auch gestimmt. (Pehnert and Berghahn 2002)

> (In some cases, we could tell from the script alone that there was something that did not suit us, that there was something that ran counter to the public opinion as it was shaped by the SED, the state, our ideology. Our state was shaped by the SED, not by the English Labour Party, but by the SED with its specific social options. And I think I can say quite confidently that it [censorship] was relatively rare. In most cases, such things could be clarified through conversation . . . There was a certain production democracy. But if nothing else worked we voted on it.)

That this ritual of discussion and comradely persuasion, which was a ubiquitous part of socialist culture, does not necessarily correspond to the mechanisms of consensus-finding in a Western-style democracy, will be explored in Chapter 4.

Film distribution and exhibition: the challenge to promote a socialist film culture

In order to ensure the promotion of a socialist film culture at the levels of film distribution and exhibition, the distribution agency Progress Film-Verleih was charged with developing so-called *Filmeinsatzpläne* (film distribution plans), which specified the release schedules and programme mix. Priority was given to DEFA productions and to films from the Soviet Union and Eastern bloc countries. Once these film distribution plans had been approved by the HV Film, publicity material was prepared and Progress supplied the *Bezirkslichtspielbetriebe* (regional film distribution and programming centres) in the GDR's fifteen *Bezirke* (regions) with the appropriate number of prints required.[14] The *Bezirkslichtspielbetriebe* circulated the copies amongst the cinemas in the area, which were managed and to a large extent owned by the district and regional councils, although in East Berlin some privately owned cinemas continued to exist up until the 1960s (Otto and Berghahn 2002). This complex administrative structure of centralised film distribution and programming ensured that even the most remote village theatre would exhibit the kind of films which the state considered appropriate.

Normally each film was circulated with a minimum of fifteen prints, one for each region. The number of prints with which a film was released was an important part of the state's film programming policy: films that did not find favour with the cultural officials were not necessarily banished into the vaults of the state film archive. Instead, ideologically deviant films or films that starred actors who had emigrated to the West were released with a small number of prints, sometimes got no mention whatsoever in the national press, were not shown in first-run cinemas and were not selected for international film festivals. By contrast, films deemed of particular artistic or ideological merit, such as the statecommissioned historical epics about the GDR's national hero, the anti-fascist resistance fighter and leader of the communist party, Ernst Thälmann,[15] were released with eighty prints and received glowing reviews in the national press, notably in *Neues Deutschland*, the daily paper which was essentially the official mouthpiece of the SED. Whole collectives were obliged to watch films of great political importance together. On such occasions it was not uncommon that tickets, which were heavily subsidised anyway, costing around 1.50 Marks for adults and 0.50 Marks for children, were given away for free. Such officially endorsed cinema attendance, though it was a comparatively rare occurrence, artificially boosted audience numbers which could then be cited as objective proof of a thriving socialist film culture.

The GDR's approximately 800 regular cinemas were by no means the only venue where films would be shown.[16] In addition, each summer around 250 temporary screening facilities were set up in tents and open-air cinemas. These were strategically placed near camping sites and domestic holiday resorts on the Baltic coast and provided entertainment to holiday-makers. This so-called *Kinosommer* (film summer) was a measure invented during the mid-1960s when audience numbers were in steady decline. The initiative seems to have been effective, attracting more than a third of the annual cinema audience in just a few weeks over the summer (Meurer 2000: 158).

Another distinctive feature of film exhibition in the GDR was the so-called *Landbespielung* (screenings in rural areas). It was originally modelled on the 'cinefication' in the Soviet Union during the 1920s, when film trains were sent across the vast country in order to target audiences in remote rural communities. In the GDR screenings in agricultural communities were set up by itinerant film projectionists who would travel from village to village, covering no less than 3,000 agricultural communities even in the late 1980s, and arrange at least two or three performances per week in club houses, village cinemas and other communal venues. Furthermore, film screenings took place in factories, schools, leisure centres and film clubs. Because the spectrum of leisure activities in the GDR was relatively limited and cinema tickets were cheap, going to the cinema was one of the prime leisure activities, particularly of young people up to the age of twenty-five. Figures for the 1980s suggest that on average GDR citizens went twice as often to the cinema as their West German compatriots, namely 4.5 times per year (Pommer 1999: 128).

Each year around 130 new films were released in the GDR. These included around fifteen new DEFA productions, approximately thirty from capitalist countries, including American imports, around thirty films from the Soviet Union, and sixty from other socialist countries (Otto 2001).

In addition, there were re-releases of previously circulated films. Film programming policies prioritised films from socialist countries, for example, by circulating these imports with many more prints than films from the West. In spite of such targeted efforts, the heavily promoted socialist film culture struggled to compete with Western imports at the box office: on average DEFA films accounted for just 20 to 25 per cent of all cinema admissions (Otto 2001: 179; Meurer 2000: 284), whereas the GDR's box-office top ten films – almost exclusively imports from capitalist countries – accounted for 50 per cent of all admissions (Wiedemann 1991: 86), suggesting that the official film policy that privileged socialist film culture was not particularly effective.

Imports from capitalist countries were a concession to audiences' tastes and a tacit admission of the failure of DEFA and other socialist film industries to produce enough films to satisfy the demand for light-hearted entertainment. The limit of on average just thirty imports from the West was imposed for ideological as well as financial reasons: DEFA-Außenhandel had only a limited amount of *Valuta* (hard, transferable currency) at its disposal to acquire film licences. This also explains why many American films were released in the GDR with a considerable time lag, sometimes two or more years later than their premiere in the US, because it was cheaper to import slightly dated films.

Another important aspect of socialist film culture was regular national film weeks and film festivals representing the film cultures of other socialist countries, not just from Eastern Europe but also from Third World or decolonising countries including Angola, Cuba, Korea, Vietnam, Mexico or Egypt. The exposure to international cinematic traditions was significant, but the kind of World Cinema which GDR audiences experienced was rather different from the kind of World Cinema known in the West. Moreover, the GDR regularly showcased its greatest artistic achievements at international film festivals. The most important venues within the socialist bloc were Moscow and Karlovy Vary (in Czechoslovakia) and Cannes and Venice in Western Europe. Following the rapprochement between the FRG and the GDR during the 1970s, which occurred as a result of Willy Brandt's *Ostpolitik* and which led to the official recognition of the GDR as a sovereign state, the GDR also participated in the International Film Festival in Berlin from 1975 onwards. Between 1949 and 1989 the GDR entered films at 300 festivals and won 155 prizes and special awards for DEFA productions (Diller and Berghahn 2002).

DEFA-Außenhandel, in charge of film import and export, was the only part of the GDR's film industry that was not state-subsidised and that was expected to generate profits which would feed back into the state budget and thus indirectly benefit the state film industry. It sold more than 3,000 film licences to partners in eighty countries and imported over 2,000 feature films from thirty-six countries (Diller and Berghahn 2002). The closest trading relations existed between the GDR and other socialist bloc countries with whom film import and export was regulated through bilateral agreements which stipulated that film was to play an important part within an extensive programme of economic and cultural exchange. Twice a year, each socialist country organised trade shows to which delegates from other socialist countries were invited in order to view and select the films they wished to import. The GDR's delegation comprised representatives from DEFA-Außenhandel, Progress, the Association of Film and Television Workers, and the HV Film. The trade currency was the rouble. Prices were fixed and reflected, amongst other things, the variable numbers of copies with which films were circulated in the different countries.[17]

Film import and export with trading partners from the West was an entirely different matter, in so far as prices and trading conditions had to be negotiated individually and the limited amount of hard currency available to DEFA's import and export division set a number of limitations. The chief export countries for DEFA productions in the West were the German-speaking countries Austria, Switzerland and the Federal Republic of Germany. However, the cinematic release of DEFA films in these countries was a rare occurrence. Even East German box-office hits like *Die Legende von Paul und Paula* (The Legend of Paul and Paula, Heiner Carow, 1973) or *Solo Sunny* (Konrad Wolf, 1980) were quickly taken off the cinema programmes in West Germany because they were culturally too specific to appeal to audiences not familiar with contemporary GDR society. The only type of DEFA films of interest to West Germans were DEFA's fairy-tale films, which were regularly broadcast on West German television. West Germany's public service television channels ARD, ZDF and the Third Channels, purchasing on average three to four licences for feature films per year, were the most important Western trading partners for DEFA-Außenhandel. Yet the general lack of interest in East Germany's film culture highlights the startling asymmetry which characterised the patterns of East and West German audio-visual consumption, a phenomenon which proved particularly problematic after unification.

Socialist Realism and the boundaries of aesthetic orthodoxy

The attempt by the GDR's political leadership to assume complete control over the cultural sphere involved the imposition of a prescriptive aesthetic doctrine upon all forms of cultural production, in particular upon narrative forms of art such as literature and film. The aesthetic doctrine of Socialist Realism, which 'was imposed as a constituent part of the Soviet hegemony over Central and Eastern Europe after 1945' (Taylor *et al.* 2000: 218), was originally developed by Zhdanov, Stalin's 'cultural commissar', and first proclaimed in 1934 at the First All Union Congress of Soviet Writers. On this occasion the Russian novelist Maxim Gorky and the Hungarian literary theorist Georg Lukács delineated their somewhat diverging interpretations of Socialist Realism. Gorky's vision of Socialist Realist art was encapsulated in works of art that glorified labour and promoted a revolutionary attitude and the Communist cause. For Gorky, Socialist Realist art had to express faith in a new and better society. Lukács's interpretation of Socialist Realism, on the other hand, was based on the aesthetic model of the nineteenth-century realist novel and was thus anti-modernist in terms of its aesthetic outlook, but at the same time allowed for a certain degree of artistic autonomy from politics.

Setting the numerous drawbacks of the Socialist Realist doctrine aside, its original rationale had been driven by a genuinely democratic and emancipatory desire, namely to create art for the masses and thus make high culture accessible to the broad middlebrow public. Socialist Realist art therefore eschewed experimentation both in form and content, which was denounced as 'formalist', bourgeois and decadent. While the debate around Socialist Realism was by no means uniform across the Eastern bloc countries, certain features such as class-consciousness, ideological orthodoxy, adherence to the Party line and typicality are ubiquitous. Further stock elements include an exemplary positive hero and a revolutionary romanticism that distinguishes Socialist Realism from critical realism. Whilst critical realism aspires to authenticity, Socialist Realism charts reality in its revolutionary development. It is this belief in continuous progress towards a better society and future that makes socialist realist art 'optimistic' and distinguishes it from the alleged pessimism and nihilism of its bourgeois counterparts, naturalism and critical realism. As Richard Taylor aptly puts it, Socialist Realism does not aim to '*reflect* reality in all its infinite variety but to *change* reality, to shape it in accordance with a predetermined mould, to convey . . . "not reality as it is, but reality as it ought to be"' (Taylor 1998: 210; emphasis in original).

Although many artists and intellectuals who were to assume leading roles in the cultural life of the GDR had contributed to the realism debate while still in exile in Moscow, it was only during the early 1950s that Socialist Realism became mandatory in the GDR. A resolution of the Politburo of the SED of 22 July 1952 ('Für den Aufschwung der fortschrittlichen deutschen Filmkunst' (For the development of progressive German film art)) and further communications at a film conference in September of the same year pronounced that film production would be harnessed more firmly to the current political and economic agenda of the construction of socialism and would have to subscribe to the aesthetic doctrine of Socialist Realism. In a speech entitled 'Über Fragen der forschrittlichen deutschen Filmkunst' (Questions regarding progressive German film art), given at the Conference of the Central Committee of the SED in September 1952, Hermann Axen dismissed forms of critical realism, which had been tolerated up till then, by stressing that they belonged to the realm of bourgeois filmmaking (Axen 1953a: 30). On the issue of 'formalist' film aesthetics, he noted:

> Gerade weil der kapitalistische Film einen niedrigen Ideengehalt hat, nicht den positiven, sondern vielmehr den negativen Helden 'verherrlicht', gerade deshalb muß er die Zuflucht nehmen zu formalen Effekten, zu einem ununterbrochenen Bilder- und Szenenwechsel; nicht zur Darstellung des Menschen, der guten schöpferischen Tat, sondern zur Häufung der Sensationen, Katastrophen, Abenteuer usw. (Axen 1953a: 35)

> (It is because capitalist films are short on ideas and, instead of promoting a positive hero, glorify a negative one, that they need to resort to formal effects and an incessant change of images and scenes; the representation of people and good creative deeds is replaced by a mere accumulation of sensations, catastrophes, adventures and so on.)

This remark also points towards the incompatibility of the Socialist Realist doctrine and genre cinema, of which more below.

In principle, Socialist Realism, or at least the filmmakers' implicit pledge to artistic orthodoxy as defined by the Party, remained binding throughout state-socialism in the GDR. However, in practice it did not provide a coherent and monolithic system of directions for filmmakers because there were several periods during which the limits of the artistically permissible were expanded and filmmakers were given leeway to renegotiate the concept of Socialist Realism. As a result, East German film history, just as much as the history of Soviet and East European cinema, provides numerous examples of occasions on which filmmakers deviated from this master narrative and stylistic paradigm. Whether such unorthodox films came under attack from the cultural officials was determined not so much by the extent of their aesthetic transgression as by the cultural climate that prevailed at the time of their production and release. For example, Gerhard Klein and Wolfgang Kohlhaase's film *Berlin – Ecke Schönhauser* (Berlin – Schönhauser Corner, 1957) was made at a time of relative ideological relaxation that was ushered in by Khrushchev's revelation of Stalin's crimes at the Twentieth CPSU Congress in 1956. In the GDR de Stalinisation was carried out rather half-heartedly but, nonetheless, it resulted in a volatile political atmosphere and a short-lived competency conflict between the DEFA studio and the HV Film which afforded the director-scriptwriter duo Klein and Kohlhaase with the freedom to start shooting the film without ever obtaining permission from the HV Film (see Heimann 1994: 255ff). However, after its completion and despite being a success at the box office, *Berlin – Ecke Schönhauser* was subsequently harshly criticised at the Party Activists Convention (*Parteiaktivtagung*) in 1958 for aligning itself with competing realist aesthetics, notably Italian Neo-Realism and a Zolaesque type of naturalism. At the second Film Conference in 1958 the spectre of revisionism was polemically evoked and even prominent filmmakers were reprimanded for returning to critical realism, for adhering to modernist aesthetics and for suggesting in their films that alienation was not a problem that besieged capitalist societies alone. Films that came under attack ranged from Martin Hellberg's adaptation of the literary classic, *Emilia Galotti* (1958), to Francesco Stefani's fairy-tale film *Das singende, klingende Bäumchen* (The Singing, Ringing Tree, 1957). In fact, only a few films produced during the past two decades escaped reproach.

In later years, prominent examples of films that transgress the aesthetic boundaries of Socialist Realism are Frank Beyer's *Königskinder* (Star Crossed Lovers, 1962) and Konrad Wolf's *Der geteilte Himmel* (Divided Heaven, 1964) which, on account of their montage sequences, achronological time structure and highly stylised cinematography, exhibit distinctly modernist aesthetics. Similarly, Jürgen Böttcher's film *Jahrgang '45* (Born'45, 1966/90), which was forbidden in the wake of the Eleventh Plenum in 1966 (see Chapter 4), foreshadows a new aesthetic trend that flies in the face of Socialist Realism by depicting the *tristesse* of everyday life in the GDR with great authenticity and without any progressive pathos. This type of realism, documentary realism, which became associated with the third generation of DEFA directors, notably Lothar Warnecke, Rainer Simon and Roland Gräf, stood in the tradition of Italian Neo-Realism, Klein and Kohlhaase's Berlin films of the 1950s and *cinéma vérité*. Though the first documentary realist films, such as *Dr. med. Sommer II* (Lothar Warnecke, 1969) and *Mein lieber Robinson* (My Dear Robinson, Roland Gräf, 1970), were produced in the late 1960s, it was not until after the considerable political and cultural relaxation which occurred after the replacement of Walter Ulbricht by Erich Honecker as the First Secretary of the SED and his much cited cultural policy of 'no taboos' (see Chapter 5) that documentary realism could establish itself temporarily as an acceptable variety of Socialist Realism.

What these examples illustrate is that although the stylistic paradigm of Socialist Realism was never officially renounced it was by no means tantamount to a monolithic orthodoxy and a formulaic style. According to Andreas Dresen, one of East Germany's most prolific new generation directors, identifying a distinctive DEFA style is difficult:[18]

> Der DEFA Stil stellt sich für mich nicht als etwas Homogenes dar, sondern als ein Bündel von unterschiedlichsten Handschriften. Natürlich hat Rainer Simon ganz andere Filme gemacht als Roland Gräf oder Kurt Maetzig. Deswegen fällt es mir schwer zu sagen, was eigentlich das Wesen des sogenannten DEFA Stils ist. Es läßt sich im Herangehen an die Themen etwas finden, was vielleicht markant ist, aber nicht nur für DEFA, sondern für die osteuropäische Filmkultur insgesamt, nämlich ein bestimmtes humanistisches Menschenbild, was sich im Film manifiestiert. Die Filme sind meistens sozial gesettled. Da ist keine Flucht in die Ästhetik, sondern sie finden auf einem sozialen Bodensatz statt. (Dresen and Berghahn 2002)

> (In my view, the DEFA style is not homogenous but, instead, a bundle of the most diverse individual approaches. Naturally, Rainer Simon's films are entirely different from those of Roland Gräf or Kurt Maetzig. That's why I find it difficult to identify a so-called DEFA style. Maybe there is something distinctive in the way in which certain themes are approached, not just with regard to DEFA, but in the entire film culture of Eastern Europe: there is a certain humanism in the way people are portrayed. Most of these films have a social relevance. They don't offer an escape into pure aestheticism but are grounded in society.)

And this is precisely, as will be shown in Chapter 6, DEFA's legacy today: the continuation of a strong realist tradition combined with a commitment to socially relevant issues.

DEFA genre cinema[19]

DEFA did not produce thrillers, but *Reißer* (the German equivalent of thriller but only used in East German parlance); DEFA did not produce Westerns, but *Indianerfilme* (Red Indian films); the East German variant of the science fiction genre was called *utopisch-abenteuerliche Filme* (utopian adventure films); DEFA had no stars, they were called *Publikumslieblinge* (audience darlings). In short, DEFA was suspicious of genre cinema and made a conscious attempt to differentiate its own, rather modest output of genre films from Western genre cinema, notably Hollywood. The different choice of terminology gives a clear signal that genre cinema made in the GDR was always a conscious attempt to offer a socialist variant to the sensationalist practices of capitalist entertainment cinema.

The obvious problem which DEFA had with genre cinema was that its goals are diametrically opposed to the function that was ascribed to cinema in the GDR: genre cinema aims to offer entertainment, whereas DEFA's mission was to educate and to promote the development of a socialist consciousness. While some of DEFA's early films were both ideologically instructive and commercially successful, it did not take long for audiences to demand an escape in the cinema from the drudgery of their daily lives.

In the FRG where, at least until the rise of Young German Cinema, film was classified as entertainment with no pretence to art or education, this demand was easily satisfied. In particular the 1950s were the heyday of home-produced popular cinema. The commercially most successful genre of all was the *Heimatfilm*. Other popular genres enjoyed by West German audiences during the 1950s and 1960s were melodramatic *Arztfilme* (medical dramas); costume dramas, notably the *Sissi* trilogy (1955–57), about the Austrian empress and featuring Romy Schneider and Karl Heinz Böhm; musical comedies and *Schlagerfilme* (pop music films); crime thrillers such as the series of Edgar Wallace films; and the West German variant of the American Western, the *Winnetou* films based on popular novels by Karl May.

Beyond Germany's national boundaries, however, the very concept of German popular cinema is almost a contradiction in terms. There are many reasons for this, the most important being that in a cultural context dominated by Hollywood imports, popular European cinema has, at least until recently, been dismissed as a pale imitation of the original. Moreover, popular European cinema tends to be nationally specific and, therefore, does not travel well. More specific to the German context, there has been a critical bias against genre cinema which has had a profound impact on its critical reception, though not on audiences' enthusiasm for popular genre traditions. The critical paradigms set in particular by the Frankfurt School and notably by Theodor Adorno's highly influential concept of the culture industry has resulted in a disdain for mass culture, including mainstream cinema. What the cultural elite promoted instead as a sufficiently 'elevated manifestation of national culture' (Bergfelder 2002: 15) was the *auteur* cinema of the late 1960s through to the mid-1980s, which embodies desirable high-cultural values and which critically engages with capitalist ideology and the perceived harmful dominance of capitalist consumer culture. Only since the mid-1980s has this position been reconsidered and German genre cinema has been revitalised both in terms of film production and critical reception.

What these cursory remarks on popular cinema in the West German context suggest is that the dominant cultural elites in both East and West Germany were united in their disdain for genre cinema, which was deemed to lack the high-cultural values they wanted to see reflected in national cinema. Of course, in West Germany the laws of commerce played a much more significant role, which explains why popular cinema was an important feature of West German film culture in particular during the 1950s, irrespective of what cultural elites considered to be desirable. In the GDR, by contrast, where ideology was valued higher than commercial success and where the state dictated what audiences were supposed to watch, the production of popular films was a reluctant concession to audience demand rather than a central aspect of national film culture. During the 1960s, when audience figures dropped by as much as ten million annually as a result of increasing competition from television (Otto 2001: 178), the production of genre films became somewhat of a rescue operation to buck the alarming trend. Consequently, the studio was encouraged to produce more popular films, often in direct response to international developments.[20] For example, DEFA's thrillers of the 1960s can be seen as the East German variant of the James Bond movies and the popular West German Edgar Wallace films of the 1960s. DEFA's hugely successful *Indianerfilme* are not only the socialist answer to the most American of all genres, the Western, but also 'successfully cashed in on the renewed popularity of the Western genre in Europe' demonstrated by the mass appeal of West German Winnetou films and the Italian Spaghetti Westerns, of which no fewer than four hundred were made in the 1960s and 1970s (Vincendeau 1995: 221).

Although DEFA had produced a number of crime and spy thrillers during the 1950s, it was really during the 1960s that DEFA crime thrillers came into their own. Some of the better-known titles include *Seilergasse 8* (8 Seiler Street, Joachim Kunert, 1960); *Nebel* (Fog, Joachim Hasler, 1963); *Die Glatzkopfenbande* (The Skin Head Gang, Richard Groschopp, 1963), a film about juvenile delinquents in the GDR; and *Schwarzer Samt* (Black Velvet, Heinz Thiel, 1964). The most famous spy thriller is János Veiczi's *For Eyes Only* (1963), in which an East German secret agent and colleague of the Stasi spy chief and Deputy Minister for State Security, Markus Wolf, manages to steal important military documents from the CIA (here called MID) and, after a dramatic escape, brings them back safely to the GDR.

Another popular genre of which DEFA produced a socialist variant was science fiction (see Soldovieri 1998b). Yet the number of DEFA's sci-fi films was limited to just four in total: *Der schweigende Stern* (Silent Planet, Kurt Mactzig, 1960); *Signale – Ein Weltraumabenteuer* (Signals – A Space Adventure, Gottfried Kolditz, 1970); *Eolomea* (Herrmann Zschoche, 1972); and *Im Staub der Sterne* (In the Dust of the Stars, Gottfried Kolditz, 1976). The production and release of these films largely coincided with the prominence the genre regained internationally through the release of Stanley Kubrick's *2001: A Space Odyssey* (USA, 1968) and Andrei Tarkovsky's *Solaris* (USSR, 1972). Despite the fact that *Solaris* became one of the most famous sci-fi classics, in general the sci-fi genre did not flourish in socialist film production – firstly, because these films placed high technological and financial demands on the studio, and secondly, because the attempt to instil political messages into what is essentially a fantasy genre proved only moderately successful. DEFA's excursions into outer space remained in many respects too close to home, since the depiction of the future was always made subservient to the demands of the present. Space missions never take the astronauts beyond the realms of the known, instead they are trips into social utopias. These utopian adventures promote a superior socialist community and peaceful co-existence, the latter being an unmistakable reference to the GDR's state doctrine. This inability to transcend the demands of Socialist Realism even in a fantasy genre makes DEFA's futuristic films appear dated from the outset.

The increased prominence of genre cinema since the late 1960s can also be seen as a consequence of the ferocious film censorship which occurred at the Eleventh Plenum (see Chapter 4). The banned films had been predominantly critical examinations of contemporary society, a thematic area which the Party had encouraged but which had proven too risky for filmmakers. Intimidated by the repercussions of the Plenum the studio directorate encouraged the production of 'safe' films which were at least ostensibly remote from sensitive contemporary issues. This explains the significant number of costume dramas (see Chapter 3); *Schlagerfilme* (pop music films) like Joachim Hasler's *Heißer Sommer* (Hot Summer, 1968); comedies like Roland Oehme's *Der Mann, der nach der Oma kam* (The Man Who Came after Granny, 1971) and, most importantly, DEFA's *Indianerfilme* from the late 1960s onwards.

The *Indianerfilme* are the only continuously successful series of genre films that DEFA ever produced. Between 1966 and 1979, the Babelsberg Studio made twelve *Indianerfilme*. The first one in the series, *Die Söhne der großen Bärin* (The Sons of the Great Mother Bear, Josef Mach, 1966), attracted more than ten million viewers. From then on *Indianerfilme* became a key attraction of the *Kinosommer* (film summer) and were invariably released in open air theatres. Titles include *Chingachgoog, die große Schlange* (Chingachgoog, the Big Snake, Richard Groschopp, 1967); *Die Spur des Falken* (The Trace of the Falcon, Gottfried Kolditz, 1968); *Weiße Wölfe* (White Wolves, Konrad Petzold, 1969); *Osceola* (Konrad Petzold, 1971); and *Apachen* (Apaches, Gottfried Kolditz, 1973). With the exception of *Blauvogel* (Blue Bird, Ulrich Weiß, 1979), all were made by the same artistic work group, Roter Kreis, which specialised in the genre. Yugoslav-born actor Gojko Mitic was the heroic Indian chief and uncontested star at the centre of nearly all *Indianerfilme*. Not only did his athletic looks and the heroic qualities he represented make him popular with audiences, more importantly, from an official point of view, his biography made him extremely well suited as an ideological role model and a model citizen in the GDR. As Gerd Gemünden points out, Mitic incorporates elements of the GDR's anti-fascist myth of origin since his father 'had fought Hitler's army as a partisan' and he himself 'had moved to East Berlin in the mid-1960s after having already acted in some English and Italian productions and some of Reinl's Karl May films. Mitic was thus a highly visible exception to the westward flow of East German actors and film professionals' (Gemünden 1998: 404).

In a more general sense, political correctness, coupled with historical authenticity, is one of the hallmarks of DEFA's *Indianerfilme*. Consequently, the good guys and the bad guys in the socialist variant of the Western swap roles: the American Indians and their chief, Gojko Mitic, are not only brave and heroic, they also promote values such as anti-imperialism and the peaceful coexistence between Indians and whites, which resonate with the GDR's official ideology. The white settlers, by contrast, are depicted as greedy, 'treaty-breaking Army colonels, corrupt sheriffs, imperialist oil magnates and despicable plantation owners' (Gemünden 1998: 399) and thus embody the value system of capitalism. What explains the mass appeal of these films is, however, not so much their ideological correctness but the fact that they offered powerful fantasies of escape and freedom. Shot on location in Yugoslavia, Czechoslovakia, Bulgaria, the Soviet Union and even Cuba – countries that boasted the kind of landscapes which could with some credibility stand in for the wide-open plains of Dakota and other famous Western landscapes the *Indianerfilme* opened new vistas to audiences who had become prisoners of their own country a few years before DEFA's first Indians fought for their land and freedom on screen (see Gemünden 1998: 406).

Fairy tales and other children's films

In view of the educational mission assigned to cinema in East Germany, it is not surprising that films targeting children and adolescents played a key role in DEFA productions. Between 1946 and 1990, the feature film studio produced around 180 feature-length films for children; this equals nearly four per year and one fifth of DEFA's entire feature film production (Wiedemann 1996: 21).[21] The importance attributed to children's films betrays the strong affinity between East German and East European film culture, where children's films were generally accorded much higher esteem than in the West. Even today imports from East European countries feature more prominently on German children's television than one would have expected given the American dominance elsewhere.

In 1953 a department was founded in the DEFA feature film studio which was exclusively dedicated to the production of children's films. Like DEFA's genre cinema, children's films are associated with a group of directors and scriptwriters who specialised in this type of film, notably Rolf Losansky, Walter Beck, Hans Kratzert, Egon Schlegel, Hannelore Unterberg, Helmut Dziuba and Christa Kožik, to mention but a few. In addition, well-known feature film directors such as Heiner Carow, Gerhard Klein, Herrmann Zschoche and Rainer Simon also contributed to this important aspect of East German film production by making either *Gegenwartsfilme* for children (e.g. *Alarm im Zirkus* (Alarm in the Circus, Gerhard Klein, 1954); *Sheriff Teddy* (Heiner Carow, 1957); *Ikarus* (Heiner Carow, 1975); *Sieben Sommersprossen* (Seven Freckles,

Herrmann Zschoche, 1978)) or films in the anti-fascist tradition with young protagonists (e.g. *Irgendwo in Berlin* (Somewhere in Berlin, Gerhard Lamprecht, 1946); *Sie nannten ihn Amigo* (They Called Him Amigo, Heiner Carow, 1959); *Mein blauer Vogel fliegt* (My Blue Bird Flies, Celino Bleiweiß, 1975)).

The most critically acclaimed type of DEFA children's films are its fairy-tale films, based on sources by the Brothers Grimm, Wilhelm Hauff and Hans Christian Andersen. Over forty were made and they include internationally well-known titles such as Paul Verhoeven's *Das kalte Herz* (The Cold Heart, 1950), Francesco Stefani's *Das singende, klingende Bäumchen* (The Singing, Ringing Tree, 1957) and Wolfgang Staudte's *Die Geschichte vom kleinen Muck* (The Story of Little Mook, 1953). Staudte's exotic fairy-tale film was seen by more than twelve million viewers in the East and the West and was allegedly Ho Chi Minh's favourite film. While the implicit message of fairy tales, that everyone is capable of changing for the better, felicitously coincides with one of socialism's fundamental tenets, often the classic sources did not adequately reflect the pedagogical aims of socialist consciousness-formation in other respects.

The preponderance of kings and queens, princes and princesses, for example, was problematic because they belonged to the 'wrong' social class. Hence the stories were often 'sanitized along the lines of domesticated proletarian good behaviour' (Bathrick 1996: 168). Thus, in the cinematic adaptation of *Dornröschen* (Sleeping Beauty, Walter Beck, 1971), the king's order to ban all spinning wheels from the country is shown to result in insufferable impoverishment for those who earn their living from spinning. Moreover, the film's colour scheme underlines the fact that the nobility and the aristocracy are doomed to be overtaken by the progressive forces of history: their complexions are of a bluish, deadly hue. Typically even princes and princesses do not get things for free but instead have to validate themselves through hard work. In *Froschkönig* (The Frog Prince, Walter Beck, 1988) the princess cannot get married to the frog-turned-prince immediately but first has to shed her long hair and precious clothes, disguise herself as a man and undertake hard physical labour before she eventually wins the frog prince's heart.

Fairy tale adaptations that failed to make the appropriate ideological adjustments, such as *Das singende, klingende Bäumchen*,[22] were harshly criticised for promoting a bourgeois class consciousness and a 'verlogene Monarchenromantik' (hypocritical idealisation of the monarchs), which was seen to be ill-suited to the development of a 'sozialistische

Erfassen solcher moralischen Werte wie z. B. "Gut und Böse", "Recht und Unrecht"' (cited in König and Wiedemann 1996: 109) (socialist understanding of moral values such as 'good and evil', 'right and wrong') in children.

State patronage and the promotion of national film culture in East and West Germany

The governments of both East and West Germany endeavoured to promote their specific variant of German national identity through the development of a distinctive national film culture. Where nothing less than the cultural and historical legitimacy of the two separate German states was at stake, the state was bound to intervene in order to ensure that domestic film production would support the construction of an officially endorsed national identity. Though the mechanisms through which East and West German governments tried to assert their control differed considerably, in both Germanys state patronage of the film industry provided an efficient form of indirect regulation and control while at the same time being an indispensable prerequisite for the survival of film industries, which were not sustainable by audience demand alone.

Whereas state patronage was the norm in East European film industries under state-socialism, West Germany was the first major capitalist country where the state extended its role as patron beyond the traditional spheres of education and 'high culture' art forms to the film industry (Elsaesser 1989: 28). Even during the 1950s, when film was considered to be 'just' a form of entertainment and still enjoyed a healthy domestic market share of 40 per cent, the state introduced a number of subsidy programmes to support the national film industry. From the 1960s onwards, when the market share of indigenous films dropped to 30 per cent and the quality became so poor that no German film was awarded a Federal Film Prize in 1961, consecutive West German governments implemented a diverse array of subsidy measures. These ranged from project-based public funding to legal frameworks for television coproduction and a system of quality ratings that attracted tax relief. These quality ratings, which were centrally awarded by the *Filmbewertungsstelle* (Film Assessment Office) in Wiesbaden, constituted a form of indirect censorship because films that displeased the members on the selection board, be it for ideological or aesthetic reasons, would not receive a quality rating and, as a result, were unlikely to find a distributor because no relief on entertainment tax would be granted. In this sense the quality ratings were a disincentive for difficult and critical films, instead encouraging conformity and mediocrity. According to Thomas Elsaesser 'the official list of "valuable" films for the 1950s reads more like a roll call of the world's worst movies than a guide to a nation's film culture' (Elsaesser 1989: 20).

On the other hand, the emergence of the Young, and subsequently, New German Cinema during the 1960s, often referred to as the second golden age of German cinema, could never have happened without state patronage. Cinema's increasing reliance on state funding automatically implied that film was no longer perceived as 'just' entertainment but was elevated in status to other forms of high culture which the government deemed worthy of subsidy. In return, West German film culture was expected to promote a distinct national identity at home and abroad. Through state legislation on film subvention West German governments ensured a certain degree of political control over film production. Similarly, during the 1970s the strong involvement of public service television, with its mission to promote 'Bildung' (education) and 'Kultur' (culture), resulted in a distinctly high-cultural bias in New German Cinema, which is characterised by an abundance of cinematic adaptations of literature (see Chapter 3).

However, the various bodies involved in making decisions relating to film subvention and control, including the Ministry of the Interior, the federal governments in charge of cultural policies of the federal states, the *Filmförderungsanstalt* (Film Subsidy Board) in Berlin, the *Filmbewertungsstelle* in Wiesbaden and German public service television, ensured a considerable degree of aesthetic and ideological diversity. In fact, the filmmakers associated with New German Cinema found that this 'cultural mode of production' (Elsaesser 1989: 40–2) afforded them a greater degree of freedom than a film industry predominantly driven by commercial considerations. After all, the international acclaim of New German Cinema is largely based on its status as counter cinema, its high degree of artistic innovation, and its critical examination of West German contemporary society. Film directors like Rainer Werner Fassbinder, Alexander Kluge and Edgar Reitz were not restrained from pointing out some uncomfortable truths about the FRG's failure to overcome the fascist legacy. Similarly, a number of films that took a rather sympathetic approach to the politically highly sensitive issue of urban terrorism, including Margarethe von Trotta's *Die bleierne Zeit* (The German Sisters/Marianne and Juliane, 1981), based on the story of the RAF terrorist Gudrun Enslin, and Reinhard Hauff's *Stammheim*

– *Baader-Meinhof vor Gericht* (Stammheim – The Trial, 1986), about the trial of the leading terrorists of the Red Army Faction in the high-security prison Stammheim, were granted subsidy while, admittedly, others such as the collaborative project *Deutschland im Herbst* (Germany in Autumn, 1978) were not eligible.

Though undeniably any form of film subsidy granted or regulated by the state is a form of indirect censorship insofar as it allows the government to influence what kind of screen images are deemed an appropriate reflection of a desirable national identity, in the case of West Germany the actual impact of state interference and indirect censorship was relatively limited. Given that many different political factions and interest groups were involved in the decision-making processes, West German films that were made with state funding reflect the democratic and pluralist political culture from which they emanated. Arguably, the increasing commercialisation of the film funding system since the 1980s has limited the diversity of artistic expression and political outlook of West German film culture far more than state intervention in the previous decades.

Since film subsidy in the Federal Republic of Germany has traditionally concentrated on domestic film production rather than on distribution and exhibition, government initiatives aimed at actively promoting a national film culture have remained relatively ineffective. Unlike in the GDR, where a centralised distribution monopoly implemented a state-approved film programming policy, the patterns of film circulation and consumption were, and after re-unification still are, largely determined by the market forces of a capitalist economy. US majors dominate distribution channels and cinema ownership is concentrated on just a few chains with strong links to the US majors. Since access to premiere and multi-screen cinemas is controlled by just a few conglomerates which favour Hollywood releases, those domestically produced and state-subsidised films, through which West German governments hope to promote a national film culture, are released by specialist, under-capitalised distributors in small cinemas and thus hardly ever reach a broad public and rarely recuperate their production costs. Under such abysmal conditions 'the market for national identity is small' with an estimated 50 per cent of all domestically produced films never being distributed commercially at all (Meurer 2000: 121–2). And while a small number of films made by famous *auteurs* of the New German Cinema, or international co-productions like Wolfgang Petersen's *Das Boot* (The Boat, 1981) and *Die unendliche Geschichte* (The Never-Ending Story, 1984)

or Sönke Wortmann's relationship comedy *Der bewegte Mann* (Maybe
... Maybe Not, 1994) found a receptive audience abroad, generally
German cinema is orientated toward the home market and international
box-office hits are the exception rather than the rule.

As has been illustrated above, in the GDR this bourgeois model of
cultural sponsorship was considered to be inadequate for steering the
course of national film culture. 'Film war Staatssache' (film was a state
affair) (Geiss 1997: 198) and nothing less than the cultural leadership of
the Party would do to ensure that the GDR's film culture reflected the
state's strategic priorities. What this meant in practice was a curtailment
of artistic freedom and the subordination of individual creativity to the
imperatives of the collective and the state. From a Western perspective,
such conditions of cultural production are seen to result in political art
or even propaganda. But more than a decade after the fall of the Wall
and the end of state-socialism, we ought to be wary of perpetuating the
clichés of the Cold War era. Instead of merely condemning the modes
of cultural production under state-socialism it is time we reassessed its
advantages as well as its disadvantages.

Admittedly, around thirty of the 750 feature films DEFA made fell
victim to various mechanisms of censorship. In the larger scheme of things
this is a small share. Hundreds of scripts were never realised and thousands of ideas were aborted through the complex mechanisms of censorship, most importantly self-censorship. But this is by no means what
filmmaking in the GDR was all about!

For a start, it would be a gross oversimplification to understand the
relationship between filmmakers and the state in terms of a straight-
forward polarisation between *Geist und Macht* (art and power). In particular during the early years of the newly founded German Democratic
Republic considerable consensus between the filmmakers and the state's
leaders existed about the kind of films they wanted to make: films that
legitimised the GDR as the better Germany on account of its anti-fascist
origins and on account of the superiority of socialism over capitalism.
Even later on, when this fundamental consensus evinced some cracks,
it would be incorrect to describe the relationship between filmmakers
and the state as one of opposition.

Similarly, distinguishing between 'conformist' and 'non-conformist'
filmmakers proves problematic. For instance, Konrad Wolf, Kurt
Maetzig and Frank Beyer all made films which the state honoured with
the bestowal of the GDR's most prestigious award, the *Nationalpreis*
(National Prize). These laurels did not, however, make them immune

to the repressive mechanisms of state intervention: censorship was inflicted upon films like *Sonnensucher* (Sun Seekers, Konrad Wolf, 1958/72), *Das Kaninchen bin ich* (The Rabbit is Me, Kurt Maetzig, 1965/90) and, most famously, *Spur der Steine* (Trace of Stones, Frank Beyer, 1966/90), and Beyer was even prohibited from making films for several years.

As this evidence suggests, the state's ideological and material investment in the film industry was a double-edged sword. No attempt should be made to play down or even deny the adverse effects of state intervention in the artistic process, but at the same time one must not forget that the state's vested interest in national film culture also had enormous benefits for the industry and everyone associated with it. Film was accorded the status of art in the GDR and was, because art and culture in general fulfilled a central legitimatory role, taken very seriously. 'Where else in the world', the writer Bertolt Brecht remarked, 'can you find a government that shows such interest in, and pays such attention to, its artists?' (cited in Bathrick 1995: 91). Consequently, DEFA's film directors, scriptwriters and other artistic staff enjoyed considerable kudos and many privileges. Being permanently employed by the state-owned studios enabled filmmakers to dedicate their efforts entirely to the creative side of their work. Thanks to state patronage, their working conditions were in many respects much more favourable than those of their colleagues in capitalist countries, where the demands of the market usually impose severe limitations on the kind of films that are realised and eventually distributed. Arguably, the percentage of East German films that were banned or withdrawn as a result of censorship is small compared with the significant proportion of West German films that never get a theatrical release: some figures suggest around 17 per cent, others as much as 50 per cent.[23] Thus, in effect, in the FRG the laws of competition and commerce have proven much more powerful in discriminating against 'unpopular' films and excluding a considerable share of domestic film production from circulation than the practice of censorship in the GDR, which identified a relatively small number of films as unsuitable for public viewing.

In spite of resenting the curtailment of their artistic freedom, ultimately DEFA filmmakers were aware of their privileged position. Weighing up the pros and cons of filmmaking in the socialist and the capitalist systems, most opted to stay in the GDR.[24] Admittedly, permission to leave the GDR was not easy to obtain even for uncomfortably critical artists and intellectuals. But neither privileges nor obstacles alone can fully

explain why most filmmakers chose to stay. Until the demise of the socialist German state they never completely gave up the goal of building
a better society, or at least the hope of contributing to the development
of a reformed and democratic socialism, through their work.

The way in which film could contribute to the building of a better
society was interpreted rather differently by filmmakers and state officials,
leading to many frictions. Party bureaucrats were so intent on using film
as an instrument to bolster political conviction and harnessing film production to the Party line that they often lost sight of the bigger picture.
The result was often formulaic films with little popular appeal, films that
replicated the drudgery of working life on screen. 'Mit dir würde ich mir
sogar einen DEFA Film angucken' (With you, I'd even go and see a DEFA
film') says Manfred Krug's character Balla in *Spur der Steine* as a proof
of his affection for Kati.

This disparity between the kind of films audiences wanted and the kind
of films the paternalistic state considered to be suitable viewing for its
'children' was one of the biggest problems from which the GDR's film
industry suffered. From the perspective of the state bureaucrats it was
only legitimate to denounce film's pretence of artistic autonomy for film
was, after all, not about diversion but about socialist education. The state
was therefore justified in devising mechanisms of ideological monitoring in order to retain control over its chosen master narratives and their
representation in the cultural realm, notably the mass medium of film.

Hence, whenever the SED Party state feared that its power and legitimisation were jeopardised it tried to re-assert its control through
crack-downs in the cultural sphere. Culture fulfilled, in more than just
one sense, a *Stellvertreterfunktion* (replacement function): film, alongside literature, filled a gap in the GDR's multiple public spheres which
had been left by the more tightly controlled news media.[25] Since the
latter had a more immediate impact on the ideological basis of the regime
they were used for overt political propaganda and came under the
direct supervision of the Central Committee. In this hierarchy of media
control, film, compared with television, radio and the press, was less closely
guarded by the state. However, because of its collective mode of production and its reliance on technology, it was harder for film to develop
outside the authorised sphere of cultural production than for literature.
Nonetheless, both film and literature fulfilled a replacement function insofar as they provided media which aired 'in an oblique fashion issues
that were otherwise taboos. Conversely, the Party leadership through encouragement or condemnation of cultural trends, sent signals about wider

political and social issues' (Feinstein 2002: 8). This explains why films and books rumoured to voice dissent gained such notoriety and fame that they frequently enjoyed great audience appeal as a result.

Despite the fact that neither East nor West German audiences were particularly enthusiastic about their domestic film productions, as their unimpressive market shares indicate, there is nevertheless considerable evidence that film culture in the East was more closely intertwined with people's daily lives than that in the West. Whether people liked it or not, what they saw on screen overlapped to a large extent with what they experienced by living and working in the GDR. The majority of DEFA films, in particular the *Gegenwartsfilme*, were something like a running social commentary on the GDR's socio-political and even economic evolution and for this reason, though not for this reason alone, a truly national cinema.

Furthermore, the GDR's national film culture was promoted in such a way that it was art by the people for the people. Notwithstanding the status and prestige which DEFA filmmakers enjoyed, they were not celebrities like some filmmakers in capitalist film industries, whom the average person can only admire from afar at televised award-giving ceremonies or on chat shows. It was common for film directors, script-writers, dramaturges and other artistic staff to go on tour with their films when they were released nationwide. They would actively engage in a dialogue with audiences and discuss their films with ordinary people. And this close rapport with audiences was not just a ritual to demonstrate that film art was art for the people.

The impetus for Konrad Wolf's last film before his untimely death in 1982 was partly derived from this kind of audience feedback. Wolf's most acclaimed films had all been concerned with German history, including such masterpieces as *Sterne* (Stars, 1959) and *Ich war neunzehn* (I Was Nineteen, 1968). In one such audience discussion a young man challenged Wolf by saying that in his eyes Wolf had no credibility as an artist unless he could make equally powerful and convincing films about contemporary GDR society (Pehnert and Berghahn 2002). With *Solo Sunny*, a hugely popular film about a young woman who aspires to be a pop star and who asserts her right to a solo performance, not just on stage but in life as well, Wolf proved he could.

It is this immediate social relevance that many DEFA films had for the people of the GDR – Andreas Dresen calls it the 'sozialen Bodensatz' (social grounding) (Dresen and Berghahn 2002) – which we have come to recognise as one of the hallmarks of DEFA feature films. The film director Gerhard Klein, famous for his closely observed milieu studies in the 'Berlin films' of the 1950s, expressed the same idea differently:

> Die Menschen in fünfzig Jahren werden sich unter anderem auch aus unserer Produktion von Filmen, aus unseren Konsumwünschen im Kino ein genaues Bild über uns machen können. Ein Bild unserer menschlichen Reife, unserer Klugheit, unserer Haltung zum Leben überhaupt. In fünfzig Jahren werden Menschen in den Sesseln eines Filmmuseums sitzen und sich auch mit Hilfe der Kunstkonserve Film ein Bild über unser Leben machen. Lassen Sie uns schon heute im Geiste ihre Plätze einnehmen. Es wird uns von Nutzen sein. (Klein cited in Schenk and Kasten 1994)

> (In fifty years' time, people will be able to get a clear idea of who we were by, amongst other things, watching our films and by studying our consumer behaviour on screen. An idea of our maturity, our wisdom, our attitude towards life in general. In fifty years' time, people will be sitting in the seats of a film museum forming a picture of our lives with the help of the film art that has been preserved. Let us imagine today that we are in their place. It will be to our advantage.)

Notes

1 When Staudte presented his screenplay of *Die Mörder sind unter uns* to Peter van Eyck, who was film officer in the American-occupied zone at the time, van Eyck refused to give Staudte a production licence, remarking that it would probably take another twenty years before Germans could make their own films again. However, just a few days after the Soviets had licensed DEFA's first feature the British military government followed suit. Film production in the American zone was not resumed until the latter part of 1947 (Greffrath 1995: 116).
2 See Mückenberger (1994: 20–40) for a detailed account of the meeting.
3 This was the precursor of the *Staatliche Komitee für Filmfragen* (State Committee for Film Issues), which was set up in 1952.
4 During the 1970s, however, a small underground film scene of painters, musicians, poets and performance artists began to develop; see the video compilation of shorts, *Gegenbilder* (GDR Underground Films, 1981/89).
5 DEFA's production centres and additional facilities were re-organised several times between 1946 and 1990 (see Schulz 2001).
6 None of these journals survived German unification. Even *Film und Fernsehen* was unable to compete with West Germany's equivalent publications, *epd film* and *Filmdienst*, and ceased to be published in 1999.
7 A DEFA film that attracted more than 500,000 viewers within twelve months of its theatrical release was considered to be a box-office hit, resulting in bonus

payments for the creative team. The highest bonus payments were awarded for films that received quality ratings (Otto and Berghahn 2002).

8 See note 23 below.

9 The KAGs in the feature film studio were: Roter Kreis, Berlin, Heinrich Greif, Johannisthal, Babelsberg and, since 1990, DaDaeR. See also Chapter 4.

10 Similar reports were also submitted by DEFA's distribution and export divisions. They appraised the film's artistic and ideological merits and specified the film's national and international target audiences.

11 This system of quality distinctions had already been used during the Third Reich and was subsequently adopted by the *Freiwillige Selbstkontrolle* (FSK, Voluntary Self-Regulation) in the FRG and by the HV Film in the GDR.

12 In the early 1960s, DEFA's chief dramaturge Klaus Wischnewski relinquished his position by demoting himself to the level of dramaturge, thus abolishing an additional layer of internal control.

13 The State Security Service, which was set up in 1950 just four months after the foundation of the GDR, provided an all-pervasive network of surveillance, control and coercion through which the government and the Party aimed to secure their position. By 1989 the number of paid employees had risen from 4,000 during the 1950s to an estimated 100,000. In addition, there was a vast network of up to 180,000 unofficial informers and collaborators. Since informers were active only for a few years and there was a high turnover, it has been estimated that 'every thirtieth citizen of the GDR . . . may have acted at one time or another as an informer' (Fulbrook 1995: 50).

14 Over the decades the administrative organisation of film exhibition was changed several times (for a detailed account see Otto 2001).

15 Kurt Maetzig, *Ernst Thälmann – Sohn seiner Klasse* (Ernst Thälmann – Son of His Class, 1953) and *Ernst Thälmann – Führer seiner Klasse* (Ernst Thälmann – Leader of His Class, 1955). Part one was seen by 3.6 million viewers and part two by 5.7 million viewers within the first thirteen weeks of the films' theatrical release (Wittfoth 1987: appendix I).

16 Figures refer to the late 1980s.

17 The Soviet Union usually required ten times as many prints as the GDR. Hence the exchange ratio was ten to one; with other socialist countries the ratio was three or four to one (Diller and Berghahn 2002).

18 See also Kannapin (2000).

19 On DEFA's genre films see Fellmer (2002); Gemünden (1998); Grisko (2002); Hanisch (2001); Soldovieri (1998b); Wehrstedt (1996; 2001).

20 Directors who specialised in genre cinema, such as Gottfried Kolditz, Richard Groschopp, Joachim Hasler, Roland Oehme and Konrad Petzold, never enjoyed the same kudos as the creators of anti-fascist films, national epics and contemporary dramas, which were officially accorded priority.

21 This figure excludes animation films or children's films commissioned by East German television.

22 *Das singende, klingende Bäumchen* became a children's classic on British tele-
    vision during the 1960s when the BBC showed it in German with an English
    narrative voice-over (see Bowlby 2002).
23 Statistics about the percentage of films produced or co-produced by West
    German producers which were never released vary considerably. According
    to SPIO (Spitzenorganisation der Filmwirtschaft e. V.), around 17 per cent
    of German films produced between 1985 and 2001 were never released
    (information courtesy of Wilfried Berauer, department for statistics, SPIO).
    Meuer, however, suggests that at least for the period between 1979 and
    1989, 'fifty per cent of all films [produced or co-produced by West German
    producers] were never ordinarily distributed in the commercial market'
    (Meurer 2000: 122). According to Herrn Berauer, the significant variance
    may be due to the fact that the terms 'produced' and 'never released' are
    ambiguous and may be interpreted in different ways.
24 Frank Beyer and Egon Günther temporarily worked in the West, but both
    had official visas and never relinquished their East German citizenship.
    The directors Helmut Nitzschke and Iris Gusner left the GDR in the 1980s
    when they were travelling abroad, but neither of them succeeded in estab-
    lishing themselves in West Germany's film industry. Hannes and Sybille
    Schönemann, who had applied for exit visas in 1984, were imprisoned
    and were eventually bought free by the Federal Republic in summer 1985;
    see Sybille Schönemann's documentary *Verriegelte Zeit* (Locked-up Time, 1990).
    Amongst the most famous DEFA actors who re-launched their careers in the
    FRG or even in Hollywood are Manfred Krug, Jutta Hoffmann, Katharina
    Thalbach, Angelika Domröse, Hilmar Thate and Armin Mueller-Stahl.
25 For a discussion of the concept of the 'public sphere' in the GDR's social
    context, see Bathrick (1995) and Silberman (1997). Bathrick argues that out-
    side the officially-controlled public sphere, there existed two additional ones:
    access to West German media and unofficial enclaves of artists and intellec-
    tuals, grassroots movements and a developing underground culture provided
    a spectrum of counter-official voices that filled the information deficit left
    by the Party-controlled public sphere.

2

Coming to terms with the Nazi legacy: DEFA's anti-fascist films[1]

Conflicting memories in a divided nation

German reunification signified the end of the Cold War division, the restoration of the German nation and the search for a new German identity. Since the only common memory of German nationhood after more than four decades of division, dated back to the Third Reich, this quest for a new and shared German identity was bound to lead back to the Nazi past and the Holocaust. Given the different interpretations of National Socialism in the GDR and in the FRG, the democratisation of memory in the wake of unification resulted in a contestation and debate about whose memory would be represented in the construction of Germany's new identity. This ongoing engagement with the Nazi legacy culminated in a veritable memory boom after unification, as is testified by a rapid succession of public debates which attracted the attention of a broad spectrum of the public during the 1990s. The origins of these public debates lead back to the early post-war years and the foundation of the two German states in 1949.

In seeking to define German national identity after the war, the Nazi past, as well as the division of the German nation, have posed major obstacles, resulting in uniquely fractured national identities in East and West Germany. Not only did both parts of the divided nation have to define a new identity in opposition to a common past, they also had to demarcate their new identities against each other, principally by subscribing to the ideologies of the superpowers whose pawns they had become during the Cold War (Fulbrook 1999: 18–24). The endeavour to come to terms with the burden of history was highly competitive since both East and West Germany wanted to prove that they had made a more decisive break with the past and were, therefore, the 'better' of the two Germanys. *Vergangenheitsbewältigung* was thus made subservient to a political agenda. While this was much more obvious in the GDR, where one monolithic interpretation of the past was officially propagated, even the pluralistic and changing engagement with the Nazi past, which characterised the discourse of *Vergangenheitsbewältigung* in the Federal Republic, ultimately served political purposes.

Soon after the Second World War, official accounts in East and West Germany began to establish simple tales of villains, victims and heroes which aimed to absolve the German population at large from the charge of collective guilt. The narratives invoked in these complex strategies of guilt denial were, however, significantly different. In the West Hitler's regime was interpreted as a totalitarian one in which the power was concentrated in the hands of a few evil men: Hitler, Himmler, Heydrich and a few others. Since in the Nuremberg trials (1945–46) and the successor trials, namely the Eichmann trial in Jerusalem (1961) and the Auschwitz trials in Frankfurt/Main (1964–65), the chief perpetrators were punished by death or long prison sentences, the Germans felt that the past had been effectively dealt with. As Mary Fulbrook points out in her study *German National Identity after the Holocaust*, 'the massive public efforts devoted to exposing Nazi crimes in the Nuremberg war trials assisted a complementary process amounting, eventually, almost to collective amnesty for the rest of the German people' (Fulbrook 1999: 50–1).

Whitewashed by the Allies in a de-Nazification campaign in which administrative and political expediency soon gained the upper hand over considerations of justice, a vast majority of civil servants and leading industrialists were reinstated in their former positions so that the challenging task of rebuilding Germany from the ruins could begin. Critics, not only from the GDR but also, amongst others, the '68-generation, kept pointing out that far from having made a clean break with the past the Federal Republic of Germany had made a series of ethically dubious compromises which resulted in a continuity of the past in the present.

Although the philosopher Karl Jaspers, among others, admonished his compatriots not to leave de-Nazification entirely to the Allies but to undertake some serious soul-searching in order to establish, if not a sense of personal guilt, then at least a sense of accountability, most Germans were too preoccupied with the sheer effort it took to survive. Building for the future and contributing to the economic miracle of the 1950s soon harnessed the energies of the West German population to such an extent that they had no spare capacity to analyse their personal investment in Nazism. Moreover, the economic miracle soon provided a new, positive self-image for most West Germans, centring on values such as work ethic, efficiency and economic success. Mourning the past was easily forgotten. The question of collective guilt was brushed aside and replaced by collective amnesia. This is one of the charges often levied against the West Germans.

Another interpretation suggests that collective shame for the atrocities that had been committed *in the name of*, but not *by*, the German people, replaced the feeling of collective guilt. It found its public expression in a political culture that encouraged collective penance and that made 'restitution' (*Wiedergutmachung*) to the victims of Nazism, who in the FRG were defined primarily as the Jews (Fulbrook 1999: 49–50, 65–7). This restitution consisted of compensation payments to Holocaust survivors or the relatives of victims and to the state of Israel. Appropriate constitutional arrangements made it easy for Jewish immigrants to obtain German citizenship. Extremely liberal asylum laws for political refugees were intended to repay the international community that had – reluctantly – opened their borders to Nazi refugees during the Third Reich. These measures, along with an almost state-ordained 'philo-Semitism', were designed to express if not a sense of collective guilt then at least a sense of collective responsibility.

Since the GDR, by contrast, disavowed historical responsibility as well as historical continuities with Nazism, *Vergangenheitsbewältigung* was much simpler than in the West. According to the GDR's official historiography the defeat of the Germans and the collapse of the Third Reich were interpreted as the victory of the fighters against fascism and the liberation of the innocent German workers and peasants from the fascist oppressors. Anti-fascism was narrowly defined as organised communist resistance. Since a considerable number of the GDR's founders and SED Party leaders had been communist resistance fighters who had been incarcerated or driven into exile, these individuals could justifiably claim to be the victims of Nazism and base their claim to leadership on their uncompromising and heroic opposition to the Nazis. The ultimate defeat of Nazism, or 'fascism', to use the term favoured in the GDR, also implied that the fighters against fascism had emerged triumphant; clever propagandists coined the term 'the victors of history' (Münkler 1998: 23). While this concept is problematic in itself, what made the GDR's foundational narrative and myth of origin, the 'anti-fascist myth', even more questionable is the fact that after the immediate period of de-Nazification the anti-fascist credentials of its founders were extended to the entire populace. In a clever re-interpretation of history, the GDR's population at large were not only exonerated, but had also collectively emerged as the victors of history.

Far from sharing the West Germans' sense of collective shame, the East Germans enjoyed a guilt- and shame-free relationship with the past and could consequently feel much more comfortable about this particular aspect of their new national identity than their compatriots in the West. The FRG, which professed to be the *Rechtsnachfolger* (legal heir or successor state) of the Third Reich and which recognised its liability for the crimes and consequences of the Hitler regime, was denounced as the home of former Nazis. In the eyes of the socialist German Democratic Republic, the capitalist Federal Republic of Germany had failed to overcome the past by eradicating the roots of fascism, which according to a Marxist interpretation of history was state-monopoly capitalism. Following Georgi Dimitrov's definition of fascism, proposed in 1935 to the Comintern as 'the overt terrorist domination of the most reactionary, the most chauvinistic, and the most imperialistic elements of German finance capital', the SED relativised the specificity of 'the Nazi phenomenon by embedding it in a critique of capitalism' (Jarausch 1991: 87). Since the GDR had replaced capitalism with socialism – thus the argument ran – it had not only made a clean break with the past but had also abolished the economic conditions which had led to, and could potentially lead again to, fascism. Moreover, this socio-economic revolution under the auspices of the Soviet occupation powers, which consisted of the land reform of 1945 and the expropriation of industry and finance in 1946, also resulted in a significant turnover of personnel, which could be conveniently cited as a measure of de-Nazification. While the majority of the GDR's population was thus spared from confronting its own complicity with the Nazis, the class enemy in the Federal Republic not only had to bear the sole burden of the Nazi legacy but was also regarded as the living proof of the conception of 'fascism as a past which never ends' (Jarausch 1991: 91).

At the centre of the GDR's founding myth was the concentration camp Buchenwald, the GDR's most significant memorial site. Close to Weimar, a cultural heritage symbol, Buchenwald became 'the national symbolic heart of the GDR' (Fulbrook 1999: 29), epitomising successful communist resistance which culminated in the alleged self-liberation of the camp.[2] On 19 April 1945 an international group of political prisoners at Buchenwald, by no means exclusively communists, swore an oath in which they committed themselves to the 'annihilation of Nazism at its very roots' (Niven 2002: 65) and the 'construction of world peace and freedom' (Fulbrook 1999: 31). In years to come the 'Buchenwald Oath' was invoked on countless occasions and interpreted by the GDR's leaders as a specifically socialist pledge to destroy fascism at its roots.

Predictably, the GDR's portrayal of resistance excluded or distorted the 'other resistance' that was remembered in the FRG, namely the resistance around Stauffenberg, which culminated in the unsuccessful attempt on Hitler's life on 20 July 1944. Because it was led by the 'wrong classes', namely the military elite, up until the early 1980s the July plot was dismissed as 'the attempt by reactionary representatives of German finance capital to prevent the inevitable collapse of German imperialism' (Niven 2002: 67). Despite timid attempts to acknowledge non-communist resistance during the 1980s, it was not until German unification that a thorough reappraisal of the anti-fascist myth and the Nazi legacy took place. Only in 1990 did Hans Modrow, the Prime Minister of the interregnum between the SED government and the new government of a reunited Germany, publicly acknowledge that the GDR shared responsibility for Germany's fascist past with the FRG (Carter 1997: 433). Yet until then, and in spite of its apparent lack of plausibility, the anti-fascist myth played a crucial role in the construction of the GDR's national identity and was instrumentalised to reinforce the GDR's legitimacy as the only anti-fascist German state and thus 'the better Germany'.

Screen memories of Germany's past

The contributions of East and West German cinema to the discourse of *Vergangenheitsbewältigung* have played a crucial role in the construction of collective identities in the two German states. Consistent with the continuous reappraisal of Germany's recent history, West German film culture takes a multifaceted approach to the theme, ranging from mainstream war films in the 1950s to a critical reassessment of the Nazi legacy by New German Cinema and a virtual memory boom on the silver screen during the 1990s. While it is not possible to provide a detailed account of the cinematic representation of the Nazi legacy in West German cinema,[3] the following brief survey is intended as a basis of comparison between East and West German memories of Germany's past on the silver screen, and will illustrate the significant role which cinema played in the construction of collective memories and the demarcation of German national identities.

In the Federal Republic screen memories of Germany's traumatic past have oscillated between phases of collective amnesia and phases of keen interest in the Third Reich. Immediately after the Second World War filmmakers in all four occupied zones, and indeed in many other European countries,[4] made *Trümmerfilme* (rubble films) – named after the characteristic *mise-en-scène* of the ruined cityscapes. These rubble films reflect the sense of disorientation and hardship experienced by millions of people who had lost relatives, their homes and their livelihood during the war and who were faced with the seemingly impossible task of rebuilding their lives from the ruins. They appealed to 'broadly humanistic cultural values as an antidote to nazism' (Byg 1992a: 206) and aimed to assist the Germans in their struggle to come to terms with their experience of war and the haunting spectre of guilt. Made under the control and licence of the Allies between 1946 and 1949, rubble films were not yet required to proclaim the conflicting alternatives of Germany's recent past and could afford to be less dogmatic in overcoming the past, a past that until 1949 was still perceived to be the shared legacy of the German people.

Thus the first wave of *West* German films about the Third Reich were principally the war films of the mid-1950s. These were in part British and American war features, in part indigenous productions – among them *Canaris* (Alfred Weidenmann, 1954); *Des Teufels General* (The Devil's General, Helmut Käutner, 1954); *Solange du lebst* (As Long as You Live, Harald Reinl, 1955); *08/15* (The Revolt of Corporal Ash, Paul May, 1954); *Taiga* (Wolfgang Liebeneiner, 1958); and *Rommel ruft Kairo* (Rommel Calling Kairo, Wolfgang Schleif, 1958). By 'distinguishing between the noble-minded rank and file and the sinister Nazis', these films attempt to 'reinstate soldiering as an admirable calling' (Rentschler 1987: 217) at a time when West Germany was joining NATO (1955), establishing the *Bundeswehr* (Federal Army) (1956) and instituting mandatory conscription. The year when the *Bundeswehr* was set up witnessed the highest number of war film releases (Silberman 1995: 129). War films, which accounted for 10 per cent of all film screenings in the 1950s (Rentschler 1987: 217), were used as a form of state propaganda to urge West Germans to support remilitarisation – a significant about-turn in postwar policy that even required a change of the *Grundgesetz* (basic law).

The New German Cinema of the 1970s and 1980s represents the second wave of films, casting a rather different light on the past: filmmakers such as Rainer Werner Fassbinder, Alexander Kluge, Volker Schlöndorff, Margarethe von Trotta and Hans-Jürgen Syberberg were imbued with the spirit of the '68 student movement, which was in many respects a rebellion of the generation of the sons and daughters against the silence of their parents' generation regarding the Second World War.

It resulted in a surge of books and films in which the post-war generation questioned the 'generation of culprits' about their complicity with
Nazi crimes. Many of the directors of the New German Cinema, themselves representatives of the inquisitive post-war generation, set out to
explore the continuities of the past in contemporary West German society. Alexander Kluge's film *Abschied von gestern* (Yesterday Girl, 1966)
contradicts the proposition of its German title (the literal translation is
'Farewell to Yesterday') by stating in its first intertitle 'Uns trennt von
gestern kein Abgrund, sondern eine veränderte Perspektive' (It is not an
abyss that separates us from yesterday, but a changed perspective).
Rainer Werner Fassbinder's FRG Trilogy, consisting of *Die Ehe der
Maria Braun* (The Marriage of Maria Braun, 1979), *Lola* (1981) and *Die
Sehnsucht der Veronika Voss* (Veronika Voss, 1982), tells the private
histories of its female protagonists during the founding years of the
FRG. In these films Fassbinder examines strategies of guilt denial and
collective amnesia that prevailed during the period of reconstruction.
Fassbinder condemns his parents' generation for having missed this unique
chance of 'founding a state that could have been the most humane and
freest ever' (cited in Kaes 1992: 79).

Women directors such as Helma Sanders-Brahms (*Deutschland – bleiche
Mutter*/Germany, Pale Mother, 1979), Jutta Brückner (*Hungerjahre –
in einem reichen Land*/The Hunger Years: In a Land of Plenty, 1979),
Jeanine Meerapfel (*Malou*, 1980) and Marianne Rosenbaum (*Peppermint Frieden*/ Peppermint Peace, 1983) approach the past from a semi-
autobiographical vantage point, emphasising that the experience of
the past and the question of guilt are gendered (Frieden *et al.* 1993;
Linville 1998; see also Chapter 5 of this volume). An investigation of the
impact of fascism on ordinary lives is another central concern that preoccupied West – as well as East – German filmmakers during the 1970s
and 1980s. Several films dwell on the moral dilemmas faced by the
Mitläufer (fellow-travellers of the Nazi regime). *Mephisto* (1981), made
by the Hungarian director István Szabó and based on Klaus Mann's novel
of 1936, tells the story of the German actor Gustav Gründgens, who
rose to fame and fortune under the Nazis but sold his soul. Likewise,
Fassbinder's film *Lili Marleen* (1980) explores the ambiguous motivations behind an artist's complicity with the Nazis. The film is a fictionalised biography of Lale Andersen, a prominent Nazi performer, whose
love song '. . . wie einst, Lili Marleen' (. . . like times gone by, Lili
Marleen) was played by German *Wehrmacht* radio stations and even heard
on Allied and Russian radio in 1943, becoming a smash hit and a kind

of signature tune for soldiers all over Europe (Elsaesser 1996: 150). While these films struck a resonant chord with a broad public, Edgar Reitz's sixteen-hour film *Heimat*, which was shown on television in 1984, was a major media event. 'No fewer than 25 million West German television viewers saw at least one of the eleven episodes of Reitz's film' (Kaes 1992: 163), which sparked a lively public debate. *Heimat* was conceived as a counter-narrative to the American television series *Holocaust* (shown on German television in 1979), through which Reitz wanted to give Germans the opportunity to repossess their own history, from which they had been expropriated because of the dominance of American films about Germany's traumatic past (Kaes 1992: 184). Like the *Holocaust* miniseries, *Heimat* chronicles German history in the shape of a family saga. Here the family is based in a remote Hunsrück village and, although the characters' personal lives are affected by fascism and the war, major historical events as well as the Holocaust are elided, thereby allowing German audiences to make peace with their problematic past.[5]

A third wave of films concerned with the past was sparked by the revived debate around Germany's shared historical legacy in the wake of reunification. This debate reached its peak in the mid-1990s, when reunited Germany celebrated the fiftieth anniversary of the end of the Second World War, when the controversial yet spectacularly popular Crimes of the *Wehrmacht* exhibition opened and when the publication of Daniel Goldhagen's best-seller *Hitler's Willing Executioners* (1996) – which is essentially an indictment of the entire German nation as a people of anti-Semites – led to a reassessment of the guilt of the 'ordinary German'.[6] Significantly, the third wave of films about the Nazi legacy consists almost exclusively of films made by West German filmmakers.

Screen memories during the 1990s are preoccupied with three thematic concerns. First, they dramatise fictive encounters in which the chief perpetrators are lent a voice (Mengele, the 'angel of death' at Auschwitz, in *Nichts als die Wahrheit*/After the Truth, Roland Suso Richter, 1999; Hitler in *Gespräch mit dem Biest*/Conversation with the Monster, Armin Mueller-Stahl, 1997). Second, family sagas pose the question of whether the guilt runs through the family beyond the generation that actually experienced and was complicit with National Socialism (*Meschugge*/ The Giraffe, Dani Levy and Maria Schrader, 1998; and the German-Hungarian co-production *Ein Hauch von Sonnenschein*/Sunshine, István Szabó, 1999). The third group comprises films about anti-Semitism, a theme which has received unprecedented attention since the 1990s (*Aimée und Jaguar*/Aimée and Jaguar, Max Färberböck, 1999; *Gloomy Sunday* –

Ein Lied von Liebe und Tod/Gloomy Sunday, Rolf Schübel, 1999; *Mutters Courage*/My Mother's Courage, Michael Verhoeven, 1995; *Meschugge*; *Hitlerjunge Salomon*/Europa, Europa, Agnieszka Holland, 1990; *Comedian Harmonists*, Joseph Vilsmaier, 1997; *Viehjud Levi*/Jew-Boy Levi, Didi Danquart, 1999; the award-winning European co-production *The Pianist* directed by the Polish filmmaker Roman Polanski, 2002; and *Rosenstraße*/ The Women of Rosenstrasse, Margarethe von Trotta, 2003).

In order to give mainstream appeal to narratives about the Third Reich and the Holocaust, filmmakers frequently resort to the conventions of genre cinema. Melodramas which portray the romantic love between a German and a Jew (*Aimée und Jaguar, Gloomy Sunday*) speak of an underlying, symbolic desire for reconciliation. In the thriller/love story *Meschugge* this German–Jewish reconciliation is eventually achieved by the third-generation protagonists: once the victims and perpetrators amongst the generation of the parents and grandparents have been identified and cases of mistaken and forged German–Jewish identities have been revealed, the burden of the past is successfully overcome in a blossoming German–Jewish romance. A number of other films recast the memory of the Holocaust by narrating tales of the miraculous survival of Jews brought about not just by fortuitous circumstances or successful camouflage but, more significantly, by the intervention of exceptional Germans who are not anti-Semitic (*Mutters Courage*; *Hitlerjunge Salomon*; *The Pianist*). In particular, those films which render the Holocaust as a tragicomedy with a 'happy end' (*Hitlerjunge Salomon* and *Mutters Courage*) construct the most unequivocal plea for a normalisation of Germany's burdensome past.

The aesthetic strategies employed in several of these films create a sense of nostalgic allure of the past for those who experienced it and for the post-war generations who rely solely on a mediated memory of that past. This mediated memory does not aspire to authenticity despite the fact that several of these films are based on the memoirs or biographies of survivors. There is little documentary footage; instead, history is shot through a coloured lens, which trivialises the suffering caused by fascism, presumably to capture audiences that have no first-hand recollection of the Nazi past and whose attention can only be won by presenting a sanitised, nostalgic account of a traumatised memory.

Compared with this multi-faceted cinematic discourse on *Vergangenheitsbewältigung*, East German cinema provides a relatively one-dimensional commentary on the fascist past that reflects the GDR's official historiography and largely supports the orthodox narrative about the state's anti-fascist myth of origin. It is thus not surprising that DEFA's anti-fascist films were the cornerstone of East German film culture and the lifeline of the studio. From its very first film, *Die Mörder sind unter uns* (The Murderers Are among Us, Wolfgang Staudte, 1946), until the end of DEFA in 1992, DEFA produced approximately one hundred anti-fascist films. This represents roughly 13 per cent of the entire feature film production.

In what follows, this chapter will examine how DEFA's anti-fascist films resonate with the GDR's *verordnetem Antifaschismus* (state-prescribed anti-fascism) by exploring the evolution of the anti-fascist genre over four and a half decades. How do these films address or avoid the question of guilt? Whom do they identify as the perpetrators, whom as the victims?

Confronting the question of guilt in *Die Mörder sind unter uns* (The Murderers Are among Us, Wolfgang Staudte, 1946) and other rubble films

The title of the first post-war German film, *Die Mörder sind unter uns*, produced under Soviet licence, promises to deliver an unapologetic if not radical confrontation with the past. Passing a harsh judgement on the Germans as a people tainted by the presence of murderers amongst them, the film's final scene appeals to the Germans to track down these murderers and to hand them over to justice. More so than other rubble films, Staudte's film lives up to the role the Allies had envisaged for indigenous German film production: to provide moral guidance to the German people by helping them to recognise the gravity of their wrong-doings during the twelve years of the Nazi regime.

The making of *Die Mörder sind unter uns* was driven by Staudte's personal need to liberate himself from the experience of fascism (Mückenberger 1994: 41). He had written the treatment for the film during the last two months of the war, taking as his starting point the obvious question as to what would happen to the Nazi criminals after the German defeat. Once the war was over he peddled the project, still entitled *Der Mann, den ich töten werde* (The Man I Am Going to Kill), to the film officers of the British, American and French forces. They all declined except for Major Dymschitz in the Russian zone. He was prepared to issue a licence on the condition that Staudte change the film's ending, in which the protagonist, Dr Mertens, avenges the war crimes committed by the former Captain of his platoon by shooting him. Dymschitz feared that the film's ending might condone similar acts of revenge causing total mayhem (Brandlmeier 1989: 39).

1 Hildegard Knef in *Die Mörder sind unter uns* (The Murderers Are among Us)

Like many other rubble films *Die Mörder sind unter uns* tells the story of a traumatised homecoming at the end of the war. The film opens with the intertitle 'Berlin 1945. Die Stadt hat kapituliert' (Berlin 1945. The city has capitulated). The first canted shots show two earth mounds marked by crosses, flowers and a *Wehrmacht* helmet – makeshift graves in the middle of a bombed-out city, a landscape of towering ruins. In the background a lonely figure is approaching, moving towards the camera. He passes by a group of children playing, who in rubble films often signify innocence and hope for the future, or who act as catalysts facilitating the traumatised homecomer's re-socialisation.[7] His unshaven face remains partly obscured by shadows that dissect his features. The cheerful, tinny piano music accompanying this opening sequence is incongruous with this setting of death and desolation. As the camera pans to the left, the source of the music is revealed – a bar advertising 'Tanz, Stimmung, Humor' (Dancing, merriment, humour). The sign above the door dissolves into an extreme canted shot of a train overloaded with passengers and the music changes to an ominous orchestrated score of non-diegetic music. In the crowd of descending passengers the camera singles out a young, beautiful woman, dressed in a light-coloured coat with a scarf loosely draped around her head. Soft violin music accompanies her first appearance. Her face is fully lit, revealing an expression of wide-eyed amazement at what she observes around her: a ruined city, inhabited by crippled and desolate POWs, homecomers without a home to go to. As the story unfolds, we learn that this woman, Susanne Wallner, played by the rising star Hildegard Knef, has just returned from a concentration camp to which she was deported 'because of her father'. Her experience of internment is left vague and obscure and has apparently left her unscathed.

Hans Mertens, with whom she shares one of the few habitable flats in ruined Berlin, by contrast, is traumatised by the experience of war and unable to reintegrate himself into society. Susanne assumes the role of comforter, lover and catalyst, enabling Mertens to work through his memories of the war and thus regain his sense of self.[8] A series of aural and visual flashbacks reveals what is at the core of Mertens' destabilised psyche. When serving as a military doctor in a platoon he tried in vain to stop his superior, Captain Brückner, from ordering the shooting of Polish hostages, women, old men and children on Christmas Eve 1942. When Mertens learns that Brückner is still alive he decides to kill him in order to avenge the murder of the innocent victims. The post-war Brückner is depicted as a successful entrepreneur and a loving family patriarch. He is the epitome of the *petit bourgeois* who bears precisely those contradictory character traits – banal and shallow, yet capable of committing monstrous atrocities in the name of duty – that Hannah Arendt later described in her seminal study *Eichmann in Jerusalem: A Report on the Banality of Evil* (1963).[9] Mertens' two attempts to exorcise the past and atone for the crimes against the Polish families by shooting Brückner are both aborted. First a mother who urgently needs a doctor's help to save her dying infant intervenes, and in the second instance, Susanne prevents Mertens from taking the law into his own hands, reminding him that 'Wir haben nicht das Recht zu richten!' (We do not have the right to judge!), whereupon Mertens replies 'Nein Susanne, aber wir haben die Pflicht, Anklage zu erheben, Sühne zu fordern im Auftrag von Millionen unschuldig hingemordeter Menschen!' (No, Susanne, but we have the duty to accuse, to demand atonement on behalf of millions of innocent people who were murdered in cold blood!).

The film concludes with Brückner behind prison bars, protesting his innocence while a series of dissolves, showing the victims of war, a war cemetery and hundreds of graves with wooden crosses, belie his words.

These crosses establish a visual link with the film's opening scene and make the symbolism of the visual leitmotif of the many window crosses, shadows of crosses and intersecting lines that runs through the entire film transparent: subliminally inverting the relationship between victims and perpetrators, the leitmotif suggests that it is the post-war Germans who have to bear their cross – the burden of the past.

A contemporary audience would have interpreted the film's relatively open ending in an unequivocal way as an implicit plea to hand over the war criminals to the legal system, that is the Allies who at the time were the executors of justice in occupied Germany. The Nuremberg War Crimes Trials, which took place between 20 November 1945 and 1 October 1946, came to an end shortly before *Die Mörder* premiered on 15 October 1946. In fact, a film review appeared in the same edition of the weekly periodical *Sonntag* as the lead article reporting on the execution of the sentences passed at the Nuremberg War Crimes Trials (Mückenberger 1994: 42). A review in the *Tägliche Rundschau* even interprets Brückner, who not coincidentally bears physical resemblance to Himmler, as a perpetrator in the same league as those sentenced to death:

> jener Hauptmann Brückner ist [. . .] Fleisch vom Fleisch und Geist vom Geiste jener Angeklagten, die auch nichts wissen wollen von der Schuld ihrer Taten und nur vollbracht zu haben behaupteten, was ihre 'Pflicht' gewesen sei. (cited in Mückenberger 1994: 42–3)

> (This Captain Brückner is [. . .] made of the very same flesh and bone as those accused who refuse to accept responsibility for their actions and who claim to have simply done their 'duty'.)

Of all the rubble films, Staudte's *Die Mörder sind unter uns* is the most explicit in apportioning guilt not only for the crimes and atrocities committed by the Germans during the war but also for their tacit acceptance of the presence of murderers in their midst. Moreover, it is the only rubble film that gives a clear answer as to how the Germans could come to terms with the burden of their past: by handing over the murderers to the executors of justice. Staudte's proposition is clearly imbued with the spirit of its time. The Nuremberg Trials were readily welcomed by the majority of Germans as a quick solution to the issue of collective guilt: with 'the murderers' being tried and punished by the Allies, it seemed no longer necessary for the Germans to examine their own involvement in the crimes against humanity. As the German writer Wolfdietrich Schnurre perceptively noted in a film review, this attitude is reflected in the film's narrative structure: the film remains equivocal about the

2 Film poster of Germany's first post-war film *Die Mörder sind unter uns* (The Murderers Are among Us)

murderers. Who are the murderers? Not just Brückner, but anyone who fought in the war; anyone who did not resist the Nazis; Mertens himself is a murderer (Schnurre 1946). Critics subsequently argued that Mertens does precisely what most Germans did in the post-war years: in order to distract from his own culpability he wants to punish Brückner, and thus, indirectly remove his own guilt.

The way Mertens is portrayed corresponds to the prevailing sentiments at the time. Not only is he absolved from any complicity in the war crimes, he – like so many of the returning soldiers of other rubble films – evokes the audience's sympathy and pity: Mertens, just like Iller in *Irgendwo in Berlin* (Somewhere in Berlin, Gerhard Lamprecht, Soviet licence, 1947) or Beckmann in *Liebe '47* (Love '47, Wolfgang Liebeneiner, British licence 1949), is assigned the role of a victim. Susanne characterises him as someone who has suffered severe injuries during the war and whose sense of identity has been destabilised. This is borne out by the fact that Mertens is predominantly shot from canted camera angles that convey this sense of destabilisation. His psyche is as wrecked as the bombed-out city around him.

Staudte uses the ruins of Berlin in an expressionistic way as the objective correlative of Mertens' haunted mind. The elongated shadows and the chiaroscuro lighting with which these landscapes of the soul are lit are reminiscent of Robert Wiene's *Das Cabinet des Dr. Caligari* (The Cabinet of Dr Caligari, 1920), a masterpiece of Weimar Expressionist cinema, which tells the story of a lunatic and murderer. The expressionist visual style used by the cinematographers Friedl Behn-Grund and Eugen Klagemann is consistent with the emphasis placed on the protagonist's psyche. A series of flashbacks, which gradually acquaint the audience with the most crucial incident of Mertens' traumatic war-time experiences, are the cinematic equivalent of what Freud and the psychoanalysts Alexander and Margarete Mitscherlich have described as the process of mourning, a 'psychological process in which the individual, by repeated painful remembering, slowly learns to bear and to work through a loss' (cited in Carter 2000: 102). The first sonic flashback is an acoustic montage of the sounds of war, a device Staudte would employ to a similar effect in the final scene of *Der Untertan* (The Subject, 1951): while the camera focuses on a close-up of Mertens' haunted face, one hears the sounds of exploding bombs and grenades, followed by a triumphant fanfare, sirens and the panic-stricken cries of a woman. The second flashback – nearly five minutes long – is introduced by a sound bridge that creates an acerbic ironic comment on Brückner's assessment of post-war Germany as a country where 'Menschlichkeit triumphiert' (humanity triumphs) and Mertens' entirely different judgement, which is based on his detailed recollection of the massacre of the Polish villagers on Christmas Eve 1942.

Staudte renders the process of *Vergangenheitsbewältigung* as a highly internalised conflict, presumably intended to give the Germans the right impetus to reflect on their own share of guilt. Yet what appears to be a radical reckoning with the past is not without an apologetic impulse in that the film's cathartic conclusion displaces the guilt: while it concedes that there were some evil Germans, namely the likes of Brückner, it also invites the viewer to identify with the film's chief pro-claimed victim, the traumatised homecomer Mertens. In their study *Die Unfähigkeit zu trauern* (The Inability to Mourn, 1967) Margarete and Alexander Mitscherlich argue that one of the strategies of guilt avoid-ance employed by the post-war German public was to identify them-selves as the primary victims of war:

> Identification with the victim is very frequently substituted for mourning; this is above all a logical defence against guilt. . . . To the conscious mind the past then appears as follows: We made many sacrifices, suffered the war, and were discriminated against for a long time afterward; yet we were innocent, since everything that is now held against us, we did under orders. (cited in Carter 2000: 108)

Consequently, the suffering of the real victims is typically marginal-ised in most rubble films, and *Die Mörder sind unter uns* is no exception in this respect. Witness the highly unspecific references to Susanne's internment in a concentration camp which has left neither physical nor psychological traces, and from which she returns with freshly ironed clothes and two pieces of substantial luggage! Mondschein's survival is only remarked upon by Susanne's inappropriately brief comment to her possibly Jewish neighbour,[10] 'Schön, daß Sie leben' (Good to find you alive). The genocide of the Jews is alluded to when the camera pro-vides a brief glimpse of the newspaper headline: 'Millionen Menschen vergast. Bericht vom Konzentrationslager Auschwitz' (Millions of people gassed. Report from Auschwitz) – but the Jews are not singled out as the chief victims of the Holocaust. The only films to adopt the suffering of the Jews as a dominant theme (*Ehe im Schatten*/Marriage in the Shadows, Soviet licence 1947; *Lang ist der Weg*/Long is the Road, US licence 1948; *Morituri*, French licence 1948; *Die Affäre Blum*/The Blum Affair, Soviet licence 1948; *Der Ruf*/The Last Illusion, US licence 1949) were motivated by the autobiographical experiences of their writers, directors or producers as half-Jews (Kurt Maetzig) or Jews (Israel Beker, Artur Brauner, Erich Engel, Fritz Kortner) during the Third Reich. Yet to some extent even in these films the Jews are assimilated into general victimhood (Shandley 2001: 77–115).

Creating a universal model of victimhood that allowed the Germans to conflate their own experience of suffering during and after the war with the experience of the primary victims is, however, only one of the manifold strategies of guilt denial employed by rubble films. Another one, best exemplified in Helmut Käutner's episodic film *In jenen Tagen* (In Those Days, British licence 1947), is to claim the position of innocence for the Germans themselves. In seven episodes that are told from the supposedly objective and unprejudiced point of view of an old car, which has witnessed the destinies of its seven owners during the Third Reich, the film portrays their private lives, set against the backdrop of the twelve years of the Nazi regime. As is typical of many rubble films, the Nazis are never mentioned and do not appear on screen. With the perpetrators being unidentifiable, history is mystified, reduced to an inexorable fate which provides the good German people with an opportunity to prove their humanity. Humanity is defined as the victory of true love over the destructive forces of time; as the willingness to risk one's own life in order to save that of others; as loyalty and self-sacrifice. People from all strata of society, the film argues, rose to the challenge of these exceptionally difficult times by proving their inherent goodness.

Käutner's apolitical confrontation with the past, which focuses on the private life of the average German, resonated particularly with all those Germans who claimed to have chosen the path of 'inner emigration' – a claim much overused by a vast majority of Germans after the war. As Shandley argues in his book *Rubble Films, In jenen Tagen*, where 'stories of death' are interpreted as 'a form of innocence and glorifications of inner emigration as a form of shutting out external political realities' (Shandley 2001: 62), creates a highly attractive collective fantasy of private resistance, inviting post-war spectators to justify their inaction as resistance and to perceive themselves as private resisters.

A third common strategy of guilt avoidance is that of sweeping the past aside and focusing on the troubled present instead. Films such as *Irgendwo in Berlin, Razzia* (Soviet licence, 1947), *Und über uns der Himmel* (And the Heavens above, American licence 1947), *Straßenbekanntschaft* (Street Acquaintance, Soviet licence 1948) and *Unser täglich Brot* (Our Daily Bread, Soviet licence 1949), displace the guilt of the past by concentrating on the guilt of the present, taking the shape of petty crimes, black marketeering, theft and prostitution. These kinds of moral trespassing can be quickly redeemed and rubble films propose two recipes for redemption. Self-doubting males, like Iller and Mertens, need to be reintegrated into the domestic sphere and a traditional social order needs to be re-established, while the all-too-independent rubble woman has to return to the homely hearth. The second remedy for the problems of the troubled present as well as the burden of the past is the catharsis achieved through hard work.

The ideological project undertaken by rubble films was designed to have limited currency. In the early post-war days, the more apologetic rubble films in particular, which portrayed the Germans as innocent bystanders, inner émigrés or victims, provided highly appealing counternarratives to the harsh judgements passed on the Germans by the Allies and the international community.

Some of these films attracted large audiences, but generally viewers were eager to seek refuge from the rubble in the cinema. Although some of the rubble films achieved very respectable audience figures – *Die Mörder sind unter uns* was seen by 5.2 million viewers, *Ehe im Schatten* by 10.1 million, and *Irgendwo in Berlin* by 3.8 million viewers between their release and 1950 – they were hard pressed to compete with the escapist entertainment offered by imports and re-runs of supposedly politically innocuous entertainment films of the UFA dream factory (Greffrath 1995: 430–1). Opinion polls conducted in the British and American zones revealed a clear preference for comedies, musicals and romances over rubble films (Greffrath 1995: 121–37). After the currency reform the competition from imports that flooded a highly lucrative market became even stronger. In order for new German films to sustain a viable position in the market it was necessary to dilute the educational mission of the rubble films by creating more entertaining hybrids or casting popular stars. Since, ultimately, the appeal of the rubble films lay in their ability to provide narratives that collectively exonerated the Germans of their share of guilt, the founding of the two German states in 1949 soon resulted in the construction of alternative collective identities that largely rendered the ideological project of the rubble films superfluous.[11]

The construction of the anti-fascist myth in DEFA films

The centrality of the anti-fascist myth of origin for East German national identity is reflected in the prominence accorded to this subject in its national film production. Organised communist resistance is by far the most common thematic angle taken in anti-fascist films,[12] but the genre also includes films which examine the political and economic causes which led to the Second World War and a comparatively small number of films about Jews in the Third Reich.

Although shortly after the founding of the GDR the SED shifted the cultural agenda from overcoming the past to building the socialist future, the anti-fascist theme flourished throughout the 1950s and 1960s.[13] In fact, some of the masterpieces of the anti-fascist tradition date from those decades. They include Slatan Dudow's *Stärker als die Nacht* (Stronger than the Night, 1954); Konrad Wolf's *Lissy* (1957), *Sterne* (Stars, 1959), *Professor Mamlock* (1961) and *Ich war neunzehn* (I Was Nineteen, 1968); Gerhard Klein's semi-documentary feature *Der Fall Gleiwitz* (The Gleiwitz Case, 1961); Frank Beyer's *Fünf Patronenhülsen* (Five Cartridges, 1960) and *Königskinder* (Star-Crossed Lovers, 1962); Joachim Kunert's popular film *Die Abenteuer des Werner Holt* (The Adventures of Werner Holt, 1965), and Heiner Carow's anti-fascist children's film *Sie nannten ihn Amigo* (They Called Him Amigo, 1959). At the other end of the spectrum are blatantly propagandist anti-fascist films such as the second part of the state-commissioned films about the national hero and communist resistance fighter, *Ernst Thälmann – Führer seiner Klasse* (Ernst Thälmann – Leader of His Class, Kurt Maetzig, 1955) and *Rat der Götter* (Council of the Gods, Kurt Maetzig, 1950), the latter of which testifies to the Cold War tensions during the early 1950s. The film argues that the same economic and political structures persist in the Federal Republic of Germany and America which led to the rise of fascism and that the West, therefore, continues to pose a threat to world peace. The film's ending emphasises the stark contrast between the two German states: while IG-Farben in the West continues to produce lethal gas and explosives, in the East people are taking to the streets of Berlin in an anti-war march on 1 May 1950.

Slatan Dudow's film *Stärker als die Nacht* is in many respects the prototype of the anti-fascist genre during the 1950s. True to the aesthetic doctrine of Socialist Realism it features a positive hero, Hans Löning, who is not only a worker and communist but whose courageous resistance to fascism makes him larger than life: after having spent seven years as a political prisoner in a concentration camp his will to resist the Nazis is unbroken. Even the threat 'beim nächsten Mal kostet es den Kopf' (next time you'll pay with your life) does not deter him from campaigning against the regime. His wife Gerda is portrayed as a self-sacrificing,

supportive comrade whose courage is based on her communist conviction and her love of Hans. Unlike earlier films such as Staudte's *Rotation*
(1949), which portrayed a *petit bourgeois* hero who changed sides from
being an opportunistic fellow-traveller of the Nazi regime to joining the
resistance, *Stärker als die Nacht* suggests that the anti-fascist resistance
movement consisted exclusively of communists. Dudow's film, based
on a script by Jeanne and Kurt Stern, who had been active in the resistance movement themselves, portrays anti-fascist resistance as a collective effort by communists whose heroism and willingness to sacrifice
their lives is based on their unflinching allegiance to communist ideals.
Moreover, and entirely in line with the SED's new agenda to enlist filmmakers in its march towards the future, this anti-fascist film makes an
obligatory reference to the present and the achievements of socialism.
Following the hero's sacrificial death and the funeral march 'Immortal
Victims', Dudow's film ends on an optimistic note: a series of images of
nationally-owned factories, students at the Humboldt University, vast
expanses of cornfields swaying in the wind and shots of the sea equate
the socialist way with nature's way, thus subliminally legitimising the
German road to socialism (Schenk 1994a: 118).

Paths of discovery in Konrad Wolf's *Lissy* (1957) and his later anti-fascist films

Konrad Wolf's film *Lissy* (1957) does not share any of the propagandist
qualities of *Stärker als die Nacht*. Instead of celebrating the heroism of
steadfast communist resistance fighters, *Lissy* sketches the inner conflicts
of wavering people, who are misled by the appeal and the promises of
the Nazis, who struggle with moral and political doubts and who are torn
between opportunism and their conscience. In the words of the film
director himself, *Lissy* explores 'wie der deutsche Faschismus es fertig-
brachte, in die Seele und in den Verstand von Millionen und aber
Millionen Deutschen Eingang zu finden' (cited in Spoden 1990: 29) (how
German fascism succeeded in penetrating the soul and mind of millions
and millions of Germans).

Based on a novel by F. C. Weiskopf and scripted by Weiskopf's
widow Alex Wedding and Konrad Wolf, the film focuses on the internal struggle of its title heroine. Taking the fate of Lissy and her husband Freddy Fromeyer as an example, the film explores how mass
unemployment at the end of the Weimar Republic made the Germans
susceptible to Nazi propaganda. Lissy is torn between the temptation of

leading a comfortable life at the side of her *petit bourgeois* husband and her communist social conscience. Her pregnancy precipitates the decision to marry Fromeyer. Like millions of other Germans he loses his job. Finding it impossible to support his wife and infant son, Fromeyer succumbs to Nazi propaganda and joins the Storm Troopers. He is not the only one in Lissy's immediate circle who is misled by the force of circumstance. Her brother Paul, whose chequered history includes a strong allegiance to the Communist Youth Movement as well as a criminal record as a petty thief, is also driven by economic need to join the SA. Initially the Nazis appear to offer the solution to Lissy's, Fromeyer's and Paul's problems, especially when Fromeyer is promoted and Lissy is able to enjoy the life of luxury she yearned for so much. Yet it comes at a price. When her brother Paul, misguided in his belief that the National Socialists were, like himself, anti-capitalist, reveals his political convictions, he is assassinated by his fellows in brown uniforms. Although the Nazis attribute the crime to the communists, Lissy discovers the truth. This event marks the turning point in her life. At Paul's funeral where his sacrificial death 'at the hands of the communists' is staged with much pomp and circumstance by the Storm Troopers, Lissy suddenly understands that the Nazis are 'murderers' and realises where she belongs. When Kaczmierczik, Freddy's friend and SA officer, addresses the mourners in the morgue, stating: 'Ein jeder muß sich entscheiden, wer nicht mit uns ist, ist gegen uns' (Each of us has to make up his mind. Those who are not with us are against us), Fromeyer turns towards the Nazi banner, but Lissy turns away from him, towards her proletarian father. Accompanied by stately extra-diegetic music, she leaves the morgue. All alone she runs along a straight, tree-lined avenue towards the camera. The off-screen voice-over commentary suggests that Lissy joins the communist resistance:

> Ja, ein jeder muß sich entscheiden. Und Lissy wußte jetzt, man kann einsam sein und doch nicht verlassen. Sie wußte jetzt, es gibt einen Weg, einen schweren und mühsamen Weg, aber einen ehrlichen Weg. Jeder geht ihn für sich allein, und doch geht ihn keiner allein.
>
> (Yes, each of us has to make up his mind. And Lissy had come to realise that one could be lonely without being abandoned. She knew of a path, a difficult and laborious path, but it was an honest path. Everyone had to take this path by themselves and yet nobody would follow this path alone.)

In the eyes of contemporary critics, the film's open ending did not do justice to Weiskopf's novel. In the novel Lissy returns to her roots, her

3 Discovering the right path, Sonja Sutter in *Lissy*

communist circle of friends, and joins the underground resistance movement. In a review entitled '... doch alle Fragen bleiben offen' (... yet
all questions remain unanswered), which appeared in *Die Weltbühne* in
September 1957, the film is criticised for its 'unverbindlichen Ausgang'
(Klaus 1957) (non-committal ending) which leaves too many questions
unanswered and therefore fails to convey a clear anti-fascist message.

Despite winning a prize at the film festival in Karlovy Vary and despite being widely praised as one of DEFA's best productions, reviewers
were concerned about the film's politically untoward deviation from
Weiskopf's novel: the communists, who play a significant role in the
workers' novel, are marginalised in Wolf's film (Joho 1957; Klaus
1957). References to their resistance activities remain sketchy; they are
passive and their chief role consists in being the targets and victims of
Nazi brutality. Although *Lissy* as well as Wolf's subsequent films leave
no doubt about the director's commitment to socialism, they eschew
the kind of bold messages that Party officials had been trying to impose
upon filmmakers since the early 1950s. Making *Lissy*, Wolf explained was
'vor allem ein Prozeß der Selbstbesinnung, der Selbsterkenntnis, war der
Beginn eines langen Weges, der ... nie ein Ende haben [wird], nicht für
mich zumindest' (cited in Herlinghaus 1980: 4) (above all a process of

self-discovery and self-knowledge. It was the beginning of a long path which . . . will never come to an end, not for me at least).

This searching, self-reflective nature of Wolf's films, one of the hall-marks of his oeuvre, is rooted in the director's biography. Konrad Wolf, the son of the Jewish communist doctor and writer Friedrich Wolf, spent his formative years in Moscow. When the Nazis came to power his family was driven into exile. Konrad Wolf, who was just eight years old at the time, became a fluent Russian speaker for whom Moscow was home. He returned to Germany as a soldier of the Red Army in 1945, a return that made him acutely aware of his ambivalent national identity. In his semi-autobiographical film, *Ich war neunzehn* (I Was Nineteen, 1968) Wolf revisits this experience of confused allegiances and a divided self. The character Gregor, a German in Russian uniform, is torn between his home, the land he is fighting for, and the as-yet-unknown land of his origin. Speaking both languages, he becomes a mediator between two peoples at war. He screams at the Germans, calling them murderers and criminals, and yet the film's final voice-over, spoken by Gregor, 'tells us what the boy has begun to discover but will only later learn to accept: "I am German, I was nineteen years old"' (Coulson 1999: 177).

After the war, Wolf studied film at the Moscow State Institute of Cinematography, VGIK, under the guidance of Grigori Alexandrov, Mikhail Romm and Sergej Gerassimow. But he eventually returned to East Germany in 1956, committed to building a socialist society and culture both through his films and through assuming key roles in the GDR's bureaucratic apparatus: he was a member of the SED, Chair of the Artists Union, member of the Central Committee of the SED (1981–82), and held the prestigious position of President of the Academy of Arts (1965–82). He became one of East Germany's foremost film-makers, making thirteen feature films with DEFA between 1955 and 1980. Despite the fact that filmmaking was a collective enterprise, incompatible with the notion of *auteur* cinema, Wolf is often referred to as DEFA's greatest *auteur* on account of the subjective authenticity of his films and their modernist aesthetics (Elsaesser and Wedel 2001).

His approach to the anti-fascist theme, with which five of his films are concerned, differs markedly from that of the 1940s rubble films and from the usual tales of heroic anti-fascist resistance. Instead Wolf is interested in sketching psychological processes that determine his protagonists' experiences of the Third Reich, tracing their 'paths of discovery' (Coulson 1999) that led them to making choices for or against fascism. Yet Wolf's films typically end once that choice has been made. They end where other anti-fascist films begin and thus eschew conventionalised depictions of anti-fascist heroism. *Lissy* ends with the mere suggestion that the protagonist goes underground. The Bulgarian co-production *Sterne* is a melodramatic story about Walter, a German sergeant stationed in Bulgaria and charged with guarding a transit camp for Greek Jews en route to Auschwitz. He falls in love with the Jewish teacher Ruth. His attempt to rescue her from deportation to Auschwitz fails, but the experience changes him from an apolitical cynic into someone who is determined to take sides. The film's ending shows Walter joining the Bulgarian partisans. *Professor Mamlock* – discussed further in the next section – ends with its protagonist's realisation of having made the wrong choice in failing to fight fascism.

Since Konrad Wolf lacked first-hand experience of the Third Reich, he had to have recourse to an eclectic range of sources for the cinematic construction of Nazi Germany. He cites Christa Wolf's novel *Kindheits-muster* (Patterns of Childhood, 1976) as one such important source, which he consulted to gain insight into how his German contemporaries experienced the Third Reich. Walther Ruttmann's documentary *Berlin. Die Sinfonie der Großstadt* (Berlin, Symphony of a City, 1927) provided Wolf with an atmospheric template for Berlin during the Weimar Republic. Wolf also derived inspiration from a considerable range of avant-garde film classics of the 1920s that he had access to while study-ing at the Moscow State Institute of Cinematography, but which had not been screened in post-war Berlin (Herlinghaus 1980: 4). Like other second-generation DEFA directors, such as Ralf Kirsten, Frank Beyer and Konrad Petzold, who joined DEFA during the mid-1950s after graduating from the Prague film academy FAMU, Wolf had been more strongly exposed to the Thaw – a period of liberalisation following Stalin's death in 1953 – than filmmakers in the GDR, where the process of de-Stalinisation was implemented in a rather haphazard fashion. But also in the GDR, Wolf's privileged position in the cultural sphere gave him greater access to the products of the Thaw.

This explains why Wolf's films are more firmly rooted in an interna-tional tradition, including Weimar left avant-garde cinema, Italian neo-realism and the New Waves, than other DEFA films of the time (Elsaesser and Wedel 2001). For example, the montage sequence which shows Fromeyer's hapless attempts at earning a living as a salesman, with his feet climbing and ascending stairways at ever increasing speed, pressing doorbells with telling names such as Mühsam (meaning 'laborious') and having doors slammed shut in his face, pays tribute to the hunt-for-work sequence in Brecht's and Dudow's film *Kuhle Wampe oder Wem gehört die Welt?* (Whither Germany?, 1932), a prime example of the proletarian film tradition of the Weimar Republic. The same montage sequence in *Lissy* also contains two frames that show the exchange of a wooden box and neatly folded bed linen for some bank notes at a pawnbrokers, a metonymic reference to the rapid economic decline of the Fromeyer family. These two frames are reminiscent of a scene in Vittorio de Sica's film *Lardi di Biciclette* (Bicycle Thieves, Italy, 1948). The cinematographer Werner Bergmann's innovative use of close-ups anticipates much more subjective camera angles and frames in Wolf's later films: the extreme close-up of Lissy's watch conveys her sense of nervous anxiety preceding her meeting with her boss at the Quick bar; the close-up of the pair of shoes in the shop window reveals Lissy's yearning for luxury, while the close-up of the spoonful of honey pouring lavishly on her bread roll epitomises the attainment of her materialistic dreams. Bergmann, who worked with Wolf on several of his film projects, 'pointed with pride to the fact that *Lissy* anticipates some of the famous camera innovations of Mikhail Kalatozov's *Letyat zhuravli* (The Cranes Are Flying, 1957)' (Byg 1999: 35), the most highly acclaimed Soviet film of the Thaw period that was also widely released in Western Europe and the GDR. Kalatozov, as well as Konrad Wolf – even more so in his autobiographical anti-fascist films *Ich war neunzehn* and *Mama, ich lebe* (Mama, I Am Alive, 1977) – employs subjective camera techniques that underscore the introspective theme of remembering and re-working the experience of the past, thus giving a highly personalised account of the war. In this respect Wolf's films anticipate a key feature of what became known as the third wave of *Bewältigung* (coming to terms with the past) in East German culture of the 1970s (Emmerich 1996: 317–34).

The deconstruction of the anti-fascist myth: *Dein unbekannter Bruder* (Your Unknown Brother, Ulrich Weiß, 1982)

When in 1971 Honecker announced that henceforth no taboos should impede cultural production, a spell of nearly thirty years was broken, setting writers and filmmakers free to embark on 'nachholende Erinnerungsarbeit' (a belated process of remembering). This was, as the writer Heiner Müller put it, an attempt 'die deutsche Geschichte bis auf die Knochen freizulegen, um zu verhindern, daß in Schuld und Unterdrückung das Verbrechen überlebt' (to strip German history to its very bones in order to prevent the survival of crime through guilt and suppression) (cited in Emmerich 1996: 318). The third wave of books and films about the Third Reich set out to challenge official historiography and the myth that the people of GDR had been the victors of history. The writer Stephan Hermlin stated that the GDR also shared the legacy of Germany's fascist past, while Heiner Müller took this view further when he said in 1975: 'Heute ist der gewöhnliche Faschismus interessant: Wir leben auch mit Leuten, für die er das Normale war, wenn nicht die Norm, Unschuld ein Glücksfall' (Today we are interested in everyday fascism. There are people amongst us for whom it was normal, if not the norm. Innocence was a happy coincidence) (cited in Emmerich 1996: 319).

DEFA films of the 1970s and 1980s, too, though arguably to a lesser extent than literature, break with the clichés that had become customary in dealing with the anti-fascist theme. Horst E. Brandt's film *KLK an PTX – Die Rote Kapelle* (KLK Calling PTZ: The Red Orchestra, 1971), a film about the resistance groups co-ordinated by Arvid Harnack and Harro-Schulze Boysen and labelled 'Red Orchestra' by the Gestapo because of its connections with Moscow, still inflates the importance of communist solidarity but at least acknowledges the existence of resistance amongst the military, the bourgeoisie and nobility. Günther Rücker's and Günter Reisch's prize-winning and extremely popular film *Die Verlobte* (The Fiancée, 1980) tells the story of a female resistance fighter who retains her strength and dignity during ten years of imprisonment amongst murderers, prostitutes and corrupt guards, not primarily because of her political convictions but because of her love and the oath she took on parting from her fiancé: 'Du bist mein Mann. Ich bin deine Frau, was auch kommt' (You are my husband. I am your wife, whatever may happen). The film's innovative quality consists in personalising and thus individualising the traditional theme of collective communist resistance. Moreover, it touches upon a taboo in that it is far more explicit than previous films about the Hitler–Stalin pact, a historical event that was glossed over in the GDR's official historiography. Frank Beyer's cinematic adaptation of Kant's novel *Der Aufenthalt* (The Turning Point, novel 1977, film 1982), the story of nineteen-year-old Mark Niebuhr, who is mistakenly arrested and put into a Warsaw POW camp in 1945, proposes that even those proven innocent share in the collective guilt of the Germans. 1987 also saw the release of a film made and banned some twenty years earlier: Heiner Carow's *Die Russen kommen* (The Russians Are Coming, 1967), which sheds new light on the state-sanctioned narrative of liberation by the Red Army, suggesting 'that the GDR as an anti-fascist state did not emerge full-blown with the arrival of the Russian liberators but instead was at the outset confronted with violence, confusion, and deep unprocessed feelings of having been betrayed' (Byg 1992: 208; see Chapter 4 of this volume).

In terms of their ideological trajectory, both Carow's censored film and Weiß's film *Dein unbekannter Bruder* are comparable to Marcel Ophüls' ground-breaking documentary *Le Chagrin et la pitié* (The Sorrow and the Pity, 1970) and Louis Malle's equally controversial feature *Lacombe Lucien* (1974), which set out to reveal the 'truth' about the occupation of France and the resistance. Malle's popular film portrays how the young Frenchman Lucien accidentally joins the *milice* and becomes receptive to the seductive allure of fascism. The film caused a considerable stir at the time of its release because – not unlike Weiß's and Carow's films – it debunked the national myth that the French under German occupation were a nation of resistance fighters. This myth, known as *le résistancialisme*, had been upheld until the end of the Gaullist dominance in post-war France in 1974 and Malle's film was the first feature film to deconstruct it (Austin 1996: 28–33).

One of the remarkable things about *Dein unbekannter Bruder*, based on Willi Bredel's novel of the same title that was written in Soviet exile in 1936–37, is that it turns this canonical anti-fascist text into a film that debunks Bredel's orthodox credo. Rather than celebrating acts of heroic resistance, the film provides a psychological account of the protagonist's internal conflict and paralysing fear.

The film, set in Hamburg in 1935, centres on Arnold Clasen, who resumes his work in the communist resistance movement after his release from a concentration camp where he was tortured. Unlike the resistance fighters typically depicted in DEFA's anti-fascist genre who are united by their common goal, Arnold lives in isolation – an isolation that springs from distrust and the fear of betrayal. He is particularly mistrustful of his contact Walter. The film's ending confirms Arnold's suspicion: Walter is actually a spy, who has betrayed several members of the resistance group to the Gestapo and who is also responsible for Arnold's second arrest. Unlike Bredel's novel, where Walter is a Gestapo spy who is smuggled into the group, in Weiß's film he comes from within the ranks of the communist resistance itself and is thus a traitor to the anti-fascist cause.

Far from passing a harsh moral judgement on the traitor, Weiß gives a differentiated account of Walter's motivations for becoming a spy: like

Arnold he is caught by the Gestapo but, unlike Arnold, he succumbs to blackmail and the fear of physical and psychological torture. As a spy, his collaboration with the Gestapo not only spares him punishment but also grants him financial rewards, which appeal to his hedonism. However, like Arnold he is haunted by ambivalence and tremendous inner turmoil. Whilst in Bredel's novel the communist resistance group fabricates what looks like Walter's suicide, in Weiß's film the resistance group does not engage in that form of punishment but simply deserts the traitor, leaving it to him to come to terms with his multiple acts of treason. Weiß's film lacks the explicit didactic ending of Bredel's novel, which is directed at the Germans at large: 'Mut, Arnold, Mut! Du ver-trittst die beste, die gerechteste Sache. Du bist ein Soldat der großen Armee der Freiheitskämpfer, der stärksten Armee der Welt!' (Bredel 1978: 368) (Courage, Arnold, courage! You represent the best and fairest cause. You are a soldier in the great army of freedom fighters, the strongest army in the world!).

Due to the highly subjective cinematic techniques which Weiß employs in the screen adaptation of Bredel's text, the film's narrative is so ambiguous that the traitor Walter can be interpreted as Arnold's alter ego. Walter's treason would then simply represent an alternative course of action that Arnold might have taken and certainly considers. As Ralf Schenk argues in his thought-provoking reading of *Dein unbekannter Bruder*, Walter could be

> nichts anderes als die nach außen projezierte Verkörperung, die Personi-fizierung der in Arnold vorhandenen Befürchtung, seine moralische Kraft zu verlieren. Der Film als Monolog: die ‚Teilung' als gedankliches Varian-tenspiel Arnolds, das letzte Drittel der ‚Handlung' als subjektive Vorstel-lung des Helden von einer möglichen zukünftigen Realität, nicht mehr als das subjektiv gebrochene Bild der Realität selbst. (Schenk 1981: 10)

> (nothing but an externally projected embodiment, a personification of Arnold's fear that he might lose his moral resilience. The film as mono-logue: the 'division' as a game of variants in Arnold's mind, the last third of the 'action' nothing but the subjective imagination of the protagonist of a possible, future reality, nothing but the subjective refracted picture of reality itself.)

Numerous clues legitimate this highly subjective reading of the film. Weiß, born in 1942, does not intend to render the anti-fascist theme in the same way as those directors who actually experienced the Third Reich. He does not aim for any sense of authenticity, instead he plays with possible realities: 'Meine Wirklichkeit ist es, ein Spiel vorzuführen, das das Publikum annehmen kann.' (cited in Kersten 1996: 195) (My kind of reality is to perform a game, which the audience may choose to accept). *Dein unbekannter Bruder* stresses the uncertainty of the (hi)story rendered. In this respect it is similar to Beyer's *Jakob der Lügner*, discussed below. Moreover, the film itself substantiates the interpretation of Walter as Arnold's weaker alter ego on several levels. In one scene he says to Walter:

> Es kommt wahrscheinlich davon, weil ich so viel allein bin. Da drehen sich die Gedanken noch einmal um. Man wendet sich hin und her, und plötzlich beschäftigt man sich mit sich selbst . . . Wir dürfen nicht gegeneinander mißtrauisch sein. Das ist, als wären wir mißtrauisch gegen uns selbst.

> (That is probably because I am on my own so much. My thoughts turn round and round in my head. You turn backwards and forwards and suddenly you are just concerned with yourself . . . We must not become suspicious of each other. That would be like being suspicious of ourselves.)

This remark hints at the blurring of boundaries between Arnold's and Walter's identities. Shortly afterwards, Arnold is arrested and interrogated by the Gestapo, whilst Walter is interrogated by the communist resistance group and charged with having betrayed several members of the group. It is in particular the cross-cutting between those two scenes which suggests that Weiß takes the psychological profile of Arnold's inner world to the extreme by depicting a hypothetical construct of Arnold's imagination.

Whether we interpret the dialectical relationship between trust and mistrust, strength and weakness that Weiß dramatises in the film as Arnold's imaginary constructs or whether we subscribe to the more conventional reading of the Judas–Jesus constellation and consider Walter and Arnold as separate individuals is open to debate. However, the fact that the film seems to invite conflicting interpretations points towards the overall ambiguity of its narrative which runs counter to the explicit didacticism and the clear message advocated by Socialist Realism. The film's ambiguity is largely due to Weiß's reliance on the visual language of images, which in his view is more appropriate to the medium of film than the dominance of dialogue: 'Film – das ist für mich die Entdeckung der sinnlichen Welt. . . . Es geht nicht einfach darum, Sprache ins Bild zu übersetzen' (cited in Gehler 1982) (For me film is the discovery of the sensory world. . . . It is not simply about translating language into image).

The film abounds in visual metaphors and symbols which are the objective correlative of Arnold's inner psychic states: recurrent images of metal grids, cages and nets form a leitmotif which corresponds to Arnold's fear of getting caught; a hunting scene which shows a pheasant being hounded down by dogs fulfils the same function. The lurid red Nazi banner opposite his window is getting bigger and bigger – but is it really? Or does the camera simply render Arnold's point of view and does the banner only grow with Arnold's growing fear?

The film's innovative visual style gave rise to serious concerns when the film was still in production. *Dein unbekannter Bruder* was charged with conflating the heroic acts of anti-fascist resistance with the anarchic terrorism of the West German Red Army Faction (cited in Geiss 1997: 155). Although Weiß was allowed to complete shooting the film, he was put under Stasi surveillance. Even after the HV Film licensed the film in September 1981, it remained highly controversial and was withdrawn from the Cannes Film Festival in 1982. Shortly after premiering in a sold-out performance in East Berlin's Colosseum cinema, the film was taken off the programme and was only released with fifteen copies, the minimum number to cover the GDR's fifteen districts.

In the official SED newspaper *Neues Deutschland*, *Dein unbekannter Bruder* received no mention. Elsewhere in the national press it was not well received either. Film critics attacked the ambiguous language of images, which was felt to make the film inaccessible (Stolze 1982; Wittfoth 1987: 53–8). *Dein unbekannter Bruder* was charged with lacking a social and historical dimension, and with reducing Bredel's novel about heroic resistance to a mere psychological study of fear. Critics found fault with the film's iconography because it tacitly equates the underground anti-fascist struggle with the undercover operations of gangsters and spies (Stolze 1982; Wittfoth 1987: 53–8). Indeed, it is not merely Walter's trench coat and the men's hats which are borrowed from the genre of *film noir*: Weiß and his cameraman Claus Neumann consciously allude to the *film noir* genre through playing with a number of its cinematic conventions.

Weiß's film blasphemously debunks the anti-fascist myth in three ways: firstly, by staging the anti-fascist theme as *film noir* and psychodrama, Weiß diminishes the heroic stature of the anti-fascists. Secondly, by turning Walter into a traitor from within the ranks of the communists, he dismantles the myth of communist solidarity. And thirdly, by blurring the boundaries of Arnold's and Walter's identities, the distinction between the heroes and the villains, the victims and the perpetrators becomes ambiguous. Weiß thus relativises the dichotomy of resistance and complicity, heroism and guilt and thus subscribes to Heiner Müller's view: innocence was a happy coincidence.

The cinematic discourse on the Holocaust in divided Germany

The suppression of Nazi anti-Semitism and the Holocaust in East and West German cinema until the 1980s is one of the most staggering characteristics of the on-screen memory discourse. In the context of West German film culture this omission is even more remarkable given the state-endorsed philo Semitism that prevailed in the FRG from the Adenauer period onwards. The impulse for German filmmakers and the German public at large to engage with this darkest aspect of their past came from abroad: in 1979 the West German television station WDR broadcast the American television mini-series *Holocaust*. This was 'the first major commercial film to deal with the persecution and systematic slaughter of millions of European Jews in a fictional form' (Kaes 1992: 28). The series tells the story of a fictitious Jewish family in order to show the systematic persecution and annihilation of the Jews between 1933 and 1945. Despite the fact that the series was controversial on account of its kitschy style and melodramatic sensationalism, it had a huge impact on the German public. It was seen by over twenty million West Germans, that is, every other adult (Kaes 1992: 30). Although *Holocaust* was not broadcast in the GDR, because the East, unlike the West, claimed to already have dealt fully with the fascist past (Grote 1979: 2), the vast majority of East Germans, who could receive West German television, were able to watch.[14]

Of course, even before the watershed year of 1979, there had been a few relatively isolated attempts to address the persecution of the Jews in West German film. Yet with the exception of *David* (Peter Lilienthal, 1978), a film that makes the persecution of the Jews its central concern, most West German films, 'made only vague or obscure references to the systematic killing of Jews that occurred under Hitler's rule' (Reimer and Reimer 1992: 132) and never assigned the theme more than a peripheral role.

From the 1980s onwards, an increasing number of West German films engaged with this most difficult chapter of German history, including *Regentropfen* (Raindrops, Michael Hoffmann and Harry Raymon, 1981) and the television film *An uns glaubt Gott nicht mehr* (God Does Not Believe in Us Anymore, Axel Corti, 1982); both films relate the flight from Nazi persecution from the perspective of young boys. *Das Boot ist voll* (The Boat Is Full, Markus Immhoof, 1980) and *Regentropfen* dispel the myth that countries like Switzerland and America welcomed the Jews with open arms. *Die Wannseekonferenz* (The Wannsee Conference, Heinz Scheik, 1984) provides a fictionalised account of the most infamous meeting in history, when high-ranking Nazi officials met at a villa in the Berlin suburb of Wannsee and decided on how to implement the genocide of the Jews.[15]

In particular in comparison with East European cinema, where the Holocaust has been a major thematic concern at least since the 1960s, the late emergence of the Holocaust discourse in the context of German cinema is astounding and begs the question as to whether indeed some form of collective amnesia prevented German filmmakers from breaking the silence earlier. While several East European films are set in ghettos or even in concentration camps, portraying the experience of the Holocaust victims,[16] others look into the minds of the perpetrators. Yet significantly, and unlike American, British or Italian films about the Third Reich, which usually invoke the stereotype of the evil Nazi officer, the perpetrators in these films are either the filmmakers' own compatriots, or Germans whose guilt and complicity is portrayed in much more subtle shades of grey. András Kovács's *Hideg napok* (Cold Days, Hungary, 1966) deals with the retrospective attempts at self-justification of Hungarian officers who sided with the Nazis and who were complicit in a massacre of Jews and Serbs that took place on the frozen Danube in the occupied Yugoslav city Novi Sad in 1942, an event that had hitherto been shrouded in silence in official Hungarian historiography (see Iordanova 2003: 76). Similarly, Andrzej Munk's *Pasażerka* (Passenger, Poland 1960/63), a film about a former female concentration camp guard in Auschwitz, deals with 'the process of readjusting memory, issues of guilt and remembrance, and the ways perpetrators construct a morally acceptable post-war account of their crimes' (Iordanova 2003: 79). Remarkably, filmmakers who worked in a highly controlled cultural context had the courage to break taboos about their nations' complicity and burden of guilt, whereas West German filmmakers, who enjoyed an incomparable degree of freedom, remained silent about the Holocaust until nearly two decades later.

As DEFA film historians usually like to point out, East German cinema has been less reluctant to engage with anti-Semitism and the Holocaust than West German cinema. Films like *Ehe im Schatten, Die Affäre Blum* (The Blum Affair, Erich Engel, 1948), *Sterne*, and *Professor*

Mamlock, made between 1947 and 1960, are generally cited as prominent examples.[17] However, this claim merits closer inspection. Given the abundance of anti-fascist films, the anti-Semitic aspects of the Nazi regime are certainly under-represented. Where the annihilation of the Jews is addressed, it is usually instrumentalised to support the Marxist interpretation of anti-Semitism. This is not surprising since due to the state-control that governed all aspects of film production, it had to reflect the official historiography. As has been pointed out by historians who revisited the GDR's *verordneten Antifaschismus* (state-prescribed anti-fascism) after the *Wende*, strict state supervision which dictated the historians' research agendas resulted in a number of politically determined blind spots in the historiography of the Third Reich, the Holocaust being one of them (Kessler 1993: 149–67; Fox 1999). The main reason for this omission is that the persecution of the Jews is not easily accommodated by a Marxist interpretation of history, which 'considered anti-Semitism [...] a peripheral phenomenon, one caused by manipulation from above in order to provide a scapegoat for anti-capitalist sentiment, thus displacing the energies of class struggle' (Fox 1999: 10). It would automatically be resolved through the overthrow of the capitalist order. Other reasons for neglecting the persecution of the Jews under the Nazis are certain obvious homologies between the anti-Semitism of the Nazis and anti-Semitic tendencies in Stalinism,[18] which also resulted in latent anti-Semitic attitudes in the GDR that found public expression in many aspects of the GDR's political culture (Danyel 1992, 1993; Kessler 1993). And finally, in the GDR's official hierarchy of victims of the fascist regime, those who were persecuted because of their active political resistance were commemorated, whilst those who were persecuted because of their race or religion and other groups tended to be forgotten because their fate was less suited to support the anti-fascist myth of origin. Hence, in the GDR's official hierarchy of victims of fascism, Jews were accorded only the twelfth position! (Jung 1998: 54).

This universalisation of the Nazi past into a general sense of victimhood 'from which the Jewish question was essentially dropped' (Kattago 2001: 7) explains the abundance of films which pay tribute to the heroes of the communist resistance compared with the dearth of films about the persecution of the Jews. Moreover, the production and release of films dealing with aspects of the Holocaust always depended upon the constantly shifting politics regarding Jews, Arabs and Israel. Witness the production history of Frank Beyer's film *Nackt unter Wölfen* (Naked among Wolves, 1963), based on Bruno Apitz's best-selling novel (1958).

Novel and film give a fictionalised account of the heroic resistance and alleged self-liberation of political prisoners in Buchenwald, who hide and thus save a Polish Jewish child. While, on the one hand, the film epitomises the heroism of organised communist resistance by showing how political conviction and loyalty impart strength and hope to the individual and ultimately lead to victory, on the other hand *Nackt unter Wölfen* was not entirely uncontroversial because it touches upon one of the lacunae of the GDR's official historiography – the Jewish victims. Therefore, 'Apitz's *Nackt unter Wölfen*, originally conceived as a film, was refused by the East German Babelsberg film studios in 1955 and could not be filmed until 1963' (Fox 1999: 113).

The dates of the film's production history illustrate how the 'Jewish question' was utilised for political ends. In the early 1950s Jewish topics were highly sensitive in the GDR since the Stalinist anti-Zionist campaign, which affected all Eastern bloc countries including the GDR, led to the disbanding of the *Vereinigung der Verfolgten des Naziregimes*, which represented the interests of all victims of the Nazi regime, including Jews, in 1953, the imprisonment of Paul Merker as a Zionist agent and the emigration of several hundred Jewish citizens to the West. In the early 1960s, by contrast, it seemed opportune to play the 'Jewish card'. The capture and subsequent trial of Adolf Eichmann in Jerusalem focused worldwide attention on Nazi crimes and the GDR exploited this opportunity to maximise the propaganda value in a campaign which was to remind the world at large that many former Nazis were living in West Germany and held high positions (Fox 1999: 12).[19] The release of a film like *Nackt unter Wölfen*, which celebrated the GDR's myth of origin while at the same time associating communist resistance with the emotionally charged topic of saving a Jewish child, was certainly well timed. Released in twenty-two prints, it was seen by an audience of well over half a million within the first thirteen weeks of its release (Wittfoth 1987). What is interesting about this film is that, despite dealing with the sensitive Jewish theme, Beyer's film reaffirms the GDR's official discourse on the Holocaust which typically portrays the Jew as a passive victim, in this case even an infantile victim, dependant upon the protection of the communist heroes. Moreover the Jewish child is principally referred to as the Polish child, which again is in line with the GDR's official Holocaust discourse in that it subsumes the Jewish victim within other groups of victims and thus underpins the notion that the persecution of the Jews was a peripheral phenomenon.

Other films addressing the subject of Jewish annihilation reinforce this stereotype by portraying Jews who escape persecution through suicide.

Kurt Maetzig's melodrama *Ehe im Schatten*, about a mixed 'Aryan'-Jewish couple, based on the fate of the popular actor Joachim Gottschalk, his wife Meta and their son Michael,[20] and Konrad Wolf's *Professor Mamlock* (1961) are paradigmatic in this context. Wolf contrasts the fate of the assimilated, bourgeois Jewish doctor, Professor Mamlock, who fails to recognise the early signs of the Nazis' policy regarding Jews and who steers well clear of any political involvement, with that of his son Rolf, a communist resistance fighter. Wolf reaffirms the fervent political pathos of his father's play *Professor Mamlock* (1933), on which the film is based, by concluding the film with the admonishing commentary: 'Es gibt kein größeres Verbrechen – nicht kämpfen zu wollen, wo man kämpfen muß!' (There is no greater crime – than not wanting to fight – when fight one must!). By condemning Mamlock's lack of political commitment, the film – utterly scandalously – attributes Mamlock's suicide to his failure to join the resistance, thus making the Jew accountable for his own fate.[21]

Unheroic resistance in *Jakob der Lügner* (Jacob the Liar, Frank Beyer, 1975)

It is in this context that we have to consider Frank Beyer's fourth film in the anti-fascist tradition, *Jakob der Lügner*, a film about life in a Polish Jewish ghetto. The idea for the film dates back to 1965, when Jurek Becker wrote the script. Yet a number of adverse circumstances resulted in a delay of some nine years. First, the Polish co-production company withdrew their support – a move which Beyer believes was due to latent anti-Semitism amongst the Poles. Beyer felt that on-location shooting in Poland was essential but, as permission was not granted, the project had to be postponed. To complicate matters, in August 1966 permission to make the film was suddenly withdrawn, presumably because Beyer's film *Spur der Steine* (Trace of Stones) was forbidden in the wake of the Eleventh Plenum of 1965 and Beyer had to leave DEFA (see Chapter 4). Jurek Becker did not want another director to take on *Jakob der Lügner* and turned the script into a hugely successful novel, published both in East and West Germany (1969/70). When in 1972 the West German television channel ZDF approached Becker about a television adaptation of the novel, Becker contacted Beyer who was working for East German television at the time. Fortunately, a clause in his contract allowed him to do occasional coproductions with DEFA. Eventually, the film was made without any Polish or West German involvement (Schenk and Beyer 1995: 72).

The eventual realisation of the project was also favoured by a significant liberalisation in the GDR's cultural climate in the early 1970s and the ensuing third wave of *Bewältigungsliteratur* discussed above. *Jakob der Lügner*, not an anti-fascist film as such, deals with a form of resistance that has little in common with the organised communist resistance glorified in the official discourse. In the face of imminent deportation and almost certain death, the Jewish community of a Polish ghetto tries to live a normal life, as far as they can. But the suicide rate is high. Against this background Jakob Heym (played by the Czech actor Vlastimil Brodský) emerges as an unlikely hero. By an unlucky coincidence he finds himself in a Gestapo office in the ghetto when news comes over the radio that the Russians are only 20 km away from Bezanika. In order to save his friend Mischa from stealing potatoes, a petty crime which in the ghetto could have cost him his life, Jakob Heym tells him what he heard on the radio. However, as nobody would believe that he was in the Gestapo office without having been arrested, he pretends to possess a radio of his own. He lies because the truth would be too incredible. Since the possession of a radio is an offence punishable by death Jakob Heym, who is anything but a heroic man, becomes a hero against his will when he supplies his companions in the ghetto with regular 'news' about the war and the Red Army's advance, in order to offer them hope and strengthen their will to survive. But ultimately neither Jakob nor the others can be saved and the film ends with their deportation to a concentration camp.

The innovative aspects in this film consist of the new approach taken to the anti-fascist and Jewish themes,[22] the use of humour and the poetic qualities of the film's plot and its *mise-en-scène*. Unlike other anti-fascist films *Jakob der Lügner* pays no tribute to the victors of history, but focuses exclusively on its victims. Book and film 'resist' the type of resistance which had become a cliché of GDR film and fiction by portraying a world in which that kind of heroic resistance is absent (Becker 1983).

Beyer's film spares the audience most of the usual harrowing images of the barbarism against the Jews; the bleak life in the ghetto is not rendered with documentary authenticity. In fact, both the film and the novel explicitly undermine any potential claim to authenticity by emphasising that the (hi)story presented is merely a speculative one. In the novel the narrator's meta-narrative comments stress the uncertainty of his tale, whilst the film is prefaced by the paradoxical comment: 'Die Geschichte von Jakob dem Lügner hat sich niemals so zugetragen. Ganz bestimmt

4 Vlastimil Brodský (Jakob) and Manuela Simon (Lina) in *Jakob der Lügner*
(Jacob the Liar)

nicht. Vielleicht hat sie sich aber doch so zugetragen.' (The story of
Jacob the liar never happened in this way. Definitely not. But maybe it
did happen like this after all.) The film's cinematography underpins this
deliberate uncertainty by consciously eschewing any sense of historical
authenticity. Beyer, who after initial reservations shot this film in
colour, does not attempt to emulate documentaries about concentration
camps; he does not try to reconstruct the past. With pictures of emaci-
ated bodies and piles of corpses having become familiar territory in this
context, he argues, there was no need to repeat this gruesome reality in
an authentic mode (Schenk and Beyer 1995: 73).

Jakob der Lügner alludes to the horrors of the Holocaust, but its central theme is the life-giving, transforming power of hope, even the false
hope conveyed by lies and fairy tales. In order to convey this sense of
hope, Beyer renders the bleak reality of the ghetto in positive terms:
instead of elaborating on the near starvation of the people in the ghetto,
Beyer shows how precious a slice of bread is, when Jakob Heym turns
his humble, solitary meal into a little feast. In order to draw our attention to the complete absence of trees or any plants in the ghetto (they

had been removed by the SS) Beyer highlights how precious even a tiny green weed is when Rosa picks it and takes the precious find home as if it were a rare botanical specimen. By turning the negatives into positives, Beyer conveys a story of hope and thus makes the powerful impact of Jakob's lie on everyday life in the ghetto tangible (Becker 1983: 272).[23]

Even the eventual deportation of the Jews is presented so poetically that one might almost share the little orphan-girl Lina's misconception that the entire ghetto is going on holiday. Beyer achieves this remarkable poetic transformation of a journey into death by granting us access to Lina's imaginary world. The final dialogue sequence between Jakob and Lina refers back to the fairy tale which Jakob had invented for Lina and broadcast, as it were, on his imaginary radio, and which parabolically summarises the central theme of hope, even if it is illusory: a young princess is fatally ill and can only be rescued if a man plucks a white fluffy cloud out of the sky for her. No man can rise to this challenge and the princess is doomed to die. However, the gardener comes to the rescue when he tells the princess that clouds are made out of cotton wool, and when he presents her with a cotton wool cloud as big as her pillow the princess' fatal illness is cured. It is to this fairy tale that the very last images of the film refer. Only briefly does the camera focus on the crammed conditions in the railway carriage and on the troubled faces of the deported Jews. When Lina asks to be lifted up in order to be able to look out, the camera assumes her point of view and with her we see green fields and trees and real white clouds, not cotton wool clouds. By assuming the innocent perspective of a child, the film sustains the sense of hope against all odds until the very end. As Beyer explained: 'Die Geschichte endet tragisch und doch nicht pessimistisch, der Gedanke von der unzerstörbaren Menschenwürde wird verteidigt bis zum Schluß' (Beyer 1974) (The story ends tragically and yet not pessimistically. The idea of indestructible human dignity is defended until the very end).[24]

The film, a co-production of DEFA and GDR television, was shown on television in December 1974 and premiered in GDR cinemas on 18 April 1975. Despite being promoted as an anti-fascist film that marked the thirtieth anniversary of Germany's liberation from fascism, it was released with only seventeen copies and was seen by just 89,279 viewers within the first thirteen weeks of its release (Wittfoth 1987). Compared with other anti-fascist films of the 1970s, which were more in line with the official anti-fascist discourse, *Jakob der Lügner* received relatively little public exposure nationally, which is indicative of its

5 The fairy tale of the fatally ill princess in *Jakob der Lügner*
(Jacob the Liar)

ideological ambiguity.[25] Abroad, by contrast, the film received considerable attention. It was the first DEFA film to be sent to the Berlinale in
West Berlin in 1975, where Vlastimil Brodský won the Silver Bear for
best actor. Moreover, *Jakob der Lügner* was the only DEFA film ever to
be nominated for an Oscar as the best foreign language film – though
it ultimately did not win this award.

It is also the only DEFA film that was remade in Hollywood, starring
Robin Williams as well as Armin Mueller-Stahl, who also plays a part
in Beyer's film. The French director and scriptwriter Peter Kassovitz and
co-scriptwriter Didier Decoin turned Becker's tale of unheroic resistance
into a star-studded tale of heroic Jewish resistance, a black comedy about
the Holocaust – a 'me-too', but a more authentic version, of the hugely
successful Holocaust comedy *La Vita È Bella* (Life Is Beautiful, Roberto
Benigni, Italy 1997) (McCarthy 1999: 51).[26] Kassovitz's film reinterprets
the concept of resistance proposed by Becker and Beyer in a more conventional, that is, heroic fashion: even under torture and when held at
gunpoint Jakob does not renounce his mission of instilling hope amidst
the horror in the ghetto – and he pays with his life.

The end of DEFA's lifeline

In the wake of German reunification, the divided memory of the Nazi past, which had been characterised by sharply divergent social constructions of remembering, became replaced by memories of a double past – the Nazi past and the communist past. In the ensuing East–West German memory contests, predictably, the West German model of internalising the Nazi legacy gained hegemony over the East German model of universalising the Nazi past. The anti-fascist myth of origin automatically lost currency. Whereas West German filmmakers became obsessed with revisiting the burdensome past, focusing more than ever before on the Holocaust, East German filmmakers quickly abandoned DEFA's anti-fascist tradition. Or rather, the majority of those filmmakers who had specialised in the anti-fascist genre had either died or were unable to make feature films after the privatisation of DEFA in 1992 (see Chapter 6). With their departure from the industry East German on-screen memories of the Third Reich disappeared, too. What the handful of films about the Third Reich that were still made by DEFA directors such as Rainer Simon, Roland Gräf and Maxim Dessau in the early 1990s have in common is that they break with the conventions of the anti-fascist tradition and instead continue a trend that had already manifested itself in a number DEFA films of the 1980s: they question the myth of heroic anti-fascist resistance and acknowledge that the East Germans, too, are not free from guilt (*Der Fall Ö*/The Case of Ö, Rainer Simon, 1991; *Die Spur des Bernsteinzimmers*/The Trail of the Amber Room, Roland Gräf, 1992). They assert that the relationship between Germans and Russians was far more ambiguous than stated in official memory (*Erster Verlust*/First Loss, Maxim Dessau, 1990).[27] The new generation of East German filmmakers that came to the fore shortly after unification was too preoccupied with coming to terms with a more recent past and its ramifications for the present. They were anxious not to repeat the sins of their fathers, who had abided by the state-ordained interpretation of the fascist past, and instead critically examined the GDR's Stalinist dictatorship through their films.

Notes

1 Some sections of this chapter were previously published in Berghahn (2002).
2 In fact, the prisoners' uprising had only prefaced the actual liberation by the American army.

3 Publications focusing on *Vergangenheitsbewältigung* in West German cinema include Kaes (1992); Kosta (1994); Linville (1998); McCormick (1991); Santer (1990). Several of the comprehensive studies on New German Cinema include relevant sections on this topic. See, for example, Corrigan (1994); Elsaesser (1989); Sandford (1981). Seeßlen (2000) and Hake (2002) provide an up-to-date account of East and West German films about the Nazi past from 1946 to the present. Koepnick (2002) examines German Holocaust films of the 1990s in the contexts of heritage cinema and post-memory.

4 Amongst the most prominent examples of other European rubble films are Roberto Rossellini's *Germania anno zero* (Germany Year Zero, Italy, 1947); *Valahol Európában* (Somewhere in Europe, Géza von Radványi, Hungary, 1947); *Piątka z ulicy Barskiej* (Five Boys from Barska Street, Aleksander Ford, Poland, 1954); and *Jeux interdits* (Forbidden Games, René Clement, France, 1952). See Iordanova (2003: 59–60) on East European rubble films.

5 Between 1975 and 1985 more than fifty new feature films dealing with National Socialism were made in West Germany (Kaes 1992: 22). They include the Academy Award-winning film *Die Blechtrommel* (The Tin Drum, Volker Schlöndorff, 1979); Wolfgang Petersen's international box-office hit *Das Boot* (The Boat, 1981); and *Bittere Ernte* (Angry Harvest, Agnieszka Holland, 1985), starring Armin Mueller-Stahl.

6 The Crimes of the *Wehrmacht* exhibition raised the controversial issue of the moral responsibility of the average *Wehrmacht* soldier. It was seen by nearly a million people in Germany and Austria between 1995 and 1999 (see Niven 2002: 71).

7 On the function of children in rubble films see Fisher (2001) and Iordanova (2003: 59–60).

8 On the role of women and male identity crisis in post-war cinema, see Byg (1997a) and Carter (2000).

9 The same character-type appears in *Tage aus einem deutschen Leben* (Days from a German Life, Theodor Kotulla, FRG, 1977), which portrays the concentration camp commander Rudolf Höß as a duty-bound officer and loving family man.

10 Barton Byg has drawn my attention to the fact that the film remains equivocal about the Jewishness of the Mondschein character. While his name suggests that he is Jewish nothing else points in this direction. His son, for example, is a *Wehrmacht* soldier.

11 While DEFA's rubble films made between 1946 and 1949 are usually also subsumed under the more general term 'anti-fascist films', their ideological agenda is markedly different from that of the anti-fascist films that developed in parallel to the GDR's nation-building myth of origin.

12 As claims of a broad-based resistance movement played a subordinate role in the discourse on West German *Vergangenheitsbewältigung*, films dealing with the theme of resistance are comparatively rare. Titles include *Es geschah*

am 20. Juli (Jackboot Mutiny, G. W. Pabst, 1955) and *Des Teufels General* (The Devil's General, Helmut Käutner, 1955), a war film that interprets acts of sabotage as a form of resistance amongst the military. Both *Die weiße Rose* (The White Rose, Michael Verhoeven, 1982) and *Fünf letzte Tage* (Five Last Days, Percy Adlon, 1982) are about the Munich-based student resistance group called 'The White Rose'. *Georg Elsner* (Klaus-Maria Brandauer, 1989) tells the story of the German carpenter Elsner, who made an attempt on Hitler's life. *Rosenstraße* (The Women of Rosenstrasse, Margarethe von Trotta, 2003) depicts the 'resistance of the heart' of German Gentile women whose protest against the internment of their Jewish husbands resulted in the release of the intermarried Jewish men.

13 At the SED's second Party Convention in July 1952, Ulbricht announced the 'planmäßigen Aufbau des Sozialismus' (the planned construction of socialism), which was to have a significant impact on culture. According to the resolution of the Politbüro of the SED on 22 July 1952 (Für den Aufschwung der fortschrittlichen deutschen Filmkunst) and a film conference (17–18 September 1952), film production would have to be harnessed more firmly to this new political and economic agenda.

14 To my knowledge no data is available on how many East Germans actually watched *Holocaust* on West German television.

15 For a useful survey of German Holocaust films made between the late 1940s and 1990 see Reimer and Reimer (1992) and Deutsches Filminstitut (2001).

16 For an illuminating account of East Central European films about the Holocaust see Iordanova (2003: 74–86, 188–9).

17 The fact that several Jewish-themed films were also made in the Western occupation zones is often forgotten in discussions of *Ehe im Schatten*.

18 In Russian cinema, the prevailing anti-Semitism is documented by the fate of Aleksandr Askoldov's classic *Komissar* (The Commissar, 1967/87). In this film the Jewish family which takes care of the abandoned baby of a female commissar during the Revolution is portrayed more sympathetically than the communist heroine. This positive portrayal of Jews was a taboo. The film was shelved and the director was banned from filmmaking. See Johnson (1997: 644–5). Moreover, during Stalin's anti-cosmopolitan campaigns Jewish directors and scriptwriters were banned from filmmaking; see Kenez (1997: 397). Turovskaya (1992) gives a brief account of the Jewish theme in Soviet cinema under Stalin.

19 Other crucial dates which demonstrate how the 'Jewish question' was utilised for political ends are 1967 and 1988: in the late 1960s the 'Jewish question' became once again a very sensitive topic due to the Arab–Israeli conflict in which the GDR alongside the Soviet Union took a pro-Arab stance. In 1988, by contrast, the GDR commemorated the fiftieth anniversary of the *Kristallnacht* with a series of ceremonies and the release of Siegfried Kühn's film *Die Schauspielerin* (The Actress), as it seemed wise to play 'the Jewish

card' in order to attain Most Favoured Nation trade status with the US. See Fox (1999: 13–15).

20 In the film the couple are portrayed as childless.

21 As Gertrud Koch (1993: 68) points out, the film's ending implies that Mamlock 'bears the guilt for his death in the very same way that had already been expressed in the propagandistic allegations of the early 1950s in the show trials against Merker. The German Jews are condemned to their own death – as part of the bourgeois class, they bear the blame for it.'

22 O'Doherty (1997), however, argues that the film conveys an orthodox image of the Jews because it omits the only significant episode of active resistance – Kirschbaum's suicide and the resultant death of a Nazi – thus reinforcing the stereotype of the passive Jewish victim.

23 In an article published in *Neues Deutschland*, Frank Beyer states that his prime aim was neither the depiction of Jewish suffering nor the commemoration of anti-fascist heroism. Instead he wanted to reflect upon truth and lies, dream and reality; see Beyer (1974).

24 The original script of 1965 had a different ending: Jakob gets shot in an attempt to escape from the ghetto just before it was liberated by the Red Army. But since no ghetto was ever liberated by the Red Army this ending was abandoned. See Schenk and Beyer (1995: 72).

25 According to Wittfoth's (1987) data, *KLK an PTX – Die Rote Kapelle* (1971) was released with fifty-eight copies and was seen by 1.3 million viewers; *Mama, ich lebe* (1977) was released with thirty copies and was seen by more than a million viewers.

26 Beyer's film is also likely to have inspired the Academy Award-winning Italian film *La Vita È Bella* (Life Is Beautiful, Roberto Benigni, 1997) – a film that was both hailed and criticised for being the *first* Holocaust comedy, presumably because in the West only a few people had ever come across Jurek Becker's and Frank Beyer's much more subtle tragicomedy. For a wide-ranging, excellent discussion of humorous Holocaust films, see Gilman (2000).

27 Other anti-fascist films produced or co-produced by DEFA shortly before its privatisation were: *Die Sprungdeckeluhr* (The Spring Lid Watch, Gunter Friedrich 1991); *Laßt mich doch eine Taube sein* (Let Me Be a Dove, Miomir Stamenkovic, co-production with Yugoslavia, 1990); *Krücke* (Crutch, Jörg Grünler, co-production with FRG, 1993); *Großvaters Reise* (Grandfather's Journey, Staffan Lamm, co-production with Sweden, 1993). Frank Beyer, who, alongside Konrad Wolf, is associated with DEFA's most acclaimed anti-fascist films, made several films for television which continue the tradition: *Ende der Unschuld* (The End of Innocence, 1991), *Das letzte U-Boot* (The Last Submarine, 1993) and *Wenn alle Deutschen schlafen* (When all the Germans are Asleep, 1993), a ghetto-film that is based on a text by Jurek Becker.

3

In the guise of costume drama: the appropriation of Germany's cultural heritage

Vying for Germany's cultural tradition

According to the *Einigungsvertrag* (unification treaty) of 31 August 1990, German art and culture were 'in den Jahren der Teilung . . . – trotz unterschiedlicher Entwicklung beider Staaten in Deutschland – eine Grundlage der fortbestehenden Einheit der deutschen Nation' (cited in Judt 1998: 336) (in the years of division . . . – in spite of the different developments of both German states – a basis for the continuing unity of the German nation). Yet, in fact, the question of Germany's cultural unity in the face of its political division had been a continuously contested issue. Notwithstanding the fact that in 1950 Otto Grotewohl, the Prime Minister of the newly-founded GDR, declared that German culture could not be divided (Judt 1998: 334), he also criticised the Americanisation of West German culture, a development that he considered to be '*Kulturverrat*' – a betrayal of Germany's indigenous culture. Paul Wandel, the new *Volksbildungsminister* (education minister) confirmed the official view by stressing that the government would 'alle Maßnahmen unterstützen, die der kulturellen Einheit der deutschen Nation dienen. Sie wird das Kulturerbe der Nation wahren' (cited in Schlenker 1977: 84) (support all measures that will serve the cultural unity of the German nation. It will preserve the cultural heritage of the nation). In the eyes of the GDR's leaders, the preservation of the nation's cultural tradition was the most powerful antidote to American cultural imperialism in West Germany, which was seen to destroy Germany's indigenous cultural tradition through 'cosmopolitan' influences, resulting in a barbaric 'boogie-woogie culture' (Schlenker 1977: 86).

Predictably, the notion of one German *Kulturnation*, 'meaning variously a cultured nation and a nation unified through its cultural achievements' (Silberman 1996: 297), was short-lived. After the erection of the Berlin

Wall in 1961, the GDR's official view was that the political division extended to the cultural sphere and that East Germany's socialist culture and West Germany's imperialist *Unkultur* (non-culture) were irreconcilable. In fact, socialist culture needed to be protected from the harmful influences of the decadent and manipulative entertainment industry in the West. In the wake of the *Ostpolitik* (West German foreign policy regarding East Germany), which resulted in a lowering of the real barriers between East and West Germany during the 1970s but paradoxically also in a policy of cultural *Abgrenzung* (demarcation), 'emphasis was laid ... on a GDR-specific culture separate from the class-biased culture of capitalist West Germany' (Fulbrook 1992: 294). In 1980, Kurt Hager, the Party's chief ideologue, openly rejected the West German view of a 'unity of culture' and a German '*Kulturgemeinschaft*' (cultural community), arguing instead that the anti-fascist and democratic restructuring and the construction of socialism in the GDR had resulted in an independent socialist national culture that was inspired by the ideas of freedom, humanism and socialism (Judt 1998: 335).

At the same time, the GDR did not want to forsake its pre-socialist cultural heritage. Just as East and West Germany competed to be 'the better Germany' with regard to overcoming the fascist past, so they vied for the title of sole legitimate heir to Germany's culture and history. While national history and cultural tradition play a decisive role in any nation's attempt to define its national identity, in the case of divided Germany, history and culture became a ferociously contested territory in the protracted processes of demarcation and legitimisation of the two German states. In a nation that had achieved political unity as late as the nineteenth century, only to experience repeated political divisions during the twentieth century, the notion of a *Kulturnation* became central to Germany's self-definition. Yet the rupture of cultural and historical continuity after the Second World War resulted in two 'highly partisan version[s] of national history fixated on the phenomenon of Fascism' (Elsaesser 1989: 49) and in an uncertainty about the meaning of national culture not found in any other European country. Arguably, culture assumed such an exaggerated centrality in the search for a new German identity after the war because it was all that remained on which to build the divided nation's self-esteem. While the anti-fascist myth of origin offered identificatory potential for East Germans, and the economic miracle and the values of a liberal democracy played a similar nation-building role in the West, it was Germany's cultural heritage that served as a *common* source of national pride in both parts of Germany.

Both German states guarded this precious core of German national identity through various cultural and educational policies, intended to promote those aspects of the cultural heritage deemed appropriate to reflect the two emerging and diverging identities of the divided nation. In the GDR the selective appropriation of Germany's *kulturelles Erbe* (cultural heritage) initially only included those periods and movements that were considered to be humanist and progressive. In terms of the literary canon, the Enlightenment, Weimar Classicism, the *Vormärz* (the period from 1815 to the March revolution of 1848), and nineteenth-century Realism were approved of, whereas the avant-garde, Modernism and – at least until the mid-1970s – Romanticism were excluded. Similarly, the appropriation of German history focused on themes in keeping with orthodox Marxist materialist historiography, in particular 'the succession of modes of production, the progressive role of the exploited and oppressed classes, and the importance of revolutions in the transition from one stage to the next' (Fulbrook 1992: 301), excluding until the 1980s the historic role of great individuals, such as Bismarck, Frederick the Great and Luther, as well as certain historic themes, most notably militarism and the legacy of Prussia. This selective focus in the appropriation of Germany's *Tradition und Erbe* (tradition and legacy) was meant to reflect and legitimise the GDR's new socialist order 'as the inevitable culmination of the past, the goal towards which all German history [and culture] had been tending' (Fulbrook 1992: 300).[1]

The promotion of Germany's cultural heritage through film

Even a cursory glance at the cinematic adaptations of literature and artist biopics made by East and West German filmmakers reveals a number of conspicuous similarities and synchronicities which seem to confirm the persistence of a common cultural tradition in spite of Germany's forty years of division. Firstly, the list of film titles suggests that in both parts of Germany, the *Land der Dichter und Denker* (country of poets and thinkers), biopics of writers feature far more prominently than biographical films about painters, composers or other figures of historical interest. Secondly, cinematic adaptations of literature are based to a large extent on the same sources, notably canonical texts by Lessing, Goethe, Fontane, Storm, Thomas Mann and, from the 1970s onwards, those of the Romantics. And thirdly, in both parts of Germany the 1950s and 1970s clearly emerge as the decades during which the largest number of films appropriating Germany's literary and cultural tradition were produced.

Furthermore, East and West German filmmakers, as well as writers, shared a fascination with counter-cultural heroes, notably writers such as Heinrich von Kleist, Georg Büchner, Friedrich Hölderlin and Reinhold Lenz, whose artistic struggles and rebellious stance *vis-à-vis* the reactionary forces of society seemed to provide identificatory reference points for artists and intellectuals on either side of the Wall during the 1970s.

In both parts of Germany cinema played a crucial role in the appropriation of the cultural and literary traditions by making Germany's cultural heritage widely available. As one would expect, DEFA's heritage films reflect the GDR's two-pronged approach to its cultural identity, which aimed to amalgamate the pre-socialist tradition with communist internationalism. Consequently, DEFA's historical epics and film biographies celebrate on the one hand East Germany's communist forebears, such as Lenin, Karl Liebknecht and Ernst Thälmann; the artist Käthe Kollwitz; and the proletarian women's rights campaigners Louise Otto Peters and Clara Zetkin.[2] On the other hand, they pay tribute to pre-socialist cultural icons such as the composers Ludwig van Beethoven and Johann Strauß; historical figures like Thomas Müntzer, Johannes Kepler and Alexander von Humboldt; artists like Riemenschneider and Goya; and the aforementioned writers.[3] Many of these historical films and costume dramas were produced and released to mark centrally organised celebrations, commemorating the anniversaries of cultural icons, which were generally celebrated with much pomp and circumstance in the GDR.

The fact that film underpinned the cultural legitimisation strategies of the two German states is further underscored by the two consecutive waves of heritage films in the 1950s and 1970s: during the 1950s DEFA made thirteen and during the 1970s eleven films appropriating the pre-socialist cultural heritage, compared with twenty and thirty made in the FRG during the respective decades (Rentschler 1986: 336–65). Of course, the need for historical and cultural self-definition and demarcation was particularly high on the agenda during the 1950s, after the founding of the two German states in 1949, and again during the 1970s, when the GDR gained international recognition as a sovereign state.

Yet in the FRG, the '*Literaturverfilmungswelle*' (wave of cinematic adaptations of literature, see Sandford 1989) of the 1970s cannot simply, or even primarily, be explained as an attempt to harness the national film production to the task of competing for the status of true heir to Germany's cultural tradition. More significantly, the high cultural status of the literary canon helped to close the cultural legitimisation gap from

which cinema was suffering. Unlike in the GDR, where film was classified as art from the outset, in the FRG film was considered to be 'just'
entertainment. Only when the filmmakers associated with the New
German Cinema appeared on the scene and combined high-cultural
literary sources with artistic aspirations was film deemed fit to play an
important role in the *Bildung* (culture and education) of West German
citizens. Through becoming a purveyor of high-cultural values cinema
had succeeded in asserting its claim to cultural respectability (Sandford
1989: 161). As a result it also attracted public funding, which in the long
run became a vital prerequisite for its establishment and survival as one
of Europe's most critically acclaimed art cinemas (see Chapter 1).

Bringing the literary canon up to date

Though cultural legitimisation was the primary and official function
assigned to cinematic adaptations of literature and artist biopics, the
temporal displacement of films set in the past coupled with their
cultural respectability afforded East and West German filmmakers the
opportunity to critically comment on contemporary society. Unlike the
European heritage film, a popular genre that emerged in the 1980s in
particular in France, Britain and some other West European countries
and that renders 'history as spectacle, as *separate* from the viewer in the
present, as something over and done with' (Higson 1993: 113), DEFA's
period dramas emphasise the relevance of the cultural tradition for
the present. In this respect they are more akin to European art cinema,
which typically updates literary adaptations or biopics, frequently insert-
ing anachronisms as distanciation devices in a Brechtian manner or
transposing historical matter into the present outright. For example,
Syberberg's adaptation of Kleist's early nineteenth-century novella *San
Domingo* (FRG, 1970) relocates the action in the Munich drop-out scene
of the 1970s; Wim Wenders' *Falsche Bewegung* (Wrong Movement,
FRG, 1975), loosely based on Goethe's novel *Wilhelm Meister*, uses
the motif of the educational journey to comment on the sociopolitical
paralysis of the Federal Republic at that time; and Derek Jarman's
biopic of the Italian baroque painter *Caravaggio* (UK, 1986) scrambles
the past of sixteenth-century Italy with the more recent past of post-1945
Italy. But even European popular cinema and American adaptations of
the literary canon are now breaking the rules of period fidelity. Richard
Loncraine's *Richard III* (UK, 1995) renders Shakespeare's history play

as a political thriller set in the 1930s, while Baz Luhrmann's *William Shakespeare's Romeo + Juliet* (USA, 1996) is located in an unidentifiable, constructed world, somewhere between the suburbs of Mexico City and contemporary LA gang culture.

Compared with these examples the updating of the cultural heritage in DEFA costume dramas lacks audacity, chiefly because the preservation and promotion of Germany's cultural heritage via the medium of film was governed by the same conservative principles as the preservation of historical monuments, leaving little room for artistic experiment. Contemporisation was permissible only insofar as it safeguarded the educational function assigned to the canon and art generally in the GDR. With the evolution of the socialist state the active appropriation of the pre-socialist tradition was subjected to a multitude of educational and ideological purposes, including the provision of an ideological basis for the construction of socialism and even increasing economic productivity during the 1960s (Schlenker 1977: 162). The critical appropriation of the cultural and literary tradition was thus never static: its dynamism was driven by the continuous endeavour to utilise the cultural values of the past to solve the tasks of the present (Dau, Haase and Kliche 1984: 1417).

Thus DEFA filmmakers frequently underscored the relevance of the past for the present by using anachronisms in their films. However, these were not as aesthetically innovative as those described above. Typically, they consisted of a few subtle references to the present that momentarily broke with the self-effacing illusionism of a traditional period drama. In the early years of the GDR, when a sense of consensus between *Geist und Macht* (intellect and power) prevailed, topical subtexts and anachronisms in heritage films were normally in keeping with the official ideology and thus contributed to the project of socialist consciousness-raising. Yet, in years to come, updating of the cultural tradition became more ambiguous and heritage films were often used to voice coded expressions of dissidence.

For example, the final scene of Horst Seemann's biopic *Beethoven – Tage aus einem Leben* (Beethoven – Days from a Life, 1976) shows the composer in period costume following a horse-drawn cart with all his belongings amidst busy traffic on the Karl-Marx-Allee in East Berlin. Similarly, in one of the opening shots of Egon Günther's Goethe-film *Lotte in Weimar* (1975), cars replace the horse-drawn carriages in the historical setting of Weimar. While the official rationale for such bold attempts at contemporising the cultural heritage would have been to make

it clear to the audience that Beethoven and Goethe are an integral part
of the cultural heritage of the German Democratic Republic, filmmakers
also used such anachronisms to signal to the audience that the social and
political ills of the past evinced certain correspondences to those of
the present. Seemann's Beethoven-biopic for instance – not unlike
Tarkovsky's famous forbidden film *Andrei Rublev* (1966/71) about a
fifteenth-century Russian icon painter – is an impassioned plea for
artistic freedom and autonomy.[4] An East German audience, well-versed
in reading between the lines, would have interpreted the film's final scene
as a barely disguised comment on the problematic relationship between
art and power in the GDR. In other words, DEFA's heritage films provided a welcome opportunity to dress up dissidence as costume drama.
Many of the political subtexts voiced in DEFA's heritage films were only
able to pass the scrutiny of the censors because they were skilfully
camouflaged as quotations from literary sources and because they
ostensibly criticised social conditions that had been transcended by the
progressive forces of history, resulting in the construction of a socialist
society.

Due to the dual strategy employed by DEFA's costume dramas, heritage films gained particular prominence during politically repressive
periods. As Harry Blunk has observed, at times when the treatment of
contemporary themes was subject to rigid state supervision, cinematic
adaptations of the bourgeois-realist literary canon offered a welcome
escape from officially imposed silencings (Blunk 1987: 160). Thus, the
preponderance of DEFA heritage films during the 1970s can partly be
explained by the high degree of volatility in cultural matters during this
decade. Honecker's famous pronouncement of 'no taboos in the realm
of art and literature' (see Chapter 5) was soon superseded by restrictive
cultural policies that culminated in the expatriation of Wolf Biermann
in 1976 and the exodus of numerous writers and other intellectuals to
the West (see Jäger 1995: 165–70).

These vicissitudes are mirrored in the cinematic oeuvre of many a DEFA
film director. Egon Günther's artistic career, for example, suggests that
he, too, sought refuge in making *Erbefilme* when his *Gegenwartsfilme*, such
as *Wenn du groß bist, lieber Adam* (When You Are Grown Up, Dear Adam
1965/90) and *Die Schlüssel* (The Keys, 1972), were banned or sparked
controversy. Although Günther had made a name for himself with
much-acclaimed films about women in contemporary society, notably *Lots
Weib* (Lot's Wife, 1965) and *Der Dritte* (Her Third, 1971), after *Die Schlüssel*
the DEFA studio directorate only offered him film projects that promised

to be safe, i.e. cinematic adaptations of literature. Günther interprets this strategy as 'Ruhigstellen von schwer Erziehbaren . . . Psychopharmaka. Arbeitend ruhigstellen, nicht an brisante Dinge heranlassen' (Günther and Schenk 2000: 70) (Sedating the maladjusted . . . Psychiatric drugs. Sedation through work, keeping me away from explosive topics).

The following case studies will explore how DEFA's heritage films employ the dual strategy of, on the one hand, supporting the cultural legitimisation of the GDR as the true heir to German culture, while on the other hand utilising costume drama as camouflage to voice critical subtexts about contemporary society. In order to gauge the degree of cultural affirmation or critique inscribed in these films, it will be indispensable to trace the complex and shifting debates surrounding the reception of the traditional literary canon (the so-called *Erbedebatte*) and to identify to what extent the films in question reflect the officially pronounced positions.[5]

Appropriating the literary canon in a cold climate: *Der Untertan* (The Kaiser's Lackey/The Subject, Wolfgang Staudte, 1951)

Wolfgang Staudte's 1951 adaptation of Heinrich Mann's novel *Der Untertan*, completed in 1914 and first published in 1918, harnesses Mann's satirical novel about the Wilhelmine Empire to the pursuit of anti-fascist re-education, a key concern of DEFA productions up to the late 1940s. Staudte's screen adaptation resonates with the official reception of Mann's novel in the GDR: *Der Untertan* featured prominently in the GDR's school curricula, being hailed as a masterpiece of bourgeois-realist literature in the struggle against imperialism and war (Emmerich 1980: 146). Mann's sarcastic depiction of the *Untertanengeist* (subservient spirit) and the authoritative personality was considered retrospectively by many critics to be a prophetic insight into the psychological predispositions that were to pave the way for the rise of fascism two decades later (Emmerich 1980: 73–9). A novel that was seen to explore the roots of fascism in the shape of chauvinism, racism and the cult of the Emperor/leader, Mann's *Der Untertan* played a crucial role in the process of anti-fascist, democratic re-education and was read by millions of East Germans in the post-war years.

Moreover, Heinrich Mann had all the right credentials to be included in the pantheon of pre-socialist German writers revered in the new socialist Germany. He was an anti-fascist, whose books were burnt by the Nazis, who was forced into exile in 1933, and whose writings were socially committed and encapsulated the spirit of humanism and democracy that the GDR was eager to inscribe on its banners. In 1949 he was awarded the *Nationalpreis erster Klasse* (first-class National Prize) and was nominated the first president of the *Akademie der Künste* (Academy of Arts) (Haupt 1980: 177). East Germany's President Wilhelm Pieck commemorated Mann – who had died in Californian exile on 12 March 1950, shortly before he could realise his plan to make the GDR his new home – as a true heir to the progressive humanist tradition of Goethe and the French Revolution, and a professed supporter of the socialist revolution (Herden 1977: 5).

The homage that was paid to Mann in East Germany made him unacceptable to the West so that Ulbricht's claim, 'er ist unser' (he is ours) (Emmerich 1996: 84), rang true in more than just one way. Unlike his brother, Thomas Mann, who was honoured in both Germanys, Heinrich Mann was dismissed as a communist writer in the West. But the distrust was mutual, for Mann was equally suspicious of the developments in West Germany, where he observed not only signs of an anti-communist hysteria but also alarming neo-fascist tendencies (Mann 1963: 139). These observations are particularly interesting with respect to Staudte's cinematic interpretation of *Der Untertan* since they seem to condone the ideological stance that informs his adaptation.

In translating Mann's social satire from page to screen, Staudte eliminated all subplots and characters that were not immediately relevant to the film's main theme: the psychological development of the *Untertan*-mentality – typified by the protagonist Diederich Heßling – in a system of shifting power structures, in which 'the victim becomes victimizer becomes victim' (Silberman 1986: 151). The film sketches the maturation of Heßling, the prototype of the bourgeois industrialist during the Wilhelmine Empire, from early infancy to the pinnacle of his material and social success. His education at home and at school teach him to adapt to the demands of authority, be it in the shape of parents, teachers, military officers or the new Emperor, William II, himself. Both novel and film demonstrate that this kind of social conditioning – 'an inversion of the classical ideal of *Bildung*' (education) (Silberman 1986: 147) – produces a deformed personality with no real sense of a true inner self, whose behaviour alternates between fearful submission to any form of authority and a domineering suppression of anyone deemed to be weaker or inferior. 'Wer treten wollte, mußte lernen, sich treten zu lassen' (Whoever wanted to kick, had to learn to be kicked), thus the motto of the *Untertan*-type.

6 Werner Peters as Diederich Heßling in *Der Untertan* (The Kaiser's Lackey/The Subject)

Staudte traces the development of Heßling's psychological deforma-
tion chiefly through three devices that together create an acerbic visual
satire: alternating high and low camera angles, extended montage sequences
and the dispassionate voice-over commentary of an extra-diegetic narrator. The narrative function of high and low camera angles is already
apparent in the film's opening sequence, which provides a compressed
account of the formative influences in Heßling's infancy and youth:
his father and mother, the policeman, doctor, teacher and – indicative
of Diederich's inability to fully recognise social hierarchies yet – even
the chimney sweep, are shot from low, often distorting camera angles,
representing young Diederich's point of view and suggesting how overpowering and intimidating he finds any form of authority. Conversely,
these representatives of authority look down upon a crouching, bowing
and scraping Diederich, invariably shot from high camera angles. These
shot-reverse-shot sequences alternating between high and low camera
angles run through the entire film, illustrating Heßling's position in
the social hierarchy. Yet the film's visual and verbal messages evaluate
Heßling's response to these existing power structures in contradictory
terms, resulting in an ironic tension between the film's various narrative elements. In a scene that shows Heßling at the mercy of a captain
at a military drill, again shot from a very high angle, the disembodied
narrator, citing verbatim from Mann's novel, reveals that Heßling de-
rives masochistic pleasure from this kind of humiliation:

> Ja, Diederich fühlte wohl, daß alles hier, die Behandlung, die geläufigen
> Ausdrücke, die ganze militärische Tätigkeit vor allem darauf hinzielte, die
> persönliche Würde auf ein Mindestmaß herabzusetzen. Und das imponierte
> ihm; gab ihm, so elend er sich befand, und gerade dann, eine tiefe Achtung
> ein und etwas wie selbstmörderische Begeisterung. (Mann 1993: 44)

> Diederich fully realised that everything here, their treatment, the language
> used, the whole military system, had only one end in view, to degrade the
> sense of self-respect to the lowest level. And that impressed him. Miserable
> as he was, indeed, precisely on that account, it inspired him with deep
> respect and a sort of suicidal enthusiasm. (Mann 1984: 34)

The same scene also exemplifies Staudte's use of montage, which he
employs repeatedly in *Der Untertan* to underscore his satirical intent.
The captain of the regiment, looking down through his monocle upon
a tiny Diederich Heßling, is reduced to just two details which are shown
in extreme close-ups: first his eye and then his moustache and lips,
which are constantly moving, shouting incomprehensible commands. A

command-shouting, disembodied mouth – that is how Staudte, and before him Georg Klaren in a similar military drill scene in his Büchner adaptation *Wozzeck* (1947), sums up Prussian militarism.

The same device is employed in the most memorable scene of *Der Untertan*, the encounter between Heßling and the Emperor in Rome. Heßling is reduced to little more than a cheering voice and a feathered hat, while the Emperor, in turn, is represented by the insignia of his power, a shining helmet with an eagle on top, the Prussian *Pickelhaube*. Through this effacement of the characters Staudte uses the Emperor–subject relationship as a parable for other, similar relationships that exist in the presence of any authoritarian order.

This reduction of characters to certain details, which metonymically refer to their functions or social roles, pays tribute to the masters of Soviet montage, notably Vsevolod Pudovkin and Sergei Eisenstein, who use such conceptual editing techniques to a similar effect. Through the use of montage style in films such as *Bronenosets Potëmkin* (The Battleship Potemkin, 1926), *Oktyabar'* (October, 1928), *Stachka* (The Strike, 1925) or *Potomok Chingis-khana* (The Heir of Genghis Khan/Storm over Asia, Vsevolod Pudovkin, 1928), Eisenstein and Pudovkin wanted to reveal the social forces at work in shaping the characters' lives, while at the same time de-emphasising the role of individual personalities as the cause of action: a group of people, an entire social class, is summed up by a close-up of a face, or an eye, or a pair of marching boots.

That Staudte was not just concerned with producing an adaptation true to the spirit of Mann's novel, but wanted to apply the lessons of the past to the present, is evident in the film's final scene. Heßling, now a wealthy industrialist and dignitary in the small town of Netzig, has the honour of unveiling the newly acquired statue of William the Great, the Emperor's grandfather, and addressing the assembled townspeople on this occasion. His long speech culminates in a call for war: 'Eine solche Blüte erreicht ein Herrenvolk aber nicht in einem schlaffen, faulen Frieden: nein, nur auf dem Schlachtfeld wird die Größe einer Nation mit Blut und Eisen geschmiedet' (A master race, however, does not achieve such an incomparable blossoming in the slackness of idle peace. No, only on the battlefield will the greatness of a nation be forged with blood and iron.)

The word 'Herrenvolk' (master race) appears in Mann's text (Mann 1993: 443), but to post-war German spectators it would have sounded like Nazi rhetoric. Similarly, for a post-war audience, 'blood and iron' will have reverberated with the Nazi slogan of 'blood and soil'. The

declamatory style, gestures and the pitch of voice with which Werner
Peters in the role of Heßling delivers this chauvinistic, war-mongering
speech further reinforces these associations. In fact, Mann himself retrospectively interpreted the type of the *Untertan* as a prefiguration of
Hitler: the 'comic figure, the German "Untertan" of his Emperor William
became deadly serious for the first time under him, only then to be in
Hitler the brutal parody of himself' (cited in Silberman 1986: 156).

The film's final sequence invokes the prophecy of fascism even more
explicitly. In an acoustic montage, reminiscent of the one in *Die Mörder
sind unter uns* (see Chapter 2), the sound of the torrential downpour,
which puts a sudden end to Heßling's public address, blends into
dissonant chords, followed by the sound of sirens, strains from the
Nazi 'Horst Wessel Song', and Franz Liszt's 'Victory fanfare', which
was the signature tune of Nazi newsreels and special newsflashes on
the *Großdeutscher Rundfunk* (Greater Germany's broadcasting).[6] The
equestrian statue is shrouded in black smoke and the square has been
transformed into a field of rubble, which rubble-women, the ubiquitous
icon of post-war Germany, are clearing away. The narrative voice-over
repeats Heßling's battle-cry, adding: 'so rief damals Diederich Heßling
und riefen nach ihm noch viele andere bis auf den heutigen Tag' (thus
called Diederich Heßling and so have many others called and still do to
this day).

From the historical vantage point of the early 1950s, and in view of
Mann's own retrospective interpretation of *Der Untertan* as a prophecy
of what was really to happen to Germany,[7] Staudte's topicalisation of
the blueprint of the original text is true to the spirit of the novel. Yet
it goes beyond the anti-fascist subtext of the literary source, since the
narrator's remark that to this day there are still many who call to war,
was also a tacit reference to the GDR's perception of the FRG as a still-
fascist and potentially belligerent state. One need only recall the endings
of Maetzig's film *Rat der Götter* (Council of the Gods, 1950) and
Dudow's *Stärker als die Nacht* (Stronger than the Night, 1954), discussed
in Chapter 2, which also explicitly vilify an allegedly warmongering FRG,
to be alerted to the Cold War stance implicit in the final commentary
of *Der Untertan*.

Given the film's ideological bias, it is not surprising that its reception
in East and West Germany was divisive. The West German news magazine *Der Spiegel* dismissed it as a 'Paradebeispiel ostzonaler Filmpolitik'
(a prime example of film policy in the Eastern Zone) which failed to
address the historical fact that in Prussia no subject was ever as repressed

as 'die volkseigenen Menschen unter Stalins Gesinnungspolizei es samt und sonders sind' (cited in Ludin 1996: 54–5) (the nationally-owned people under Stalin's secret political police are without exception). In the FRG, the film was not released until 1957, and even then it was shortened by some twelve minutes and prefaced by a disclaimer that was intended to blunt its political edge, stating that Heßling was a fictional character and in no way representative of the German people (Schenk 1994: 72). In the GDR, by contrast, Der Untertan became a flagship of socialist film culture that promoted DEFA's national and international reputation. In Karolvy Vary Der Untertan was awarded the prize for social progress; in the GDR Staudte and Werner Peters, the leading actor, were awarded the prestigious Nationalpreis (National Prize) and the film was widely acclaimed by East German film critics. Reviews generally focused on the film's educational and political messages, hailing it as warning against militarism and nationalism and as a satirical masterpiece in the tradition of Simplicissimus (Orbanz 1977: 116–30; Müller 1951; Ramseger 1951). Remarkably, reviews turned a blind eye to the film's undeniably 'formalist' aesthetics, an issue that was not even mentioned when the film was discussed at the 1952 film conference.[8]

The re-evaluation of Goethe, Hölderlin and the Romantics in the debate about the Classical tradition (Erbedebatte)[9]

The foundation of both German states in 1949 coincided with the bicentenary of Goethe's birth. Both Germanys laid claim to Goethe as their national poet, perceiving the great humanistic ideals represented in his work 'as a basis for the regeneration of a German national culture' (Herminghouse 1983: 274) and for the moral and intellectual renewal of the German people after the years of fascism. With respect to the GDR, it is perhaps astonishing that neither Marx nor Engels were invoked as the pillars of the new socialist culture but rather Weimar Classicists like Goethe and Schiller, essentially bourgeois writers. In 1945 Walter Ulbricht, who was to become the leader of the SED, had advised communist functionaries that 'it was futile to attempt the immediate establishment of a specifically socialist culture, pointing out that Marx and Engels could not be assimilated by people still imbued with Nazi ideology' (Herminghouse 1983: 274) and who were more likely to associate cultural barbarism with Soviet communism than with fascism. Moreover, Ulbricht's advice was in line with Lenin's own thoughts on the continuum between socialist culture and its bourgeois antecedents: 'Proletarian

culture does not drop out of the skies. It . . . has to be the regular, continued development of the sum of knowledge achieved by mankind under
the yoke of capitalist society' (cited in Farrelly 1998: 5). Since proletarian culture is by definition mass culture, in the East the benefits of the
classical literary tradition were extended from the privileged elite to the
entire population. The GDR's leaders thus felt legitimised in laying
exclusive claim to the inheritance of Goethe and the classical tradition,
maintaining that the workers and peasants of the GDR were putting the
humanist utopia that Goethe had expounded in his works into practice.

Yet from the late 1960s onwards and in particular after the change of
the GDR's leadership from Ulbricht to Honecker in 1971, the appropriation of the cultural tradition took a new turn: the new cultural agenda
emphasised a discontinuity between the Classical bourgeois tradition and
the different ideals of socialist culture. Hand in hand with this revised
view of the German literary tradition went a critical reappraisal of those
movements which had been hitherto marginalised, notably Romanticism.
While the humanist bourgeois tradition, in particular Weimar Classicism,
was interpreted as the antecedent to socialist humanism, Romanticism
had hitherto been denounced as its irrational, reactionary counterpart,
culminating in fascism. Instead of professing to the progressive powers
of reason, the Romantics celebrated subjectivity. Classical writers epitom-
ised totality and the ideal of the well-rounded personality, whereas some
of the chief proponents of Romanticism were associated with insanity
and suicide, which were regarded as pathological expressions of extreme
forms of alienation. Indeed the rising interest in the Romantics, which
was paralleled, if not sparked, by a similar change of focus in the FRG
at the time,[10] was also associated with a more general thematic shift which
focused on the conflicting needs of the individual and society – a
conflict which becomes most apparent in the artist's role in society.

These developments explain the plethora of artist biographies and adaptations of Romantic literary texts which flooded both East and West
German cinema screens during the 1970s and early 1980s. These include
Die Elixiere des Teufels (The Devil's Elixirs), an adaptation of E. T. A.
Hoffmann's novel, first made by DEFA director Ralf Kirsten in 1973 and
three years later by the West German Manfred Purzer; *Aus dem Leben
eines Taugenichts* (The Life of a Good-for-Nothing, DEFA 1973) based
on a novella by Eichendorff, first made by Celino Bleiweiß for DEFA in
1973 and subsequently by the West German Bernhard Sinkel in 1978;
Caspar David Friedrich (Peter Schamoni, 1986, East and West German
coproduction); a considerable number of Heinrich von Kleist adaptations

made by *auteurs* of the New German Cinema, notably Volker Schlöndorff's *Michael Kohlhaas – Der Rebell* (Michael Kohlhaas – The Rebel, 1969); Hans-Jürgen Syberberg's *San Domingo* (1970), Helma Sanders-Brahms' television film *Erdbeben in Chili* (The Earthquake in Chile, 1975); *Marquise von O*... (Marquise O, 1976, directed by the French filmmaker Eric Rohmer); *Heinrich Penthesilea von Kleist* (1983) by Hans Neuenfels; and Helma Sanders-Brahms' critically acclaimed Kleist biography, *Heinrich* (1977). Elsaesser contends that Kleist was bound to become 'the patron saint of the New German Cinema' because the *auteurs* of the 1970s saw their own experience as artists reflected in the 'conflicts of art and politics, of absolute subjectivity within an absolutist Prussian monarchy [... and in] the person and work of Heinrich von Kleist' (Elsaesser 1989: 87, 48–9).[11]

Similarly, Friedrich Hölderlin, hailed in the GDR as the 'poetic archetype of the revolutionary bourgeois period' (Fehervary 1977: 77), whose personal and political defeat culminated in insanity and isolation, became the hypertrophied image of their own suffering for filmmakers and writers in both Germanys. However, this subjective reception of Hölderlin, which largely reflected his reception by the Romantics, did not emerge until the 1970s. Roughly until the bicentenary of Hölderlin's birth in 1970 he was celebrated as a Classical writer who, unlike the other Classic authors, was 'a consciously political writer whose work voiced the Jacobin spirit of the French Revolution' (Fehervary 1977: 47). This political interpretation, which rescued Hölderlin from his falsification by the Nazis and elevated him to being a 'harbinger of socialism' (Fehervary 1977: 45), dates back to Georg Lukács' and Johannes R. Becher's Hölderlin reception during their years of exile in the 1930s. Its chief tenets remained basically unchallenged until the *Erbedebatte* during the 1970s: in the wake of Honecker's much-cited 'no-taboo-speech' of 1971, East German artists were finally given leeway to broach the taboo of Hölderlin's madness. In Stefan Hermlin's radio play *Scardanelli* (1970) and Gerhard Wolf's novel *Der arme Hölderlin* (Poor Hölderlin, 1972) he becomes 'a paradigm of human alienation' (Fehervary 1977: 121), whose suffering from the discrepancy between his revolutionary ideals and reality was so extreme that he became insane.[12] In 1978 the influential journal *Sinn und Form* published an investigation into Hölderlin's madness, by Pierre Bertaux, one of the leading French Hölderlin scholars (Bertaux 1978b).

This reassessment of Hölderlin, which emphasises the poet's pathological side and asserts his affinity with the Romantics, enhanced his identificatory potential and explains the considerable number of books and films dedicated to him since the 1970s. When it came to making a choice between Goethe and Hölderlin, GDR's artists knew where they stood. Goethe, who had arrogantly advised the much younger and unknown Hölderlin to try his hand at writing little poems, fell out of favour. His overpowering stature, his political accommodation to the Restoration, and the hitherto unchallenged role as Germany's chief cultural icon made him a less appealing figure for both East and West German filmmakers when, in the wake of the *Erbedebatte* and the '68 movement, rebels and Romantics became the heroes of the day. Hence the wealth of Romanticism films and the dearth of Goethe films during the decades in question.[13]

Where Goethe does feature, be it on page or screen, he is usually treated with a certain degree of irreverence. Goethe was dethroned, not by GDR's cultural officialdom but by its artists.[14] It is in this context that Egon Günther's Goethe film, *Lotte in Weimer*, has to be considered.

Lotte in Weimar (Egon Günther, 1975) – Goethe cult or iconoclasm?

Though Goethe is the film's main concern and secret protagonist, it is not an artist biopic as such but an adaptation of a novel written by Thomas Mann in exile from Nazi Germany between 1936 and 1939. Mann centres his novel on a historically verified brief reunion between Goethe and his erstwhile beloved Lotte Kestner, née Buff, which took place in 1816. In other words, book and film present merely a brief glimpse of the poet of genius, aged sixty-eight, when he had already reached the pinnacle of his fame as one of the greatest writers of his time. As both Mann and Günther project certain aspects of their own socio-political situation onto Goethe, the images they render do not purport to be historically accurate but are in equal measure a reflection of the cultural and political conditions under which Mann and Günther created these images. Mann's approach to Goethe is to some extent coloured by the specific historical situation of Germany during the 1930s. In *Lotte in Weimar* Goethe becomes his creator's mouthpiece, voicing the latter's indictments of Nazi Germany. Günther's appraisal of Goethe is similarly anachronistic. It is indebted to the pro-Romantic spirit which prevailed among many writers and intellectuals in the GDR during the 1970s and which in many instances went hand in hand with an anti-Goethe tendency.

In order to convey this critical image of Goethe, Günther did not have to invent anything that was not already contained in Mann's text: he merely had to omit certain crucial scenes. Günther cuts Goethe down to size by the almost complete omission of chapter seven, or rather, as Mann terms it, 'The Seventh Chapter'. The centrality of this chapter in the novel is marked by the use of the definite article, which singles it out from the other eight. If one reads *Lotte in Weimar* in the light of Mann's own remarks, 'The Seventh Chapter' would seem to stand for Mann's sense of rapture, his 'unio mystica' (Mann 1960, vol. 11: 147) with the creative genius he so loved and admired, whereas the remaining chapters enunciate more or less explicitly 'die Bosheiten und ironischen Verismen, in die diese Liebe sich kleidet' (Mann 1960, vol. 2: 134) (the malice and irony in which this love is cloaked). It is the pivotal chapter, in which Mann attempts to give a 'Charakterbild Goethes, ja des Genies überhaupt' (Mann 1960, vol. 9: 655) (character sketch of Goethe, indeed of the genius *per se*), and in which he explores that which constitutes artistic genius.

In the film adaptation of the novel, the focus clearly lies elsewhere: Günther is less interested in the poet of genius himself than in the 'Goethe-cult' that surrounds him. It is thus only logical that the film assigns far greater importance to such scenes which render variously refracted images of Goethe, who, in a series of conversations, is presented from the vantage point of his Weimar circle and his erstwhile beloved, Lotte, who had served the young Goethe as inspiration for the character of Lotte in his best-selling epistolary novel *Die Leiden des jungen Werthers* (The Sorrows of Young Werther). These conversations between Lotte and Goethe's famulus Riemer, his son August, and Adele Schopenhauer take up more than three quarters of the film, indicating Günther's primary concern: he investigates the process of idolisation and myth-making only in order to totally demystify the elaborately constructed image when finally the genius himself appears in the banquet scene towards the end of the film.

The prominence assigned to the personality cult has tempted critics from the West to interpret the film *Lotte in Weimar* as a political parable attacking this phenomenon in socialist society. However, this reading seems somewhat foreshortened: with Stalin's death in 1953, the worst manifestations of the cult of personality in socialist states were over and this theme was of no particular topical relevance any more in 1975. It would seem that Günther's criticism is subtler and has to be read against the backdrop of the reappraisal of the Romantics. What literary texts of the 1970s, such as de Bruyn's *Leben des Jean Paul Friedrich Richter* (The Life of Jean Paul Friedrich Richter), Kunert's *Pamphlet für K.* (Pamphlet

for K.), Gerhard Wolf's *Der arme Hölderlin* (Poor Hölderlin), Christa
Wolf's *Kein Ort. Nirgends.* (No Place on Earth) as well as the Hölderlin
biopics discussed below, all have in common is that they aim to redress
the balance between the absolutised Weimar Classicists, notably the cult
figure Goethe, and the hitherto denigrated Romantics. Goethe is presented as insensitive to and intolerant of artistic talent that differs from
his own. Moreover, he is exposed as exploiting his privileged position
in Weimar by using his power to either foster or stifle the creativity of
less well-established poets. Given that the authors of the 1970s saw their
own role as artists in GDR society reflected in the sufferings of their
Romantic predecessors, certain correspondences between the powerful
Weimar poet and cultural functionaries cannot be entirely dismissed.
Through this critical subtext Goethe is revealed as someone who did not
translate the ideals of his writings into reality. In short, the humanistic
ideal which Goethe represented is dismantled.

   While on one level Günther's portrayal of Goethe as the most revered
poet worshipped by the whole of Weimar seems to subscribe to the
officially endorsed view, on another level Günther follows the anti-
Goethe spirit which prevailed in the literary reception of Romanticism
by questioning whether Goethe deserves this esteem. Significantly,
Günther chooses not to portray the supreme artist. He elides that side
of Goethe's character which merits respect and admiration and which
redeems his darker sides – his need to dominate and even to inflict a
certain degree of impairment upon those close to him, especially his son
August. Having suppressed the individuality of others around him to such
an extent that they merely echo his own words – as is illustrated in the
long dinner scene – Goethe's authority and greatness are uncontested
because he is, as he rightly observes, quoting Frederick the Great's
famous remark, ruling over slaves. Goethe, who was upheld in the GDR
as the embodiment of the humanistic ideal, is presented here as a
narcissistic egomaniac, whose humanity is impaired and who fails in the
human sphere. In this way Günther calls the legitimacy of Goethe as a
role model into question.

   Rather than being a political parable of the socialist cult of personality, Günther's film can be read as a parable of the hypocrisy underlying
the project of raising the socialist consciousness by implying that this
project is bound to fail if its role models are less than perfect themselves.
That this attack is directed not so much at the historical persona of Goethe
but rather at what he represents in the context of the GDR becomes
evident during the banquet scene. While Goethe keeps pontificating in

a long, almost uninterrupted monologue, the camera pans to and focuses on a decoration on his chest, establishing a rather tenuous associative link between the pompous educator Goethe and high-ranking officials in contemporary GDR society. The topical thrust of Günther's implicit criticism is further underscored by the aforementioned anachronistic opening sequence. It obliquely comments upon the hypocritical relationship between the proclaimed objective of raising the socialist consciousness and its actual outcomes: while pretending to promote the development of the well-rounded individual, it actually breeds a nation of slaves, of impaired individuals, who only parrot their supreme educator's words and never dare voice their own opinions. Through the almost grotesque portrayal of the entourage of slaves that gather at Goethe's Weimar residence Günther passes a harsh but hidden verdict on the constrictiveness and hypocrisy of the GDR.

Yet since this judgement was well camouflaged in the guise of a costume drama for which some of the GDR's most respected stars – Martin Hellberg (as Goethe), Katharina Thalbach, Jutta Hoffmann and, rather exceptionally, even a West German star, Lilli Palmer (as Lotte) – had been cast, the censors did not bat an eyelid. This jubilee-film with production costs of 4 million Marks was heavily promoted nationally and internationally. The casting of an international star like Lilli Palmer was meant to enhance the film's exportability. After its premiere in Weimar on 6 June 1975, which marked the centenary of Thomas Mann's birth and the thousandth anniversary of the city of Weimar, the film became so popular with East Germans that its box-office figures of nearly six million viewers compared favourably with those of DEFA's *Indianerfilme*, the most popular genre per se (Günther and Hanisch 1993).

While GDR reviewers were fairly unanimous in their praise, West German critics were disappointed by this conventional adaptation of Mann's novel that lacked the subtlety and finesse of Visconti's Mann adaptation, *Death in Venice* (1971), which was still fresh in people's minds and to which Günther's film alludes by playing some strains of Mahler's Sixth Symphony in *Lotte in Weimar*. The disrespectful portrayal of Germany's foremost national poet made Goethe look like a 'Popanz-Goethe' (bogey Goethe) as a reviewer in *Der Spiegel* (DDR-Film 1975) noted. Even the popularity of Palmer could not appease Western critics, for this 'diätschlanke Make-up Wunder' (diet-slim make-up miracle) was considered to be a most inappropriate casting for Lotte, 'einer leicht rundlichen, mit ersten Altersbeschwerden ringenden Sympathiefigur, der man ihre mehr als zehn Kinder glauben könnte' (Seidel 1975) (a slightly

7 Lilli Palmer (Lotte) and Martin Hellberg (Goethe) in *Lotte in Weimar*

plump, sympathetic character, afflicted by the first complaints of old age, and who is a credible mother of ten). *Lotte in Weimar* was DEFA's first contribution to the Cannes Film Festival. Yet no prize was bestowed on this flagship film commissioned in the service of appropriating the very best of Germany's cultural heritage.

Die Braut (The Mask of Desire, Egon Günther, 1999): Germany's answer to European heritage cinema?

Despite Günther's claim that the heritage films which he made for DEFA were 'nur aus der Not geboren' (Günther and Hanisch 1993) (only born out of necessity), he stayed true to this genre even after he left the GDR and was no longer enlisted by the state-owned studio to promote Germany's national heritage and its most enduring cultural icon, Goethe. His two DEFA films about Goethe, *Lotte in Weimar* and *Die Leiden des jungen Werthers* (The Sufferings of Young Werther, 1976), were followed by three television productions concerned with Goethe, including a film that portrays the relationship between Goethe and his contemporary *Lenz* (1992). In 1999 when the German media wanted to mark the two hundred and fiftieth anniversary of Goethe's birth, Günther was the obvious filmmaker to be approached because he was the uncontested Goethe film expert of the reunited Germany.

What does it say about the reunited *Kulturnation* that the only Goethe film to celebrate this anniversary was made by an ex-DEFA director, with financial aid from film funds of the new federal states, and distributed by Progress, the former film distribution arm of DEFA? Significantly, the best-selling book about Goethe in the Goethe year, *Christiane und Goethe. Eine Recherche* (Christiane and Goethe. An Investigation), was also written by an East German author, Sigrid Damm. The book and the film are less interested in Goethe than in Christiane Vulpius, the woman with whom he spent twenty-eight years in a *mesalliance* frowned upon by society.[15] Do the East Germans then prove, after the contest is over, that they are after all the true and only legitimate heir to Germany's cultural heritage because they are more expert at making one of Germany's chief high-cultural icons accessible to the man on the street? Or do the East Germans simply feel closer to Goethe, since Weimar, which became the focal point of a flourishing heritage industry during the Goethe year and which was awarded the title of European capital of culture in 1999, lies in the former East? Not quite, for *Die Braut* is an illustrative example of the joint efforts of an all-German jubilee production.

Günther relied on the artistic and technical skills of former DEFA colleagues, including art director Harald Horn, costume designer Christiane Dorst and cameraman Peter Brandt, whereas the film's cast is mainly recruited from the young stars who became famous through film and television productions made in the old federal states. Christiane Vulpius

8 Egon Günther

is played by one of Germany's most popular actresses, Veronica Ferres. Goethe is played by Herbert Knaup, familiar to German and international audiences from *Lola rennt* (Run Lola Run, Tom Tykwer, 1999), in which he plays Lola's father. *Die Braut* was produced by Tellux Film GmbH,[16] in co-production with a number of television companies from the old and the new federal states, Austrian television, ARTE and Studio Babelsberg Independents, a production company that was established when the Babelsberg studio site was privatised. The result of this all-German jubilee initiative is a peculiar blend of DEFA period drama and European heritage cinema.

According to Andrew Higson (1993), Richard Dyer and Ginette Vincendeau (1992) and Claire Monk (2002), some of the key scholars who have contributed to the debate about this 'new genre' – if it can be called that – European heritage cinema creates nostalgic fantasies about the past, or rather specific national pasts, generating clichéd notions of quintessential 'Englishness' or 'Frenchness'. European heritage cinema, according to some critics a sub-genre of costume drama (Higson 1995: 27), is popular cinema with a peculiarly cultured façade: often based on sources that reflect the established canon of a nation's literature, it is infused with cultural prestige that appeals to the educated middle class. Heritage films evoke the past through a distinctive look and the careful recreation of period details, which has, not just in the British context, become almost synonymous with Merchant Ivory Productions, which 'invented' this distinctive look in E. M. Forster adaptations such as *A Room with a View* (1985), *Maurice* (1987) and *Howards End* (1992). In spite of their historical subject matter, heritage films lack historicity since they eschew any critical perspective on the past, displaying instead a self-indulgent fascination with décor and period costumes. The past 'stands removed from history' because it is essentially a postmodern pastiche of the past, 'where the reference point is not the past itself, but other images, other texts' (Higson 1993: 113, 112). Although heritage films cannot be defined in terms of a unified iconography, except maybe for period costume, shots of country mansions set in beautiful gardens, pastoral idylls and lavishly furnished interiors. The pictorialist style of the 'museum aesthetics' (Vincendeau 2001: xviii) and high production values are an indispensable prerequisite for the success of heritage cinema on the American market.

Against this background, the similarities and differences between *Die Braut* and its popular European counterpart are thrown into stark relief: largely shot on location in Weimar, the film lavishly displays Goethe's house at the Frauenplan (now a museum) and other famous locations, thus promoting Weimar's heritage industry. But with a meagre budget of just 7 million DM the film achieves the museum look without the grandeur and is, consequently, more akin to the aesthetics of a DEFA costume drama than its recent pan-European inflection. Unlike in European heritage films, the props and décor in *Die Braut* do not take priority over the narrative, but rather assume narrative functions themselves: recurrent shots of staircases reflect the class difference that sets Christiane Vulpius, a woman of poor and uneducated background, apart from the aristocratic circle around the Weimar court to which Goethe belongs. A Greek vase that Christiane accidentally knocks over, when she trespasses on those quarters of Goethe's house to which she is usually denied access, is shot in a close-up tumbling down. The fall of the vase, captured in a slow-motion shot to indicate Christiane's shock and the momentousness of the accident, tells the whole story of her ambiguous role as Goethe's 'Haus- und Bettschatz' (treasure of the home and bed), as he referred to her. As manager of Goethe's domestic affairs, as his lover and mother to his son, she is not deemed presentable on public occasions and is excluded from Goethe's official engagements for eighteen years, until Goethe eventually marries her.

Insofar as *Die Braut* is a romantic biopic about the love life of Germany's most famous poet, it can be read as Germany's answer to *Shakespeare in Love* (John Madden, USA, 1999). Insofar as the film focuses on a woman's struggle to define her role in the public and private spheres, it reworks a theme around which numerous recently made heritage films revolve. Like these, *Die Braut* contributes to the (pseudo-)feminist project through which many women-hidden-from-history have recently been rescued from obscurity: Clara, the wife of Robert Schuhmann in *Frühlingssinfonie* (Spring Symphony, Peter Schamoni, FRG, 1983); *Céleste* Albaret, Proust's housekeeper and amanuensis (Percy Adlon, FRG, 1981); *Nora* Barnacle, James Joyce's wife (Pat Murphy, IR, 2000); the artist Dora *Carrington* (Christopher Hampton, UK, 1995), Lytton Strachey's long-term companion; Auguste, the second wife of the Romantic poet Clemens Brentano in *Requiem für eine romantische Frau* (Requiem for a Romantic Woman, Dagmar Knöpfel, FRG, 1998); and the hugely successful French biopic, *Camille Claudel* (Bruno Nuytten, 1988), lover and muse of Rodin and sculptor in her own right, whose life ended in madness.

What sets most of the German films listed here apart from their French and British counterparts is that they do not cast international stars with 'heritage credentials' and concomitant box-office success like Emma Thompson, Helena Bonham Carter, Isabelle Adjani, Emmanuelle Béart and Gérard Depardieu. This may indicate that the genre has yet to establish itself in Germany, enabling stars like Veronica Ferres to adapt their performance to the requirements of period drama with its emphasis on period authenticity in terms of demeanour and linguistic register.

In contrast to this convention of European heritage cinema, Ferres and Knaup instil their roles with a sense of contemporaneity that constantly disrupts the sense of period fidelity. Their language is timeless, neither eighteenth- nor twentieth-century. It is a register that Günther himself created in order to emphasise that he was not interested in historical authenticity. We possess no reliable records of how people spoke with each other in those days, he explained, 'denn was wir haben ist ja alles nur Briefdeutsch. Als ob die alle immer so steifleinern gesprochen hätten ... Mich hat das Historische nie interessiert!' (Günther and Berghahn 2002) (all we have is the language of letters. As if they had always spoken to each other in such a stiff and formal manner ... I have never been interested in the historical!). This deliberate attempt to disrupt the illusion of 'pastness' is of course a distinctive feature, which characterises the actors' performance in many historical films which Günther made when still working for DEFA. Indebted to the principles of Brechtian theatre, Günther has always favoured ironic distanciation over historic authenticity and escapist illusion. But whereas in films such as *Lotte in Weimar* and *Die Leiden des jungen Werthers* subtle devices of distanciation and contemporisation of the past served to underscore oblique references to the present, in *Die Braut* no such critical intent can be identified.

Arguably, the contemporaneity of Christiane emphasises her independence. An uneducated woman of humble origins rises to the social and emotional challenges which living with Goethe brings and turns into something of an eighteenth-century superwoman, allowing Ferres to transpose her most successful role to date in *Das Superweib* (Super Woman, Sönke Wortmann, 1996) to a historical context. Yet the film's approach is self-contradictory, for it omits the real independence Christiane demonstrated outside the private sphere when she travelled on her own to Lauchstädt spa and even managed the theatre there on behalf of her husband.[17] Günther's Christiane is a pseudo-emancipated woman who promotes the conservative ideal of the 'strong woman' who is allegedly behind every successful man. Accordingly, Goethe is portrayed as a chauvinistic and exploitative husband whose geniality – which, incidentally, is never dramatised in the film – comes at a price. As Lotte in *Lotte in Weimar* noted, 'es riecht nach Menschenopfern in seiner Nähe' (you can smell the human victims around him); the victim in this case is Christiane. *Die Braut* thus reconfirms Günther's previous iconoclastic reappraisal of Goethe. However, it lacks some of the subtle ironies that made his earlier Goethe film stand out among DEFA's occasionally pedestrian adaptations.

Not that the director is to blame, though, since many of the subtle ironies and scenes through which Günther endeavoured 'nicht im Historischen [zu] versinken, sondern die Haltung des Filmemachers [zu] zeigen' (Günther and Berghahn 2002) (not to become immersed in the historical but, instead, to demonstrate the filmmaker's attitude) have fallen victim to commercial censorship. The original version of *Die Braut* was three hours long – too long, the producers felt, to capture the attention span of the average viewer. Numerous scenes had to be cut. For example, the film's original ending made Christiane's death appear almost light-hearted, for Günther had given the scene the kind of ironic, playful twist that is a hallmark of his style. Whereas Goethe is too cowardly to face the torment of Christiane's dying moments, the poet and already deceased fatherly friend Wieland comes to her bedside, and makes her levitate above her deathbed. This poetic metaphor for death was considered to be some-what surreal by the film's producers and, notwithstanding the fact that during test screenings audiences had enthusiastically applauded this scene, Günther was urged to take out the scene. Such magical realism was considered to potentially jeopardise the mass appeal of what was hoped to be Germany's answer to popular European heritage cinema.

The response of German audiences and critics to *Die Braut* was rather lukewarm: just over one hundred thousand viewers saw the film during the Goethe year. Reviewers took it amiss that Günther has taken rather too many liberties in filling the blanks which Goethe scholarship had left with his own fantasies (Kühn 1999a) and blamed him for not having adapted Damm's Vulpius biography, *Christiane und Goethe* – which itself fuses archival sources with speculation – for the screen. The German public was asking for '*Bildung*' (culture and education), when all that Günther had in mind was entertainment: to make a film that shows 'wie jemand jemanden liebt' (Günther and Berghahn 2002) (how somebody loves somebody).

Hälfte des Lebens (Half of Life, Herrmann Zschoche, 1985): recasting the progressive poet as romantic lover

Friedrich Hölderlin's (1770–1843) biography has all the ingredients that make it an ideal choice for an artist biopic. According to John Walker (1993), artist biopics tend to perpetuate certain stereotypes which prom-ise to ensure popular appeal. They typically portray idealistic, radical artists who are neglected during their lifetime and achieve fame only posthumously; focus on the passionate love life of the artist; present him (or her, but there are comparatively few biopics about female artists) as different from ordinary people, on account of eccentricity, bohemian lifestyle, rebelliousness, or madness. What biopics about the creative genius gone mad, such as the Van Gogh biopics, *Lust for Life* (Vincente Minelli, 1956) and *Van Gogh* (Maurice Pialat, 1991), and Agnieszka Holland's Rimbaud film, *Total Eclipse* (1996), have in common is that they tacitly assume madness to be a prerequisite for genius.

Hölderlin's biography matches Walker's blueprint of the artist biopic on all counts: both his professional and private life were fraught with failure and tragedy. His poetic genius was unrecognised during his lifetime. To earn a living he had to assume the humble position of a private tutor educating the children of the rich. His passionate and clandestine love for his employer's wife, Susette Gontard, was ill-fated and her untimely death is presumed to have triggered Hölderlin's psychological decline into madness. Moreover, as a fervent supporter of the French Revolution, even of its most radical faction, the Jacobins, he was disillusioned by its outcome. His utopian dream, shared with his aristocratic friend and patron Isaak von Sinclair and a small circle of German Jacobins, of establishing a republic in southern Germany, also failed. The project of launching a literary journal failed, not least because established literary figures, amongst them Goethe and Schiller, denied him their support. In 1805 Sinclair was arrested and charged with conspiracy. A doctor's attestation of Hölderlin's madness saved the poet from getting embroiled in the conspiracy trials. He was eventually sent to Autenrieth's clinic in Tübingen, where he was 'treated' for *dementia praecox*. In 1807, after seven months, he was released as incurable, with a predicted life expectancy of just three years. Yet he had only lived half of his life and would spend another thirty-six years in a tower in Tübingen. The few poems he wrote during the latter half of his life were signed with pseudonyms, such as Scardanelli or Buonarotti – generally taken to be another indication of the genius's total loss of self.

While most Hölderlin scholars take the poet's madness for granted, the French Hölderlin scholar Bertaux has put forward the controversial hypothesis that he simulated insanity, using madness as a mask in order to escape persecution in the conspiracy trials and to withdraw from a world that had disappointed him on all counts. He sagely chose the life of a hermit, Bertaux concludes, but was mistaken for a lunatic (Bertaux 1978a, 1978b; Wackwitz 1997: 54–9).

It is this controversy that preoccupies Herwig Kipping in his poetic film essay *Hommage à Hölderlin* (1983), his graduation project at the Babelsberg Film and Television Academy. This obscure film, overburdened with ambiguous visual symbols, selects the spectre of Hölderlin's insanity and alienation as a focal point and thus redresses the hitherto

officially-propagated image of Hölderlin as revolutionary poet. Kipping's
debut film revisits Bertaux's investigation, asking explicitly in an extra-
diegetic voice-over: 'Ist diese Krankheit eine Maske? Schmiedet der ehe-
malige Jakobiner hochverräterische Pläne, oder ist er wirklich verrückt?
(Is this illness a mask? Is the former Jacobin hatching treacherous
plans or is he really mad?). The film explores this question by means of
an extremely subjective discourse that traces the meandering reflections
of a madman or poetic genius through a collage of images and textual
montage, consisting of Hölderlin's extended soliloquies, a cacophony
of sounds, choral music and some of his poems set to music. Although
the film's title suggests that homage is paid to one of the GDR's most
revered national poets, the film itself eulogises that aspect of Hölderlin's
life that had been deliberately ignored until the 1970s. Such a complete
about-turn in the reception of Hölderlin was not welcome and Kipping's
film was only shown once, at the Academy of Arts in Berlin, before it
was eventually broadcast on television after the *Wende*.

The DEFA biopic *Hälfte des Lebens*, as well as the more recent film
Feuerreiter (Fire Rider, Nina Grosse, 1999), takes a much more conventional approach to Hölderlin's biography. Both take his mental illness
for granted and ask what precipitated his madness: was it his tragic love
for Susette? Was it his disappointment at the outcome of the French
Revolution? Was it his lack of success as a writer? By dramatising the ten
years preceding Hölderlin's mental breakdown (1796–1806), namely the
years spent with Susette Gontard, the lovers' painful separation and
Susette's death, both films attribute Hölderlin's illness primarily to his
ill-fated love affair.

Herrmann Zschoche's film *Hälfte des Lebens*, based on a script by Christa
Kožik, endeavours to popularise Hölderlin's life story, while at the same
time aspiring to a biographically accurate image of Hölderlin that is both
'politically correct' and in keeping with the official Hölderlin discourse
during the 1980s. The film achieves a delicate balance between these
potentially conflicting aims by ensuring popular appeal through fore-
grounding the tragic love story and by soliciting official approval through
alluding to the poet's political conviction as a German Jacobin.

Kožik and Zschoche attempt to give a multi-dimensional account of
the genius on the brink of madness. In addition to some sparse references to the 'German misery' and Hölderlin's disappointment at the
outcome of the French Revolution, they stress Hölderlin's marginalisation at the hands of the Weimar Olympians, notably Goethe. 'Er rät mir
zu kleinen Gedichten ... Der sagte immer Herr Hölterlein zu mir' (He

9 Tragic love triangle: Susette Gontard (Jenny Gröllmann), Jakob Gontard (Michael Gwisdek) and Hölderlin (Ulrich Mühe) in *Hälfte des Lebens* (Half of Life)

advised me to write little poems and kept calling me Mr Hölterlein), Hölderlin reports to Susette after a meeting with Goethe in Frankfurt, a meeting that is historically authenticated (Bertaux 1978a: 476). While these and other references to significant biographical details, such as his problematic relationship with his mother or the trial of Sinclair for high treason, can only be fully appreciated by those who are familiar with Hölderlin's life story, the film's primary focus lies on the ill-fated love, which aims to enhance the film's wider appeal but occasionally trivialises the tragedy of Hölderlin's life. As the West German film critic Peter Buchka sarcastically commented, 'Einen der fähig war, sich sein Dienstbotenzimmer zum Olymp der Götter Griechenlands zu machen, den darf man nicht wegen einer heimlichen Liebe in den Wahnsinn treiben' (Buchka 1987) (Someone who was capable of transforming his humble servant's abode into the Olympus of the Greek gods could not be driven to madness by a clandestine love affair).

Kožik, however, had argued that her approach to the tormented poetic genius was intended to counter-balance the overtly political (and official) appropriation of Hölderlin, which male writers in particular had adopted (see Miltschitzky 1998: 117–20). Moreover, and in contrast to *Feuerreiter*, which really reduces Hölderlin to one of history's most tragic lovers, *Hälfte des Lebens* repeatedly posits an identity between the poet's life and his writings and successfully intertwines the two. Hölderlin's love for Susette is equated with Hyperion's love for Diotima in Hölderlin's epistolary novel, *Hyperion – oder der Eremit in Griechenland* (Hyperion – or the Hermit in Greece). Hence, Susette's white, floating dresses and hairstyle lend her appearance a statuesque grace, reminiscent of the Greek statues which are a visual leitmotif of the film. Conversely, in one of Hölderlin's hallucinations a white, bleeding statue bears Susette's facial expressions. By establishing correspondences between Hölderlin's tragic love and his writings, Kožik and Zschoche try to bring Hölderlin's writings to life on screen and to make them accessible to a wide audience.

That the endeavour to synthesise education and entertainment was bound to result in a certain degree of trivialisation becomes particularly apparent in the film's use of visual symbols. The leitmotif of the matching halves of an apple symbolises the Platonic ideal of love and leaves the audience in no doubt that Hölderlin and Susette are these two halves who need to be together to achieve wholeness and perfection. Moreover, it encapsulates Hölderlin's central dilemma, a life only half-realised, in which perfection and fulfilment were never attained. The art director Dieter Adam and the director of photography Günther Jaeuthe seem to have distrusted the power of Hölderlin's poetry when duplicating the words of his most famous poem, 'Hälfte des Lebens' (Half of Life), on screen. The 'wild roses' and 'gracious swans' dipping their heads into the 'sobering holy' lake, which are described in the poem's first stanza, are depicted in several shots before the spectator gets a chance to eavesdrop on the poetic genius at work, writing this poem as he is approaching his mental breakdown.

Ulrich Mühe's widely acclaimed portrayal of Hölderlin, however, rescues the film from being a melodramatic costume drama by emphasising Hölderlin's contemporaneity. Mühe's convincing performance, in fact his first film role, successfully conveys the dual coding of certain messages, typically quotations from original sources. The film's penultimate scene shows Hölderlin incarcerated in a cell in Autenrieth's clinic, sedated and silenced after three days of 'treatment' with the infamous Autenrieth mask. This brown leather mask, which covers the entire head except for the eyes and the mouth, looks like an instrument of torture. Speaking straight to the camera and looking at the audience, thus underscoring the contemporary relevance of this quotation from

Hölderlin's elegy 'Brod und Wein' (Bread and Wine), he expresses not just his own dilemma as a poet, but that of any poet writing in a less than perfect socio-historical context: 'wozu Dichter in dürftiger Zeit?' (why be a poet in wretched times?). Zschoche's film thus follows Gerhard Wolf's interpretation of Hölderlin in *Der arme Hölderlin* as an allegory of the writer's dilemma in a society that affords him just one type of freedom, namely that of isolation.

In spite of the film's dissident subtext, it was commended as an important contribution to the appropriation of the cultural national heritage (Spangenberg 1984) that underscored Hölderlin's 'humanistisch-progressive Haltung zur Welt' (Mäde 1984) (humanist-progressive attitude towards the world) by the HV Film and the DEFA studio. Although Horst Knietzsch, the film critic for *Neues Deutschland*, bemoaned the fact that Zschoche and Kožik had paid too little attention to the political-historical discourse and had thus rendered only half of Hölderlin's tragedy (Knietzsch 1985), nobody in the GDR found fault with what looked on the surface like a politically innocuous costume drama. After all, any oblique criticism of contemporary society had been carefully camouflaged in quotations from Hölderlin's writings, a strategy that ostensibly supported the film's educational mission. This mission was successfully completed: after the film's theatrical release a collection of Hölderlin's poems became a literary best-seller in the GDR (Kersten 1985). Critics in the Federal Republic were largely oblivious of the film's critical undertones and only saw their usual prejudices regarding DEFA period dramas confirmed: criticising *Hälfte des Lebens* on account of its quotation-laden language and conventional cinematography, they dismissed this 'Hölderlin für Einsteiger' (Hölderlin for beginners) film as yet another uninspired attempt to popularise Germany's cultural heritage (see Miltschitzky 1998: 238).

Cultural heritage on a split screen

The less than enthusiastic reception which the majority of DEFA's heritage films encountered in the Federal Republic suggests that the years of political division also resulted in a demarcation of socialist and bourgeois culture that ultimately led to an estrangement between East and West Germans in the cultural sphere. At least in the GDR, Germany's shared cultural heritage became a contested site for ideological demarcation from the bourgeois culture of the West. As has been outlined, great emphasis was placed on an ideologically correct appropriation of the cultural heritage that reflected the tenets of a Marxist-Leninist worldview – hence the recurrent claim that artists such as Hölderlin, Beethoven and Forster were fervent supporters of the French Revolution, and thus harbingers of socialism. Since aesthetic orthodoxy and an educational mission were part and parcel of such a partisan appropriation of the national heritage, critics and audiences in the West frequently dismissed DEFA's heritage films as didactic, if not propagandist, period dramas at the service of socialist cultural policies. Such a harsh dismissal testified to the longevity of Cold War prejudices and to the different aesthetic sensibilities which audiences and critics had developed in the East and the West. In particular in the context of the New German Cinema any self-respecting *auteur* imbued his or her period drama with a carefully measured dose of artistic experimentation. Admittedly, there were exceptions, such as the aesthetically rather conventional Thomas Mann adaptations by Franz Seitz; and even Volker Schlöndorff, arguably West Germany's expert at cinematic adaptations of literature, frequently eschewed the kind of artistic experimentation that had become de rigeur ever since film had gained cultural respectability.

Although the same cultural icons and literary traditions were upheld, East–West German co-productions were few and far between, resulting in a duplication of the same source material on Germany's split screen. Nonetheless, after unification Germany's shared cultural heritage was frequently invoked as proof of the 'artificiality of the border line drawn in 1945' (Bruyn 1991: 60). As the East German writer Günter de Bruyn remarked shortly after unification, 'the concept of the cultural nation has become important for me in the last two decades, because it was an expression of the fact that culture in the widest sense (from the Ninth Symphony to the way we celebrate Christmas) still connected the inhabitants of the two German states' (Bruyn 1991: 60).

Notes

1 Marxist historians and literary historians distinguish between *Tradition* and *Erbe*, whereby *Erbe* denotes only those carefully chosen strands of the German cultural tradition that are actively appropriated on account of their humanistic and progressive tendencies; see Mandelkow (1983: 78–117).

2 See *Unterwegs zu Lenin* (On the Way to Lenin, Günter Reisch, 1970, co-production with Mosfilm, USSR); Liebknecht features in *Solange Leben in mir ist* (As Long as There Is Life in Me, 1965) and in *Trotz alledem* (In Spite of Everything, 1972), both directed by Günter Reisch; for the Thälmann films

see Chapter 1, note 15; *Käthe Kollwitz – Bilder eines Lebens* (Käthe Kollwitz – Pictures of a Life, Ralf Kirsten, 1987); *Nur eine Frau* (Just a Woman, Karl Ballhaus, 1958, about Louise Otto Peters); *Wo andere schweigen* (Where Others Remain Silent, Ralf Kirsten, 1984, about Clara Zetkin). Interestingly, the biopic *Rosa Luxemburg* (1986) was made by the West German filmmaker Margarethe von Trotta.

3 *Beethoven – Tage aus einem Leben* (Beethoven – Days from a Life, Horst Seemann, 1976) and *Johann Strauß – der ungekürte König* (Johann Strauß – the Uncrowned King, Franz Antel, 1987, co-production with Austria) are in fact DEFA's only films about composers. Other notable biopics include: *Thomas Müntzer* (Martin Hellberg, 1956); *Tilmann Riemenschneider* (Helmut Spieß, 1958); *Goya* (Konrad Wolf, 1971); *Der verlorene Engel* (The Lost Angel, Ralf Kirsten, 1966/71, about the sculptor Ernst Barlach); *Johannes Kepler* (Frank Vogel, 1974); *Addio, piccolo mia* (Lothar Warnecke, 1979, about the poet Georg Büchner); *Die Besteigung des Chimborazo* (The Ascent of the Chimborazo, Rainer Simon, 1989, co-production with FRG, about Alexander von Humboldt); *Pestalozzis Berg* (Pestalozzi's Mountain, Peter von Gunten, 1989, co-production with Switzerland); and *Treffen in Travers* (Meeting in Travers, Michael Gwisdek, 1989, about Georg Forster).

4 *Andrei Rublev* is a famous example of an artist biopic which employs such a dual strategy. The controversial issue of artistic freedom, though here addressed in the context of fifteenth-century Russia, was nonetheless considered to be too topical and the film was suppressed for several years (see Engel 1999: 153–6).

5 Given the prominence of cinematic adaptations of literature and biopics about writers, I have decided to focus on this particular group of heritage films.

6 The 'Horst Wessel Song', named after SA storm trooper Horst Wessel, who upon his assassination became one of the Nazi's prominent martyrs, was, alongside the 'Deutschlandlied', the national anthem of the Third Reich.

7 In a letter to Karl Lemke dated 27 May 1949, Mann wrote: 'Ich schrieb im voraus, was aus Deutschland dann wirklich wurde' (Mann 1963: 139) (I wrote in advance what eventually really happened to Germany).

8 Staudte's film is representative of the ideological trajectory of other literary adaptations made during the 1950s. *Kabale und Liebe* (Intrigue and Love, Martin Hellberg, 1959) updates Schiller's canonical text by elaborating on the sale of young men who are to serve as mercenaries in the American war, which was interpreted as a topical reference to the 'sale' of young West German men to the NATO forces (Knoll 1959).

9 This section can only provide a glimpse of the wide-ranging academic and literary discourse of the *Erbedebatte* in the GDR. For a detailed account, see Farrelly (1998); Herminghouse (1981 and 1983); Grimm and Hermand (1971); Leistner (1977); Mandelkow (1977 and 1983); and Schlenker (1977).

Some parts of this and the subsequent section have been previously published in Berghahn (1999a).

10 In the context of the 1968 student movement, when Herbert Marcuse's concept of the 'affirmative character of culture' was widely adopted and applied to the climate of cultural restoration that had prevailed under Adenauer's government, the West German cult of Weimar Classicism was critically reappraised. At the same time the Romantics, hitherto tarnished by the stigma of irrationalism, nationalism and the National Socialist cult of the Romantics, were re-discovered (see Mandelkow 1983).

11 The only East German Kleist film is *Jungfer, sie gefällt mir* (The Maid Pleases Me, Günter Reisch, 1969). However, Kleist features prominently in a number of East German literary texts, including Günter Kunert's 'Pamphlet für K.' (Pamphlet for K, 1975) and Christa Wolf's *Kein Ort. Nirgends* (No Place on Earth, 1979), both giving a favourable account of Kleist and a critical one of Goethe.

12 Both writers had used *Friedrich Hölderlins Leben: Dichtung und Wahnsinn* (Friedrich Hölderlin's Life: Poetry and Madness, 1831) by the Romantic writer Wilhelm Waiblinger as source material (Fehervary 1977: 124). Wolf Biermann's polemical poem 'Das Hölderlin-Lied' (The Hölderlin Song, 1967) even explicitly equates Hölderlin with the GDR's writers, who are strangers in their own country and cut off from the outside world.

13 Filmmakers and writers were particularly interested in the *Frühromantiker* (Early Romantics), such as Hölderlin, Kleist, von Günderrode and Jean Paul. Films about Goethe or adaptations of his works not mentioned elsewhere in this chapter include the West German *Begegnung mit Werther* (Encounter with Werther, Stroux, 1949); *Faust* (Gründgens and Gorski, FRG, 1970); *Die Wahlverwandtschaften* (Elective Affinities, Siegfried Kühn, GDR, 1974) and the French–West German co-production for television of the same title (1981), directed by Claude Chabrol.

14 Ulrich Plenzdorf's *Die neuen Leiden des jungen W.* (The New Sorrows of Young W., 1972) is paradigmatic in this context. The irreverent reception of Goethe's epistolary novel *Die Leiden des jungen Werthers* (The Sorrows of Young Werther) by an adolescent dropout was seen as a desecration of the classical canon.

15 Despite the staggering similarities between Damm's book and Günther's film, the director-scriptwriter claims not to have been influenced by Damm's investigation (Günther and Berghahn 2002). This is true insofar as Damm aspires to a high degree of biographical accuracy, carefully distinguishing between authenticated source material, on the one hand, and any form of speculation, on the other, to fill the gaps. Günther's film, by contrast, is biographical fiction, and thus not particularly concerned with authenticity.

16 Tellux Film GmbH with its headquarters in Munich became one of the co-owners of Progress Film-Verleih when DEFA's distribution arm was privatised in 1997. Since 2001 Tellux has been the sole owner of Progress.

17 This characterisation of Christiane as a capable and, in her later years, independent woman is emphasised in *Christiane und Goethe*, whereas Günther vehemently rejects the notion of Christiane's autonomy: 'Das ist 'ne Verklärung von ihr. Im Zeitalter des Feminismus noch mehr. Man wollte dem Goethe nicht antun, daß er ein so dummes Kind geheiratet hat. Fähigkeiten, das bestreitet ja keiner, seelisch oder so. Aber im Kopfe, nein!' (Günther and Berghahn 2002) (This is a transfiguration of her, necessary, in particular, in the age of feminism. People simply did not want to admit that Goethe had married such a stupid child. Nobody denies that she had certain talents, spiritual ones and so forth. But no intellectual talents, no!).

4

The forbidden films

Film censorship on either side of the Wall

Although freedom from censorship was guaranteed in the three consecutive constitutions of the German Democratic Republic and in the *Grundgesetz* (basic law) of the Federal Republic, both German states sought to regulate the production and circulation of films through appropriate laws and various other mechanisms of control. Since the GDR was a highly politicised society in which film was used to promote and protect the Party's ideological objectives, the degree of state intervention was much higher than in the West. In fact, as has been outlined in Chapter 1, in the GDR state control was all-encompassing, since the state acted both as patron and censor of the nationalised film industry. Film censorship affected domestic productions as well as foreign imports and the state employed every imaginable mechanism of censorship, ranging from prior censorship of annual production plans and scripts, to the surveillance of filmmakers and the outright ban of films. Notwithstanding the rigour of censorship which affected the entire cultural sphere, officially the GDR claimed that there was no place for censorship in socialist society, since this was deemed to be an instrument of control which only less advanced, capitalist societies utilised.

While state control of the film industry was generally far less strict in the Federal Republic and consisted primarily of indirect censorship through subventions and funding, mechanisms of direct film censorship were also in existence. The *Freiwillige Selbstkontrolle der Filmwirtschaft* (FSK, the Voluntary Self-Regulatory Body of the Film Industry), which played a prominent role between 1949 and the early 1970s, was anything but 'voluntary' and 'self-regulatory', for its officially appointed members were recruited from the film industry, as well as from the federal and central governments and the church. Effectively the FSK was a censorship body that had to approve all films prior to their theatrical release.

Though the criteria for censorship and the number of films suppressed were never made public 'FSK practice seems to have corresponded to the political directives of the Cold War' (Loiperdinger 2002: 155).[1] In other words, censorship was mainly of a political nature and directed at film imports from communist countries. This also explains why in the 1970s, in the wake of the *Ostpolitik*, which resulted in more liberal policies towards the East, the powers of the FSK were significantly reduced. Moreover, the relaxation of moral attitudes from the late 1960s onwards resulted in the FSK by and large limiting its role to approving films for minors. In view of the curtailed role of the FSK, new laws were passed that aimed to protect the public at large from the glorification of violence and the dissemination of pornography, but institutionalised mechanisms of political and moral censorship as such were abolished in the 1970s.

In the GDR, by contrast, censorship had a significant impact on film culture until the late 1980s. Between 1951, the year which marks the first outright ban of a DEFA film, and 1989, when the HV Film relinquished control over the film industry and censorship was abolished, around thirty films were banned, never completed or never released (Schenk 1994b: 537–41). In addition to the twelve films which were shelved in the wake of the Eleventh Plenum of the Central Committee of the SED in 1965 – and which will be the focus of this chapter – the list of banned films also comprises numerous other examples: *Das Beil von Wandsbek* (The Axe of Wandsbek, Falk Harnack, 1951/62/81); *Die Schönste* (The Most Beautiful One, Ernesto Remani, 1957/2002); *Sonnensucher* (Sun Seekers, Konrad Wolf, 1959/72); *Das Kleid* (The Suit, Konrad Petzold and Egon Günther, 1961/91); *Die Russen kommen* (The Russians are Coming, Heiner Carow, 1967/87); *Die Taube auf dem Dach* (The Pigeon on the Roof, Iris Gusner, 1973/91); *Jadup und Boel* (Jadup and Boel, Rainer Simon, 1980/87); and *Schnauzer* (Maxim Dessau, 1984). While in some cases film censorship resulted in the destruction of all prints and the negative, in most cases the banned films were shelved in the state film archive and could therefore be released at a later date when the political mood had changed. The number of films that fell victim to pre-censorship during the development and production phase is much more difficult to gauge. It has been suggested that during the 1950s and 1960s up to half of all film projects were abandoned at script stage or beyond, costing the studio some 7 million Marks (Feinstein 1999: 203; Soldovieri 1998: 57). However, the reasons for abandoning projects at script stage were varied and did not always relate to issues of censorship, as the dramaturge Dieter

Wolf amply documents in his book *Gruppe Babelsberg: Unsere nicht gedrehten Filme* (The Babelsberg Group: The Films We Didn't Make, 2000). According to DEFA's filmmakers themselves, far more harmful than institutionalised forms of censorship imposed from above was self-censorship. In the words of Frank Beyer:

> Am liebsten war es dem obersten Zensor, wenn er gar nicht in Erscheinung treten oder zumindest nicht öffentlich auftreten musste, wenn er seine Entscheidungen nach unten delegieren konnte: also Honecker an das für Kultur verantwortliche Politbüromitglied, das Politbüromitglied an den Abteilungsleiter für Kultur im ZK, der Abteilungsleiter an den Kulturminister, der Kulturminister an seinen Stellvertreter, der Stellvertreter an den Studiodirektor der DEFA, der Studiodirektor an den Chefdramaturgen, der Chefdramaturg an den Arbeitsgruppenleiter, der Gruppenleiter an Regisseur und Autor. Wenn die Zensur dort ankam, wurde sie am wirkungsvollsten ausgeübt. Sie trat als Selbstzensur auf, wenn Autor und Regisseur gar nicht erst versuchten Geschichten zu erzählen, in denen Tabuthemen steckten. [...] Die Zensur saß also nicht in *einer* Behörde, sie war wie Krebs, der den ganzen Organismus der Gesellschaft befallen hatte. (Beyer 2002: 283)

> (The chief censor preferred not to appear at all, at least not in public, he preferred to delegate decisions to a lower level: in other words, Honecker delegated to the member of the Politburo in charge of culture, the member of the Politburo delegated to the head of the Cultural Section in the Central Committee, the head of this section to the Minister of Culture, the Minister of Culture delegated to the Deputy Minister of Culture, the Deputy to the director of the DEFA studio, the studio director to the chief dramaturge, the chief dramaturge to the head of the Artistic Working Group, the head of the Group to the director and the author. When censorship reached this level it was at its most effective. Once author and director no longer even tried to tell stories that broached taboos, censorship had become self-censorship. [...] Thus, censorship was not located in *one* office. It was like a cancer attacking the entire social organism.)

Self-censorship was the most effective censorship practice because it conveyed the misleading – but desirable – impression that a consensus existed between *Geist und Macht* – between intellect and power – which, rather ironically, seems to confirm Erich Honecker's bold declaration after the *Wende*: 'Wir hatten ja keine Zensur . . . Bei uns gibt es sie nur kraft des Bewußtseins' (cited in Emmerich 1996: 52) (We did not have censorship . . . It only exists by virtue of our consciousness).

Even a cursory glance at the films listed above indicates that the reasons for censorship were diverse and often arbitrary, for they depended not just upon a film's subject matter and its aesthetic orthodoxy, but also on the prevailing political climate. Sometimes it even sufficed for a high-ranking individual to raise objections, as the case of Egon Günther's film *Abschied* (Farewell, 1968) illustrates. The film, based on an autobiographical novel by the GDR's first Minister of Culture, Johannes R. Becher, had been awarded the rating 'besonders wertvoll' (particularly valuable) and Günther received the accompanying prize money of 40,000 Marks. But within a week of its official premiere, which was also attended by many figureheads of the state, the film was taken off cinema programmes. Rumour had it that Walter and Lotte Ulbricht left the cinema even before the screening had begun, because the wife of the head of state had objected to the portrayal of Becher, remarking, 'Das soll unser Hans sein?' (That's supposed to be our Hans?) (Günther and Schenk 2000: 63). Only then was the film discredited in the national press on account of its modernist aesthetics, its scepticism and its subversion of Becher's revolutionary pathos.

Similarly, the final impetus to delay the theatrical release of Rainer Simon's depiction of contemporary society in a provincial town in *Jadup und Boel* in 1981 came from the very top. The film had been suspect from the very outset and its development and production were carefully monitored by the Stasi. The film is essentially an indictment of the stagnation of East German society. In a pivotal scene, the protagonist and mayor of the small town, Jadup, addresses a group of adolescents on the occasion of their *Jugendweihe* (ceremony in which fourteen-year-olds are given adult social status), giving them the following provocative advice: 'Hütet Euch davor, alle Fragen endgültig lösen zu wollen. Ich habe es immer versucht, und ich weiß, es geht nicht. Das Leben ist keine Frage, die man endgültig löst. Es bliebe ja dann nur Stillstand und Tod.' (Beware of trying to solve all questions once and for all. I have always tried to do that and I have learnt that it is impossible. Life is not a question one can solve once and for all. The result would be stagnation and death.)

According to the former film minister, Horst Pehnert, this speech in particular was seen to be a barely camouflaged critique of one of the fundamental problems of real existing socialism in the GDR: the denial of irresolvable problems and a sense of stagnation. Such provocation put the DEFA studio director, Dieter Mäde, and cultural functionaries in the Ministry of Culture and even in the Politburo on high alert.[2] Protracted negotiations as to whether *Jadup und Boel* could be released at all took place over a period of three years between 1980 and 1983, when the film was eventually banned.

However, on 9 October 1981 the HV Film actually certified the theatrical release, albeit only on a small scale with just eight copies. The film's premiere was planned for 17 December 1981. During those two months continued uncertainty prevailed in the HV Film, which was reinforced through the publication of a lead article in *Neues Deutschland* on 17 November 1981, which has become known as the 'Hubert Vater letter'. Camouflaged as a letter from Mr Hubert Vater, a reader of *Neues Deutschland* and a humble car mechanic from the town of Erfurt, the real author of the letter was most likely Erich Honecker himself, who expressed his disappointment with East German film production (see Chapter 5). This letter sent a clear signal about a change in the cultural climate. Consequently, the HV Film's earlier certification of *Jadup und Boel* became even more questionable and Horst Pehnert sought backing from the highest echelons, asking Kurt Hager from the culture section in the Politburo for his opinion. Horst Pehnert remembers this incident as follows: 'Da sah sich Hager den Film an. Ich saß neben ihm und ich spürte, wie Hager vor Empörung förmlich bebte. Und da sagte er am Schluß, "Wir haben doch die DEFA nicht gegründet, daß sie uns anpinkelt" – wörtlich!' (Pehnert and Berghahn 2002) (Then Hager watched the film. I was sitting next to him and I sensed how Hager was literally quivering with indignation. And at the very end he said, verbatim, 'We did not found DEFA for them to take the piss out of us'). This was the definitive verdict. The film's premiere was delayed again and again until, in April 1983, the HV Film renounced its former judgement and withdrew the licence for *Jadup und Boel*.

While, generally, films with a historical subject matter were considered to be a much safer bet than films about contemporary society, East German film history also includes numerous instances of controversial films belonging to the anti-fascist genre. On the one hand, films about the GDR's anti-fascist myth of origin featured prominently during times of crisis when this myth was re-invoked to legitimise the rule of the SED. On the other hand, the artistic treatment of the GDR's anti-fascist origin was a potential minefield, especially if certain tacitly agreed conventions were disregarded. The Hitler–Stalin pact of 1939 was best left unmentioned; Russians had to be portrayed as warmly welcomed liberators of the German people from the yoke of fascism, never as looters and rapists; communists held a monopoly on anti-fascist resistance; traitors and Nazi fellow-travellers came from the *petit bourgeoisie*, not the proletariat, and were to be portrayed unsympathetically. Falk Harnack's debut film *Das Beil von Wandsbek* ran counter to the last convention. Notwithstanding the film director's anti-fascist credentials – he had barely escaped a sentence in the trial of the resistance group Weiße Rose and, after having deserted the *Wehrmacht*, had joined a Greek resistance group – *Das Beil von Wandsbek* was charged with encouraging viewers to sympathise with one of Hitler's henchmen and was banned a few weeks after its theatrical release (Schenk 1994a: 65–70).

Heiner Carow's *Die Russen kommen* challenged the GDR's official historiography even more overtly, by asserting that the Russians had not been perceived as the eagerly awaited liberators but instead as the 'Bolshevik menace' or simply the enemy. Moreover, the film's adolescent protagonist is anything but an anti-fascist hero: he is complicit in the murder of a Russian foreign worker and volunteers to join the German *Wehrmacht* in an attempt to achieve the final victory. Not surprisingly, this – by East German standards – unorthodox account of German history was entirely unacceptable during the late 1960s and was banned and supposedly destroyed on account of its assuming the vantage point of a Hitler Youth, denying the historical truth, denigrating the anti-fascist cause and adopting modernist aesthetics (BArch Film 1969; Richter 2001). Thanks to Evelyn Carow, the director's wife and the editor of *Die Russen kommen*, a copy of the film was preserved which could be duplicated when, in 1987, the HV Film revised its former decision and certified the film's release.

The belated release during the late 1980s of films such as *Die Russen kommen, Jadup und Boel* and others that had been previously banned can be seen as the GDR's response to the spirit of *glasnost* and *perestroika*, which had led to an unprecedented liberalisation in all spheres of culture and society in the Soviet Union, following the appointment of Mikhail Gorbachev as Communist Party General Secretary in 1985. Initially Erich Honecker had dismissed the need for a similar cultural and social renewal in the GDR, stating that there was no need to redecorate one's home just because one's neighbour chose to do so. But ultimately it was impossible for the GDR, which had always to a greater or lesser extent followed the policies of its big brother, to resist the tidal wave of change that swept across the Eastern bloc countries. Everywhere filmmakers demanded that films which had been banned, often decades ago, be taken off the shelves and shown at last.

In the Soviet Union this epoch-making event occurred in 1986, when the Filmmakers' Union set up a Conflict Commission that lobbied for the release of more than two hundred previously shelved films (see Graffy 2001: 2118). Amongst them were Tengiz Abuladze's allegory of Stalinist repression, *Monanieba* (Repentance, 1984), Andrej Tarkovsky's *Zerkalo* (The Mirror, 1975) and Aleksei German's *Moi drug Ivan Lapshin* (My Friend Ivan Lapshin, 1984). Many filmmakers, including Aleksandr Sokurov, Alesksei German and Kira Muratova, whose careers had become submerged as a consequence of ideological censorship, were rehabilitated at last.

Yet the GDR's leadership was clearly confused by the cultural relaxation implemented by its big brother and, as a result, sent out mixed messages. In October 1988 the German edition of the popular Soviet journal *Sputnik* was banned because one of its articles suggested that Hitler's atrocities would never have been possible without Stalin (see Beyer 2002: 418). In the same month a number of *perestroika* films, including *Kholodnoye leto '53* (Cold Summer of '53, Aleksandr Proshkin, 1988), *Zavatra byla vojna* (Tomorrow Was the War, Yuri Kara, 1987) and the previously banned *Komissar* (The Commissar, Aleksandr Askoldov, 1967/87), premiered at the GDR's festival of Soviet film and were subsequently released nationwide. Controversy ensued and they were taken off the programmes at short notice, only to be re-released a few months later. These incidents of untimely censorship sent ambiguous signals that the policy of repression was not entirely a thing of the past. And although several of the aforementioned East German films were released in the late 1980s, one group of films still remained locked away in the state film archives. These were the ones that had been banned at or in the wake of the Eleventh Plenum of the Central Committee of the SED, which convened between 15 and 18 December 1965. Twelve films, most of them *Gegenwartsfilme*, fell victim to one of the most ferocious instances of film censorship that ever affected East German film production.[3] The Eleventh Plenum, also appropriately referred to as *Kahlschlag* (clearing the ground), led to the shelving of nearly the entire annual production of the feature film studio and to the suspension from office of several figureheads of the film industry. Among them were one of DEFA's best-known directors, Frank Beyer, the head of the DEFA studio, Jochen Mückenberger, the studio's Party Secretary, Werner Kühn, and even the Minister and Deputy Minister of Culture, Hans Bentzien and Günter Witt.

The grand scale of the censorship, as well as the fact that the guardians of socialist film culture in addition to its creators were implicated, raises a number of questions that this chapter will address. First, how could the mechanisms of film regulation and control be rendered so ineffective that nothing short of a radical *Kahlschlag* would do to ensure ideological and aesthetic orthodoxy on East German screens?

Second, if we believe the protestations of numerous prominent filmmakers who claimed that they had no intention of making subversive films but, on the contrary, wanted to further the progress of socialist society, then how was it possible that their films were attacked for undermining the fundamental principles on which socialist society was based? And third, what impact did the Plenum have on the future development of East German cinema in relation to other East European cinemas during the 1960s and beyond?

Kahlschlag in a politically volatile climate[4]

Film censorship across the Soviet bloc countries, where the state usually acted as both patron and censor, has been notoriously volatile, making the degree of creative autonomy enjoyed by filmmakers a rather unpredictable matter, as the film historian A. J. Liehm notes:

> As long as the state . . . knows exactly what it wants and what it doesn't . . . all the benefits the cinema could obtain from its nationalized structure are, so to speak, suspended . . . On the other hand, whenever the state . . . does not know exactly where it stands, . . . that is, in moments of political, economic and social crisis, and periods of uncertainty, all the advantages of subsidized film production begin to function . . . the film-makers are in charge, and their art functions to an astonishing extent. (cited in Garrett 2001: 805)

The years following Stalin's death in 1953 and the ensuing phases of de-Stalinisation initiated in the Soviet Union by Khrushchev in 1956 resulted in socially and aesthetically challenging films, most notably the New Waves in Czech, Polish and Hungarian cinema during the 1960s. But typically phases of relaxation were followed by political backlashes, such as the Warsaw Pact invasion, which put a sudden end to the Prague Spring in 1968. Invariably, the result was a clampdown in the cultural sphere. In Czechoslovakia alone bans were imposed on over one hundred films during the so-called 'normalisation' that followed the Soviet invasion. Amongst the forbidden films was Miloš Forman's *Hoří má panenko* (The Firemen's Ball, 1967), which provides a particularly instructive example of the arbitrariness of censorship. The film 'was initially banned, then released in 1968, nominated for an Oscar, banned the following year after the Warsaw Pact invasion, and listed as banned "forever" in 1973' (Hames 2001: 839). It was eventually re-released in the summer of 1989, prior to the Velvet Revolution.

The ferocious film censorship that occurred during the mid-1960s in the GDR is but one of many similar instances in East European film history that points towards the significance which critical political junctures had for the type of films that were possible. It occurred when de-Stalinisation, which had been implemented rather half-heartedly in the GDR anyway, was superseded by a return to the hard-line. The development of the films thus took place in a climate of ideological flux and uncertainty, when 'die Kulturpolitk ... zwischen der Duldung künstlerischer Experimente und ihrer exemplarischen Unterbindung konzeptionslos hin und her [pendelte]' (Engler 2000: 17) (cultural politics ... oscillated without a definitive line between tolerating some artistic experiments and intercepting others to set a precedent). In other words, the films which were to be forbidden could be made in the first place not because the sophisticated apparatus of censorship had failed, but because both cultural officials and film-makers had not fully appre-ciated the vicissitudes of the political climate during the mid-1960s and had overestimated the degree of ideolo-gical latitude.

Several factors had encouraged the filmmakers' optimism. In order to counteract the rapidly declining audience numbers for DEFA films in the late 1950s and early 1960s – the result of increasing competi-tion from television and the loss of audience appeal of films over-burdened with Party doctrine – filmmakers and administrators agreed on a strategy that promised to draw in audiences without relinquish-ing the educational mission of the national film culture: a new type of *Gegenwartsfilm* (film about contemporary society) which examined socialist society more critically and more honestly. In a repressed society a greater degree of openness and criticism promised to have nearly as much popular appeal as sheer escapist entertainment. These films are based on observation of everyday life and typically revolve around conflicts at the workplace. Consistent with the doctrine of Socialist Realism and, more significantly, the agenda set at the Bitterfeld Con-ferences, the socialist workplace plays a formative role in the personal development of the protagonists and is portrayed as a prime site of socialist consciousness formation.[5] Like the literary heroes and heroines of the so-called *Ankunftsliteratur* (arrival literature) of the early 1960s, the protagonists of the new critical *Gegenwartsfilm* are forced to recon-cile their high socialist ideals with the sobering reality of 'socialism as it actually exists rather than as a still-distant aspiration. In contrast to many examples of later GDR literature [and film], these works, however, still posited East Germany as a perfectible society, one clearly and rapidly advancing toward the future' (Feinstein 2002: 125).

Another factor which contributed to a relaxation of the political and cultural climate was, rather paradoxically, the erection of the Berlin Wall on 13 August 1961. Despite a sense of shock, many artists and intellectuals who had decided to stay in the GDR because of their belief in the socialist project accepted the Wall as a necessary sacrifice to ensure the GDR's inner stability. And indeed, with the GDR populace practically imprisoned in their own country, the regime's internal vigilance was relaxed and a more liberal atmosphere began to prevail which lasted until winter 1965. As Kurt Maetzig, one of DEFA's founding members and best-known directors, put it when interviewed upon the release of *Das Kaninchen bin ich* after the *Wende*:

> Nach dem Mauerbau kam es zu einer gewissen Beruhigung, Stabilisierung des Landes. Wir hielten den Zeitpunkt jetzt für gekommen, uns den inneren Problemen ohne Rücksichtnahme, kritisch und mit prinzipieller Deutlichkeit zu nähern. (Maetzig 1990)
>
> (After the erection of the Wall, the situation in the country stabilised and became calmer. We thought the time had come to tackle the problems in our country more critically and more outspokenly.)

In particular, the year 1963 heralded a number of liberalising and democratising measures in the legal system, the economic sector and youth culture which were indicative of a greater degree of tolerance and a more open-minded attitude toward Western culture.[6] Significant structural changes in the DEFA studio mirrored the all-embracing reform trend. Following the example of the Polish film industry, DEFA's management structure was decentralised by the introduction of *Künstlerische Arbeitsgruppen* (or KAGs, Artistic Working Groups, see Chapter 1). Political supervision of film production was further loosened because DEFA's chief dramaturge, Klaus Wischnewski, relinquished his post.

More significantly, several bureaucrats in the Ministry of Culture shared the desire of the filmmakers who wanted to liberate socialism from the horrible deformations which were inflicted upon it by Stalinism through their socially critical films. Yet, before the crippling effects of Stalinism could be eliminated in the GDR, the period of Thaw came to an end in the Soviet Union when Khrushchev was ousted from power in October 1964 and Brezhnev took over. This resulted in a massive political backlash in the GDR and a re-strengthening of the allegiance with the Soviet bloc.

By that time, the development of the screenplays and scripts of several of the forbidden films was well under way and filmmakers were aware
that they were working against the clock, anticipating that the changed
political agenda would soon have repercussions in the cultural sphere.
A number of warning signs underscored the volatility of the political
climate. Just a month after the erection of the Wall the first significant
cultural backlash occurred when an exhibition at the Academy of Arts,
'Junge Kunst' (Young Art), met with severe criticism and Kurella, head
of the Committee for Culture of the SED, himself took abstract paint-
ings off the wall. A few weeks later Heiner Müller's play *Die Umsiedlerin
oder Das Leben auf dem Lande* (The Resettler or Life in the Country)
was withdrawn on the night of its premiere and Müller was expelled from
the *Schriftstellerverband* (Writers' Association). Controversies sparked
by the Kafka conference in Liblice in 1963 also signalled that the cultural climate had not fundamentally changed. Modernism was still
denounced as formalism and thus an expression of bourgeois decadence;
alienation, a prominent theme in the works of Kafka, was declared to
be an inappropriate topic for art since, allegedly, alienation did not exist
in a socialist society.

In the sphere of film, too, restrictions persisted more tenaciously
than in other Soviet bloc countries. While DEFA directors wanted to
emulate Soviet directors like Kalatozov, Tarkovsky, Chukhrai and the
New Wave directors in Poland, Hungary and Czechoslovakia, cultural
officials in the GDR were not ready to accept films that overtly challenged
the Socialist Realist formula. Internationally acclaimed and prize-winning
Soviet films such as Tarkovsky's feature film debut *Ivanovo detstvo*
(Ivan's Childhood, 1962) and Kalatozov's *Letyat zhuravli* (The Cranes
Are Flying, 1957) were controversial in the GDR. Jean Paul Sartre's
review of Tarkovsky's debut, in which he singled out the expressionistic and surrealistic quality of its symbolism, suddenly disappeared a
few hours before it was due to go to print (see Netzeband 1990: 45).
And yet, in this climate of ideological instability, DEFA filmmakers saw
a window of opportunity and mustered the courage at least to begin to
compete with their colleagues across the Eastern borders. Only at or in
the aftermath of the Eleventh Plenum did they fathom the full extent of
the about-turn.

Of the dozen films which were banned or withdrawn in the context
of the Eleventh Plenum only two were actually discussed at the meeting. These were Frank Vogel's *Denk bloß nicht, ich heule* (Just Don't Think
I'll Cry) and Kurt Maetzig's *Das Kaninchen bin ich*, whilst Günter

Stahnke's film with the prophetic title, *Der Frühling braucht Zeit* (Spring Takes Time) had been screened once in November 1965 and then been recalled. Frank Beyer's *Spur der Steine* (Trace of the Stones) was already completed before the Eleventh Plenum, whereas the other forbidden films were still in production. Some were never completed or released, either because the new DEFA studio director, Franz Bruk, who replaced Jochen Mückenberger after his dismissal, pre-empted censorship by not applying to the HV Film for permission to license the films, or because of direct state intervention. Like dangerous ammunition these films – weapons in the struggle against the class enemy – were put under lock and key in the state film archives. Even the filmmakers were denied access to them until the *Wende*. But, in 1989, following the example of the Soviet Filmmakers' Union, the film historian Ralf Richter founded the Commission of the Association of Film and Television Workers of the GDR which urged the cultural functionaries to revisit the censorship decisions of the past. The commission, together with the filmmakers, retrieved the films from the archives and raised the necessary funds to reconstruct or complete them. With the exception of three films which remained unfinished, and two which had been released earlier, the forbidden films of 1965–66 were eventually shown in February 1990 at the *Akademie der Künste* (Academy of Arts) and shortly afterwards at the International Film Festival of Berlin.

While the censorship history of each of the forbidden films is unique, they share certain common denominators: with a few exceptions, they belong to the genre of the *Gegenwartsfilm*, which carried considerable weight since it was by definition suited to promote the state's current socio-political and economic agenda. Consequently, nearly all of the forbidden films bear some relation to the reform measures introduced in 1963: *Das Kaninchen bin ich* deals with the reforms in the legal system, while *Der Frühling braucht Zeit* and *Berlin um die Ecke* (Berlin around the Corner, Gerhard Klein, 1966) endorse the reform plans proposed by the New Economic System. *Denk bloß nicht, ich heule, Karla* (Carla, Herrmann Zschoche, 1966), *Jahrgang '45* (Born in '45, Jürgen Böttcher, 1966) and *Berlin um die Ecke* are in keeping with the liberal attitude expressed in the 1963 Youth Communiqué which advocated the development of a distinctive youth culture, and even took a surprisingly permissive stance on issues such as sexual morals, dance and Western beat music, hitherto vilified as an expression of capitalist decadence. This seems to suggest that filmmakers were indeed acting in good faith when making the forbidden films for, arguably, all of the films promote topical reforms which promised to restructure GDR society by opening it up to Western cultural and economic influences. However, by December 1965, the Party's views on reform had changed so that the liberal attitudes expressed in these films were at odds with the Party's revisionist notion of 'ein sauberer Staat mit unverrückbaren Maßstäben' (Honecker 1965: 19) (a clean state with unshakeable ethical and moral standards), as described in the Politburo's official report, read by Honecker at the Eleventh Plenum.

Turning a forbidden book into a forbidden film: *Das Kaninchen bin ich* (The Rabbit is Me, Kurt Maetzig, 1965)

Licensed by the HV Film on 3 November 1965 and banned just a few weeks later at the Eleventh Plenum, Maetzig's film *Das Kaninchen bin ich* set a precedent which foreshadowed the crackdown on other films that was to follow in the weeks and months after the Plenum. It also lent its name to these films, which are variously referred to as *Kaninchenfilme* (rabbit films), *Verbotsfilme* (forbidden films) or *Regalfilme* (shelved films). In fact, *Das Kaninchen* was considered to be such a prime example of subversive film art that it was used at the *Stasi* Training Academy, teaching *Stasi* officials how to detect traces of ideological diversion on celluloid (Geiss 1997: 43). Moreover, the history of its censorship exemplifies the strategies that were commonly employed to camouflage censorship in order to convey the impression that the relationship between the GDR's artists and its political leaders was based on consensus.

The film tells the story of Maria, a nineteen-year-old girl from East Berlin who is denied access to university because her brother, Dieter, has been charged with openly provocative behaviour against the state and has been sentenced to three years in prison. When Maria falls in love with Paul Deister, a married man much older than herself, she soon finds out that he is the judge who passed the inordinately severe verdict on Dieter. Initially, she tries to separate her love for Paul from his involvement in her brother's case. But when the penal code is reformed and Maria witnesses a similar case, a tribunal in which the fisherman Grambow is tried for slander against the state, she is amazed that Grambow gets away with just one hundred hours' community service. She begins to surmise that justice is relative. The legal reforms provide Maria with the opportunity to plead for mitigation in her brother's case. For Deister, however, these reforms are disadvantageous because they make his former verdict appear too dogmatic. For the second time he tries to use Dieter's case to advance his career by suggesting that he,

10 *Das Kaninchen bin ich* (The Rabbit Is Me) – a manifestation of Western immorality

instead of Maria, ought to propose that the case be reviewed. Maria realises that her lover's motivations are exploitative and opportunist and leaves him. Her brother's sentence is curtailed and Maria is offered a place at the university. The final scene shows Maria moving into her student digs accompanied by the jubilant chords of baroque music. In a voice-over she proudly states that she is a citizen of the German Democratic Republic.

In spite of the film's positive ending and its convincing demonstration that the GDR's system of jurisprudence has been much improved as a result of the *Rechtspflegeerlaß* (Resolution on Jurisprudence), the film was harshly criticised at the Eleventh Plenum, where it was shown to members of the Central Committee in a private screening.[7] One of the issues raised was how the film could have been made in the first place, since it was based on a book that had been banned in 1963 and that was never to be published in the GDR. When the film minister Günter Witt was asked at the Eleventh Plenum why he had given permission to adapt Manfred Bieler's novel *Maria Morzeck oder Das Kaninchen bin ich* (Maria Morzeck or the Rabbit is Me) in the first place, he justified his decision by pointing out that the ideological thrust of the film differed significantly from the literary text. For example, the film makes explicit references to reforms of the administration of justice between 1961 and 1963, leading to an increased democratisation of criminal justice. In fact, the director Kurt Maetzig and the scriptwriter Manfred Bieler had included a number of alibi scenes in the script, notably the one showing the trial of Grambow at the hands of a conflict commission, which had no correspondences in the novel. These scenes convey what Maetzig and Bieler believed to be a politically desirable message, namely that certain aspects of Stalinist dogmatism within the legal system had been replaced by a reformed and democratic form of jurisdiction. These good intentions are stressed in the studio assessment which the DEFA studio director Jochen Mückenberger submitted to the HV Film:

> Es ist die Absicht des Films anhand des Erlebens von Maria deutlich zu machen, wie sich die sozialistische Demokratie in unserer Republik gefestigt hat, und daß hierin Kraftquellen liegen, die Maria erkennen lassen: nicht Heuchelei, sondern Wahrheit und Aufrichtigkeit . . . sind Kennzeichen eines Sozialisten. (Mückenberger 1965)

> (It is the intention of this film to show through Maria's experience how the socialist democracy of our Republic has been consolidated and how this provides a source of strength, which results in Maria's realisation that honesty and truth, not hypocrisy . . . are the hallmarks of a socialist.)

However, neither the alibi scenes nor the defence put forward by the DEFA studio director himself were sufficient to placate the censors. Maetzig's representation of the justice system was considered to distort reality since it equated the penal code prior to the legal reform of 1963 with the dogmatism of a careerist and opportunist judge. This implied that the Resolution on Jurisprudence was a reform necessary to correct certain previous shortcomings. Naturally, the Party did not want to admit to any mistakes, past or present, and argued that these legal reforms had gradually evolved in synchronicity with the overall progression of socialist society (BArch SAPMO DY30 /IV/A2/9.06/124, 1965). Moreover, the fundamental question raised by Maria – whether justice is absolute or relative – remains unanswered, leaving it to the audience to draw their own conclusions. Such uncertainty, as well as the portrayal of one of the figureheads of socialist society as a ruthless opportunist and adulterer, was regarded as heresy.

In addition to its ideological shortcomings, *Das Kaninchen bin ich* was criticised on account of its aesthetic principles, which were seen to be incommensurate with the doctrine of Socialist Realism (see Chapter 1). The film's subjectivity was considered to result in a dangerous lack of partisanship. The entire narrative is rendered from Maria's perspective, whose disrespectful views on certain aspects of society are conveyed in a number of voice-over comments. As in Maetzig's post-war newsreel *Der Augenzeuge* (The Eyewitness), where the audience is invited to 'Watch for yourself. Listen for yourself. Judge for yourself', Maria in *Das Kaninchen bin ich* also appeals to the audience to make up their own minds about the events rendered by directly addressing them. The point of view of a young girl who is anything but a positive heroine was perceived to be incompatible with the ideological guidance which film was expected to provide.

Party functionaries from the highest echelons spoke out against *Das Kaninchen* at the Eleventh Plenum. Kurt Hager, a member of the Politburo and the Party's chief ideologue, claimed to have discovered a Kafkaesque sense of alienation in Maetzig's film and in *Der Frühling braucht Zeit* (withdrawn in November 1965), which indicated that the filmmakers had a 'gebrochenes Verhältnis zu unserem Staat' (Hager 1965: 62) (a broken relationship with our state). In his keynote address, 'Ein sauberer Staat mit unverrückbaren Maßstäben' (a clean state with unshakeable moral standards) at the Eleventh Plenum, Erich Honecker, at the time in charge of security matters in the Central Committee and the second man behind Walter Ulbricht, denounced Maetzig's film, alongside Biermann's poems, Werner Bräuning's novel *Rummelplatz* (Fairground) and Frank Vogel's film *Denk bloß nicht, ich heule*, as manifestations of Western ideological subversiveness. Through infusing socialist society with a sense of pessimism, and through weakening its moral substance with pornography, trash literature and decadent beat music, the class enemy was trying to undermine the unshakeable principles and convictions of the socialist state. This resulted, Honecker declared, in a generalised scepticism and nihilism, in particular amongst artists and intellectuals (Honecker 1965: 21).

Against this background any attempt to justify the making and certification of *Das Kaninchen bin ich* was doomed to fail. Nonetheless – and this was part of the pseudo-democratic ritual of censorship – the film minister Günter Witt was given the opportunity to defend his decisions at the Eleventh Plenum. His speech provides an illustrative example of the rhetoric employed in such ritualised retractions. He begins by expressing his gratitude to the leading comrades in the Ministry of Culture and the Party for having helped him recognise the errors of his ways. He then concedes that he has 'meine Verantwortung in diesem Falle nicht wahrgenommen und meinen Parteiauftrag, mit jedem Film unsere sozialistische Sache zu stärken' (Witt 1965: 23) (not fulfilled my responsibility and my order from the Party to further our socialist cause through each film) and identifies the fundamental flaw of the film as follows:

> Die richtige Auffassung von dem gewachsenen politischen Reifegrad der Bevölkerung, also unseres Publikums, führte zu dem Fehlschluß, man könne deshalb dem Publikum das Denken über die Lösung der im Film gezeigten Widerprüche und Konflikte überlassen. Die Folge dieser Auffassung ist die Aufgabe der erzieherischen Funktion des Films, der Verzicht auf das Hineintragen der sozialistischen Ideen in die Massen durch die Kunst. (Witt 1965: 24)

> (A correct view of the growing political maturity of the population, that is to say, our audience, led to the false conclusion that the audience would be able to solve the contradictions and conflicts shown in the film by themselves. As a result the film abandons its educational mission, which consists in disseminating the ideas of socialism amongst the masses through art.)

The self-criticism which Witt exercised at the Eleventh Plenum could not save him. He was dismissed from office. Kurt Maetzig learnt of the banning of his film from the press and was invited by Kurt Hager to discuss the film with him. During a four-hour conversation Hager persuaded Maetzig to write an open letter to Ulbricht, the head of state, recanting the critical point of view and nihilistic propaganda expressed in his controversial film. On 5 January 1966 an article appeared in *Neues Deutschland* entitled 'Der Künstler steht nicht außerhalb des Kampfes' (Maetzig 1966) (The artist does not stand outside the class struggle) in which Maetzig admits to having made a detrimental film and to having committed a political error.

A few days later, Walter Ulbricht wrote a letter of reply to Maetzig that also appeared in *Neues Deutschland*. Whilst reiterating Maetzig's self-accusation – 'Ihr Film war ein Irrtum, und Sie haben ihn als solchen öffentlich erklärt' (Ulbricht 1966) (your film was an error, and you have openly declared it as such) – Ulbricht refers to the film itself only in passing. Primarily, the letter is a treatise on the role of art in socialist society, dwelling on the political commitment expected of artists.

> Unsere Schriftsteller und Künstler müssen ihre Reihen fester um die Partei zusammenschließen, sie müssen ideologische Diversion, das Gift des Skeptizismus, die Negation alles Heroischen, aller großen Empfindungen, offen und hart bekämpfen. Also Freiheit für alles, was unserem Staat nützt, aber keine Freiheit für Schmutz und Pornographie, keine Freiheit für ein ideologisches Paktieren mit den Feinden des Sozialismus, keine Freiheit für das Beschmutzen unseres Staates, der auf der Tradition unzähliger Opfer, unzähliger heroischer Taten guter Deutscher entstanden ist. (Ulbricht 1966)

> (Writers and artists must close rank more tightly around the Party. They must fight openly and with determination against ideological diversion, the poison of scepticism, the negation of any heroism and of great emotions. In other words, there exists freedom for everything that benefits our state, but no freedom for filth and pornography, no freedom for an ideological pact with the enemies of socialism, no freedom to sully our state, which is founded on the tradition of countless victims and the countless heroic deeds of good Germans.)

Maeztig, one of DEFA's founders and figureheads, who had made no less than fourteen films by 1965 and who had been awarded the GDR's most prestigious prize, the *Nationalpreis* (National Prize) five times, survived the Eleventh Plenum unscathed. Sceptics who surmised that through his public retraction of *Das Kaninchen bin ich* Maetzig may have compromised his artistic integrity got the following explanation to pon der: his letter to Ulbricht was not an opportunist act of self-protection but a strategy through which he had hoped to avert a similar fate for the films which were still in production at the time (Maetzig 1990).

11 Manfred Krug as Balla in *Spur der Steine* (Trace of Stones)

A flagship of socialist film culture? *Spur der Steine* (Trace of Stones, Frank Beyer, 1966/90)

Of the twelve forbidden films *Spur der Steine* is the most famous. It enjoyed considerable box-office appeal when it was released in East and West German cinemas after the *Wende* and was the most success-ful German film of 1990. The fact that Manfred Krug, who had been a *Publikumsliebling* (audience darling) in the East and became a popular West German television star after his emigration in 1976, plays a lead-ing part in *Spur der Steine* certainly contributed to the film's positive reception. But arguably, its notorious censorship history is equally significant in explaining why a twenty-four-year-old, black-and-white film, set on a large construction site in the GDR's industrial heartland, sparked any interest at all.

Frank Beyer's film is based on Erich Neutsch's best-selling novel of the same name, which had been reprinted eight times since its publica-tion in 1963, had been awarded the National Prize and occupied a prime position in the GDR's literary canon.[8] It epitomises the genre of the *Produktionsroman* (production novel), which posits the workplace as a 'uniquely privileged locus of progressive consciousness formation' (Feinstein 2002: 186). The novel had also inspired Heiner Müller's play *Der Bau* (The Building Site, 1965), one of the literary texts severely criticised at the Eleventh Plenum and not performed in the GDR until 1980. Beyer's film, by contrast, was not even mentioned among the controversial films and texts at the Plenum. In fact, the suggestion to turn Neutsch's novel into a *Gegenwartsfilm* had come from up high. Frank Beyer was the right person to approach. By the time the thirty-three-year-old director embarked on the project, he had already made a name for himself through his anti-fascist trilogy, *Fünf Patronenhülsen* (Five Cartridges, 1960), *Königskinder* (Star-Crossed Lovers, 1962) and the prize-winning Buchenwald film, *Nackt unter Wölfen* (Naked among Wolves, 1963).

Spur der Steine had been scripted between May 1964 and January 1965 and was shot between April and October 1965. In November, the rough-cut had been approved. When Beyer and his team, the KAG Heinrich Greif, realised that the Eleventh Plenum signalled a change of the political climate, they re-edited parts of the film and re-shot a number of scenes in order to make its political message more acceptable in this highly charged atmosphere. In March 1966 high-ranking cultural functionaries, including Kurt Hager, Alexander Abusch, the new Minister of Culture, Klaus Gysi and representatives from the DEFA studio and the HV Film, met to scrutinise the final cut. The ensuing discussion was devastating. But instead of banning the film, Kurt Hager delegated the responsibility for the final verdict on *Spur der Steine* to the *Filmbeirat*, which had an advisory role in matters relating to film in the Ministry of Culture. Since the *Filmbeirat* did not suggest banning the film, the to-ing and fro-ing continued throughout spring and summer 1966 and views on the film's ideological position oscillated considerably (see Beyer 2002: 126–53).

The DEFA studio report, for example, refers to it as one of the 'bedeutendsten und wirksamsten Gegenwartsfilmen' (most important and effective films about contemporary society), which is likely to have 'eine parteiliche, aktivierende Wirkung bei einem relativ breiten Publikum' (Bruk 1966) (a partisan and agitational effect on a relatively wide audience). Such a whole-hearted recommendation by the DEFA studio director was by no means the rule after the Eleventh Plenum. Franz Bruk, a reliable functionary from outside the cultural sphere, who had been appointed two months after the Plenum as DEFA's new head, was careful not to jeopardise his position and took no risks when submitting the studio's assessments on those critical *Gegegenwartsfilme* to the HV Film which were to be certified after the Eleventh Plenum. *Karla, Fräulein Schmetterling* and *Jahrgang '45* were not even submitted to the HV Film for certification but withdrawn by the studio itself. However, *Spur der Steine* was the flagship determining the future of the critical *Gegenwartsfilm*.

Notwithstanding the controversy which surrounded Beyer's film, to one side in the divided camp it still seemed as if the film had all the ingredients for success: set on a large construction site, featuring a proletarian hero, it adheres to the aesthetic doctrine of Socialist Realism and the Bitterfeld Way. Moreover, the film promised to have great popular appeal, with Manfred Krug in the lead and a witty screenplay that had significant political import. When *Spur der Steine* was first shown at the Potsdam Workers' Festival on 15 June 1966 all screenings were sold out for an entire week. In addition, the film was earmarked for the film festival in Karlovy Vary, the East European equivalent of Cannes, and was to be released with fifty-six copies – by GDR standards a very high number – in cinemas across the country on 1 July. Two days before the film's official premiere the Politburo convened and reconsidered Beyer's film. The next day the Central Committee devised a strategy whereby *Spur der Steine* would be taken off cinema programmes at short notice. The billboards at East Berlin's Alexanderplatz and elsewhere which advertised the film's official premiere were removed. Nevertheless, the six hundred seats of the first-run cinema International in East Berlin were sold out. Ten minutes into the screening youth gangs, which had been planted in the cinema by SED hard-liners, disrupted the film screening, expressing their indignation at the film's portrayal of society. Recalling this event in his autobiography, Beyer remarked that he could not believe that his own Party – for he was a member of the SED – would resort to the very same measures which the Nazis had used to discredit films they wanted to ban (Beyer 2002: 149). Similar organised protests were staged in cinemas in Leipzig and Rostock. The only press coverage which *Spur der Steine* received was in *Neues Deutschland*. However, this review was essentially an extract from the Politburo's directives – a fake review published under the pseudonym Hans Konrad. The official film critic of the *Neues Deutschland*, Horst Knietzsch, had refused to put his name to a slating review when his favourable commendation of Beyer's film was withdrawn from print (Schenk 1995: 114–18). Alongside those films which had already been banned at the Eleventh Plenum *Spur der Steine* was shelved in the state film archives.

The sudden reversal in the reception of *Spur der Steine* documents the ideological volatility which prevailed at the time. Was it a film which toed the Party line, or was it a subversive attack on the Party?

The film, set before 1961, opens with Party disciplinary proceedings against the Party secretary Werner Horrath, who is charged with 'unmoralischem Verhalten, Karrierismus und politisch-ideologischem Versagen' (immoral behaviour, careerism and political-ideological failure). A series of extended flashbacks reveals what is at the bottom of these charges: when Horrath arrives at the construction site of Schkona both his leadership qualities and his moral integrity are put to the test. Foreman Hannes Balla, played by Manfred Krug, is the unchallenged king of the site. He is an ebullient, hard-drinking and hard-working carpenter with little interest in socialism and absolutely no interest in the Party. In spite of that his brigade, 'the Ballas', is successful in attaining the goals and meeting the schedules on the Schkona site. Horrath, a pale and diffident intellectual who is out of touch with the workmen, is Balla's opposite in all respects. The men's personalities clash, but they fall in love with the same woman, Kati Klee, a young engineer on the site. She chooses Horrath, despite the fact that he is married and has a family. When Kati falls pregnant, Horrath is too weak to make a choice between the two women in his life or to acknowledge that he is the father of Kati's child. Telling the truth might indeed have cost him his position as Party secretary, for the Party was intolerant of marital infidelity. Even when Kati is ostracised by the men on site for expecting an illegitimate child, she remains loyal to Horrath. Balla, who soon gets to the truth of the matter, proves to be the better man of the two: he respects Kati's decision for secrecy, while at the same time trying to protect her honour and being generally supportive. But not only on a personal level does Balla take the moral high-ground, he is also professionally more competent than Horrath. Intuitively, he chooses what is right for his brigade and for the efficient running of the construction site. The fact that he is not committed to toeing the Party line makes him a better judge of what is required. Although Balla's rebellious behaviour provokes the leading functionaries at Schkona, they cannot afford to get rid of him because they depend on him and his brigade. Horrath is clever enough to realise this and – at least temporarily – the men become allies. Personal and ideological differences, however, make this allegiance short-lived. The film ends where it began, with the Party proceedings against Horrath. Horrath, who eventually divorces his wife and admits to being the father of Kati's child, is deemed morally unfit to hold the post of Party

secretary at Schkona. As Balla rightly points out, he is dismissed and punished not for the mistakes he made, but for telling the truth. Kati does
not attend the trial but leaves Schkona to start a new life elsewhere.

Whereas the other forbidden films were considered to be unacceptable on account of specific scenes, *Spur der Steine* was perceived to
be harmful throughout. According to Maaß, the new film minister, the
depiction of the Party and its representatives was particularly offensive.
In the contrasting character portrayal of Party members and non-Party
members the latter invariably fare better. The fact that Balla and his brigade
are portrayed in the most positive terms, that they epitomise the values
of a model collective without being SED members, was seen to be a
distortion of reality which would bias the audience against the Party
(BArch Film 1966: 2, 6–7). The leading functionaries at Schkona, on
the other hand, are portrayed as autocratic and incompetent in their
decision-making processes. The moment Horrath arrives on the site
he witnesses how the foundation and pillars of a nearly completed
building are blown up. This is a not altogether subtle reference to the
mismanagement and economic inefficiency prevalent in the GDR's
command economy.

To make things worse, the HV Film even detected ideological tendencies
in Beyer's film which echoed the convictions of Havemann and other
dissidents: the film undermines the Marxist doctrine which posits that
the Party is the vanguard of the proletariat and, possessing unique insight into the progressive forces of history, should therefore direct the
socialist nation's march towards the realisation of the socialist utopia.
Instead, the HV Film argued, *Spur der Steine* insinuates that the people
in the first workers' and peasants' state would have achieved even more
if the Party had not hindered them (Argumentation zum Film *Spur der
Steine* 1966: 8).

In order to convey the impression that the withdrawal of *Spur der Steine*
had been demanded by the voice of the people another public protest
was staged. On 5 July 1966 twelve workers wrote a letter to Frank Beyer
expressing their disapproval of *Spur der Steine*. Reiterating the arguments
which dominated the controversy surrounding the film, the workers
accused Beyer of misrepresenting the Party and of focusing exclusively
on negative aspects of socialism, and even suggested that 'Säufer, Rowdys
und moralisch verkommene Subjekte [in unseren Betrieben] den Ton
angeben' (cited in Schenk 1995: 111) (drunkards, hooligans and morally
debased individuals set the tone [in our enterprises]). Frank Beyer responded in a letter, stating that he had made the film convinced that

with *Spur der Steine* he was making 'einen Film *für* die Partei . . . , einen Film der unserer Gesellschaft nützt' (cited in Schenk 1995: 112) (a film *for* the Party, a film which benefits our society).

Except for this timid act of self-justification, Beyer did little to defend himself. Unlike his colleague Kurt Maetzig he did not avail himself of the opportunity to exercise self-criticism. He stuck to his guns, lost his job at DEFA and was exiled from Berlin for several years. At first he worked for the theatre in Dresden, then he was invited to direct two films for television. Only in 1974 was he given the opportunity to make *Jakob der Lügner* (Jacob the Liar, 1975), a co-production of DEFA and East German television.

The only person who dared to defend Beyer openly was his colleague Konrad Wolf, who had just been appointed to the prestigious position of President of the Academy of Arts. Precisely because of this important position it was particularly dangerous for Wolf to speak his mind. When *Spur der Steine* was discussed at two *Parteiaktivtagungen* (Party Activists' Conventions) at the DEFA studio on 5 and 13 July 1966, he decided to make his views known in a letter instead of taking the risk of being subjected to an inquisition by the representatives of the Central Committee and the Ministry of Culture. In this letter, Wolf dismisses most of the charges raised against *Spur der Steine* and finally reminds the cultural functionaries that they share collective responsibility for the film: Beyer, he argues, did not make this film in isolation. The film had been discussed more than once with Party leaders and cultural functionaries. Notwithstanding certain reservations, Wolf pointed out, the decision to release *Spur der Steine* had been made collectively (cited in Schenk 1995: 121).

Such outspokenness could not be tolerated. Konrad Wolf was asked to reconsider his views and to issue a statement that matched the Party's position. Wolf's renunciation of his original assessment of *Spur der Steine* was circulated by Kurt Hager among members of the Politburo. It follows the protocol of such customary retractions in all respects. Wolf raises the question as to where he went wrong and where he failed to take responsibility, and admits that his judgement was flawed, that Beyer's film is indeed a hostile attack on the Party. Wolf's self-accusation ends with the plea that the studio's central Party leadership may grant him the opportunity to make amends through his own artistic work in which he will endeavour to correct his error. He pleads allegiance to the Party and accepts the Party's reprimand. However, instead of using his next film, *Goya* (1971), as an opportunity to make amends, Wolf used this historical artist biopic to comment upon the censorship of the Eleventh Plenum (see Schenk 1995: 122–3).

The film *Goya*, based on Lion Feuchtwanger's novel *Goya oder Der arge Weg der Erkenntnis* (Goya, or the Arduous Path of Discovery, 1951) brings to life the eighteenth-century painter Goya, who was employed as court painter to Their Catholic Majesties Charles IV and Maria Luisa of Spain. When he becomes involved with politics and criticises the Spanish Inquisition in a cycle of satirical sketches, the *Caprichos*, he falls from grace. He is tried by the Grand Inquisitor but, despite the pressure put upon him, he does not recant but goes into exile instead.

One scene in particular is crucial in this context: the Grand Inquisitor questions Goya about the hidden meaning of his *Caprichos*, suggesting that Goya has levied an attack upon the Church. The Grand Inquisitor asks: 'Wem dienen diese Zeichnungen? Dienen Sie dem Wohl der Kirche?' (Who benefits from these drawings? Does the church benefit?), whereupon Goya replies: 'Sie dienen der Wahrheit' (They benefit the truth) – The Inquisitor: 'Wenn ich recht verstehe, unterscheiden Sie zwischen der Kirche und der Wahrheit. Ich frage, ob Sie einen Unterschied machen zwischen der Kirche und der Wahrheit? (If I understand you correctly, you are distinguishing between the church and the truth. I am asking you, is there a difference between the church and the truth?) – Goya responds equivocally: 'Die Kirche steht über der Wahrheit. (The church is above the truth.)

Despite its historical remoteness this artist biopic was not exactly politically innocuous. Konrad Wolf uses the inquisition scene as a compelling comment on a theme that preoccupied GDR artists – the relationship between *Geist und Macht*. More specifically, it is a reflection upon Konrad Wolf's own experience of the aftermath of the Eleventh Plenum.

Generation conflict in the GDR? *Berlin um die Ecke* (Berlin around the Corner, Gerhard Klein, 1966/87)

Berlin um die Ecke is the fourth 'Berlin film' of the director-scriptwriter duo Gerhard Klein and Wolfgang Kohlhaase. Like *Alarm im Zirkus* (Circus Alarm, 1953), *Eine Berliner Romanze* (A Berlin Romance, 1956) and the popular but controversial *Berlin – Ecke Schönhauser* (Berlin – Schönhauser Corner, 1957), this fourth 'Berlin film' explores the everyday life of adolescents in the divided city. While *Berlin – Ecke Schönhauser* came under attack on account of its Neo-Realist aesthetics,

Berlin um die Ecke promised to have all the ingredients of a flagship of socialist film culture: the plot focuses on the workers and the trials and tribulations of socialist production in a Berlin metal processing plant. It also features stock characters such as Hütte, the anti-fascist around whom the GDR's foundational narratives are constructed, and Paul Krautmann, the dedicated socialist worker whose entire raison d'être revolves around the nationalised enterprise. Moreover, the film is in line with the state-endorsed strategy at the time to develop films that specifically target the youth sector (BArch/DR117/A/240 1965).

The depiction of adolescents was, in principle, desirable because films were expected to make a significant contribution to the formation of a socialist identity by portraying suitable role models. Following the Youth Communiqué of 1963, this had become an even more pressing goal since the Party wanted to involve young people more actively in the building of the socialist state, culminating in the slogan 'Die Mädchen und Jungen von heute werden in wenigen Jahrzehnten die Hausherren des sozialistischen Deutschland sein. Die Stunde der jungen Leute ist gekommen' (Rauhaut 1991: 53) (Within a few decades today's girls and boys will be the patrons of socialist Germany. The hour of the young people has come).

Several of the forbidden films make more or less explicit reference to this slogan – and yet, ideologically, they were off-target. The young heroes and heroines portrayed take the official rhetoric at face value and as a result become disillusioned. Karla, the young teacher in Ulrich Plenzdorf's and Hermann Zschoche's eponymous film, takes up her first teaching position in a small rural school, encouraging her pupils to examine the tenets of real, existing socialism critically. She soon realises that her youthful idealism is not liked by her superiors. Her boyfriend Kaspar had to learn his lesson earlier. When he was still working as a journalist he was asked to write about the crimes of Stalinism – but then the GDR's views on de-Stalinisation changed and he was fired. In Frank Vogel's film *Denk bloß nicht, ich heule*, eighteen-year-old Peter Neumann is asked to write an essay on the topic 'Die Republik braucht Dich. Du brauchst die Republik' (The Republic needs you, you need the Republic). When he expresses a rather critical view of socialism he is expelled from school. Regarding himself as a product of socialist education, Peter fails to comprehend how it is possible to have grown up under socialism yet not be a socialist.

Similarly, *Berlin um die Ecke* is the story of two adolescents, Olaf and Horst, who are members of a *Jugendbrigade* (youth brigade) in a Berlin metal processing plant. This socialist enterprise suffers from all the problems that East Germany's planned economy was renowned for: shortages of materials, low work morale and flawed production plans. Olaf and Horst exploit and expose the shortcomings of the system by forging their payslips and by cynically turning down the honorary title of *Aktivist*,[9] explaining that through over-achieving the production target by 250 per cent they had merely intended to demonstrate that the production norms were unrealistic and that the enterprise could be much more efficient if everyone worked to their full capacity.

Such provocative behaviour does not go down well with the older workers in the plant. To committed socialists like Hütte and Krautmann, Horst's and Olaf's attitude is incomprehensible. The conflict between old and young workers does not end here but culminates in Olaf's physical attack on Hütte. However, in the end the workplace emerges as a prime site of socialist consciousness formation: Olaf's rebellious attitude towards certain aspects of socialism becomes superseded by a deeper insight into its merits as well as its shortcomings.

Much of the controversy that surrounded Klein and Kohlhaase's film concerned the generational conflict. This was a highly sensitive topic since it belied the official view that old and young agreed upon all fundamental issues in life and shared the common goal of developing socialism. Yet *Berlin um die Ecke* was seen to tell a different story. In particular the functionary Hütte is the chief antagonist of the young. He accuses the members of the *Jugendbrigade* of crimes against the socialist state and 'is portrayed as a fossil, as an intolerant zealot' (Mückenberger 1999: 72). However, in the pivotal scene in which Olaf physically attacks him, the audience's sympathies shift in favour of Hütte: his victimisation and the slow-paced depiction of his lonely and impoverished existence evoke a sense of pity. This feeling is reinforced by Hütte's revelation: 'Das letzte Mal haben sie mich auf dem Appellplatz geschlagen. Einer, der so jung war wie du. 24. April '45' (The last person to hit me was a guard at roll call. He was a young chap like you. That was on 24 April '45), making a laconic reference to his incarceration in a concentration camp, which in the context of East German cinema identifies him as an anti-fascist resistance fighter. Because of his anti-fascist past, the film implies, he deserves respect and Olaf responds accordingly. As Christiane Mückenberger notes, 'when relations [between the generations] have all but reached breaking point, the innate respect of the younger generation for the anti-fascist past of their elders prevents total rupture' (Mückenberger 1999: 71).

The relationship between old and young is by no means presented in negative terms throughout. The closest ally of the young heroes is Krautmann, played by the popular actor Erwin Geschonneck. Modelled on Kohlhaase's father, he is cast in the most favourable light: idealistic and dedicated to his work, humane and open-minded. Although he epitomises the virtues of hard work and total commitment to the people-owned enterprise, he is also critical of the flaws of the socialist economic system, which he compares with his pre-war experience of the capitalist economy. Krautmann is a role model for the young generation and in fact, Olaf's work ethos changes as a result of his friendship with this father-figure. When Krautmann unexpectedly dies, Olaf writes an obituary, addressing his deceased friend directly, which suggests that dialogue between the generations does exist after all:

> Ich denke, Paul, daß du immer noch da sein wirst, wenn wir die Halle neu einrichten, und wenn wir ruhiger geworden sind, weil wir die Sachen besser hinkriegen, und wenn kein Strom mehr verschwendet wird und wenn es 16 Millimeter Muttern gibt wie Sand am Meer.

> (I think, Paul, that you will still be here with us when we refurbish the hall, and when we have calmed down because we have learnt to manage things better, and when we no longer waste electricity and when 16 millimetre nuts will be a penny a dozen.)

This obituary is a summative expression of a firm belief in the unstoppable progress of socialism, conceding that problems exist but that they will be solved.

The dialectical structure which Klein and Kohlhaase use in the film when dealing with such sensitive issues as conflict and corruption in socialist society was actually in line with the aesthetic agenda set for the *Gegenwartsfilm* in the early 1960s. Thematising the existence of conflicts and contradictions was acceptable as long as positive solutions were offered. This is precisely what Klein and Kohlhaase do: the generational conflict is not presented as an unbridgeable chasm but as a formative experience on the way to adulthood. The shortcomings of the command economy are rendered as evolutionary problems which will eventually be overcome. The overall tenor of the film is one of reconciliation and affirmation. And yet the censors did not see it this way.

The HV Film criticised the makers of this film for suggesting that 'in unserer Republik ein Generationskonflikt besteht, der nicht aufzulösen geht' (Jahrow 1966) (an irresolvable generation conflict exists in our Republic). Further charges concerned the film's 'kapitalistische

Unmoral' (capitalist immorality) which consisted in the reduction of loving relationships to quick sexual gratification, and a distorted representation of the socialist enterprise (Jahrow 1966). Jahrow, head of the production department of the HV Film, coerced the studio into abandoning the project immediately. In an act of preventive obedience the DEFA studio director, Bruk, ordered a production stop. *Berlin um die Ecke* was shelved in its rough-cut version. The sound track was not finished and the film music by Georg Katzer had not yet been composed.

The film's portrayal of the young touches upon an issue that was highly sensitive at the time of the Plenum: it advocates tolerance towards a distinctive youth culture with all its paraphernalia such as its own music and dance styles, its own dress codes, sexual morals and attitudes towards work and the socialist collective. In many respects the film endorses precisely those measures of liberalisation that had been outlined in the Youth Communiqué a few years earlier. Addressing areas as diverse as literature, dance, sexual morals and sport, it placed particular emphasis on beat music, a cultural phenomenon that had been hitherto vilified as an expression of capitalist decadence. Yet, for a short while, the GDR's youth could enjoy beat music and even Beatles songs on DT 64, a radio channel targeting the young, and generally benefit from a cultural relaxation that no longer attempted to seal the GDR off from Western youth culture.

By September 1965 the SED had changed tack: after fans rioted at a Rolling Stones concert at the Berlin Waldbühne the national press levied a rabble-rousing attack against beat music fans and youth culture at large. Licences for amateur bands were withdrawn and beat music fans and other rebellious youths suspected of criminal activity were sent to labour camps. Young people with long hair and a Western dress code were denounced as 'fascists' and treated as if they were enemies of the state (Dalichow 1992). At the Eleventh Plenum Erich Honecker explained in his keynote speech why this clampdown on youth culture had become necessary:

> Unsere DDR ist ein sauberer Staat. In ihr gibt es unverrückbare Maßstäbe der Ethik und Moral, für Anstand und gute Sitte. Unsere Partei tritt entschieden gegen die von den Imperialisten betriebene Propaganda der Unmoral auf, die das Ziel verfolgt, dem Sozialismus Schaden zuzufügen. ... In den letzten Monaten gab es Vorfälle, die unsere besondere Aufmerksamkeit erforderten. Einzelne Jugendliche schlossen sich zu Gruppen zusammen und begingen kriminelle Handlungen. Es gab

Vergewaltigungen und Erscheinungen des Rowdytums. Es gibt mehrere Fälle ernster Disziplinverstöße [...] Hier zeigt sich wiederum der negative Einfluß von Westfernsehen und Westrundfunk auf Teile unserer Bevölkerung. [...] Den Erscheinungen der amerikanischen Unmoral und Dekadenz wird nicht offen entgegengetreten. (Honecker 1965: 19)

(The GDR is a clean state with unshakeable standards of ethics, morality, decency and good manners. Our Party is vehemently opposed to the imperialist propaganda of immorality, which aims to harm socialism. . . . During the last few months there have been a number of incidents that have demanded our particular attention. Individual young people have ganged up and committed criminal offences. There have been rapes and examples of hooliganism. There are several serious violations of discipline [...] Here we can witness again the negative influence of West German television and radio on certain sections of the population. [...] Manifestations of American immorality and decadence are not opposed openly enough.)

Although *Berlin um die Ecke* does not feature long-haired hippies or hooligans the film was nonetheless implicated in Honecker's attack on youth culture: alongside *Denk bloß nicht, ich heule* and *Jahrgang '45*, *Berlin um die Ecke* was advocating that young people had a right to their own way of life and their own opinions. Implicitly, these films called the authority of the state, which recruited its leaders from the founding generation of anti-fascists, into question. Moreover, since young people were open to Western influence – thus the argument ran at the Eleventh Plenum – they were endeavouring 'im Zuge einer sogenannten Liberalisierung die Deutsche Demokratische Republik von innen her aufzuweichen' (Honecker 1965: 21) (to destabilise the GDR from within in the course of a so-called liberalisation).

Klein and Kohlhaase did not avail themselves of the opportunity to make the significant alterations to the rough cut, which Bruk had recommended in an attempt to save the film. As a result, *Berlin um die Ecke* was consigned to the archives until 1987, when it was shown in its unfinished form during the celebrations marking the 750th anniversary of the founding of the city of Berlin. Even today, *Berlin um die Ecke* is a film without music, finished but still bearing the visible scars of censorship. Though the film was re-edited in 1990, Kohlhaase decided that there was no point in concealing the film's fate and therefore deliberately retained its somewhat fragmentary form – a testimony to the filmmakers' courageous resistance to censure (Kohlhaase 1990). In contrast to colleagues such as Egon Günther and Frank Beyer, who kept changing their films in line with the censors' requests only to find them banned eventually, Klein and Kohlhaase stuck to their guns. As the scriptwriter Kohlhaase explained retrospectively: 'Bestimmte Vorwürfe nicht zu akzeptieren, war für mich wesentlich für meine weitere Arbeitsfähigkeit. Sonst hätte ich etwas von mir selbst verloren' (cited in Sylvester 1992) (In order to preserve my future ability to work it was essential for me not to accept certain charges. Otherwise I would have lost part of myself).

Wenn du groß bist, lieber Adam (When You Are Grown Up, Dear Adam, Egon Günther, 1966/90): a humorous indictment of hypocrisy

Egon Günther's career at DEFA suggests that he was one of the studio's *enfants terribles*, albeit one with a good guardian angel. Four of the nine films which Günther directed or co-directed at DEFA were forbidden in some form or another but, surprisingly, he was never banned from filmmaking. As he commented in hindsight: 'Es war immer wieder, als wenn man ein verirrtes Kind auf die rechte Bahn zurückbringen wollte' (Günther and Schenk 2000: 55) (It always seemed to me as if they were trying to bring a wayward child back to the straight and narrow).

After studying German and Psychology in Leipzig under the tutelage of such famous thinkers as Ernst Bloch and Hans Mayer, he worked as an editor in the Mitteldeutscher Verlag before joining DEFA as a dramaturge in 1958. One of the first projects in which he became involved as a scriptwriter and co-director, *Das Kleid* (The Suit, 1961/90), based on Hans Christian Andersen's classic fairy tale *The Emperor's New Clothes*, was effectively banned. The film closely follows the plot of the original tale, mocking the emperor's desire for adulation and suggesting that the emperor does not have the support of his people. Although the film eschews overt anachronistic references to contemporary GDR society, the fact that the story is set in a walled city was enough to alarm cultural officials during the politically tense climate prior to the erection of the Berlin Wall. After 13 August 1961 this political parable in the guise of a fairy tale had become unsupportable: the studio director Mückenberger withdrew it himself, aware that it would not have stood a chance (see Günther and Schenk 2000: 54–5).

Five years later, in the aftermath of the Eleventh Plenum, *Wenn du groß bist, lieber Adam* was forbidden. In 1968, the year when the Prague Spring was suppressed by military force, and when Egon Günther's son was charged with slander against the state and imprisoned, *Abschied* was withdrawn but never officially forbidden. In 1972 *Die Schlüssel* (The Keys) proved controversial on several counts: the film is aesthetically unorthodox insofar as it blends fictional and documentary scenes. The fact that these documentary interludes were improvised and thus evaded any form of pre-censorship was perceived to jeopardise the censors' authority (Günther and Berghahn 2002). And indeed some of these improvised documentary scenes touched upon areas that were taboo in East Germany or Poland at the time. Günther and his crew filmed a religious procession in Krakow which shows Cardinal Wyszynski – who at the time was an 'unperson' in Poland – blessing the film crew; this scene was cut immediately. Another subsequently censored documentary scene was shot in a morgue and showed the corpse of a young woman whose private parts were covered with peonies (Günther and Berghahn 2002). Actors abandon their roles and speak directly to the camera using Brechtian distanciation techniques which fly in the face of Socialist Realism. In other respects, too, *Die Schlüssel* broaches several taboos: it suggests that socialist society is ridden with class divisions; it denies socialism's utopian conviction that man can change for the better. And, most significantly, *Die Schlüssel* runs counter to socialism's obligatory optimism by making death one of its central concerns. In a country in which even the weather report was euphemistically enhanced, forecasting sunshine instead rain, the truism that life ends in death was unacceptable. The film was never officially banned; however, it was not released until 1974 and then only shown rarely in a few cinemas.

After *Die Schlüssel* Günther was no longer trusted with *Gegenwartsfilme* and was assigned to cinematic adaptations of the literary canon instead (see Chapter 3). Ultimately this remedy proved ineffective as well, for he could not resist instilling topical messages into heritage films. In 1978 he was given permission to work in the West. In spite of numerous offences, such as holding an East as well as a West German passport, and keeping a substantial part of his hard currency earnings, which under East German law was regarded as a breach of exchange control regulations, he was never expelled from the GDR. Maybe Günther was too valuable as a cultural ambassador. After all, he had not just made subversive films but also films like *Der Dritte* (Her Third, 1971) and *Lotte in Weimar* (1975), which brought DEFA considerable international recognition. Miraculously, someone at the very top seems to have taken this non-conformist artist under his wing and granted Günther liberties that others could only dream of.[10]

Günther's film *Wenn du groß bist, lieber Adam* betrays a degree of audacity that pushes the boundaries of the permissible to the very limit. It is essentially a treatise on the hypocrisy and mendacity that undermined all human relations in the GDR. In order to be able to address such an obvious taboo, the scriptwriters Helga Schütz and Egon Günther came up with the idea of couching this provocative message in a comic fairy tale for adults. For Günther, an ardent admirer of Brecht, this provided the opportunity to explore Brecht's dictum 'daß die Komödie die Dinge des Lebens auf die viel schwerere Achsel nimmt, als es die Tragödie vorgibt zu tun. Wenn's Ihnen ernst ist, können Sie's doch auch lustig ausdrücken' (cited in Kasten and Gehler 1997) (that comedy takes life much more seriously than tragedy purports to do. If you're serious about something, then you can poke fun at it).

Wenn du groß bist, lieber Adam clearly displays the influence of East European, notably Czech, comedy which, according to Peter Hames, combines a 'heretical and ironic attitude towards those that have [power], a humour of the everyday, allusion to social realities . . . and a workplace locale' (Hames 2000: 72–3). In fact, the inspiration for Günther's and Schütz's film had come from Vojtěch Jasný's film *Až přijde kocour* (When the Cat Comes/Cassandra Cat), which was released in the GDR in 1963. In Jasný's fairy tale a black tomcat wearing magic spectacles sees the people around him in the different colours of their souls. The magic spectacles reveal what people really feel and think. Jasný's film is a playful, humorous attack on the prevailing hypocrisy and opportunism in society.

Like the Czech film, *Wenn du groß bist, lieber Adam* employs elements of magical realism and is essentially a hybrid between a fairy-tale and a *Gegenwartsfilm*. Fairy-tale elements, such as an eloquent swan and a torch with magic properties, as well as the voice-over commentary introducing the cast at the beginning, underscore the fictional status of the story. This creates an ironic contrast since the genre of the *Gegenwartsfilm* typically renders problematic aspects of everyday life.

The film tells the story of Sepp Tember and his eight-year-old son Adam, who are given a torch by a swan on the riverbank of the Elbe in Dresden. Soon they find out that this torch has magic properties: if it is directed at someone who does not tell the truth the liar is revealed and sent up into the sky. Sepp, who works in the research and development department of an electrical goods company, tries to persuade the company director to mass-produce the L-catcher. At first sceptical

12 Magical realism in *Wenn du groß bist, lieber Adam* (When You Are Grown Up, Dear Adam)

as to whether such a lie detector would sell at all, he eventually welcomes the project, confessing:

> Was mich angeht, ich wäre ein ideales Prüfungsobjekt. . . . Vom Scheitel bis zur Sohle eine einzige wandelnde Lüge. Wenn Sie mich anleuchten, bin ich schon verschwunden. [the following part was cut:] Na und? Glauben Sie, ich bin so lange Direktor trotz meiner moralischen Verwerflichkeit? Wegen! Weil! Deshalb! (Günther and Schütz 1965: 71)

> (As far as I am concerned, I'd make an ideal guinea pig. . . . There is nothing truthful about me. I am false from top to toe. I shall disappear the moment you shine the torch on me [the following part was cut:] Well? Do you think I have been company director for so long in spite of my moral reprehensibility? Because of it. That's why!)

The mass production of the magic torch is a failure: thousands of lookalike torches simply shine but cast no light on the truth. However, the new company director does not mind this technical fault since there is obviously no demand for the L-catcher anyway. Even Sepp and his son Adam are relieved because they realise that the magic torch does not necessarily bring happiness to its owner. A minister who pays the

company a visit considers the torch to be an unnecessary gadget anyway, commenting equivocally:

> Nehmen wir mal an, es hätte die Lampe wirklich gegeben. . . . ich hätte sie
> auch vernichtet. Es ist unnötig, einander so ins Herz zu sehen. Entweder
> bekennen wir uns dazu, den Menschen zu vertrauen, oder es wird alles
> nur ein Fortstolpern sein, und das ist nicht die glücklichste Art der
> Vorwärtsbewegung. (Günther and Schütz 1965: 151)

> (Assuming the flashlight had ever really existed . . . I would also have de-
> stroyed it. It is unnecessary to look into each other's hearts so deeply. Either
> we decide to trust people, or we simply keep stumbling along. And that is
> not the most felicitous way of moving forward.)

This kind of trust did not exist in the mid-1960s – hence the censors
ensured that this incisive remark was deleted from the film's soundtrack.
Like numerous other scenes and dialogue sequences which went missing in the process of the film's continual revision, the above comment
appears as a written insert in the film's final version which Günther prepared for the premiere in 1990. These written inserts, which replace lost
or destroyed scenes, draw particular attention to those aspects of *Wenn
du groß bist, lieber Adam* that were deemed particularly heretical in the
mid-1960s. Examples of such eliminations include a scene where the soldiers of the GDR's *Nationale Volksarmee* (National People's Army) are
taking an oath of allegiance and go up in the air when the torch is shone
on them,[11] as well as Sepp Tember's remark, which ran counter to the
GDR's official historiography that he never experienced the bombing
of Dresden, since he was a soldier at the time: 'Ich habe eine Heinkel
geflogen. An der Ostfront. Ich bin einer der Spätbelehrten (Günther and
Schütz 1965: 149) (I flew a Heinkel. I was at the East front. I am one
of those who learnt his lesson late). Similarly, the casual observation,
'Das Schändlichste ist, jemandem Angst zu machen' (Günther and Schütz
1965: 88) (The most disgraceful thing you can do is to instil fear in somebody), and the joke 'Schalten ist kein Geheimnis, das kann jeder hören'
(Changing the gears is no secret. Anyone can hear it) were cut. The joke's
ambiguous meaning ostensibly alluded to the fact that East German cars
like the Trabi were known for their noisy gearboxes while, at the same
time, the frequently used tag, 'kann ja jeder hören', was understood by
audiences as an oblique reference to the realisation that certain things
were better left unsaid because of the omnipresence of the *Stasi*
(Günther and Berghahn 2002).

In numerous self-referential scenes the film pokes fun at the short-comings of East German film production and even at censorship itself. In one such scene a film crew ponder the difficulties of making a comedy, wondering: 'Über wen lachen . . . über wen muß . . . darf . . . soll gelacht werden? . . . das ist die zentrale Frage' (Günther and Schütz 1965: 71) (Who to laugh at . . . who must we . . . may we . . . should we laugh at . . . that is the central question). Then they write down all the topics that can be safely laughed at, but the film director becomes so scared that he eats the piece of paper.

The censorship history of *Wenn du groß bist, lieber Adam* proves that finding a suitable topic for comedy was not easy. This is not to say that censors had no sense of humour, but frequently they even had to censor their own laughter. Günther recalled how the cultural functionaries who saw this scene were trying to pretend that they were not amused. Hans Rodenberg, a high-ranking official in the Central Committee, confessed later: 'Ich hab' auch gelacht bei dieser Stelle. Aber ich muß mich berichtigen, nicht ich habe gelacht, sondern mein innerer Schweinehund' (cited in Günther and Berghahn 2002) (I also laughed at this point. But I must correct myself, it was not me who laughed but my weaker self).

In the debate surrounding the film nobody gave the real reasons for the ban. Helga Schütz recollects numerous discussions revolving around the film's humour, its ambiguity and its inaccessibility (Günther 1990). According to Schauer, the deputy head of the HV Film, the film was overly intellectual and rendered a distorted picture of the spirit of truthfulness, trust and humanism that prevailed in GDR society (cited in Richter 1994: 205). Taking the HV Film's views into account, the DEFA studio director suggested that further changes be made. However Günther, who had complied with numerous requests from the scriptwriting to the shooting and post-production stages, was unwilling to mutilate the film any more. Many scenes had been sacrificed, jokes had been eradicated, compliance and cunning had been employed in order to increase the film's slim chance of survival. All in vain!

More visibly than in any of the other forbidden films *Wenn du groß bist, lieber Adam* bears the scars of censorship. When in 1989 the film-makers were granted access to the reels of film which had been kept in the state film archives for nearly a quarter of a century they discovered that certain scenes had gone missing and that the soundtrack had been partly damaged. Günther and his team made no attempt to gloss over the traces of censorship: the film's final version includes several silent scenes and excerpts from the script which replace cut scenes. Through this unconventional form of restoration, a Brechtian *Verfremdungseffekt* is achieved, which highlights censorial interference and comments upon what was deemed to be subversive.

The fetters of Stalinism

Günther's light-hearted and stylistically innovative film provides a mere glimpse of a nascent East German New Wave that never happened. There were a few other, albeit isolated attempts by reformist forces at the DEFA studio during the 1960s. These include Konrad Wolf's aesthetically modernist but ideologically partisan *Der geteilte Himmel* (Divided Heaven, 1964) and Jürgen Böttcher's forbidden film *Jahrgang '45* (Born '45, 1966/90), which rejects a conventional narrative and simply records the ordinary life of a young couple in a documentary realist style. But on the whole, DEFA did not partake in the all-encompassing artistic renewal for which other East European cinemas during the 1960s have become renowned. The reasons for this are necessarily complex and hinge, as I have tried to outline in this chapter, on a cluster of socio-historical circumstances. Yet one factor in particular has been identified as crucial in explaining the suppression of an emergent New Wave in East German cinema: the conflation of Stalinism with anti-fascism. It prevented East Germany's artists and intellectuals from fighting for the kind of more radical de-Stalinsation that occurred during the post-Stalinist Thaw in other Eastern bloc countries and which paved the way for an artistic renaissance that manifested itself, amongst other things, in the East European New Waves. As Frank Beyer and others have noted, in the GDR such a radical de-Stalinisation was impossible

> Weil es Antifaschisten waren, die den Sozialismus stalinistischer Prägung bei uns eingeführt haben. Man hätte Antifaschisten bekämpfen müssen, um den Stalinismus zu bekämpfen. Das wollten viele nicht. Es gibt einen großen Respekt im Lande vor denjenigen, die viele Jahre ihres Lebens in der Emigration oder in Gefängnissen und Lagern verbringen mußten. (Beyer 2002: 421–2)

> (Because it was anti-fascists who had introduced a Stalinist type of socialism in our country. In order to fight Stalinism, one would have had to fight anti-fascists. Many people were not prepared to do so. Those who had spent several years of their lives in emigration, in prisons or in camps were held in high esteem in our country.)

As a result, Stalinist power structures were never eradicated in the GDR and, consequently, even the slightest form of dissent was instantly suppressed by the appartus of power:

> Wer sich auflehnt, wird isoliert, aus dem Lande gedrängt, ausgebürgert. Die lange Reihe von Namen beginnt nicht erst mit Ernst Bloch, Hans Mayer und Wolf Biermann, und sie endet nicht mit meinen Freunden Jurek Becker und Klaus Poche, Jutta Hoffman, Manfred Krug und Armin Mueller-Stahl, sie endet mit Zehntausenden junger Leute, die das Land seit dem Sommer [1989] verlassen und es immer noch verlassen und die wir hier so bitter nötig brauchcn. (Beyer 2002: 422)

> (Anyone who opposes the regime is isolated, expelled and expatriated from the country. The long list of names does not begin with Ernst Bloch, Hans Mayer and Wolf Biermann, it does not end with my friends Jurek Becker, Klaus Poche, Jutta Hoffmann, Manfred Krug and Armin Mueller-Stahl, it ends with tens of thousands of young people who have been leaving this country since this summer [1989] and are still leaving it, people we badly need here.)

Film at the service of politics

The ferocious film censorship that occurred in the context of the Eleventh Plenum highlights the importance assigned to the GDR's national film culture. As a form of mass communication, film was considered to be a potentially dangerous weapon of propaganda and mass mobilisation, and was therefore hit harder than other forms of art. For many years to come DEFA film production was curtailed artistically and financially, resulting in a much-reduced annual output.[12] In 1966, only eight feature films (among them three for children) were released, just a third of the annual output of the early 1960s. And, after the Plenum, the DEFA feature film studio never regained the high production figures of previous decades. Filmmakers had had their fingers burnt and had become more cautious. It was certainly not coincidental that the wake of the Eleventh Plenum witnessed the emergence of a politically innocuous and tremendously popular genre – the *Indianerfilm*, DEFA's answer to the American Western, and a preponderance of genre and heritage films amongst DEFA's productions.

But did cultural officials really fear the subversive power of these twelve forbidden films? Critics and filmmakers alike have suggested that the cultural backlash that occurred at the Eleventh Plenum was in fact a strategy designed to divert attention from the economic problems that besieged the country. Günter Netzeband contends:

> Es ging nicht um Kunst, es ging um Politik. Von Anfang an wurde Kunst in den Dienst der Tagespolitik gestellt und daher auch beurteilt. Man konnte nur allzuoft den Eindruck gewinnen, daß Künstler als Prügel-knaben herhalten mußten für Vorgänge, die sie nicht zu verantworten hatten, wenn im Staate Krisenentscheidungen sich häuften, die die Macht der Herrscher zu gefährden schienen. (Netzeband 1990)

> (What was at stake was not art but politics. From the very beginning, art was made subservient to day-to-day politics and judged accordingly. One could not but get the impression that artists served as whipping boys for events which were beyond their sphere of responsibility. This occurred when-ever a crisis point was reached and the state was faced with decisions which jeopardised the power of the leaders.)

The Eleventh Plenum was originally intended to address the economic situation of the GDR and to assess the viability of the New Economic System, which aimed to combine the advantages of a Western-style capitalist economy with those of the centralised socialist economies. But even before the Central Committee convened on 15 December it was clear that many aspects of the economic reform had failed to resolve the persistent economic problems, since it was not underpinned by the more encompassing measures of decentralisation and democrat-isation in other spheres that would have been necessary to make it a success. Erich Apel, head of the State Planning Commission and one of the chief architects of the NES, committed suicide on the eve of the Eleventh Plenum, presumably because he foresaw its imminent renun-ciation (Eckert 1991). Although the GDR's economy still featured on the agenda, debates about film, literature, the arts and media took centre stage, arguably to detract from the country's irresolvable economic problems. The harsh attack on the GDR's cultural instead of its economic production can be explained by the *Stellvertreter Funktion* (replacement function) that art, in particular literature and film, had in the GDR. Art was used to articulate issues which could not be publicly discussed but which were, nonetheless, decoded by a public that was well versed in reading between the lines. The Eleventh Plenum is a prime example: the Party leadership attacked cultural trends and associated them with socio-political issues, such as youth unrest, Western decadence and nihilism. In so doing signals were sent out about wider political and social issues. The Eleventh Plenum was never forgotten by DEFA filmmakers, not only because it had such a devastating effect on the film industry, but also because the complex relationship between *Geist und Macht* continued to affect artists and intellectuals until the demise of the GDR in 1989.

Notes

1 Political censorship, in particular of film imports from communist countries, was further reinforced when, in 1954, a so-called 'Interministerial Committee' was established at the behest of the *Amt für Verfassungsschutz* (Office for the Defence of the Constitution) which was charged with carefully monitoring all imports from Eastern bloc countries. This form of political censorship 'subsequently gained a legal basis through the introduction in 1961 of the Impoundage Act, which explicitly outlawed the import of films "that might function as propaganda against the free democratic order or the spirit of international understanding"' (Loiperdinger 2002: 154). It is estimated that 130 films in total fell victim to politically motivated import control until the 1970s.

2 The censorship history of *Jadup und Boel* is documented in the respective files at BArch Film (1980–83), HV Film 'Jadup und Boel' 3 and 3B; see also Geiss (1997: 116–47); and Schieber (1994: 281–5).

3 In addition to the films discussed in this chapter, these films were Ralf Kirsten, *Der verlorene Engel* (The Lost Angel, 1966/71); Kurt Barthel, *Fräulein Schmetterling* (Miss Butterfly, 1966/never released); Hans-Joachim Kasprzik, *Hände hoch – oder ich schieße!* (Hands up – or I'll Shoot, 1966/never released); Egon Schlegel and Dieter Roth, *Ritter des Regens* (Knights of the Rain, 1965, a debut film co-produced with the Hochschule für Film und Fernsehen, never released). For a concise account of the impact of the Plenum on DEFA, see Wischnewski (2000).

4 Some parts of this and the following sections have been previously published in Berghahn (1999a; 2000).

5 At the first Bitterfeld Conference in 1959, 150 writers and 300 workers initiated a cultural revolution in the literary sphere which envisaged writers and workers swapping roles: writers were to work in production and workers were encouraged to reach for their pens. The second Bitterfeld Conference of 1964 slightly shifted the focus of the production-based literature from the simple workers to the planners and leaders in socialist enterprises. The agenda set at these conferences is usually referred to as the *Bitterfelder Weg* (Bitterfeld Way); see Emmerich (1996: 129 and 181).

6 These measures were in particular the *Rechtspflegeerlaß* (Resolution on Jurisprudence), the *Jugend-Kommuniqué* (Youth Communiqué) and the *Neue ökonomische System* (New Economic System); see Mückenberger (1990: 7–21).

7 Maetzig's colleague Egon Günther cites the film's propagandist end as an example of how DEFA directors resorted to the most sickening strategies to placate the censors; see Günther and Schenk (2000: 59).

8 Beyer, however, suggests that Neutsch's novel itself had been controversial when it was published and that its nomination for the National Prize had been a strategy to mute the novel's critics; see Beyer (2002: 127–8).

9 This award was an important aspect of the activist movement which aimed to improve socialist competitiveness and was granted in particular to workers or collectives who surpassed their production goals.

10 While he was working in Munich he received a birthday card from the studio director, Mäde, and the Minister of Culture, Hoffmann, in which the latter wrote: 'Solange ich meine schützende Hand über Dich halten kann, werde ich sie halten. Alles Gute für Dich' (cited in Günther and Berghahn 2002) (As long as I can take you under my wing, I shall do so. All the best!).

11 This scene had already been eliminated from the script.

12 After the Plenum state interference even at the earliest stages of the creative process significantly increased. The studio director lost the authority to commission scripts independently (Feinstein 2002: 1997). The Artistic Working Groups were either disbanded (Heinrich Greif) or lost a large part of their artistic autonomy. The KAGs Berlin, Johannisthal, Babelsberg and Roter Kreis existed until DEFA's demise but were essentially reduced to teams of dramaturges that recruited directors only on a project basis (Wolf 2000: 10–11).

5

Women on film, or:
how political is the private sphere?

'Women's cinema' on either side of the ideological divide

Roughly from the late 1960s onwards, filmmakers on either side of
the ideological divide began to focus their attention on women's issues.
In the Soviet Union and West Germany a new genre came to the fore,
zhenskie film'my (women's film) and the *Frauenfilm* (feminist film), while
in the GDR the genre of the *Gegenwartsfilm* (film about contemporary
society) began to prominently feature female protagonists. Despite their
shared focus on women, at closer inspection the 'women's films' that
emerged roughly at the same time in capitalist and socialist countries
prove as different as their ideological bases.[1] It is, therefore, instructive
to contextualise the examination of DEFA's 'women's films' by first looking at women's status in society and their representation in films on
either side of the Iron Curtain.

Although women's equality was constitutionally guaranteed in the GDR,
the FRG and the Soviet Union, in practice there were considerable differences as to how equality was actually interpreted. If it meant that
a high percentage of women contributed to the country's labour force,
then indeed the Soviet Union and the GDR were way ahead of the FRG.
Since the Stalin era, women's participation in the workforce had been
mandatory and was vital in order to achieve the targets set by the centralised command economy. Moreover, the need for women's work
coincided happily with Marxist-Leninist ideology. According to Lenin,
woman's emancipation could only be achieved through her gainful
employment, the basis of her economic independence from patriarchy,
and through her liberation from the private world of the family.
Originally, the proletarian women's movement at the turn of the century envisaged rendering the traditional marriage and the nuclear family superfluous, in particular since the raising of children, legitimate
and illegitimate alike, would be handed over to collective institutions.

However, this view was renounced both by Stalin and by Brezhnev when demographic crises made it necessary to extol the virtues of motherhood and the family.

In the GDR, the self-proclaimed workers' and peasants' state, the very notion of citizenship was associated with work. Not surprisingly, in a state that routinely addressed its citizens as *Werktätige* (working people), 'the constitutional promise of equal rights for men and women was tied to employment' (Kolinsky 1993: 259). Everybody had the right but also the duty to work, and non-working was stigmatised as antisocial. During the 1950s women's participation in the labour force was as high as 40 per cent, while on the eve of German unification it had risen to 49 per cent, making East Germany the country with the highest proportion of female labour in Europe (Kolinsky 1993: 259).

In West Germany, women's employment was viewed entirely differently. At least until the rise of the women's movement in the late 1960s, female labour was associated with economic necessity, whereas the full-time mother and homemaker was regarded as a symbol of affluence. Thus, in effect, the constitutional promise of gender equality was perceived as a threat to traditional gender roles and the stability of the family. Even when this conservative attitude became superseded in the wake of the women's movement, a significant share of West German women remained excluded from the labour force partly because the inadequate provision of childcare tied them to their homes.

These differences in women's social status on either side of the ideological divide had a visible impact on the representation of women on screen. The depiction of women in West German films of the 1950s was harnessed to the restorative agenda that characterised the Adenauer period: the independence of the *Trümmerfrau* (rubble woman) was incompatible with the reestablishment of the patriarchal order and women's employment was perceived as unwelcome competition for scarce jobs. Back to the homely hearth was the order of the decade. In the ostensibly depoliticised cinema of the 1950s, this message was conveyed more subliminally than in the often overtly propagandist DEFA films of the time. The *Heimatfilm*, West Germany's most successful indigenous genre ever, including such box-office hits as Hans Deppe's *Schwarzwaldmädel* (Black Forest Girl, 1950) and *Grün ist die Heide* (Green Is the Heath, 1951), constructs female identity around the idealised concepts of *Heimat* (homeland) and matrimony, thus rooting the German woman firmly in a mythical community and in a traditional system of values (Fehrenbach 1995: 148–68).

The small number of career women who appear in West German films of the 1950s, notably the fruit wholesaler in *Eine Frau von heute* (A Woman of Today, Paul Verhoeven, 1954), the physician in *Liebe ohne Illusion* (Love without Illusion, Erich Engel, 1955) and the small-town mayor in *Die ideale Frau* (The Ideal Woman, Josef von Báky, 1959),[2] never pose a real threat to traditional gender roles, for they strive to combine a successful career with traditional female qualities. To quote the protagonist of *Eine Frau von heute*: 'Man kann doch beides – einen Beruf haben und trotzdem Frau sein, mit Chic und Charme!' (One can do both things – have a career and still be a woman, with dress-sense and charm).

The depiction of women in West German popular cinema of the 1950s provides a broad spectrum of stereotypes, which is partly explained by the fact that many of these popular films were star vehicles for actresses whose star personae complemented each other in the construction of the modern woman (Hake 2001: 104–14). Romy Schneider, best known for her three films about the Austrian Empress '*Sissi*' (1955–57), is the archetypal devoted daughter; Maria Schell, referred to by German audiences as 'das Seelchen' (the little soul), became known for her tearful performances and excessive emotionality in melodramas; Sonja Ziemann espoused the values of the *Heimat* and the patriarchal family; Ruth Leuwerik and Luise Ulrich stake out their positions by being cast as the competent and practical modern woman; while Hildegard Knef's star persona took a dramatic development when she swapped her image as rubble woman for that of the fallen woman in *Die Sünderin* (The Sinful Woman, Willi Frost, 1951).

Screen images of women in DEFA films during the 1950s are harnessed to the political and economic agenda of the *Aufbau* (construction of socialism) and consequently espouse women's integration into the workforce and the collective. With an overwhelming majority of women working in agriculture at the time, the Party wanted to increase women's participation in the production process and even tried to steer women towards traditionally male domains such as mining and heavy industry (Strauß 1996: 58). In this respect the GDR's policies mirrored those of the Soviet Union where women were also recruited to jobs requiring hard physical labour, something which was advertised as a sign of real gender equality. Consequently, Soviet films of the Stalinist era and East German films of the early founding years promote similar female role models: the 'new woman' is hard-working, a good communist, and her ordinary, often de-feminised looks make her typical and plebeian rather than beautiful in a conventional sense. On Soviet screens the 'new woman' emerged during the 1930s in the shape of the female tractor driver, *stakhanovite* (a shock-worker who over-exceeds the production target), brigade leader, pilot and engineer (see Attwood 1993; Bulgakova 1993; Taylor 2000). These screen heroines choose their men on the grounds of high labour productivity, not looks or sex appeal. Similarly, DEFA's screen heroines of the 1950s are predominantly women working in production, often in the textile industry, a specifically female domain of industrial production (e.g. *Besondere Kennzeichen: Keine* (Particular Characteristics: None, Joachim Kunert, 1951) and *Modell Bianka* (Model Bianca, Richard Groschopp, 1951)), and sometimes even heavy industry (e.g. *Frauenschicksale* (Destinies of Women, Slatan Dudow, 1952)). As partners they choose good comrades. Typically gender relationships are portrayed as devoid of sensuality but full of socialist consciousness-raising discourse.

Given the fundamental disparities in woman's social status under socialism and capitalism, the concrete issues of gender equality, which came to the fore during the 1970s, were evidently very different on either side of the Iron Curtain. Yet in both ideological camps film played an important role in publicising these issues. The West German *Frauenfilm* emerged as a result of the women's movement during the late 1960s and is typically driven by a sense of personal trajectory. Made by women with a common cause, the prime objective of feminist films of the late 1960s and 1970s was to raise awareness about women's discrimination and oppression. Early examples of such consciousness-raising films often adopt a documentary format or *cinéma vérité* style, focusing on working-class women and concrete political issues such as the legality of abortion or equal pay.[3] They advocate the end of women's confinement to the domestic sphere and the patriarchal family, which was perceived by many feminists to be the focal point of male oppression.

Many of these films adopt an autobiographical mode in examining woman's troubled identity. The preponderance of autobiographical modes of narrative in the medium of film, television documentaries and literature is symptomatic of the attempt to highlight the feminist slogan, 'das Private ist politisch' (the private sphere is political). Helke Sander's trilogy, *Die allseitig reduzierte Persönlichkeit – Redupers* (Redupers – The All-Round Reduced Personality, 1977), *Der subjektive Faktor* (The Subjective Factor, 1981) and *Der Beginn aller Schrecken ist Liebe* (Love is the Beginning of All Terrors, 1984), explicitly links the filmmaker's private history with public history by documenting her involvement in the student movement or by juxtaposing the division of the female self with the division of the city of Berlin. The films' autobiographical impetus is further underscored by Sander being the leading actress in two of these films. All three films investigate 'the divisions of the female self in the various apparatuses of male power' (Elsaesser 1989: 191) and in so doing make a significant and artistically innovative contribution to the feminist agenda.

Helma Sanders-Brahms and Jutta Brückner take the exploration of the female self further, dealing with pathological states. Sanders-Brahms' film *Die Berührte* (No Mercy, No Future, 1981), focusing on a history of schizophrenia, takes the problem of a coherent female identity to the extreme. Brückner's *Hungerjahre in einem reichen Land* (The Hunger Years: In a Land of Plenty, 1980) is an autobiographical case history of the filmmaker's upbringing during the time of the economic miracle. It dwells on the contrast between material affluence and emotional starvation which is interpreted as the trigger for a specifically female identity crisis that manifests itself in anorexia and bulimia (Kosta 1994: 153–81; Linville 1998: 64–83).

Many women's films link women's biographies to Germany's history.[4] Nowhere is this more apparent than in Helma Sanders-Brahms' equally successful and controversial *Deutschland – bleiche Mutter* (Germany, Pale Mother, 1979).[5] On one level the film gives a semi-autobiographical account of the filmmaker's own mother and her experience of the Second World War and the reinstatement of patriarchy in the post-war period. On the other hand, the protagonist, Lene, is an allegorical representation of Germany's national history and its division. This division is inscribed on the protagonist's face, one half of which becomes paralysed. This psychosomatic illness is linked to the reassertion of the male order after the war, whereby the film constructs a close connection between 'private male violence and politically sanctioned violence' (Kaes 1989: 156).

While on the one hand the use of woman as allegory of national history reiterates the feminist slogan that the personal is political, on the other hand it 'works counter to the autobiographical attempt to present the characters in a differentiated, "realistic" – that is, contradictory – way' (Kaes 1989: 148). This would explain why such allegorical constructions of women are more commonly adopted by male filmmakers. Witness, for example, Konrad Wolf's film *Der geteilte Himmel* (Divided Heaven, 1964), to be discussed below, and in the West German context, most prominently Rainer Werner Fassbinder's FRG trilogy. Here, the biographies of the title heroines represent the early days of the FRG in that they reflect the dominant mentality of their time: *Die Ehe der Maria Braun* (The Marriage of Maria Braun, 1979) evokes 'the subjugation of emotions to mercenary material greed in the reconstruction years'; *Lola* (1981) documents 'the ubiquitous corruption . . . in the years of opportunistic conformity'; and *Die Sehnsucht der Veronika Voss* (Veronika Voss, 1982) explores 'the neurosis about one's own past and traumatic memories that had to be exorcised' (Kaes 1989: 82).

Fassbinder's preference for women as allegories of national history builds on a long tradition in pictorial representation and is a common representational strategy employed in many other national cinemas. Well-known examples include Alain Resnais' *Hiroshima mon amour* (France, 1959), Régis Warnier's *Indochine* (France, 1992) and Aleksandr Askoldov's *Komissar* (The Commissar, Russia 1967/87). Fassbinder explained his preference for female protagonists in this context by the greater degree of flexibility afforded to women in society: women, he argued, are less rooted in a rigid social framework; they can break away from their social roles and thus be less conformist than men. They are therefore more interesting than men as dramatic characters. Moreover, by rendering women as politically unaware and absorbed in their private lives, they are better suited to Fassbinder's declared aim to render 'history from below' (Kaes 1989: 82).

It is interesting to note that Fassbinder's rationale for portraying women in these films in some respects coincides with the reasoning behind the predilection of DEFA filmmakers for women protagonists from the 1970s onwards. As Regine Kühn, a prominent DEFA scriptwriter, explained:

> Frauenfiguren wurden in dieser Zeit oftmals erzählt im Film, nicht um Frauenfiguren zu erzählen, sondern weil es möglich war, Gegenwartsprobleme, die an die Grenze dessen gingen, was man uns erlaubt hat, zu erzählen, oftmals leichter durchzusetzen waren, wenn man sie anhand von Frauen erzählt hat . . . (cited in Gräf 2001: 108)
>
> (Many films of this time narrate women's lives, not in order to narrate women's lives, but because it was easier to address problems of contemporary society which were on the borderline of what we were allowed to narrate when they concerned women. . . .)

This explanation betrays some undeniably sexist assumptions, which led DEFA filmmakers during the 1970s and 1980s 'to construct a gender-specific binary opposition of "male" and "female" qualities on screen', associating men with 'external authority and the public sphere as well as stagnation, entrapment and denial' whereas women were linked with the 'private sphere' and qualities such as 'vitality and emotional excess' (Rinke 2001: 226). Utilising this female gender stereotype afforded DEFA filmmakers a certain degree of ideological latitude, which they used not to campaign for women's liberation in socialist society but for the liberation of the individual from the demands of the collective.

What distinguishes Soviet and East German films about women made during the 1970s and 1980s from those made in the West is that they pursue no feminist agenda as such. Nor were they linked to a women's movement. The issue of women's rights was appropriated by the state, which set up official bodies (such as the Committee of Soviet Women and the German Democratic Women's Association) which were supposed to take care of gender issues but which essentially subjugated them to the Party's ever-changing political and cultural agenda. In fact, in both the GDR and the Soviet Union Western-style feminism was 'discredited as a "bourgeois" protest against the oppression of women under capitalism which was deemed to be uncalled for in a socialist society, an alleged community of equals' (Rinke 2001: 42). The predominant image of the feminist in the media was that of a 'woman dressed in overalls, who both hated men and yet wanted to be like them' (Attwood 1993: 79).

In fact, many socialist women's films ostensibly invert the aims of the women's movement.[6] By the 1970s women in socialist societies had sufficient experience with emancipation, largely defined as their participation in the production process, to realise that it was tantamount to another form of exploitation: they alone had to shoulder the double burden of working inside and outside their homes. Hence they wanted to emancipate themselves from competing with men in a men's world, demanding a reduction of women's work outside the home in order to be able to spend more time with their families. Thus most of the Soviet women's films of the 1970s follow a similar plot: the heroine is a fully emancipated, professionally successful woman, married or divorced, usually with children, who realises that she has to pay too high a price for her independence and equality. She loses either her husband or her child and is lonely and unfulfilled.

There are numerous films which propose that love and a family should be a woman's priorities since neither education nor professional success can give her happiness. Some of the better-known films include Kira Muratova's *Korotkie vstrechi* (Short Meetings/Brief Encounter, 1967) and *Dolgie provody* (Long Farewells, 1971), Gleb Panilov's *Proshu slova* (I Wish to Speak, 1975) and, most famously, Vladimir Menshov's *Moskva slezam ne verit* (Moscow Doesn't Believe in Tears, 1979). This film approaches the question of women's rights in Hollywood-style fashion. It attracted eighty million domestic viewers and even won an Oscar (Attwood 1993: 90). The film's narrative epitomises the Soviet dream, but ironically also the American dream, which Lenin pronounced in his famous dictum that every cook is fit to govern. Katya, a woman of provincial origin, a single mother and humble factory worker, is promoted to manager of a large factory. Yet she only achieves true happiness when she meets Gosha, a simple manual worker but a 'real man'. In order to compensate for her husband's professional inferiority, she grants Gosha full patriarchal supremacy at home. The film thus promotes traditional gender roles which had become jeopardised through the 'masculinisation' of women and which had resulted in an alarming drop in the birth rate in the European republics of the Soviet Union. As Lynne Attwood argues in her study *Red Women on the Silver Screen*, the ostensibly anti-feminist message of the *zhenskie film'my* can be largely attributed to the demographic crisis during the 1970s which resulted in a heavily promoted pro-family campaign.[7]

It seems, however, that the ideological agenda of the Soviet women's films is more complex. Many of these films can also be read as a covert critique of the communist ethos of collectivism, which was increasingly perceived as a social system that was insensitive to the needs of the individual. It is certainly no coincidence that several of the films' women protagonists hold positions which closely associate them with Soviet officialdom, making them representatives of the system which is ultimately to blame for the collapse of their relationships and their personal unhappiness. Thus the oppressor in these films is not so much patriarchy as the state which insists that the social good always has to take precedence over the personal (see Attwood 1993: 93).

As will become clear in the course of this chapter, the thematic focus of the *zhenskie film'my* is remarkably similar to that of DEFA's women's films made during the 1970s and 1980s. Both East German and Soviet films about women explore the tensions between the common good and individual happiness. They aim to stake out a private sphere that is beyond the intervention of the state and the excessive demands of the collective. They advocate that women – and by extension all members of society – should be given the freedom of self-determination.

Whilst the principal agenda of DEFA's films about women from the mid-1960s until the collapse of state socialism and the GDR in the late

1980s was a critique of the relationship between the individual and society, the agenda of West German *Frauenfilme* shifted in the mid-1980s, presumably because their emancipatory mission had largely been achieved. Furthermore, the women's movement experienced divisions, resulting in socialist vs. feminist, reformist vs. autonomous and heterosexual vs. lesbian factions, which marginalised the women's film as a dominant genre (Hake 2002: 165). Thus the different ideological bases and circumstances surrounding the question of women's rights in the East and the West have caused women's films on either side of the ideological divide to be curiously out of step at any one time.

The following close readings of four paradigmatic texts will endeavour to sketch how DEFA films portray woman's role in society, whereby the term 'portrayal' denotes either the representation of what actually existed or, in accordance with the revolutionary romanticism of the Socialist Realist doctrine, the representation of what should be. The oscillating and ambiguous relationship between the individual and the socialist collective, traced over four decades, will emerge as an aspect of particular relevance.

Frauenschicksale (Destinies of Women, Slatan Dudow, 1952): women at work and the warm embrace of the collective

Slatan Dudow's *Frauenschicksale*, DEFA's first 'women's film', combines all the features that characterise the portrayal of women in DEFA films during the 1950s. It harnesses the portrayal of women and women's issues to the wider political agenda of the *Aufbau*, the construction of socialism, and to Cold War propaganda that espoused socialism as the superior political order.

In keeping with the film's propagandist intent and the doctrine of Socialist Realism, which called for the depiction of the typical, all characters are cast as types. Like the heroines of other women's films of the 1950s, such as the war widow Gerda in Joachim Kunert's film with the telling title *Besondere Kennzeichen: Keine* (Particular Characteristics: None, 1956) or the ordinary girl Uschi in *Eine Berliner Romanze* (A Berlin Romance, Gerhard Klein, 1956), the protagonists of *Frauenschicksale* represent the lives of ordinary women, standing for thousands of others. Barbara, Anni and Renate are in search of happiness which, as the film argues, they mistakenly equate with romantic love. All three fall in love with and are deserted by Conny Lohmüller, who epitomises the moral corruption and lasciviousness that is associated with the capitalist West.

Not surprisingly, he lives in *West* Berlin. His favourite motto, 'Man lebt ja nur einmal' (You only live once) encapsulates his hedonism which stands in stark contrast to the future-oriented outlook of socialism.

Barbara, one of Conny's conquests, is an attractive and intelligent law student training to become a judge, who spent most of her youth in a concentration camp during the war. Her high-flying career testifies to the GDR's commitment to women's equality. Anni, a pretty working-class girl, succumbs to Conny's charm and falls pregnant. When she loses her job as a milliner in an elegant fashion shop on West Berlin's Kurfürstendamm she finds herself unable to compete with the thousands of unemployed job-seekers in the West and looks for work in a textile factory in Berlin's 'democratic sector'. Thanks to the excellent childcare facilities provided by this *Volkseigener Betrieb* (socialist corporation) Anni can successfully combine motherhood with a career. Renate's involvement with Conny has the most disastrous consequences: she commits theft and manslaughter and is sentenced to prison. Thanks to Barbara's legal intervention, however, Renate is given the opportunity to work as a day-release prisoner in a metal-processing plant, where she is trained as an engine driver. Not only does she obtain a qualification that will facilitate her reintegration into society, she also meets an honest and unprejudiced steelworker with whom she starts a new life upon her release.

Hertha Scholz, the fourth woman in *Frauenschicksale*, represents a slightly older generation. She is a war widow and concentration camp survivor, who channels her previous political engagement as an anti-fascist resistance fighter in a new direction by campaigning for women's equality. As Conny's positive antipode she, too, acts as an integrative device that provides a tenuous link between the three female biographies of Barbara, Anni and Renate. Hertha is the mouthpiece of the film's educational mission, quoting from some of the most frequently invoked texts on women's equality in the GDR, amongst them August Bebel's *Die Frau und der Sozialismus* (Woman and Socialism): 'Es gibt keine Befreiung der Menschheit ohne die soziale Unabhängigkeit der Frau' (Without the social independence of women, humanity cannot be emancipated).

This plot summary alone leaves no doubt as to the film's propagandist agenda. At the second Party Conference in July 1952, the SED declared the construction of socialism to be the GDR's chief goal, while DEFA's filmmakers were enlisted to capture 'diese aufgehende Sonne der sozialistischen Arbeit, des sozialistischen Bewußtseins in Ihren Scheinwerfern und Kameralinsen' (Axen 1953a: 26) (the rising sun of socialist work and socialist consciousness with your floodlights and your camera

13 Film poster *Frauenschicksale* (Destinies of Women)

lenses). To this end several women's films of the 1950s aimed to educate women about the crucial role they were expected to play in the construction of socialism. *Frauenschicksale* overtly promotes the government drive to recruit women to what were traditionally male domains, such as mining and heavy industry, by showing Renate working at the blast furnace and as an engine driver (Strauß 1996: 58). These scenes in particular betray unmistakable affinities with Soviet films of the Stalinist era in which women are typically depicted in male professions, radiating optimism in the secure knowledge that for the new woman all paths are open. Arguably, the only difference is that Renate, played by the rather glamorous Sonja Sutter, does not run the risk of coming across as de-feminised, which was applauded by one critic who noted with relief:

> Alle Frauen erkennen schließlich, daß ein dauerhaftes Lebensglück nur in der Mitarbeit am großen Aufbauwerk unserer Republik zu erringen ist. Mit der Frage nach dem Glück wird auch die nach der Gleichberechtigung beantwortet. Gleichberechtigung – und doch keine Vermännlichung! (Rostin 1952: 18)

> (All of the women finally realise that permanent happiness can only be attained through participating in the great construction of our Republic. The quest for happiness and women's equality are both accomplished. Women's equality – without masculinisation!)

In addition to being a recruitment vehicle, *Frauenschicksale* promotes a number of other SED policies, including the state's commitment to women's training and vocational qualifications. Although this aspect of women's policy making was only systematically tackled during the 1960s, *Frauenschicksale* makes several references to this target: Renate receives training as an engine driver; Ursel, a minor character and worker in a lightbulb factory, has been selected to go to university; and Barbara graduates from university and attains the socially prestigious position of a judge.

While in Dudow's tendentious film *Frauenschicksale* the opportunities for women's further training are still seen in the most positive terms, in Egon Günther's film *Die Schlüssel* (The Keys), made two decades later in 1972, a more critical view is voiced by the female protagonist and factory worker: 'Wir Mädchen . . . erschrecken zu Tode, wenn es wieder losgeht mit den Forderungen, sich zu qualifizieren' (We girls . . . get terribly scared by all this talk about the need to obtain further qualifications). She believes in the natural differences between people and thus denies the possibility of change and perfectibility, one of the chief credos of socialist society. This is just one of the many signs that the unbridled spirit of optimism that was so palpable in the films of the construction years had been dampened some twenty years down the line.

Hand in hand with this faith in the unstoppable progress of socialism went the stern conviction in the superiority of socialism over capitalism. In true Cold War spirit *Frauenschicksale* sharply contrasts the decadence and debauchery of the West with the progress and productivity of the East. One memorable montage sequence in particular encapsulates the film's unequivocal ideological position. The first scene shows Conny and his aristocratic lover dancing in a West Berlin jazz club. Their bodies shake to the jazz rhythms in uncontrollable convulsions; their faces are distorted. The camera cross-cuts between drawings on the wall, depicting ape-like figures and the dancing couples, thus suggesting that the latter are not really humans any more! The rapid camera movements of this scene stand in stark contrast to the calm flow of the next scene in the steelworks where Renate is employed. The music, a female choir singing 'Das Lied vom Glück' (The song of happiness), which was written by Bertolt Brecht and composed by Hanns Eisler, is essentially a eulogy of the socialist work ethos and collectivism. It is meant to leave the viewer in no doubt that working in socialist production, melting the iron and contributing to the GDR's industrial growth, is a much greater source of happiness than the shallow amusement offered in the West. Dudow himself commented upon these contrasting scenes, pointing out that the scene in the jazz bar is steeped in 'grünlich-violettes, fast leichenhaftes Farblicht' (green-violet, almost corpse-like coloured light), whereas red-golden hues dominate the factory scene. Whilst the bar represents 'die Untergangsstimmung der kapitalistischen Welt' (the atmosphere of decline of the capitalist world), the site of production stands for the 'gesunden Optimismus einer neuen Welt, wo für das Glück aller schaffenden Menschen gearbeitet wird' (Dudow 1952) (healthy optimism of a new world, where work will result in the happiness of all working people).

The film also promotes the GDR as the land of golden opportunities for women, where they enjoy equal rights with men, where they can find work and gain independence, where being a single mother is no blemish,[8] and where, above all, they can attain happiness in what is presented as the warm embrace of the collective. Dudow stated that the chief objective of this film was the ideological re-education of women who were still prejudiced by bourgeois ideology and were, therefore, unable to see that das Schicksal des einzelnen nicht unabhängig von den gesellschaftlichen Verhältnissen gesehen werden kann . . . Millionen von Frauen, befangen in der bürgerlichen Ideologie . . . führen den Kampf um ein bißchen Glück auf eigene Faust, jede für sich, und glauben so, alle Schwierigkeiten meistern zu können. Und gerade diesen Teil der Frauen will der Film in erster Linie ansprechen und ihnen helfen, sich von ihrem gefährlichen Irrtum zu befreien. (Dudow 1952)

(the destiny of the individual has to be seen in the larger social context. . . . Millions of women, still prejudiced by bourgeois ideology . . . pursue their little happiness on their own, all by themselves, and they believe that they can thus master all of life's adversities. It is in particular this group of women whom I want to reach with this film, in order to help them realise their dangerous error.)

In order to convey this message, Dudow espouses the virtues of life and work in the socialist collective. Not only is the collective presented as a nucleus of socialist solidarity, it also functions as a substitute for the traditional family. Hertha Scholz, for example, accepts her widowhood without grief, for her career as a trade unionist takes up all her time and energy, and for love and affection she goes to the factory crèche, where Anni's toddler son Steff is raised. Hertha always finds time to dispense some maternal affection to the children, who in turn are shown to love and embrace her, having apparently accepted her as their daytime socialist supermum.[9] Similarly Anni, who was ostracised in the West on account of being a single mother, encounters nothing but tolerance and support in the socialist collective, while her son experiences the blessings of a collective upbringing, another social policy promoted by this film.

In spite of the film's obvious propagandist intent and, notwithstanding the fact that it had garnered the director's prize at the film festival at Karlovy Vary and been a major box-office success, *Frauenschicksale* came under vehement attack from the *Demokratischer Frauenbund Deutschlands* (Democratic German Women's Association) and, subsequently, from the Central Committee of the SED. Dudow was criticised for not conveying 'typische Schicksale in typischen Situationen' (Führmann 1953: 137) (typical destinies in typical situations) and thus, by implication, for failing to create role models that would offer templates for social change. Objections were also raised against the character of Conny, the kind of man no socialist woman would fall for. Why did the film eschew the depiction of men who took care of domestic chores while their wives were away on further training courses? In short, the new socialist man was allegedly absent from the screen, whilst the new socialist woman was not true to life (Führmann 1953: 138). Dudow duly responded, expounding on his interpretation of 'the typical' and invoking the authority of Engels, Marx and Hegel to make his point that the typical, without traces of individuality, is lifeless and boring (Dudow 1952).

Dudow, who was revered as the father of German proletarian cinema on account of *Kuhle Wampe oder wem gehört die Welt* (Whither Germany?, 1932), and who had proven his commitment to socialism in two earlier tendentious DEFA films, *Unser täglich Brot* (Our Daily Bread, 1949) and *Familie Benthin* (The Benthin Family, co-directed with Kurt Maetzig and Richard Groschopp, 1950), was spared any negative repercussions. After *Frauenschicksale* he went on to make four more films, yet did not return to the depiction of women's lives until *Christine* (1963), the completion of which was curtailed by Dudow's untimely death in a car accident.

Der geteilte Himmel (Divided Heaven, Konrad Wolf, 1964): woman as allegory of national history

The wholehearted belief in the socialist utopia and the consensus between the common and the individual good that had governed the construction years was indisputably shaken by the erection of the Berlin Wall on 13 August 1961. Ultimately, the Wall signalled the defeat of the socialist system, which was struggling to compete with the allure of capitalist prosperity. Between 1949 and 1961 2.6 million people had left the GDR for the West, depriving the young socialist state of its badly needed labour force. The erection of the Wall was an attempt to stem the flood of fugitives, whilst the official explanation suggested that the Wall, which in GDR-speak was referred to as the 'antifaschistischer Schutzwall' (anti-fascist protection rampart), had prevented a West German invasion and, therefore, marked a historic victory for peace.

One of the immediate effects of the erection of the Wall on East Germany's film industry was that the Babelsberg studio, located just outside the sealed-off Western zone of Berlin, had to make do without the expertise of a considerable number of staff. The response of DEFA's employees was divided: DEFA's *Kampfgruppe* (battle group), a paramilitary unit that was expected to support the state's military action by securing the border, could muster only sixty-two men on 13 August (Feinstein 2002: 124). Morale was low, absenteeism at crucial meetings high. Several studio members refused to sign a declaration of support addressed to Walter Ulbricht, whereas others supported the Party's decisions through agitation and a series of so-called *Mauerfilme* (Wall films), feature films that portrayed the division of Germany in the most positive and partisan terms (see Richter 1994).... *Und Deine Liebe auch* (... And Your Love Too, Frank Vogel, 1962), Heinz Thiel's *Der Kinnhaken* (The Knock-out Punch, Heinz Thiel, 1962) and *Sonntagsfahrer* (Sunday Driver, Gerhard Klein, Karl-Georg Egel and Wolfgang Kohlhaase, 1963) are all more or less propagandist affirmations of the construction of the Wall. As Joshua Feinstein notes, these films look like state-commissioned propaganda pieces, but in fact are a testament to the filmmakers' misplaced idealism, for they were undertaken with little prodding from cultural officials (Feinstein 2002: 126).[10]

Not a *Mauerfilm* as such, for the film makes no explicit reference to the closure of the border, Konrad Wolf's *Der geteilte Himmel* provides a much more balanced and discursive comment on this momentous historical event. Although Konrad Wolf did not intend to make a film about the problems affecting the divided nation, as he commented at the film festival at Karolovy Vary where *Der geteilte Himmel* was shown, he nevertheless conceded that Rita's fate and that of Germany are inextricably intertwined (Traube 1966). The film is based on Christa Wolf's (no relation) novel of the same title, published in 1963, which, following a vigorous debate surrounding its thematic audacity and its subjective and innovative aesthetics, became one of the GDR's canonical texts.

The film script, written by Christa, Gerhard and Konrad Wolf, Willi Brückner and Kurt Barthel, closely follows its literary template. It adopts an a-chronological time structure, which in seven extended flashbacks blends the present, the late summer of 1961, with the protagonist's memory of the past two years. The film attempts – in the words of the director – 'die Wirklichkeit auf zwei Ebenen gleichzeitig wiederzugeben, nämlich auf der Ebene des geistigen Erfassens und auf der Ebene des unmittelbaren Erlebens' (Wolf 1964: 56) (to represent reality on two levels, namely on the level of intellectual comprehension and on the level of immediate experience).

Der geteilte Himmel traces the development and eventual failure of Rita's and Manfred's romance, culminating in Rita's nervous breakdown and suicide attempt. The nineteen-year-old girl from a small village follows Manfred, ten years her senior and a talented graduate student of chemistry, to the big city of Halle. During her summer job in industrial production and her subsequent studies at a teacher training college she learns to reconcile her ideals of socialism with the less than perfect reality. In spite of the setbacks and conflicts she experiences daily, she remains idealistic and is ultimately at one with the collective-orientated culture of the GDR. Manfred, by contrast, is portrayed as a lonely figure whose self-exclusion from the new social order leads to the gradual estrangement of the couple. When one of his inventions is not used for industrial production he becomes so disenchanted with the system that he decides not to return to the GDR from one of his business trips to West Berlin. Rita, who is supposed to join him, is faced with a dilemma which mirrored that of the millions of East Germans who contemplated leaving the GDR prior to the erection of the Wall. In the end Rita forsakes her love of Manfred and returns to the GDR.

In depicting Rita's visit to West Berlin, Konrad Wolf and his cameraman Werner Bergmann sparingly use the clichés that had become customary in DEFA's depiction of the West. Still, West Berlin is rendered as a somewhat inhospitable place with neon lights, sterile architecture and, above all, a mega-size billboard advertising Persil washing powder. The low-angle shot which shows Rita and Manfred in front of the looming billboard is not just a critique of capitalist consumer culture but also an oblique reference to the so-called 'Persilscheine' (Persil certificates), which were issued after the war by Western Allies exonerating many Nazi fellow-travellers without having properly tried them. Nonetheless, the critique of the West is subtle and the film in no way condemns Manfred's decision. In fact the blame for his defection to the West is attributed in equal measure to his individual failure and to the failure of the collective, which did not succeed in finding a suitable role for such a gifted but critical person.

Rita's decision to return to the GDR ultimately affirms the new social order and even suggests that the ties of the collective are stronger than the personal bonds of love. That is why, upon her return and during her convalescence, Rita seeks the support of her fatherly mentors at the factory and the college, upright socialists like Meternagel and Schwarzenbach who, despite some character flaws, can show Rita the way and help her attain the socialist consciousness to which she aspires.

While the thematic correspondences between Rita's private history and Germany's national history are fairly obvious, they alone would not suffice to underpin the claim, made by several scholars, that Rita is an allegorical representation of Germany's history.[11] What legitimises this interpretation is first and foremost an abundance of visual metaphors, which allude to the film's title and construct a syntagma of referents which allegorically intertwine Rita's personal trauma with the national trauma of Germany's division. The montage sequence at the film's beginning is

14 Renate Blume (Rita) and Eberhard Esche (Manfred) in *Der geteilte Himmel*
(Divided Heaven)

replete with images of a sky dissected by towers, smoking chimneys and
a double row of poplar trees shot from a very low angle against the sky.
The screenplay reads: 'Doppeltürme ragen steil in den Himmel und
zerteilen ihn.... Der Himmel eingezwängt zwischen Häuserfronten'
(Double towers jut steeply into the sky and divide it... The sky is
squeezed in between the fronts of houses) (Wolf 1963: 1). These and
further images of a divided heaven, such as the repeated shot of the
motorway bridge that horizontally cuts the sky above Rita's home in half,
function as visual leitmotifs and are invariably linked to Rita's personal
history. Similarly, the attic room, Manfred's and Rita's shared abode in
Halle, has an enormous sky light window, the grid-like pattern of which
dissects the sky. Stating the obvious, these visual leitmotifs are fully explained in a dialogue sequence preceding the couple's inevitable separation in West Berlin. Manfred, looking up at the star-lit sky, remarks
'Den Himmel wenigstens können sie nicht zerteilen' (At least they
cannot divide heaven), whereupon Rita replies 'Doch. Der Himmel teilt
sich zu allererst' (They can. Heaven is divided first).

Ironically, as outlined in Chapter 4, the closure of the border in August
1961 resulted in a liberalised climate which gave the novelist Christa Wolf
and the filmmaker Konrad Wolf the leeway to explore taboo topics and
aesthetic conventions that tested the limits of what might be tolerated.
In terms of its aesthetics *Der geteilte Himmel* marks one of the first bold
attempts to incorporate the impulses of modernism and the French

nouvelle vague into socialist film art. Wolf's film represents the beginning of East Germany's nascent New Wave that was crushed at the Eleventh
Plenum just over a year later. *Der geteilte Himmel* has been compared
to Alan Resnais' *Hiroshima mon amour* (1959) (Byg 1992; Feinstein 2002:
110–36; Wolf and Gregor 1966: 336), a prototype of modernist film
aesthetics. Both films intertwine the personal history of a woman with
a momentous historical event that deeply affects the female protagonist;
both films employ female subjectivity (constructed by men) as an integral narrative device that propels the narrative forward; and finally, both
films render the theme of memory through abundant use of flashbacks
and elliptical editing.

In the GDR the modernist aesthetics of *Der geteilte Himmel* were, to
say the least, controversial. In particular, it was feared that the complexity
of the montage sequences and the achronological time structure would
make the film inaccessible to a wide audience and thus undermine
the mass appeal that film was supposed to have (Karl 1964). Proving the
functionaries wrong, the film was tremendously successful in the GDR
where it was seen by over 1.5 million viewers during the first year of
its release (Quett 1986: 180). In West Germany it also received considerable attention on account of its daring attempt to deal with such a
sensitive topic. Hans Helmut Prinzler, one of West Germany's most
renowned film scholars and critics, praised it as the 'ersten Ernst zu
nehmenden Versuch, das nationale Bewußtsein des Ulbricht-Staates in
einem Film zu formulieren' (cited in Roos 1964) (as the first serious
attempt to express the national consciousness of the Ulbricht-state in a
film).

Clearly, *Der geteilte Himmel* is not a women's film in the sense
defined above. Instead it utilises a woman as a historical allegory that
mirrors and affirms the GDR's redefined national identity. The construction of the central character, Rita, is comparable to that of Klavida,
the female Red Army Commissar in Aleksandr Askoldov's *The Commissar*,
one of the most widely-cited examples of female allegory in film history.
Klavdia, too, renounces her personal desires, when she leaves her new-
born son with Jewish foster parents in a small village in order to return
to her battalion and serve the revolutionary cause of the Civil War. She
sacrifices her personal good in order to change the path of history.
However, heroic as Klavdia's decision may seem, it is at the same time
morally ambiguous since it entails the cruel and unnatural act of abandoning her baby, thus calling the ethics of revolution into question (see
Stishova 1993: 181).[12]

By demonstrating an unqualified commitment to a shared higher mission to which they feel destined to contribute, both heroines suffer from an existential crisis that is inextricably linked to a historical caesura – in Rita's case the erection of the Wall and the German nation's ensuing political and identity crisis. As was pointed out when the film was discussed at the Academy of Arts, Rita's biography embodies both the trauma of division as well as the rebirth of the GDR as an increasingly autonomous German state:

> Der Widerspruch zwischen beiden Gesellschaftsordnungen auf deutschem Boden geht mitten durch ihre [Ritas] Liebe hindurch. . . . Die Kraft zur Überwindung ihrer eigenen Konflikte schöpft Rita aus der Erkenntnis: Die Lösung der Widersprüche zugunsten des Sozialismus und der DDR ist eine Lösung zugunsten des Menschen und des Menschlichen, des Lebens und der Zukunft. Wir werden mit der Erkenntnis und Gewißheit aus diesem Film entlassen, daß zwar eine Liebe sterben mußte, weil sie das Leben zu leicht befand, daß aber ein neuer Mensch geboren wurde. (Dahlke 1964: 18–19)

> (The contradiction between the two social orders on German territory goes right through her [Rita's] love. . . . Rita derives the strength to overcome her own conflicts from the insight that the resolution of these conflicts in socialism and in the GDR is a resolution in favour of human beings and humanity, of life and the future. The film dismisses us with the insight and conviction that admittedly, a love had to die, because it was too lightweight to survive, but a new human being was born.)

In spite of the optimistic pathos that was officially ascribed to Wolf's film it heralds the disappearance of the happy end for the majority of DEFA films to come, in particular for films about women. Against the fully-fledged utopia of the construction films of the fifties, the utopian dimension of *Der geteilte Himmel* already shows first cracks: sacrifice and trauma are the price to pay, not just for Rita, but for all those Germans who had chosen to stay in the GDR because they believed that this was the better Germany.

Die Legende von Paul und Paula (The Legend of Paul and Paula, Heiner Carow, 1973): a plea for individual self-realisation

Paula, the heroine of Heiner Carow's East German cult film *Die Legende von Paul und Paula* is the complete opposite of Rita: to her, love means everything and she locates the source of happiness exclusively in the private sphere. Although in many respects she represents the typical GDR

woman, being a single, full-time working mother, her daily life is largely
untouched by the opportunities which socialist society held in store for
women of her generation. The kind of ideological conflict that deeply
affects Rita's life is of no concern to Paula – a woman of an entirely different intellectual make-up. She earns her living as a sales assistant at
the bottle deposit counter of a supermarket with no interest or energy
to spare for politics, social engagement or further training. In short, Paula
is anything but the socialist female role model that was advertised in other
DEFA films at the time.

For instance, *Das siebente Jahr* (The Seventh Year, Frank Vogel,
1969) and *Liebeserklärung an G. T.* (Love Declaration to G. T., Horst
Seemann, 1971) portray what was in reality the exception rather than
the rule: women with intellectually challenging careers whose professional
success is complemented by a happy family life. Admittedly, both
Barbara in *Das siebente Jahr* and Dr Gisa Tonius in *Liebeserklärung an
G. T.* are struggling to reconcile their demanding careers as heart sur-
geon and as leader of a prestigious scientific research project with their
roles as (step)mothers and wives. Both films concede that women have
to work harder than men to achieve top positions. And yet they validate
the ambitious *modus vivendi* of their heroines by contrasting their lives
with alternative female biographies: the masculine spinster who has
dedicated her entire life to science; the Russian scientist who sees her
husband only once or twice a year; or the beautiful wife and homemaker
who idles her days away – all of which are presented as lacking. In promoting the ideal of the socialist superwoman these films are set in the
realm of socialist fairy-tale land and are truly the last DEFA films to
portray women who can have it all.

Against this background the title heroine of *Die Legende von Paul und
Paula* is a novelty that would set the agenda for women's films of the
1970s and 1980s. The female protagonist with a respectable profession
is replaced or at least joined by protagonists with far more modest
occupations: sales assistants (*Bis daß der Tod Euch scheidet*/Until Death
Do Us Part, Heiner Carow, 1979); manual workers in a lightbulb factory
(*Die Schlüssel* and *Alle meine Mädchen*/All My Girls, Iris Gusner, 1979);
and unskilled workers (*Das Fahrrad*/The Bicycle, Evelyn Schmidt, 1982
and *Bürgschaft für ein Jahr*/On Probation, Herrmann Zschoche, 1980),
whose daily lives are drudgery and who live on the margins of social
respectability.

DEFA's women's films of the 1970s and 1980s break new ground,
thematically and aesthetically: the female role-model joins ranks with the

social misfit and rebel; documentary realism, a style that had still been deemed highly objectionable when Böttcher's *Jahrgang '45* (Born in '45, 1966/90) was banned in the mid-sixties, now becomes an acceptable and widely used inflection or even transgression of Socialist Realism. The semi-documentary mode adopted in particular by DEFA directors of the third generation such as Lothar Warnecke, Rainer Simon and Roland Gräf pays tribute to the dictum of the Italian Neo-Realist Cesare Zavattini that each trivial moment of everyday existence is infinitely rich. This stylistic and thematic turn also explains the dominance of female subjectivity and female protagonists during the 1970s and beyond, when the *Gegenwartsfilm* (literally: film about the present day) became superseded by the *Alltagsfilm* (film about everyday life). In his study *The Triumph of the Ordinary* Joshua Feinstein argues that the *Gegenwartsfilm* 'implies a strong sense of historical progression' and a forward-moving society, whereas the *Alltagsfilm* 'emphazises ahistorical existence, the diurnal' and a static society, thereby reflecting the Party's 'toning down [of] its millennialism' which occurred by the 1970s (Feinstein 2002: 6–7).

The gritty realism of many of these *Alltagsfilme*, which openly address social problems and contradictions and abandon the ever-optimistic faith in a perfectible society, was officially licensed by Erich Honecker shortly after he had replaced Walter Ulbricht as First Secretary of the SED in May 1971. He encouraged artists to explore new creative paths by employing a broadened range of artistic modes of expression. At the fourth convention of the Central Committee of the SED in December 1971, Honecker made a pronouncement that was to be one of the most-quoted in the history of the GDR:

> Wenn man von der festen Position des Sozialismus ausgeht, kann es meines Erachtens auf dem Gebiet von Kunst und Literatur keine Tabus geben. Das betrifft sowohl die Fragen der inhaltlichen Gestaltung als auch des Stils – kurz gesagt: die Fragen dessen, was man die künstlerische Meisterschaft nennt. (cited in Jäger 1995: 140)

> (Provided one starts from an established socialist standpoint, there cannot, in my opinion, be any taboo subjects for art and literature. This concerns issues of both content and style – in short: all issues relating to artistic mastery.)

Honecker's statement by no means signalled that the Party leadership had abandoned the aesthetic doctrine of Socialist Realism. It had simply renounced the tenet that it represented a coherent artistic style. The Party's insistence on the artists' *Parteilichkeit* (partisanship), however, remained uncontested. Nevertheless, Honecker's pronouncements ushered in a period in which the limits of the artistically permissible were expanded.

It was in this climate that films like *Der Dritte* (Her Third, Egon Günther, 1971) and *Die Legende von Paul und Paula* were made. And badly needed they were, too, since box-office figures for DEFA films had been steadily declining since the mid-1950s, making the GDR's film industry a loss leader that relied heavily on state subsidy for its continued existence (Otto 2001). The *Gegenwartsfilm*, which had been introduced as an antidote to this trend in the early 1960s, had not proven successful, mainly because the Eleventh Plenum had signalled that authentic films, which cast a critical light on contemporary society, were uncalled for. Consequently, the *Gegenwartsfilme* made during the latter years of the Ulbricht regime had reverted to the portrayal of unrealistic heroes, one-dimensional textbook models that were lifeless, gross over-simplifications of the socialist personality and, therefore, failed to inspire audiences.

With *Die Legende von Paul und Paula*, the film director Heiner Carow and the scriptwriter Ulrich Plenzdorf wanted to buck this trend by making a film that would be a major box-office hit.[13] The formula for their success included two ingredients: the creation of a heroine who was a far cry from the ideal of the socialist personality, a 'real person' with whom the audience could identify; and the transgression of the by then customary gritty documentary realism through fantasy, which the narrative form of the legend afforded.[14]

The film tells the story of Paula (starring Angelica Domröse in her break-through role), a twenty-three-year-old single mother of two children from two different fathers, who yearns for a life beyond the daily routine of monotonous work, childcare and sleep. The only escape from this drudgery she can conceive of is finding true love. However, the persistent courtship of her elderly suitor, 'Reifen-Saft', a small-time entrepreneur who could offer her and her children a comparatively prosperous standard of living, is ill-suited to make this dream come true. Then Paula meets Paul, played by Winfried Glatzleder, and falls in love with him. Paul, who lives just across the road from Paula, belongs to an entirely different social class. As a government official he enjoys numerous privileges, including a car and a comfortable flat in a modern apartment block. Yet on a personal level his life is far from perfect. His wife betrays him constantly and is primarily interested in the material gains this marriage affords her. Entrapped behind a façade of social obligations and conformity, Paul lacks the courage to leave his wife and son to be with Paula. When Paula's little son tragically dies in a car accident, she

15 DEFA's cult film *Die Legende von Paul und Paula* (The Legend of Paul and Paula), starring Angelica Domröse and Winfried Glatzleder

superstitiously interprets his death as a punishment for her adultery and ceases all contact with Paul. This results in a dramatic change in Paul's behaviour: no longer concerned about the adverse effects which a divorce might have on his career, he now pursues Paula passionately. Day and night he camps outside her flat, sleeping on a copy of the Party newspaper *Neues Deutschland*, until finally he decides to axe down the door to Paula's flat. Paula accepts him back with a passionate embrace. But the film does not end with what would constitute a traditional happy end. Instead, Paula soon finds herself pregnant and is faced with the decision of having Paul's baby – and in all probability dying in child-birth – or forsaking what is essentially the embodiment of the absolutism of her romantic love of Paul. She takes the risk and dies.

The film's end is, however, not a sad one. According to Plenzdorf, Paula's sacrificial death transforms the depressing outcome of the authentic case on which the film is based into a legend.

> Die Geschichte ist bis zu einem bestimmten Punkt authentisch. Nur wenn man sie so erzählt hätte, wie sie wirklich verläuft, wäre sie absolut de-primierend gewesen, demprimierender als es Paulas Tod ist. Sie geht so aus, daß sie den Reifen-Saft geheiratet hat. Das finde ich hoffnungsloser als unseren Schluß, der die Sache überhöht. (cited in Sylvester and Lohmann 1973: 34)

> (Up to a point the story is authentic. However, if we had told what really happened, it would have been absolutely depressing, much more depress-ing than Paula's death. The story ends with her marrying Reifen-Saft. This is much more hopeless than our end, which transfigures the matter.)

The film elides the compromise and shabbiness of real life, celebrating instead the absolutism of true love. Paula thus attains the stature of a legendary saint, who fought and died for her belief.

Die Legende von Paul und Paula is an uncompromising plea for the right to individual self-realisation and the pursuit of happiness in the private sphere. In the film's most memorable scene, a fantasy episode during which the couple indulge in an opulent feast of food, wine and sex in Paula's flower-decorated bedroom, Paula takes care to shut out any traces of the outside world. Upon his arrival she makes Paul swap the uniform of his 'Betriebskampfgruppe' (a paramilitary unit at his place of work) for just a garland of yellow flowers, evoking clichéd notions of South Sea island utopias. When, intoxicated by wine, Paul hallucinates that two of his colleagues, in Mafiosi suits, have intruded and are spying upon him, Paula reassures him that they cannot see because they are blindfolded. Whereupon, in a highly surreal scene, Paul's two colleagues from the ministry are transformed into a blindfolded musical band accompanying Paul and Paula's love-making with dissonant percussion.

In contrast to many other DEFA films, including Carow's film *Bis daß der Tod Euch scheidet*, where work colleagues offer support when the couple's marriage is in trouble, here representatives of the socialist collective are satirically portrayed as intruding into the lovers' private sphere. Worse still, this scene is 'a surrealist allusion to the omnipresence of surveillance in the GDR where even intimate relationships were a matter of social relevance subjected to public scrutiny' (Rinke 2001: 135).

What follows is an extended dream sequence showing Paul and Paula in their bed on an old wooden boat floating down a river, which is intercut with close-ups of Paula's face, Paul's naked back and other parts of the lovers' bodies making love in Paula's bedroom. The setting of the dream sequence with its phallic factory chimneys and the thumping rhythms of a rock song with the crudely suggestive lyrics, 'Geh zu ihr und laß deinen Drachen steigen' (go to her and let your kite fly high) underscore the overt sexuality of the scene. Performed by the GDR's most popular rock group, Die Puhdies, this song contributed to the film's cult status, while the ironic intertextuality of this otherwise controversial scene may have taken the wind out of the censors' sails.

Plenzdorf and Carow were fully aware that such an explicit portrayal of sex on screen would be regarded as a decadent manifestation of Western pornography. As if to pre-empt the officials' prudishness, Paul's spying colleagues from the ministry offer a practical solution to this problem. When one of them witnesses Paul and Paula's love-making on the boat, commenting, 'Das ist doch Porno!' (But that's porn!), the other suggests 'Dann guck doch nicht hin' (You don't have to look), while peeping through his fingers. In terms of sexual permissiveness, *Die Legende von Paul und Paula* was a novelty for the GDR, suggesting that the morally liberal attitude that found expression in many films of the East European New Waves, with *Lásky jedné plavovlásky* (A Blonde in Love/Loves of a Blonde, 1965) by the Czech director Miloš Forman being a famous example, had finally reached the last bastion of socialist prudishness. In the GDR, a country with a flourishing nudist culture, the general ban of sex on screen was not primarily directed at the display of naked bodies, but at sex as an uncontrollable and hence potentially subversive force.

Predictably, *Die Legende von Paul und Paula* met with a mixed response from the official and the public side. With more than three million viewers within the first year of its release Carow's film was DEFA's biggest

16 Drifting away from the demands of socialist society, *Die Legende von Paul und Paula* (The Legend of Paul and Paula)

success story (Blunk 1984: 236). Angelica Domröse emerged as a new star; women could identify with her emotional absolutism and thousands christened their baby daughters Paula.

Cultural officials, on the other hand, did not share the enthusiasm of the public. Many were displeased with what was referred to as the GDR's 'first socialist love story' and 'DEFA's first porn film' (Schreiter 1973). The film's subversive potential was ascribed not just to the portrayal of physical intimacy, but in particular to the social isolation of the hero and heroine (Knietzsch 1973), their lack of social commitment and their disinterest in work (Rother 1973) – in short, the triumph of individualism over the demands and the offerings of the socialist collective.

In addition, Paula's death proved controversial. According to the SED's chief ideologue, Kurt Hager, the portrayal of death in art was only acceptable if it was of wider social or philosophical relevance. Thus the deaths of anti-fascist resistance fighters were an acceptable topic of art, whereas Paula's sacrificial death for the sake of romantic love lacked precisely this social dimension. In fact, the film lends heroic stature to an ideologically rather questionable protagonist, whose attempt to find fulfilment in a private niche runs counter to the official view that the happiness of the individual depends on her successful integration into the collective.

While *Die Legende von Paul und Paula* was an exciting novelty in the GDR, in the FRG, where the primacy of love and individual self-determination was nothing new, nobody fathomed its audacity (Jung 1997: 53). The West German filmmakers and critics Sander and Schlesier wrote a long review in the feminist film journal *frauen und film*, maligning *Die Legende von Paul und Paula* as a 'frauenverachtende schnulze aus der DDR' (a misogynist melodrama made in the GDR) and a slap in the face of feminism (Sander and Schlesier 1974: 8). Their criticism not only documents how out of synch women's emancipation was on either side of the ideological divide, but also bears testimony to the divergence of cultural identities in the two German states.

Heiner Carow revisited the theme of women's pursuit of happiness in three of his subsequent films, *Bis daß der Tod Euch scheidet, So viele Träume* (So Many Dreams, 1986) and *Verfehlung* (meaning both Near Miss and Misdemeanour, 1992). *Bis daß der Tod Euch scheidet* is the antipode of *Die Legende von Paul und Paula* in that it argues that love and happiness will be suffocated in an atmosphere of social isolation. With *Verfehlung*, his last film before he died in 1997, Carow tried to capitalise on the legendary success of *Die Legende* by winning over Angelica Domröse, who had left the GDR in the wake of the Biermann affair and had embarked on a successful acting career in the West, to return to Babelsberg and play what is essentially Paula at fifty. Still a child-woman, naïve and passionate, she seeks fulfilment through love. Paul, twenty years on, is played by the West German actor Gottfried John, a familiar face from many Fassbinder films and a more mature, almost-lookalike of Winfried Glatzleder. Only this time love does not triumph over society. The forbidden love of Elisabeth, a cleaning woman in a desolate East German village, and Jacob, a dockworker from Hamburg, is tragically destroyed through the German–German border and a system of all-pervasive surveillance.

Though Paula and her mature counterpart, Elisabeth, are by no means the only DEFA heroines to voice an immoderate plea for individual self-realisation, the only other one that deserves mention here is Sunny in Wolfgang Kohlhaase's and Konrad Wolf's *Solo Sunny* (1980). Sunny, who lives in Prenzlauer Berg, an East Berlin neighbourhood that was emerging as a centre of counter-culture during the 1980s, abandons her mundane factory job to become a singer in a mediocre rock band.

'Man muß doch eine Persönlichkeit sein können, ohne berühmt zu sein' (Why can't one be a personality without being famous), she wonders, thus voicing her desire to be recognised as an individual. Her bohemian life style and her insistence on a 'solo performance' not just on stage but in all spheres of life, mark her as yet another non-conformist individualist who enthused the public and provoked the politicians.

Single mothers on the margin in *Das Fahrrad* (The Bicycle, Evelyn Schmidt, 1982) and in other films of the eighties

With Evelyn Schmidt's *Das Fahrrad*, the protagonists of DEFA women's films are moving down yet another rung on the social ladder. Susanne, a divorced single mother of four-year-old Jenny, is an unskilled worker in her early thirties. She resigns from her lowly job in a bleak factory because she feels suffocated by the monotony and loneliness of her work at a metal-punching machine. In a society that assigned work a prime role in the process of self-realisation, such self-inflicted unemployment constituted a moral offence. Yet things get worse when Susanne can no longer support herself and her daughter and she commits an insurance fraud: she pretends that her bicycle has been stolen in order to claim the insurance money – 450 Marks, the equivalent of an entire month's wages. Meanwhile she embarks on a relationship with Thomas, the socialist version of the knight in shining armour. He has worked his way up and now holds a respectable managerial position as an engineer. Although he is supportive of Susanne on a practical level, on an emotional level he is entirely insensitive to her needs. In a heated argument he blames Susanne for not having achieved anything in her life, whereupon she replies, 'Ich hab Jenny erzogen' (I have brought up Jenny). Thomas dismisses Susanne's greatest achievement, commenting sarcastically, 'Ja, die irgendwann mal klaut' (Yes, who will also steal one day). The implication that Susanne is not fit to be a mother is such a blow to her that she leaves Thomas there and then. The film's final scene shows Susanne, again alone with her daughter, cheering Jenny whom she has successfully taught to ride her bike.

Das Fahrrad is one of the few DEFA women's films that was made by a female director and that overtly engages with feminist issues, namely sexual discrimination and the problems of being a single mother. Amongst the thirty or so feature film directors employed by the Babelsberg studio between 1946 and 1992 there were only three women: Ingrid Reschke, Iris Gusner and Evelyn Schmidt. Compared to West Germany, 'which possesses proportionally more women film-makers than any other film-producing country' (Elsaesser 1989: 185), these figures look unimpressive. However, one needs to take into account that DEFA employed additional female directors in the documentary division, including well-known names such as Annelie Thorndike, Gitta Nickel and Helke Misselwitz, and Bärbel Bergmann and Hannelore Unterberg in the children's film division. In addition, women had a strong input into DEFA's feature film production in their capacity as scriptwriters and as *Dramaturginnen* (dramaturges or script editors, see Chapter 1). Amongst the most prolific dramaturges in the feature film studio were Marieluise Steinhauer, Erika Richter, Anne Pfeuffer and Christel Gräf; women scriptwriters included Helga Schütz, Regine Kühn and Regine Sylvester. Women also shaped the look of DEFA films in that design, make-up, costume and editing were specifically female domains. Interestingly, DEFA women filmmakers and their counterparts in other socialist countries did not feel that the small proportion of female directors – who chose to be referred to by the masculine job designation '*Regisseur*' (as opposed to the female title of '*Regisseurin*' (woman director)) – was due to sexual discrimination, for they considered the tough and demanding career of film director to be irreconcilable with raising a family and, therefore, unsuitable for women (see Frýdlová 1996: 47; Schieber and Berghahn 2002).

Another aspect that makes *Das Fahrrad* stand out amongst DEFA's *Alltagsfilme* is its thematic focus on the joys and constraints of motherhood. Although the majority of DEFA films depicting women feature protagonists who have children, the portrayal of motherhood normally plays a subordinate role. Even in films where issues of parenting give rise to marital conflict (such as *Bis daß der Tod Euch scheidet, Leben mit Uwe*/Living with Uwe, Lothar Warnecke, 1974) the interaction between mothers and children is hardly ever dramatised. In several films children function merely as a potential stumbling block to a woman's successful career. Alla in *Leben mit Uwe* resents the fact that her career suffers as a result of being the main caretaker of the children, whilst her husband can be fully committed to his academic research as a geneticist. Gisa Tonius (*Liebeserklärung an G. T.*) keeps delaying having a baby since motherhood is likely to have an adverse affect on her high-profile career as a scientist. Sepp's mother in *Wenn du groß bist, lieber Adam* (When You Are Grown Up, Dear Adam, Egon Günther, 1965/90) has temporarily suspended motherhood and family life in order to pursue her studies in a city far away from her husband and son. These socialist superwomen are by no means cast as negative examples, yet they draw attention to the price of women's emancipation.

By comparison, the portrayal of single mothers in East German films of the 1970s and 1980s is rendered in far more ambiguous terms. They are a far cry from Anni in *Frauenschicksale*, who encapsulates the officially promoted image of the socially secure single mother who could rely on the patriarchal state for support. Christine, the protagonist of Carow's film *So viele Träume*, is a middle-aged midwife who has brought thousands of babies into the world but who abandoned her own baby daughter when escaping from an unhappy marriage. Nina Kern, a divorced single mother of three in *Bürgschaft für ein Jahr* (On Probation, Herrmann Zschoche, 1981) is too absorbed in her troubled relationships with men to assume responsibility as a mother. In fact, the neglect of her children has been such that they have been taken away from her and put into a home. Arguably, even Paula is rather too preoccupied with Paul and, as a result, unable to give her children the attention they deserve. Her son's fatal accident is the tragic consequence. Christine, another divorced single mum in *Die Alleinseglerin* (Lone Female Sailor, Herrmann Zschoche, 1987) has literally no time to spare for her son, dividing her time between doing up a sailing boat and her academic career.

The troubled state of the average family – in reality as well as on screen – is ironically commented upon in *Die Alleinseglerin* when Christine asks her best friend, 'Sag mal, gibt's denn gar keine glücklichen Ehen mehr, wo sich Mann und Frau lieben und ein Leben lang treu sind?' (Tell me, are there no happy marriages any more, where man and wife love each other and are forever faithful to each other?), whereupon Veronika remarks, 'Die wird's schon geben – und wenn im Kino' (I suppose they exist, if only in the cinema). According to Christine, even that is no longer the case, 'Von wegen. Nur Kummergeschichten' (Not even there. Only agony stories). DEFA *Alltagsfilme* of the 1970s and 1980s denounce the Party-promoted ideal of the happy two-parent family, the nucleus of socialist society, as a fiction that sharply contrasts with the reality of the family in crisis.[15]

In terms of the conventional system of socialist values, the one-parent-family at the centre of *Das Fahrrad* is a representative example of such a family in crisis. And yet the film director, Evelyn Schmidt, and the scriptwriter, Ernst Wenig, take great pains to argue the opposite: this delinquent, impoverished and isolated protagonist is, in the face of all social conventions, a very good mother who always puts her daughter's

17 *Das Fahrrad* (The Bicycle) with Heidemarie Schneider as a mother on the margins of society

wellbeing first. When searching for a new job, she rejects a job offer that entails night-shifts because she is not prepared to relinquish Jenny to a semi-permanent childcare facility over night. In contradistinction to Party policies, which promoted the ideal of the full-time working mother but placed the emphasis on woman's fulfilment through work, Susanne's chosen path of self-realisation is motherhood.

The film's *mise-en-scène* and cinematography underscore the opposition between frustrating work and fulfilling motherhood by typically associating the mother–daughter bond with outdoor scenes, one even depicting a sunlit pastoral idyll, whilst the world of work is rendered in claustrophobic and gloomy terms steeped in hues of bluish-grey. Likewise, the stern face of Heidemarie Schneider, who plays Susanne, lights up when she plays with her daughter or tells her fairy tales. These devices underscore the film's chief social criticism, namely that those who put 'die Qualität menschlicher Beziehungen über reines Leistungsdenken' (Kersten 1982) (the quality of human relationships over an excessive focus on achievement) will be marginalised in society – a society that prided itself on its humanity.

Schmidt also wanted to draw attention to the persistence of sexual discrimination in East Germany's allegedly classless society of equals. A mere glance at Susanne's and Thomas' jobs and their different standards of living, however, suggests that men and women in the GDR were set apart by a gender-biased class divide (see Gerhard 1994; Merkel 1994). The circumstances and setting of the couple's first encounter underscore this message: Thomas celebrates his promotion in the brightly-lit upper levels of the club-house, whereas Susanne's sphere is the dark underworld of the disco cellar below. Whilst Thomas, the successful careerist with a Party badge on his lapel, enjoys the warm embrace of the collective, Susanne seeks comfort and consolation amongst her clique, which is ultimately unable to help Susanne with her problems. Why, one wonders, is the brigade, the concrete manifestation of the socialist collective at the workplace, virtually non-existent in Susanne's life? Is Susanne to blame for her isolation and marginalisation, or has the system failed her? The truth lies somewhere in the middle: as Evelyn Schmidt commented, Susanne has high expectations of society without being able to offer much in return (see Reichelt 1983: 1).

While conceding her heroine's shortcomings, Schmidt also wanted to draw attention to the fact that women were far more likely to be at the bottom of the social hierarchy in the GDR then men. This officially-denied social injustice is also reflected in a number of other films such as *Die Schlüssel* and *Solo Sunny* which highlight the gender inequalities. Only in the fantasy world of *Die Legende von Paul und Paula* can this educational and social chasm be overcome through the power of love.

Predictably, such a high dose of social criticism was not palatable to the political functionaries, in particular at a time when East Germany was encountering a severe economic crisis and political instability, which the government tried to combat with a tightening of control in all spheres.[16] Surprisingly, and despite a number of reservations shared by the studio director, Dieter Mäde, and the HV Film, *Das Fahrrad* was licensed on 25 September 1981. But before the film got into the cinemas, a reader's letter was published as a lead article in *Neues Deutschland* on 17 November 1981 which signalled a change of the cultural climate. In this letter with the title 'Was ich mir von unseren Filmemachern wünsche' (What I wish our filmmakers would do) the disappointed reader, ostensibly a humble car mechanic with the name of Hubert Vater but in all probability Erich Honecker himself, harshly criticises DEFA filmmakers for depicting 'belanglose Problemchen' (insignificant little problems) without any 'gesellschafliche Wirkung' (social relevance), instead of focusing on 'das Titanische . . . der Leistung . . . die in der Errichtung, im Werden und Wachsen unseres stabilen und blühenden Arbeiter- und Bauernstaates besteht' (Vater 1981) (the titanic . . . achievement . . . which the construction, development and growth of our stable and blossoming workers' and peasants' state represents).

The so-called 'Vater-letter' was the death knell for *Das Fahrrad*. Though not officially banned, the film was subjected to measures of severe indirect censorship: its release was postponed until June 1982, when most people were on summer holiday. Without any advertising and low distribution figures, the release of *Das Fahrrad* was barely noticed by the public. Only the scathing reviews in the national press drew some attention to this controversial film (see Knietzsch 1982; Sebe 1982). *Das Fahrrad* had negative repercussions for Schmidt's budding career as DEFA director: she was forced to decline all invitations to present her film at international festivals; the controversy surrounding *Das Fahrrad* nearly resulted in a legal dispute between Schmidt and the studio director Mäde; and though she directed three more films with DEFA,[17] she never made it into the ranks of DEFA's salaried directors on permanent contracts (Schmidt 1993: 131–4).

The loss of utopia: from the collective into the private niche

Having traced how DEFA films portray the shifting relationship between women and society from the 1950s through to the 1980s one cannot fail to diagnose a gradual loss of a utopian vision. In the films of the 1950s, work is presented as the chief place of woman's self-realisation, granting her economic independence and assigning her a central role in the collective project of constructing socialism. The common good and individual happiness are in perfect harmony. Women protagonists in films of the 1960s by and large still share the socialist utopian vision but are painfully aware of the fact that it comes at a high price and requires personal sacrifice. As these films gradually move away from extolling the virtues of collectivism, type-cast protagonists are replaced by individualised characters, often of considerable psychological depth. From the 1970s onwards an increasing number of heroines disassociate themselves from the ethos of collectivism. They withdraw into a private niche, a phenomenon so widespread in the GDR that the term *Nischengesellschaft* (niche society) has been applied to East German society. By investing their energy and enthusiasm in such varied pursuits as cultivating their allotments, participating in church discussion groups, or reading between the lines of literature, East Germans created a sanctuary of 'private authenticity' for themselves that allowed them to adapt to a regime that made a total claim on its citizens (Fulbrook 1991: 309). Yet whilst Paula and Sunny at least personify what Marc Silberman aptly calls 'the emancipatory power of desire' that 'undermines society's rules' (Silberman 1995: 174), the disenchanted heroines of the majority of DEFA's women's films of the 1980s are left without a vision or a mission, alone and untouched by the warm embrace of the collective.

Like in the cinemas of other socialist countries, the portrayal of women's destinies in DEFA films is not first and foremost harnessed to a feminist agenda. In fact, East German filmmakers and their socialist sisters dissociated themselves from the feminist causes that preoccupied feminist filmmakers in the West, campaigning instead for more general humanitarian issues. Since women's changing role within society was considered to function as a highly sensitive seismograph of society's development, female protagonists in East European films are usually instrumentalised in a discourse that critiques society at large. Neither patriarchy nor men were perceived as women's chief antagonists, but rather a totalitarian state that assumed the role of a patriarch oppressing male and female citizens alike. The preponderance of heroines who withdraw into a private niche or who are marginalised by the system in DEFA films of the 1980s is thus a coded diagnosis of the ill-health of socialist society and of the failure of a type of collectivism that was in denial of the needs of the individual.

Notes

1 The term 'women's film' is used here to denote films portraying women or dealing with women's issues and not in the sense of films made for and about women, which are usually ideologically affirmative and melodramatic; see Hayward (2000: 213–27).

2 *Die ideale Frau* lends itself to a comparison with the DEFA film *Bürgermeister Anna* (Mayor Anna, Hans Müller, 1950) that also depicts a female mayor, while *Eine Frau von heute* is thematically very similar to the DEFA film *Ehesache Lorenz* (Matrimonial Matter Lorenz, Joachim Kunert, 1959) in that both films address the threats that women's commitment to their careers pose to married life.

3 Examples include Helma Sanders-Brahm's *Angelika Urban, Verkäuferin, 24 Jahre* (Angelika Urban, Salesgirl, 24, 1969); Claudia Alemann's portrait of female factory workers, *Es kommt darauf an, sie zu verändern* (The Point

Is, to Change It, 1973); and Helke Sanders' *Macht die Pille frei?* (Does the Pill Liberate Us?, 1972).

4 See also Jeanine Meerapfel's *Malou* (1980) and *Im Land meiner Eltern* (In My Parents' Country, 1981) and Marianne Rosenbaum's *Peppermint Frieden* (Peppermint Peace, 1982).

5 The film's autobiographical impetus is underscored by the fact that Sanders-Brahms speaks the voice-over commentary herself, while her two-year-old daughter plays Sanders-Brahms as a small girl. For a detailed analysis of the film see McCormick (1993: 185–206), Kosta (1994: 121–52) and Linville (1998: 41–63).

6 On the role of Soviet women in society and on screen see Navailh (1992), Attwood (1993) and Turovskaya (1993a, 1993b).

7 See also Yuri Yegorov's film *Odnazhdy dvadtsat let spustya* (Once Upon a Time Twenty Years Later/One Day Twenty Years Later, 1980), which rehabilitates the full-time housewife and mother.

8 In order to boost the birth rate and thus counterbalance the demographic effects of the war and migration to the West, the GDR tightened the relatively liberal law on abortion, while at the same time stating explicitly in the *Gesetz über Mutter- und Kinderschutz* (law on the protection of mothers and children) that illegitimate birth was no blemish. Moreover, unmarried mothers enjoyed a number of legally protected privileges.

9 In *Roman einer jungen Ehe* (Story of a Young Romance, Kurt Maetzig, 1952) the collective also functions as a substitute family for Agnes when her marriage goes wrong.

10 Other DEFA films which make the division of Germany and the Wall a central theme are *Geschichten jener Nacht* (Stories of That Night, Karlheinz Carpentier, Ulrich Thein, Frank Vogel and Gerhard Klein, 1967); *Die Flucht* (The Escape, Roland Gräf, 1977); *Das Leben beginnt* (Life Begins, Heiner Carow, 1960); and *Verfehlung* (Near Miss/Misdemeanour, Heiner Carow, 1992). For an analysis of West German films which address the division of Germany, see Aurich (1991) and Kuhlbrodt (1991).

11 See Byg (1992b: 111), who argues that Rita's trauma and fractured identity mirror the trauma of Germany's division. Feinstein (2002: 119) refers to the love story as 'a parable for Germany's division'.

12 *The Commissar* was banned because it critiqued the nation-building myth of the revolution and because of the positive portrayal of the Jewish foster parents.

13 Plenzdorf's main claim to fame at the time was his enormously popular play *Die neuen Leiden des jungen W.* (The New Sorrows of Young W., 1972), about a young drop-out.

14 In its original meaning 'legend' denotes the story of the life of a saint who fought and died for his/her belief. Subsequently its meaning was extended to an unverified popular tale or romanticised myth, often comprising

miraculous and fairy-tale elements about a person who achieved legendary fame. See Blunk (1984: 250–1) and Rinke (2001: 133).

15 Roughly from the mid-1960s onwards, marital conflict, adultery and separation became central concerns in a number of films, including *Beschreibung eines Sommers* (Description of a Summer, Ralf Kirsten, 1963); *Lots Weib* (Lot's Wife, Egon Günther, 1965); *Wir lassen uns scheiden* (We Are Getting Divorced, Ingrid Reschke, 1968); *Spur der Steine* (Trace of Stones, Frank Beyer, 1966/89); *Jahrgang '45* (Born '45, Jürgen Böttcher 1966/89); *Die unverbesserliche Barbara* (The Incorrigible Barbara, Lothar Warnecke, 1977); and *Das Versteck* (The Hiding Place, Frank Beyer, 1978).

16 By the early 1980s the GDR was on the brink of bankruptcy. Due to expensive technology imports from the West, the cost of welfare and subsidies and an increase in oil prices, East Germany had encountered an insupportable level of debt. In addition, international political events contributed to an overall sense of destabilisation in the GDR: the Soviet invasion of Afghanistan in 1979 and NATO's response, as well as strikes in Poland and the massive support of the Solidarity movement were perceived to be threats which the SED tried to counteract with tight measures of internal control. See Rinke (2001: 57–8) and Schittly (2002: 215–21).

17 These were *Auf dem Sprung* (About to Go, 1983), the children's film *Felix und der Wolf* (Felix and the Wolf, 1988) and another film featuring a mother as protagonist, *Der Hut* (The Hat, 1990).

6

German cinema after unification

German unification: one nation, two identities?

At a time when *Ostalgie* (nostalgia for the former GDR) is fashionable and traumatic memories of the last German dictatorship are superseded by a media campaign that transfigures 'die DDR zum lustigsten Diktatürchen aller Zeiten' (Haußmann 2003: 220) (the GDR to the funniest little dictatorship of all times), it is easy to forget how problematic the process of overcoming the past and forging a new German identity after unification has been, and still is, for the new citizens of the Federal Republic. While the *Ostalgie* phenomenon seems to suggest that East Germans are gradually abandoning collective memories of guilt, shame and victimisation, seeking instead a positive identification with their past, they are still fighting not to see those values on which their specifically East German identity was based entirely discredited in the construction of a new all-German identity that centres almost exclusively on West German values.

When, after forty years of division, the two Germanys were reunited, a wave of unification euphoria seized the entire country. But it was not to last long. The East Germans soon realised that in the rush to unification, which had brought them the freedom of democracy coupled with hard currency and instant consumer gratification, they had been unable to foresee the enormous readjustments that would be required of them. What lay ahead was an assimilation process between two very unequal partners: for most East Germans the economic miracle, this time called *Aufschwung Ost* (up-swing of the East), never happened. Privatisation, rationalisation and de-industrialisation in the East led to unemployment levels of around 30 per cent in the new federal states. Although the overall standard of living significantly increased, a considerable wealth gap still separates East and West Germans. Since the Treuhand, the agency in charge of privatising the GDR's entire nationalised economy, did little to ensure that East Germans had the opportunity to acquire ownership of these state enterprises, the economic transformation of the former GDR appears in many respects like the second expropriation of East German citizens. Instead of seizing the opportunity to develop a new system of social, political and economic practices which incorporated the best of the capitalist and the socialist models, reunification in effect amounted to a take-over of the East by the West. While, for the citizens of the old federal states, unification signalled continuity and confirmed the superiority of their political and socio-economic order, for the citizens of the new federal states unification signalled transformation on an unprecedented scale. The 1990 Treaties on Social and Economic Union and on German Unity essentially proposed a systems transfer from the West to the East which implicitly credited the West German socio-economic model with unconditional approval and success, while it devalued whatever achievements and advantages state socialism could boast in one big sweep.

It is not surprising that the union between such unequal partners has resulted in estrangement rather than in a convergence of East and West German identity patterns. The unequal distribution of wealth and power among *Ossis* and *Wessis* (Easterners and Westerners) and the retrospective denigration of everything that forty years of state socialism stood for have resulted in feelings of antagonism and inferiority in many East Germans. What Konrad Jarausch terms 'the symbolic contests over public memory' (Jarausch 1997: 11) signal a further attempt to impose a West German identity upon East Germans: monuments of East German history have been dismantled; countless street names which had been named in honour of communist heroes have been changed, and residents have been excluded from this decision-making process. Invoking the spectre of the GDR's totalitarian dictatorship West German politicians have felt legitimised to rewrite East German history and tradition and thus obliterate key symbols of East German identification (see Welsh, Pickel and Rosenberg 1997: 129–34).

Coupled with such disparities and inequalities between East and West Germans, cognitive distances and stereotyping – the proverbial 'Mauer im Kopf' (Wall in the head) – provide major obstacles to community building and the formation of an all-German identity. To find possible spheres of convergence and commonality is not easy, especially since more recently many East Germans have reacted to the radical transformation of their country and culture by developing a positive identification with certain aspects of the GDR's past, notably a nostalgic memory of the all-encompassing state provision and social security which they now sorely miss (see Flockton, Kolinsky and Pritchard 2000: 11–13).

However, scholars have identified precisely this 'preoccupation with security and stability' (Welsh, Pickel and Rosenberg 1997: 112) as a significant commonality between East and West Germans. The strongest unifying bond between Easterners and Westerners is their 'unequivocal consensus that the economic dimension is crucial to identity building', which suggests that East Germans are ready to adopt the same model of regime identification, one based on economic performance, which West Germans had adopted during the economic miracle of the 1950s (Welsh, Pickel and Rosenberg 1997: 114). That this model proves problematic in the absence of a second economic miracle has become all too clear. Identity convergence based on a shared history, normally a core aspect of national identity, has proved equally problematic, because of the different approaches the FRG and the GDR have taken to coming to terms with the burden of the Nazi past (see Chapter 2). Moreover, forty years of radically divergent acculturation and everyday life experiences have resulted in an estrangement that is not easy to overcome. So what remains as a residue of a shared German identity is 'a sense of cultural community' (Jarausch 1997: 9) and the underlying feeling that unification, at last, has resolved the national issue which had been lingering ever since the end of the Second World War.

If, then, traces of a shared German identity are to be located in a certain cultural commonality, it is worth exploring what impact unification has had on the two German cultures that are still working on becoming one. This chapter sets out to explore how unification has affected East Germany's film industry. What happened to the centralised, vertically integrated system of film production and distribution in the wake of privatisation? To what extent have East German filmmakers succeeded in establishing themselves in the new German media landscape? How do East and West German filmmakers depict post-Wall Germany and what contribution do their films make to the re-fashioning of German national identity?

From mythical film city to media city: Babelsberg

When state socialism in the GDR collapsed and one of the most dramatic and rapid transformations of a country's political and economic system that history had ever witnessed began, DEFA, just like all other state-owned enterprises, was privatised. DEFA's employees soon realised that the blessings of a capitalist economy would not work exclusively in their favour. With mass redundancies looming, they reinterpreted the acronym DEFA, Deutsche Film AG, for the second time. Klering's motto of 1946, 'Diene ehrlich friedlichem Aufbau' (Serve peaceful reconstruction honestly) (Schenk 1993: 80) was replaced by the ominous slogan 'Das Ende für alle' (The end for everyone).

On 17 July 1990 the East German government relinquished control of DEFA and all other sectors of the state-owned film industry,[1] which was put under the trusteeship of the Treuhand. At the time of privatisation the assets of the Babelsberg-based feature film studio were highly qualified staff, the biggest costume and props department in Europe with over a million props, a 46-hectare studio site in a prime location on the outskirts of Berlin and the kudos of the Babelsberg site and name, which was associated with the golden age of German cinema during the 1920s. Even now, at the time of writing, the company logo of Studio Babelsberg Motion Pictures GmbH, as the new studio is called, pays tribute to Fritz Lang's film *Metropolis* (1927), which was also made in the film city Babelsberg in the days of UFA.

The other side of the coin was that DEFA's feature film studio was economically unviable, suffering from over-staffing and an outdated infrastructure in need of rationalisation and modernisation.[2] On 25 August 1992 the studio complex at Babelsberg was sold to the Compagnie Immobilière Phénix Deutschland GmbH (Phoenix Real Estate Company Germany) for 130 million DM.[3] CIP was supposedly a fully-owned subsidiary of CGE, Compagnie Générale des Eaux (subsequently Vivendi Universal), which had emerged as the favoured buyer because, in addition to being a consortium engaged in French water supply, urban development and real estate, it had a stake in the pay television channel Canal Plus, owned the Paris-based film studios Boulogne and Billancourt and could therefore claim relevant expertise in the film industry (Dalichow 1994: 347). Moreover, CIP joined forces with a business partner with multi-media expertise: the Bertelsmann Group, at the time the largest media conglomerate in Europe and the second largest, after Time Warner, in the world (Sandford 1995: 217). Through these business relations, CIP's investment in the DEFA studio complex promised to vouchsafe the continuation of a flourishing film industry on this historic site.

As there were rumours at the time of the deal that the new owners were primarily interested in the valuable real estate of the Babelsberg site (see Weishaupt 1993; Wenk 1997), a clause in the contract ensured that Babelsberg would stay in the business of film production. CIP was contractually bound for ten years to use two-thirds of the studio complex for film and television productions, develop a state-of-the-art European media centre, and to keep 750 of DEFA's remaining staff at least until 1994, while at the same time creating new jobs for a total of 3,500 employees in Babelsberg by 2002.[4] The contract further stipulated that CIP would have to invest 410 million DM, of which 60 million was earmarked for film production and 150 million DM for studio maintenance over a period of three years (Weishaupt 1993). The federal state of Brandenburg and the German government also heavily subsidised the Babelsberg venture in an attempt to create attractive business and employment opportunities in the region.

By 2002 a thriving media city had developed. The Babelsberg site had become home to over one hundred firms and numerous institutions related to the film sector, including the Babelsberg Film and Television Academy Konrad Wolf, the Filmboard Berlin-Brandenburg and the regional television station ORB. The most lucrative business of the media city is the Babelsberg Studio Tour, essentially a theme park that successfully exploits the Babelsberg heritage, attracting nearly half a million visitors per year. Yet film production is no longer the core business of Babelsberg. What generates profits are television productions and the vast array of post-production and new media services offered at Studio Babelsberg.

When the West German film director Volker Schlöndorff was appointed Artistic Director of the new Babelsberg Studio, he had visions of creating a Hollywood in Europe. His dream never came true, for instead of developing a new creative centre of German or European film production, the studio's management strategy was to create state-of-the-art facilities in order to attract international big-budget productions. But European films typically do not command big budgets and Hollywood did not see the need to come so far to produce films in a foreign-language country with high wages. In the competition for Hollywood runaway productions the Prague-based Barrandov film studio emerged as the undisputed winner on account of its excellent facilities and its competitive prices (Iordanova 2003: 26).

By 1997, when Schlöndorff relinquished his post as Artistic Director, it had become apparent that the former myth of Babelsberg could never be revived. Taking stock, Schlöndorff conceded that in the three years between 1992 and 1995 just seventeen feature films had been produced, only slightly more than the *annual* output of DEFA's feature film studio. None of these had been a success, including his own film *Der Unhold* (The Ogre, 1995), which proved a critical and commercial disaster. The studio's high-point came in 2000 when Frenchman Jean-Jacques Annaud shot his 80-million-dollar Stalingrad epic, *Duel – Enemy at the Gates*, at Babelsberg. Though a flop with critics at the International Film Festival in Berlin, the film was a box-office hit in the US and in this respect just the kind of good publicity the studio badly needed. The merger between Vivendi and Hollywood Universal Studios in summer 2002 (Schayan 2001: 46) attracted further foreign productions, including István Szabós's *Taking Sides* (2000) with Harvey Keitel, and Roman Polanski's *The Pianist* (2002), both of which enjoyed considerable critical acclaim.

Yet these commercial successes could not be perpetuated. In order to stay economically viable, the loss-making Babelsberg studios had to focus increasingly on television productions, in particular lucrative soaps and chat shows. However, even in the television sector competition from studios in Hamburg, Cologne and Munich is fierce. The future of film production at Babelsberg remains uncertain: at the end of 2002, Vivendi Universal, the new owner of the media city Babelsberg, was 35 million Euros in debt, and at the time of writing Studio Babelsberg has not succeeded in establishing itself in Germany's struggling film industry. Still, when the ten-year period during which CIP and subsequently Vivendi Universal was contractually bound to keep the Babelsberg Studios came to an end in 2002, to everyone's surprise the debt-laden conglomerate declared that it had no intention of selling the loss-making studios. Nonetheless, the prospects for Babelsberg are bleak, or as Bärbel Dalichow put it, 'Ein drittes Leben der Filmstadt Babelsberg ist unwahrscheinlich, aber nicht ausgeschlossen' (Dalichow 1994: 353) (A third life for the film city of Babelsberg is unlikely, but not impossible).

The changing media landscape

The asymmetries that pertained to the process of reunification as a whole were also apparent in the pattern of changes in East Germany's media landscape. The centralised, vertically integrated system of film production, distribution and exhibition was dismantled and replaced by the decentralised structure of West Germany's ailing film industry. East German television DFF (Deutscher Fernsehfunk) was incorporated into the federal structure of West Germany's public service television network. Both measures ensured that East Germans were henceforth better integrated into the media culture of the new Germany, but also implied that East Germans had to abandon vital aspects of their own media culture.

As a result of the privatisation of cinemas in the new federal states, nearly half of the eight hundred cinemas were gradually closed down, in particular those in small towns (Klingsporn 1991: 795; Hennings 1993). This massive closure severely diminished local access to what used to be a prime leisure activity in particular for young people in the East. The majority of the remaining cinemas were taken over by West German cinema chains, which modernised them or turned them into multiplexes. The change in cinema ownership had significant repercussions for the type of films that were shown. Whilst in the past DEFA productions had been promoted through centrally-devised programming policies which ensured the high visibility of the GDR's national film culture across the country, this form of artificial protection no longer existed after the privatisation of the cinemas. Suddenly German films faced unmitigated competition from Hollywood blockbusters. As Leonie Naughton poignantly states in her study of post-Wall cinema, by the time DEFA's last films reached the film theatres, 'cinema owners had realized that they could make more money selling popcorn than from screening DEFA films' (Naughton 2002: 67). When the West German currency was introduced and state subvention of cinema tickets was abandoned, ticket prices surged from 0.25–0.50 Marks for children and 1.50 Marks for adults to DM 6 (Wiedemann 1991: 81), making a visit to the cinema an almost unaffordable luxury for many East Germans at a time when they were facing major economic insecurities. The prominent role which cinema had been accorded in the GDR was further eroded by the abolition of the so-called 'Landbespielung' (film screenings in rural areas), run by itinerant projectionists, and the disbanding of hundreds of film clubs,[5] while alternative forms of film distribution such as video, DVD, cable and digital television also took their toll.

The general transformation of East Germany's cultural economy from a cultural economy of shortage, lacking amongst other things a developed entertainment industry, to one of hitherto unknown variety further contributed to audience decline. If one gives credence to the GDR's centrally collated audience statistics, in 1988 East German citizens went to the cinema four times a year on average (as often as Americans), but by 1992 this figure had dwindled to just one visit per year (Klingsporn 1991: 794; Naughton 2002: 74).[6] The films they went to see were no longer indigenous productions or imports from other Soviet bloc countries, which had accounted for 74 per cent of all new releases in the GDR in 1987 (Wiedemann 1991: 86), but recent West German releases and a flood of Hollywood films.[7]

Not only did East Germany's film industry lose most of its domestic market, it also lost its key export markets in Eastern Europe: the collapse of communism and the abolition of a centralised management of culture across Eastern Europe meant that the agreements which had regulated cultural exchange, including film import and export, became invalid. Moreover, the introduction of the Deutschmark made licences for East German films uncompetitive and the new private distributors in former Soviet bloc countries favoured Hollywood mainstream cinema anyway. What was worse, the market in the old federal states remained largely impenetrable. Since the 1980s, Hollywood films have accounted for around 80 per cent of all box-office receipts, leaving only a small share for other foreign imports and domestic productions. Moreover, West German audiences had traditionally shown little interest in the film culture of their brothers and sisters on the other side of the Wall, and unification did not spark a sudden interest in films made in the 'other' part of Germany. To date the only East German film that has appealed to audiences in the old and the new federal states alike has been Leander Haußmann's *Ostalgie* comedy *Sonnenallee* (Sun Alley, 1999).

This asymmetry in the orientation towards each other's film and media culture had been a prominent feature throughout the years of division. During the 1970s and 1980s, for example, West Germans showed more interest in film imports from such foreign and remote cultures as Hong Kong and Japan than in films made by their close neighbour across the Wall (Naughton 2002: 71). Similarly, those viewers in the West who could receive East German television dismissed it as sheer propaganda – which to a large extent it was – and hardly ever tuned in. By contrast, those 80 per cent of East Germans capable of receiving West German television avidly watched 'the class enemy's' current affairs, news and entertainment programmes. West German television had thus provided not only a window in the Wall but had played a crucial role in binding the German nation together. However, when the centralised East German broadcasting services DFF (Deutscher Fernsehfunk) were dismantled and were 'fully restructured in accordance with the federal West German pattern' (Sandford 1995: 204), a majority of East Germans deplored the loss of a platform that reflected a specifically Eastern perspective. As Naughton rightly notes, the decentralisation of East

Television and the dominance of West German public broadcasters in the new federal states 'entailed the erasure of a further component of GDR screen culture' (Naughton 2002: 79) in that it expedited the further disintegration of East Germany's film industry.

DFF had been DEFA's most important client, commissioning around thirty films for television per year, worth around 42 million Marks.[8] When DFF was absorbed by West German public service television these commissions and contracts were not resumed, resulting in staff losses at DFF and DEFA. Although the establishment of the regional channels ORB (Ostdeutscher Rundfunk Brandenburg) and MDR (Mitteldeutscher Rundfunk), which jointly serve four of the five new *Länder*, has somewhat softened the blow, there has, nevertheless, been 'a sharp drop in eastern content and eastern-based production' (Naugthon 2002: 87). These broadcasters now provide the chief outlet for DEFA's repertoire of films which rarely make their way onto the big screen (Haase 2002).

Undeniably, the dismantling of the former GDR's centralised film industry and its broadcasting services has significantly curtailed the spaces in which East German film and television makers can articulate the experience of unification from their vantage point. Given that, in terms of demographics and media policies, the Eastern point of view is critically disadvantaged, the gains achieved through the newly found freedom of expression have been severely compromised through the concurrent losses in a hotly contested media landscape, in which Western corporations and voices have emerged as the clear winner.

Filmmakers' struggle for artistic survival

When in autumn 1989 the newly installed minister of culture, Dietmar Keller, granted all sectors of culture autonomy from state control, DEFA's filmmakers were exhilarated by the prospect of being able to make films without having to worry about censorial interference. Although nominally the HV Film continued to exist until March 1990, when it was transformed into the department of film and video in the GDR's Ministry of Culture, the GDR's last film minister, Horst Pehnert, and other cultural functionaries relinquished their posts in November 1989. Henceforth films could be produced and distributed without the approval of the HV Film. Better still, the GDR's last government granted DEFA some 18 million DM for the production of eight last films, the so-called *Überläuferfilme* (run-over films, films that had been conceptualised before but were only realised after the *Wende*). Thus the period of transition afforded filmmakers the unique opportunity of still receiving funding from the state without having to conform to its supervisory rigour. When this money ran out the situation changed dramatically. The majority of ex-DEFA personnel struggled to adapt to the unfamiliar and complex conditions of the West German film industry. DEFA's directors, scriptwriters, dramaturges and other artistic personnel had been permanently employed and received salaries even when they did not make films. For most of them the dismantling of East Germany's film industry meant a free-fall from ultimate security to total independence, from the status of a once-revered artist to a nobody. They lacked vital contacts with producers in the West, and independent East German production companies were only gradually being set up. Inexperienced in raising funding, since they had never had to worry about film production budgets, which had been centrally allocated by the HV Film and the studio management, DEFA's filmmakers lost their way in Germany's notorious film subsidy jungle.

Only a handful of DEFA's old guard of directors and scriptwriters succeeded in adjusting to these new conditions (Schenk 1996a/b). Many took early retirement, others work for television. Frank Beyer, best known in the West for his forbidden film *Spur der Steine*, has worked extensively for television since unification. His productions include an adaptation of Erich Loest's novel about one of the centres of the *sanfte Revolution* (Velvet Revolution) in the GDR, the *Nikolaikirche* (Nicolai Church, 1995) in Leipzig, which was subsequently released in cinemas, and *Wenn alle Deutschen schlafen* (When All the Germans Are Asleep, 1994). Like Beyer's Oscar-nominated film *Jakob der Lügner* (Jakob the Liar, 1974), this television production is based on a text by Jurek Becker and depicts life in a Polish ghetto. Egon Günther, who had left the GDR in 1978 and worked in Munich for twelve years, returned to Babelsberg to direct two feature films: *Stein* (1991), a dreamlike parable about the lost socialist utopia, and *Die Braut* (The Mask of Desire, 1998), a film about Goethe's relationship with Christiane Vulpius (see Chapter 3). Roland Gräf and Rainer Simon both made one more feature film, *Die Spur des Bernsteinzimmers* (The Trail of the Amber Room, 1991) and *Fernes Land Pa-isch* (Distant Country Pa-isch, 1993/2000). Heiner Carow, an exceptionally popular director with a dozen feature films to his name, made *Verfehlung* (Misdemeanour/Near Miss, 1991), and thereafter worked for television until his untimely death in 1997. Rolf Losansky successfully continued DEFA's strong tradition of children's films. Several of DEFA's scriptwriters, including Christel Gräf, Stefan

Kolditz, Christa Kožik and Wolfgang Kohlhaase continued to write screenplays for East and West German feature and television productions. Similarly, many East German actors such as Michael Gwisdek, Sylvester Groth, Ulrich Mühe and Corinna Harfouch, to mention but a few, who made a name for themselves through DEFA productions but who were never permanently employed by the studio, successfully adapted to the changed conditions of film production.

For DEFA's *Nachwuchsregisseure* (next-generation directors) the radical transformation of the cultural sphere was a blessing in disguise. If DEFA had continued to exist, they would have had to embark on a drawn-out studio apprenticeship as assistant directors before they would – if they were lucky – have been assigned to their own projects. Instead, the dissolution of the rigid hierarchy in the DEFA studio at the time of the *Wende* resulted in the establishment of an autonomous Artistic Working Group, DaDaeR, in January 1990. The Group is associated with a number of aesthetically innovative or ideologically provocative debut films, notably Jörg Foth's *Letztes aus der DaDaeR* (Last from the DaDaeR, 1990), Herwig Kipping's *Das Land hinter dem Regenbogen* (The Country behind the Rainbow, 1992) and Peter Welz's *Banale Tage* (Banal Days, 1992). After the *Wende* Thomas Wilkening, one of the unit's co-founders, was commercially astute enough to transform it into a limited company, making Thomas Wilkening Filmgesellschaft mbH East Germany's first private production company. Helke Misselwitz's feature film debut *Herzsprung* (Herzsprung is the name of a village, but literally means 'crack in the heart', 1992) and her next film, *Engelchen* (Little Angel, 1996), as well as Kipping's enigmatic artist biopic *Novalis* (1994) were among the first films to be produced or co-produced by Wilkening. Several of the co-founders of DaDaeR have so far also managed to survive in the new competitive climate, which Andreas Kleinert, one of East Germany's most successful young directors, so aptly described in his *bon mot*, 'Besser im Dschungel, als im Zoo' (It's better to be in the jungle than in the zoo') (cited in Dresen and Berghahn 2002).

What the list of these names and film titles suggests is not so much that East German filmmakers have already mastered the art of survival in a hostile climate, but rather that DEFA's demise facilitated a generational change that might otherwise have been impeded by the 'old guard' (see Hochmuth 1994). A similar generational change had occurred in the mid-1980s both in the Soviet and the West German film industries, though the factors that determined these changes were, of course, rather different. The decentralisation of the Soviet film industry after

1986 resulted in a restructuring of artistic hierarchies during which the once revered old guard of directors had to relinquish their privileged positions to hitherto discredited filmmakers (e.g. Kira Muratova, Alexei German, Aleksandr Sokurov) and a new generation of directors (e.g. Vasili Pichul, Rashid Nugmanov, Sergei Selyanov) (Engel 1999: 284–5). In West Germany a new generation of filmmakers came to the fore who rejected the New German Cinema as elitist, economically unviable and intellectually pompous. Like the signatories of the Oberhausen Manifesto in 1962, who had proclaimed the death of the cinema of their fathers, some twenty years later the next generation also turned their backs on 'their fathers', proclaiming the artistically innovative counter-cinema a thing of the past. The course of West German post-war cinema has come full circle: whilst the *auteurs* rejected lightweight entertainment cinema, the next generation considers popular cinema to be the salvation for an ailing film industry (Coury 1997; Rentschler 2000). Their strategy is not unique – national film industries everywhere in Europe try to combat American dominance by replicating the Hollywood success formula. Pan-European film subsidy schemes further promote the development of mainstream European co-productions, which command larger budgets and achieve production values that compare more favourably with Hollywood.[9]

Adjusting to West Germany's increasingly commerce-driven film industry was only one obstacle which East German filmmakers faced. Of equal significance was the fact that audience expectations in the new federal states had changed as the entire cultural sphere underwent a fundamental transformation: entertainment not enlightenment was the order of the day and the majority of ex-DEFA filmmakers were ill-equipped to cater to this new agenda. Genre cinema had never been DEFA's forte (see Chapter 1) and, as the scriptwriter Wolfgang Kohlhaase had already noted in 1977, to beat a capitalist film industry at what it did best would be impossible:

> Wenn wir uns, ob wir wollen oder nicht, mit dem bürgerlichem Film messen, können wir es, wie mir scheint, nicht teurer machen, nicht bunter, nicht nackter, nicht modischer, wir können keine größeren Autos von höheren Brücken stürzen lassen. Was also dann? Vielleicht können wir vor allem eines tun, und niemand außer uns könnte es. Wir können Filme machen, die von uns selbst handeln. . . . Wir können auch im Kino miteinander ehrlich sein. (Kohlhaase 1977: 56)

> (If, whether we want to or not, we try to compete with bourgeois film production, we will never be able to be more extravagant, more colourful, more naked, more fashionable, or afford to let even bigger cars drop from even

higher bridges. So what can we do? Maybe, above all, we can do one thing
which nobody else can do. We can make films about ourselves. . . . And
we can also be honest with each other in the cinema.)

Unfortunately, in post-Wall Germany, even this formula for moderate
audience appeal no longer worked. The transformation of a tightly controlled and supervised socialist public sphere in which art constituted an
intermediary site of oblique criticism into a public sphere in which freedom of expression was a given deprived film of its *Stellvertreterfunktion*
(replacement function) and thus a significant aspect of its audience
appeal. While in the past rumours that the authorities had reluctantly
approved a film's release ensured, if not mass appeal, then at least that
a large share of the educated public would go and see it, the lure of the
forbidden or controversial has lost its magic spell. Thus filmmakers
who continued to use film as a medium to explore the social ills of the
past or the social malaise of the present failed to attract audiences both
in the new federal states and even more so in the old ones. And yet, to
penetrate the West German market where 80 per cent of all German screens
are located has to be the prime objective of any East German filmmaker
who wants to have a presence in the new Germany.

East German filmmakers have a vital contribution to make in assist-
ing both East and West Germans in their search for a new identity that
does not ignore what has been termed *Ostidentität* (Eastern identity) outright. As long as West Germans are not prepared to consider the GDR's
recent history as part of their own, however, and as long as the majority of East Germans are all too eager to remodel their sense of identity
according to Western templates, films of the truth-telling Eastern variety
are bound to struggle. It is thus not surprising that East German filmmakers find it hard to strike the right chord with a recently reunited
German audience.

East and West German cinema in the wake of unification

A comparison between the themes which preoccupied East and West
German filmmakers at the time of unification and throughout the 1990s
suggests that their focus remained predominantly on the social spheres
with which they were familiar and that cinematic explorations of life
beyond the former boundaries of the German–German border was the
exception rather than the rule.[10] The bulk of feature films made by West
German filmmakers are not concerned with the repercussions of unification. The dominant trend of the 1990s was what Eric Rentschler so aptly
calls the 'cinema of consensus' (Rentschler 2000): glossy relationship

comedies set in a middle-class milieu, centring on superficial, resolvable conflicts and promoting a post-feminist agenda which essentially restores traditional femininity and masculinity. The precursor of these lightweight romantic comedies was Doris Dörrie's box-office hit *Männer* (Men, 1985), which was imitated by a vast number of films, including Katja von Garnier's debut film *Abgeschminkt!* (Making Up, 1993); Sönke Wortmann's *Der bewegte Mann* (Maybe . . . Maybe Not, 1994), which even found an audience across the Atlantic; *Das Superweib* (Superwoman, Sönke Wortmann, 1996); Detlev Buck's *Männerpension* (Jailbirds, 1996); and Helmut Dietl's *Rossini* (1996).

Two other prominent themes that preoccupied filmmakers based in West Germany during the 1990s are reflections on Germany's Nazi legacy (see Chapter 2) and films about ethnic minorities, predominantly made by first- and second-generation Turkish immigrant filmmakers.[11] Apart from the fact that Germany's new post-Wall capital, Berlin, emerged as arguably the most-filmed city during the 1990s, the impact of unification is hardly noticeable in films made in the old federal states, thus confirming the asymmetrical impact which reunification has had on the forging of a new German identity.

The limited number of films made by West German filmmakers that focus on the changes in Germany's geopolitical landscape favour satirical depictions ranging from road movie comedies like Peter Timm's *Go Trabi, Go* (1990) and its sequel *Das war der wilde Osten* (That Was the Wild East, Wolfgang Büld and Reinhard Klooss, 1992), or Detlev Buck's *Wir können auch anders* (No More Mr Nice Guy, 1993), to a splatter movie like Christoph Schlingensief's *Das deutsche Kettensägemassaker* (The German Chainsaw Massacre, 1990). The latter is so far-fetched in its critique of unification and its representation in the media that it adds little to the discourse on German nation-building in the wake of the *Wende*. Similarly, the road movie comedies either reinforce stereotypical notions of the 'other Germans' behind the Wall or, like *Wir können auch anders*, take the sting out of East Germany's take-over by Westerners by representing them as Laurel and Hardy lookalikes and harmless dupes. The tenor of the East–West German co-production *Der Brocken* (Rising to the Bait, Vadim Glowna, 1992) is similarly optimistic: while it acknowledges the havoc which the transformation of East Germany's economy has wrought on most communities, leading to unemployment and closure of businesses, it presents the East Germans as highly adaptable to a market economy, even beating the West Germans at their own game.

Only a few West German film productions seriously engage in the realities of unification and post-Wall Germany. Margarethe von Trotta's

Das Versprechen (The Promise, 1994), promoted as a '*Wende* film', resorts
to the melodramatic constellation of two lovers, Sophie and Konrad, who
become separated during their attempt to escape from the GDR but whose
love survives decades of separation, as a backdrop for a history lesson
on the shortcomings of both East and West German societies. While
the West is criticised for its materialism and a consumer culture that
involves the wholesale adoption of American values, the East – and in
particular its intelligentsia – is criticised for its continued conformity to
an oppressive system that revealed its true colours when it condoned
the military suppression of the Prague Spring. The film concludes with
the fall of the Berlin Wall to which Sophie, who has spent the largest
part of her adult life in the West, responds with disenchantment. She
embodies the stance that many East and West German intellectuals,
who had hoped that the Velvet Revolution would result in a reformed,
democratic socialism, adopted at the time.

Even more profound is the disappointment experienced by the protagonist of Oskar Roehler's film *Die Unberührbare* (No Place to Go, 1999)
as she watches televised images of the euphoria sparked by the collapse
of the Wall. The West German novelist Hanna Flanders, based on the
film director's mother and writer Gisela Elsner, picks up the phone to
call a friend to announce her intention to commit suicide. The prospect
of a reunified Germany instils her with horror since it deprives her, a
woman whose fame and fortune have tumbled to rock bottom, of her
spiritual home, an idealised notion of socialism and the other Germany.

Hannes Stöhr is another West German film director who interprets
unification as a deeply disorientating experience – this time for an East
German protagonist. *Berlin is in Germany* (2001) tells the story of
Martin Schulz, imprisoned at the time of the fall of the Wall and
released eleven years later into a world that has changed almost beyond
recognition. His East German identification card is no longer valid;
the Ostmark is no longer legal tender; and even the map of East Berlin
has changed, as Martin realises when, in preparation for an examination to obtain a licence as a taxi driver, he has to re-learn East Berlin's
street names, many of which have been renamed in the meantime in an
attempt to obliterate East Germany's communist heritage. Yet Martin's
dislocation in the new Germany is not presented in gloomy terms. The
film's ending optimistically suggests that he will establish himself in
this transformed society though, significantly, his closest friends and
allies are not West Germans but his former East German wife and
immigrants.

The impossibility of close bonds between East and West Germans is a motif that occurs in many post-unification films made by East German directors, notably in Misselwitz's films *Herzsprung* and *Engelchen* and in Kleinert's *Neben der Zeit* (Outside Time, Andreas Kleinert, 1995). Invariably the female protagonists choose foreign men, originating from Africa, Poland or Russia, as their lovers, never West Germans, thus implicitly making a rather pessimistic comment on the possibilities of German unification on a personal level.

As in other post-communist countries the themes that East German filmmakers tackled, once censorship had been lifted, were the taboos of the past. In East European cinema the early communist years were revisited, looking at issues such as forced collectivisation and the oppression of intellectuals under Stalin. Taboos addressed in films made in the first few years after the *Wende* were the destruction of the environment (*Biologie!* (Biology!, Jörg Foth, 1990); *Abschiedsdisco* (Farewell Disco, Rolf Losansky 1990)); Stalinism (*Das Land hinter dem Regenbogen*); the military suppression of the Prague Spring in 1968 (*Stein, Der Tangospieler* (The Tango Player, Roland Gräf, 1991)); and the all-pervasive surveillance by the Stasi, East Germany's secret police (*Der Tangospieler*; *Der Verdacht* (The Suspicion, Frank Beyer, 1991); *Der Blaue* (The Informant, Lienhard Wawrzyn, 1991); *Abschied von Agnes* (Farewell to Agnes, Michael Gwisdek, 1993)). Above all, East German filmmakers were keen to tell the truth about life in East Germany before and after the *Wende* instead of having to gloss over all those aspects that contradicted the euphemistic representation of the GDR that had hitherto been mandatory. Yet, in contrast to a trend in post-Soviet cinema that has been labelled *chernukha* (literally 'dark stuff'; see Faraday 2000: 176–7) and that also manifested itself in other post-communist cinemas which gorged themselves on the representation of sex, violence, drug abuse, prostitution and other expressions associated with Western debauchery, East German filmmakers by and large eschewed such a voyeuristic and depressing take on social ills.[12]

Still, a sense of gloom prevails in many East German post-unification films, not least on account of the number of violent deaths and suicides occurring. The victims of manslaughter and murder are not just the people who worked for a surveillance system that sowed mistrust and fear, such as the Stasi informer in *Abschied von Agnes* who is thrown out of the window by the man he spied on, or the village mayor in *Verfehlung* whom Elisabeth shoots in an act of despair and revenge. Entirely innocent people, too, like Sophie's Russian lover Sergej in *Neben der Zeit* or

Johanna in *Herzsprung*, fall victim to unpredictable outbursts of violence. The suicides and suicide attempts that occur in numerous films, including *Herzsprung*, *Engelchen*, *Burning Life* (Peter Welz, 1994), *Wege in die Nacht* (Paths in the Night, Andreas Kleinert, 1999), *Verlorene Landschaft* (Lost Landscape, Andreas Kleinert, 1992) and *Bis zum Horizont und weiter* (To the Horizon and Beyond, Peter Kahane 1999), are inextricably linked to the social upheaval brought about by the transformation of the East German economy and of East German society during which thousands of East Germans faced social marginalisation through unemployment and poverty.

It was not until nearly a decade after unification that East German filmmakers were ready to take a more lighthearted approach – if not to post-Wall Germany, then at least to the former East Germany. In 1999 two films were released that reflected the phenomenon that came to be known as *Ostalgie*: *Helden wie wir* (Heroes Like Us, Sebastian Peterson) and *Sonnenallee* (Sun Alley, Leander Haußmann), to be discussed in more detail later on. The resounding commercial success of *Sonnenallee*, which attracted over 2.6 million viewers, suggests that people had had enough of gloomy films about the East and that the time had come to reveal the comical side of life under communism.

The most successful *Ostalgie* comedy to date, however, *Good Bye Lenin!* (*Goodbye Lenin!*, 2003), was made by a West German director and scriptwriter team, Wolfgang Becker and Bernd Lichtenberg. The film tells the story of twenty-two-year-old Alex and his sister, whose mother, Christiane, falls into a coma shortly before the fall of the Berlin Wall. When she regains consciousness eight months later, her condition is unstable and doctors fear that the shock that the GDR is no more could prove fatal. To save his mother's life, Alex restores the 79 square metre East Berlin flat to its former outdated and tacky East German decor. He also supplies his bedridden mother with Spreewald gherkins and other familiar East German brands that have disappeared overnight from the grocery stores by repackaging foodstuffs into old jars. To keep up appearances, Alex and his friend Denis even recreate the GDR's news programme *Aktuelle Kamera* by transmitting from the room next door a carefully edited video-montage that euphemistically enhances reality. The unprecedented presence of West Germans in the East is explained by the fact that they have become disenchanted with the daily battle for survival in the West and have chosen to emigrate to the GDR. Of course, nowhere does the film seriously claim that the GDR was the better Germany for, like *Sonnenallee*, it presents a self-consciously fictionalised account of the East as it might have been. As Alex explains in the film's voice-over, 'Die DDR, die ich für meine Mutter schuf, wurde immer mehr die DDR, die ich mir selbst gewünscht hätte' (The GDR that I created for my mother increasingly became the one I myself had always wished for).

Good Bye Lenin! marks a breakthrough in the establishment of a unified German film culture. It is one of a small number of films originating in the West that look eastwards and that speak to audiences in the new and the old federal states. Unlike the post-unification comedies about the East made by West German directors in the early 1990s, which are often dismissive of socialist values and condescending in their portrayal of Easterners, this most recent *Ostalgie* comedy is a much more incisive examination of East Germany's everyday culture that culminates in the tacit acknowledgement of the utopian dimension of socialism. *Good Bye Lenin!* is a humorous yet serious attempt to revalidate the specifically East German experience in the construction of Germany's new identity.

The fact that it took ten years or more before *Ostalgie* comedies came to the fore is symptomatic. In many post-communist countries, such nostalgic retrostyle films became extremely popular but generally only after the wave of truthtelling social problem films, made immediately after the collapse of communism, had ebbed away. Their popularity is explained by the fact that they offered audiences a much-needed affirmation of their cultural tradition and thus re-instilled a sense of national pride in people.

In order to understand what contribution East German post-Wall films make to the construction of a new German identity, it is necessary to explore some of the thematic concerns and stylistic trends outlined above in more detail. The following analysis of four representative films examines what images of the new Germany and East–West German relations are projected in these films. What impact has the freedom from state control and the Westernisation of Eastern German culture had on filmmakers' aesthetic sensibilities? Are they looking to DEFA or to Hollywood for stylistic inspiration?

Burning Life (Peter Welz, 1994), or *Thelma & Louise* go East

Burning Life is one of numerous road movies made in the wake of unification. The popularity which this genre enjoyed throughout the 1990s can be attributed to three key factors: the newly gained freedom to travel; the peculiarities of film funding in Germany; and the Americanisation of German culture beyond the former barrier of the Iron Curtain.

Made in 1975, Wim Wenders' road movie *Im Lauf der Zeit* (Kings of the Road) plays with the road movie convention of boundless open spaces by locating the route alongside the German–German border, thus highlighting the limits which this indigenously American genre encounters when being transposed into the German context. The more recent examples of German road movies, by contrast, benefit from the opportunity to cross the frontier of the unfamiliar. Yet a surprisingly small number of post-Wall road movies actually do so. In *Go Trabi, Go*, the Struuz family leave their Bitterfeld home behind to travel via West Germany towards Italy in their Trabi, a quintessentially East German car. In *Wir können auch anders* two dumb and illiterate West German brothers set out to claim the property they inherited from their grandmother near the Baltic Sea. Significantly, these two road movies, alongside *Das war der wilde Osten*, are the only ones in which the protagonists cross what was once the German–German border. In all the other road movies the routes remain confined either to the old or to the new federal states, suggesting that the desire to explore the 'other Germany' is rather limited – an attitude that stands in stark contrast to the actual mass migration of East Germans to the Federal Republic. However, even without encapsulating the spirit of the frontier, commonly associated with American road movies, the sense of freedom and mobility which is celebrated in the post-Wall road movies explains the prominence of this genre at this specific historic juncture.

Cynics on the other hand have argued that it is not so much the *Zeitgeist* but rather the peculiarities of the German film-funding system that have led to the recent popularity of the genre. Since the federal states often act as the chief investors in film projects and regional interest-free loans are awarded on the condition that 50 per cent of the loan is spent in the relevant region, road movies are an ideal vehicle for scooping up funding from several federal pots of film subsidy (see Finney 1996: 118–26; Storm 2000: 24). Hence the recent surge of road movies, criss-crossing Germany from north to south and, albeit far more rarely, from east to west.

'The Yanks have colonised our subconscious', says one of the protagonists in Wenders' *Im Lauf der Zeit*, referring to the Americanisation of West German culture after 1945. It is with this culture of pinball machines, juke-boxes, comics, chewing gum, its myths and image-makers that Wenders has been consistently engaged in his own cinematic oeuvre. He has Europeanised, if not 'Germanified', the American genre of the road movie by significantly introverting the quest motif that fuels the physical wanderings of all itinerant heroes, but nowhere more so than in Wenders' road movies.

East German post-Wall road movies such as *Burning Life* and *Bis zum Horizont und weiter*, by contrast, are much more indebted to the American template than to Wenders' inflection of the genre, featuring outlaws on the run rather than brooding buddies in search of themselves. Moroever, the genre of the road movie was intrinsically alien to GDR culture for it would have painfully alerted everyone to their precarious state of confinement and isolation. Though *Karbid und Sauerampfer* (Carbide and Sorrell, Frank Beyer, 1963) and *Ete und Ali* (Ete and Ali, Peter Kahane, 1985) have occasionally been cited as the East German equivalent of the American road movie, it was not really until the Iron Curtain fell and American culture moved its frontier eastwards that the road movie evolved in an East European context.

Thus Peter Welz's *Burning Life* (1994), the director's first feature after his graduation film at Babelsberg Film and Television Academy, *Banale Tage*, is so unmistakably indebted to Ridley Scott's *Thelma & Louise* (1991) that it is hard to believe Welz's contention that the script had already been completed when *Thelma & Louise* was released in Europe (Lemke and Welz 1993). The two films' similarities in terms of plot, character constellation and ending suggest that director Peter Welz and ex-DEFA scriptwriter Stefan Kolditz tried to copy a Hollywood success formula. Both films re-codify the male gendering of the road movie by assigning the role of outlaws and fugitives to a female couple, who replace the male buddies or heterosexual couples of older road movies. Unlike their famous forebears, such as *Butch Cassidy and the Sundance Kid* (George Roy Hill, 1969) and *Bonnie and Clyde* (Arthur Penn, 1967), Thelma and Louise are not professional gangsters but become outlaws by accident, when Louise shoots the man who is trying to rape her friend Thelma. From that moment on, they are on the run trying to escape the law, committing other crimes on impulse and out of despair on their way.

The motivation behind Lisa and Anna's renegade existence on East Germany's roads in *Burning Life* is altogether less compelling and less credible. Lisa becomes a bank robber to reinstate social justice after capitalism and West German developers have seized the East. She robs banks in order to redistribute the loot amongst East Germany's poor and deserving. Anna, whom she meets on the occasion of her first robbery, spontaneously decides to become her accomplice in crime, though her motivation is less altruistic: she is an unemployed singer who needs some cash. At the end of their seven robberies, the gangster duo asks their hostages to accompany their departure by singing the German national anthem. Which one, ask the hostages, the real one or the one from the past? This humorous reference is intended to highlight the confusion about German national identity after unification, which, as the film argues, is at the bottom of Lisa's and Anna's criminal activity.

This lack of psychological credibility might be excused by the fact that Welz and Kolditz intended to make a road movie spoof. But in fact their film works neither particularly well as a spoof of the genre, nor as a spoof on *Thelma & Louise*, for it duplicates rather than parodies Scott's film. In the words of a review that appeared in the American magazine *Variety*, 'in essence the film is a collage of hand-me-down sequences with no soul of its own' (Hansen 1995: 51).

Notwithstanding this damning but justified criticism, it is instructive to examine how *Burning Life* bends the generic conventions of the female road movie, which were principally established by *Thelma & Louise* in the early nineties, to make them fit the cultural context of post-Wall Germany. In terms of character constellation, *Burning Life* is a rough copy of its blueprint. Thelma and Louise, Lisa and Anna are good teams that complement each other – one woman is innocent and naïve, the other more streetwise. Yet they vastly differ in terms of psychological depth and the trajectories of their journeys: Thelma and Louise's journey is propelled by a feminist cause. They flee patriarchy to achieve self-determination. Anna and Lisa's quest is motivated by a host of social ills: the arrival of capitalism and its traumatic consequences; the physical violence of Anna's husband; and Anna's desire to achieve fame, if not as a singer then at least as a bandit.

Following the convention of the road movie, the buddies are joined by a third party, who shares part of their journey but ultimately has to leave the two central characters to meet their destiny alone. In *Thelma & Louise* the itinerant stranger J. D., who first sleeps with Thelma and then steals the women's entire savings, assumes this role. In *Burning Life* a new-age traveller and conjurer takes on the equivalent part, but since this is the Wild East and not the Wild West, things are not half as nasty: the mysterious stranger offers his help to Lisa and Anna and, when Lisa finally succumbs to his charm, there is more to it than just a one night stand. Whereas in the capitalist system everyone is for himself, the film suggests, in the East, there is a sense of solidarity amongst these outlaws and vagrants who until recently adhered to the ethical codes of socialism.

In the classic road movie and in its feminine inflection the car, the road, and the wide and wild open spaces are key to the genre's iconography. They signify freedom and a reprieve from social conventions and the law. In line with the different cultural context, Louise's bluish-green Thunderbird convertible becomes substituted for Anna's black Tschaika, a Russian cruiser that allegedly once belonged to Khrushchev; the wide open spaces of the American West with its highways and its oil rigs become the desolate landscape of the Wild East with its tree-lined country roads, its busy motorways, dilapidated small towns and cultivated fields; the Grand Canyon is replaced by the de-industrialised wasteland of deserted brown coal mines and the cliffs of Rügen, a small island in the Baltic Sea. The simple fact that everything is on a much smaller scale in the Wild East and that the next provincial town is just around the corner renders the road movie with the outlaw plot farcical in the German context: there is not enough space to escape from society and the law. There is not even enough space to employ those wide-angle aerial shots which capture a tiny car in the middle of nowhere, as it speeds along a rough road leaving a trail of dust behind. These shots are notoriously absent in *Burning Life* – and so is the sense of freedom and adventure. Wenders' Europeanised road movies are a different story: they are introverted quests that are equally credible in the densely populated Ruhr or the Texan desert.

Burning Life and *Thelma & Louise* both end with the women being chased by a veritable battalion of policemen in cars and a helicopter. Realising that they cannot escape, Thelma and Louise decide to escape the law by choosing 'a bittersweet freedom from patriarchy through their suicidal acceleration into the Grand Canyon' (Roberts 1997: 66). Yet, significantly, as the Thunderbird flies forward and is in midair, the image freezes and fades to white, leaving the audience with the ambiguous message of suicide (if they read the film's ending literally) and freedom (if they accept the powerful final image and its figurative meaning). Scott had actually filmed two alternative endings and it seems as if the discarded version served as the template for *Burning Life*: the Thunderbird flies and then descends into the canyon. But 'in the final shot we see a car driving down the road that opened the film leaving a cloud of dust' (Sturken 2000: 75). This ending spells out the figurative meaning as well as the literal meaning more clearly, at the same time leaving the contradiction unresolved. The creators of *Burning Life* did not challenge their audience with such a puzzling ending: the chase ends with the Tschaika taking off from the cliffs of Rügen – an unmistakable reference to *Thelma & Louise* – then exploding over the sea. Clearly, the heroines' suicide would have been an inappropriate narrative closure for a road movie comedy. Therefore, Kolditz and Welz translated what remains a mere metaphor in Scott's movie into cinematic reality. In an ending that suspends disbelief, the heroines hijack the police helicopter and have a lucky escape. As the helicopter flies off into the distance, one hears Anna and Lisa arguing whether they should head for Africa or Australia.

The list of parallels and similarities between the American and the German road movie could be continued only to prove that *Burning Life* is much too close to *Thelma & Louise* to be an effective parody. Recent road movie parodies like the Australian *The Adventures of Priscilla, Queen of the Desert* (Stephan Elliott, 1994) and the American *The Straight Story* (David Lynch, 1999) successfully subvert essential aspects of the generic conventions. *Priscilla* satirises the macho-masculinity of the genre by selecting three protagonists with more fluid gender identities; two drag queens and a transsexual. *The Straight Story* ironises the iconography of the genre, replacing the fast car, usually driven by young, adventurous heroes, by an ultra-slow motorised lawnmower that serves an old man as a mode of transport for a journey that takes him 350 miles across the Midwestern plains. But *Burning Life* simply translates these generic conventions into a German context, reducing everything in scale. Not only is the Wild East much smaller than the Wild West, it is also less dangerous: toy guns are wielded instead of real guns; the outlaws are no real criminals but rather modern-day Robin Hoods; the police are no real threat to the fugitives either, being as foolish and incompetent as they are ruthless. Everything is toned down to such an extent that there is no suspense and no conflict that could not easily be resolved.

Even the social critique lacks depth and focus: *Burning Life* purports to criticise the West German take-over of the GDR and the social injustice of capitalism. But the film's controlling idea is flawed and incoherent. Anna, who would rather keep the stolen money and enjoy the good life, is capitalist at heart. It also suffers from an inconsistency in mood in that it translates a sun-drenched feel-good movie with a somewhat downbeat ending into a road movie comedy with an unconvincing happy ending that takes place in a wintry wet climate. As in the West German relationship comedies of the 1990s that focus on 'pseudo-crises [which] have no depth of despair, no true suffering, no true joy' (Rentschler 2000: 263), this film has many of the trappings of a road movie without capturing the essence of the genre. Thus *Burning Life* comes across as a somewhat inconsistent, downsized, low-budget version of the real thing, a pastiche without a clearly discernible satirical intent.

Produced in the new federal states but starring two of West Germany's most popular young actors, Maria Schrader and Dani Levy, the film clearly aimed for an all-German audience. When it received unflattering reviews in the press just twenty-five of the forty prints made went into distribution, attracting just over thirty thousand viewers (information courtesy of VdF/Verband der Filmverleiher). In comparison with post-Wall road movies made in the West, notably the Trabi comedies and Buck's *Wir können auch anders*, which attracted around 2.8 million viewers, *Burning Life* was commercially disappointing.

Wege in die Nacht (Paths in the Night, Andreas Kleinert, 1999): unification as identity crisis

Andreas Kleinert's film *Wege in die Nacht*, his fourth feature film after graduating from the Babelsberg Film and Television Academy Konrad Wolf in 1989,[13] represents a trend in post-Wall German cinema that consciously eschews the trend towards a more commerce-orientated German film culture during the 1990s. His films are indebted to East European and Soviet cinema. Notably Andrej Tarkovsky has been a strong influence on Kleinert: in his graduation thesis he explored the representation of levels of consciousness in Tarkovsky's oeuvre, while most of his films to date can be described as complex psychographs that explore the depths of the human mind and soul. What Kleinert's films also share with those of Tarkovsky are a moral seriousness and a preoccupation with existential themes. *Wege in die Nacht* has been compared to Tarkovsky's dystopian sci-fi film *Stalker* (1979) (Decker 2001: 338) which, like Kleinert's film, depicts a sombre journey of self-discovery. *Verlorene Landschaft* displays obvious correspondences with Tarkovsky's poetic style: obscure allegorical symbols, such as an angel and death, are embedded in an otherwise realistic context and lend many of the film's sequences a dreamlike feel. Kleinert's thematic concern with moral dilemmas and the solid grounding of his characters in the social malaise of post-Wall Germany also reveal certain affinities to what has been labelled the 'cinema of moral concern', which emerged in Poland during the mid-1970s, though Kleinert's films eschew semi-documentary aesthetics, favouring a highly stylised and symbolic film language. Kleinert has thus remained faithful to the cultural allegiances and influences that were shaped by the Soviet Union's political and cultural hegemony over East Central Europe instead of second-guessing what kind of films there might be a market for in the new Germany (Kleinert and Stargard 1991: 32).

Kleinert's films are subtle psychological portrayals of characters that, notwithstanding the universality of their conflicts and moral dilemmas, are deeply embedded in the social context of East Germany's past and present. They explore how people react to change, more specifically, the changes brought about by unification. *Verlorene Landschaft* succeeds at being both a highly subjective psychograph of the film's protagonist, Elias, and a parable, not just about the 'fenced-in' state of the GDR, but also about fences and barriers in a more figurative sense: the barrier of estrangement that Elias finds almost impossible to overcome when he visits his parents in the former GDR after decades of separation corresponds to the estrangement East and West Germans experienced when the Wall came down.

Neben der Zeit transposes what could be the plot of a Greek tragedy into the desolate reality of a provincial town in Brandenburg that is becoming increasingly cut off from the world in the wake of reunification: it is a place that has fallen outside time. As so often in Kleinert's films the family functions as a microcosm of the larger historical and political context that shapes the characters' lives. This combination of the universal with the socio-specific lends the films a parabolic dimension: both Sophie and her mother choose Russian men as lovers; both do so at historically significant moments which mark the beginning and the end of the GDR; in both cases the involvement with a Russian results in tragedy – the suicide of the mother's jealous husband and the murder of Sophie's Russian boyfriend at the hands of her jealous brother. Within the microcosm of the family, Russian men become the pivot of complex family dynamics, evoking passionate and conflicting feelings and triggering a twofold tragedy. Within the macrocosm of East Germany's geopolitical context, this character constellation mirrors the ambivalence which characterised the relationship between East Germans and Russians, the GDR and the Soviet Union (Rother 1996). It embodies the changing power structures between the Russians and the East Germans after the collapse of communism: once the victors and imposers of communism, they are now the losers who have to withdraw after the ideological battle has been won by capitalism (Kleinert and Richter 1996: 53).

In *Wege in die Nacht* Kleinert explores again how changed power structures and role reversals can affect peoples' lives. Walter, a man in his late fifties used to be the powerful and well-respected director of an electricity combine. But in the wake of unification and the ensuing privatisation of industry, he has lost his job. At first it may seem as if Walter's social decline is the cause of his tragic end. However, Walter is not depicted solely as a victim who deserves our pity. Admittedly, he is a victim of the West German take-over of the East as well as a victim of 'decades of tutelage and crippling authoritarian structures [that have made him master] in the art of self-deception, disavowal and denial' (Lewis 2002: 106). But he is also a perpetrator who has been complicit with the totalitarian system and who has internalised the authoritarian principle to such an extent that it ultimately leads to his self-destruction. To give his life meaning and in order to regain self-respect, Walter becomes the self-appointed boss of a vigilante team, consisting of himself, Gina and René, who patrol Berlin's commuter and underground trains at night. At Walter's command the two adolescents beat up hooligans who molest passengers, seemingly to enforce law and order in a world that has gone out of kilter, but in reality to find an outlet for their pent-up aggression. Walter sees himself and his violent helpmates as precursors of a better time to come in which he is to occupy a central place as a new leader. Driven by his frustrated will to power Walter becomes more and more entangled in a series of acts of violence randomly directed at hooligans but also at his helpmate, Gina, when she renounces her obedience and respect. A moral abyss opens up as Walter's self-deception begins to crumble and he realises what is at the bottom of his declared mission to reinstate justice and order – an obsession with power and authority that he is unable to satisfy in the new social order of post-Wall Germany in which he has been degraded to a powerless underdog. Unable to adjust to the new social order, Walter commits suicide.

Aesthetically, *Wege in die Nacht* is minimalist through and through. The film gets by with just two pieces of music, a bass tune and a percussion piece, which are used very sparingly. The increasingly loud and haunting percussion piece, though introduced as diegetic music, functions as an objective correlative to the protagonist's inner state of turmoil. As for dialogue, this too is reduced to a bare minimum. Instead, this black-and-white film relies on the powerful language of its images and the nuanced performance of its actors to convey its message. Jürgen Jürges, the director of photography, uses the camera in a Tarkovskian manner as if endeavouring to penetrate the surface of objects and characters and capture their very essence. Contemplative tracking shots reveal empty landscapes and the deserted no man's land of former industrial

18 Walter (Hilmar Thate) and his helpers (Dirk Borchardt and Henriette Heinze) in *Wege in die Nacht* (Paths in the Night)

production; long, almost static close-ups explore the actors' facial expressions and reveal their inner states. Their faces are carefully lit, with dark shadows intersecting the lines that worry, sorrow and laughter have engraved in the mature faces of Hilmar Thate and Cornelia Schmaus, creating chiaroscuro-like effects.

Highly symmetrical image compositions are another hallmark of Jürges' outstanding cinematography. It is a device he uses to express the film's fundamental message, as the following two examples will illustrate. Early on in the film, Walter is shown on the dark and derelict factory site where he used to be the boss, firing two shots into the empty space. The small silhouette of Walter is off set against a brightly lit background and framed by towering walls on either side that cast long dark shadows. The image composition and the combination of side- and back-lighting make the setting look like a deserted town in a Western, in which Walter stars as the sheriff who will see justice done. The iconography of this shot alludes to the heroic aspirations of this anti-hero. Yet significantly, unlike in a Western, Walter faces no antagonist other than himself. That is why he aims his gun at the empty space and later, at the end of the film, at himself.

Another equally memorable shot that is repeated several times over shows Walter, Gina and René moving along platforms and staircases of Berlin's underground stations. Invariably, Walter is at the centre of this triad, invariably a step or two ahead of his gang. The symmetrical choreography of this shot, which is reminiscent of images of the Führer in Leni Riefenstahl's famous Nazi propaganda film *Triumph des Willens* (Triumph of the Will, 1935), reveals Walter's obsession with leadership and authority and thus suggests what is at the core of Walter's declared mission to reinstate justice and order: a fascist will to power.

The protagonist's path into the night is charged with dramatic irony which enables the audience to feel empathy and compassion for what is essentially a rather unsympathetic character. In fact, in Johann Bergk's original screenplay Walter had been conceived as a former high-ranking Stasi agent but Hilmar Thate insisted that Walter's professional background be changed in order to ensure the audience's empathy (Rother 1999: 8). In the actual film, Walter is sufficiently complex to invite both the audience's identification with and rejection of the character. Thanks to the central character's ambiguity as both victim and perpetrator, *Wege in die Nacht* avoids the polarised portrayal of post-Wall Germany that lays the blame for the social malaise of the East squarely on the West.

That accommodation to the new system does not necessarily have to go hand in hand with opportunism and corruption is demonstrated by Walter's wife Sylvia, who has found employment and contentment without compromising her moral integrity. While Walter's failure is indisputably triggered by the take-over of the East through the West, his life would not have ended in tragedy had it not been for his obsession with power, the film argues. Scriptwriter Bergk thus locates the cause of tragedy not primarily in the radical social change after 1989 but in a character disposition that proves resistant to change. In fact, in all of Kleinert's post-*Wende* films those characters who embrace change survive, or better still are granted a new lease of life, whereas those that resist change perish, either literally or psychologically.

The same holds true for Hanna in *Die Unberührbare*, mentioned above and regarded by many critics as the West German counterpart of Kleinert's *Wege in die Nacht*. Hanna also refuses to accept the need for change as the outdatedness of her 1960s' make-up and hairstyle suggest. More significantly, she clings to an ideal of communism that dates back to Lenin but has little in common with the realities of socialism in the GDR. Like Walter she too is deluded about her own identity: she considers herself to be a radical left-winger, a communist at heart whose spiritual home is the GDR, while indulging in the most decadent forms of consumerism. Like Walter she pays with her life for her self-deception and mental inertia.

What distinguishes *Wege in die Nacht* as well as *Die Unberührbare* from the majority of post-Wall films is that they succeed in addressing problems of existential relevance, while at the same time grounding them in a unique historical and social context. In fact, it was Kleinert's intention to make a film that would be more than just a historical document, he stated at the Cannes Film Festival in 1999, where *Wege in die Nacht* was the opening film of the *Quinzaine des Réalisateurs* (Directors' Fortnight). Instead, he wanted to tell a story that would be equally relevant in Bochum, East Berlin or Honolulu (cited in Wiegand 1999). And yet in spite of considerable critical acclaim and a number of prizes at film festivals in Germany and abroad, in the eyes of the public the film has not been able to transcend the socio-historical specificity that triggered its creation. It has been labelled the 'Dokument eines ostdeutschen Seelenzustandes' (document of an East German psychological state) (Wiegand 1999) or a 'DDR-Psychogramm' (psychograph of the GDR) (Wengierek 1999) and has thus been relegated to the status of a historical document and a quintessentially East German film. Regrettably, such labelling has not worked in favour of the film's commercial success. According to Katrin Schlösser and Frank Löprich, the founders of the East German Ö-Film production company that produced *Wege in die Nacht*, from the mid-1990s onwards East German depictions of post-socialist drabness were definitely passé amongst West German viewers, which explains the rather disappointing box-office figures for *Wege in die Nacht*: it had just 11,600 viewers in the first year of its release (www.ffa.de).

Nachtgestalten (Night Shapes, Andreas Dresen, 1999) and the humanist realist tradition

Andreas Kleinert and Andreas Dresen are often mentioned in the same breath: both were born shortly after the Berlin Wall was erected, both graduated from the Babelsberg Film Academy when the Wall came down and, a few years later, DEFA ceased to exist. Though both Kleinert and Dresen have made a name for themselves with films that reflect the social and moral dilemmas of reunification, they wish to shake off the label 'East German filmmaker', arguing that they address themes of universal significance, albeit in most cases in a specifically East German social setting. Admittedly, more than a decade after reunification this label is becoming increasingly problematic, implying that both East and West German culture have resisted the forces of unification. On the other hand, both directors spent their formative years in a cultural climate that heavily exposed them to East European and Soviet cinema and thus imbued them with a tradition that is to a large extent unfamiliar to West German filmmakers. As Dresen remarked in an interview:

> Die Erfahrung and das Großwerden mit der osteuropäischen Filmkultur haben mich in starkem Maße geprägt. Vom Menschenbild her, nicht unbedingt von der Ästhetik her. Es gibt sowjetische Filmemacher, die im Westen kaum bekannt sind . . . die unter Gorbatschow in der Tauwetter-Periode angefangen haben, die mit einer großen Offenheit, Warmherzigkeit, mit einer gewissen Sympathie für die Leute über Menschen erzählen. Darin verbirgt sich ja auch eine gewisse Art von Religiosität, oder Glauben. Glauben ist vielleicht treffender, gerade wenn man über sozialistische Länder redet. (Dresen and Berghahn 2002)

> (Experiencing and growing up with East European film culture has been a formative influence on me. Not so much in terms of aesthetics, but rather in the way people are portrayed. There are Soviet filmmakers who are largely unknown in the West. . . . who emerged under Gorbachev during the Thaw, who tell of people's lives with great open-mindedness, warmth and a certain sympathy for others. Herein lies also a certain kind of religious-ness, or faith. Faith is perhaps more appropriate, especially in the context of socialist countries.)

Films which according to Dresen's own testimony were inspirational are in particular the popular Soviet comedies of the eighties, notably the most successful film of the decade, *Vokzal dlya dvoikh* (Station for Two, Eldar Ryazanov, 1983) and *Golubye gory* (Blue Mountains, Eldar Shengelaya, 1984), as well as Alexander Mitta's earlier *Gori, gori, moya zvezda* (Shine My Star, Shine, 1969). These Soviet cult films reflect the inadequacies of communist culture in a humorous or grotesque way without ever extinguishing a glimmer of hope. In a similar vein, *Nachtgestalten*, which depicts people on the margins of society, takes a lighthearted approach to what is essentially a drab and miserable life.

At the same time, *Nachtgestalten* is unmistakably indebted to DEFA's documentary realist tradition. Dresen's training at the Babelsberg Film Academy and DEFA's masters of documentary realism, notably Lothar Warnecke, Rainer Simon, Jürgen Böttcher and Roland Gräf, have taught the director to use images rather than words, to carefully research and observe his characters and their social environment rather than invent them, and to apply this approach to feature films as well as to documentaries.

In particular Dresen's three most recent feature films – *Nachtgestalten*, *Die Polizistin* (The Policewoman, 2000) and *Halbe Treppe* (Grill Point, 2002) – suggest that he has taken these stylistic templates merely as a starting point from which to develop a distinctive style of his own:[14] the shaky handheld camera, the grainy film stock, jump cuts and tracking shots, the near absence of floodlights, often combined with improvised acting, are the hallmarks of Dresen's true-to-life aesthetics. Many critics have pointed out similarities with Dogma '95. Yet Dresen denies having been influenced by this provocative aesthetic creed proposed by the Danish filmmakers Thomas Vinterberg and Lars van Trier. In his view Dogma '95 is essentially nothing but an attention-grabbing PR gimmick (Dresen and Nagy 2002). Instead the filmmaker refers to DEFA's strong documentary tradition, which led him to develop a style that has now become associated with Dogma '95, but that might as well be associated with DEFA's documentary realist filmmakers or *cinéma vérité* of the 1960s.

In fact, with regard to *Nachtgestalten*, a film scripted and directed by Dresen, critics have not tired of searching for influences and affinities. The British filmmaker Ken Loach has been cited on account of his semi-documentary aesthetics and his preference for characters on the margins of society. Robert Altman's *Short Cuts* (1993) and Jim Jarmusch's *Night on Earth* (1992) have been cited as classic models of multi-plot films. A further parallel with Jarmusch's film consists in the use of a taxi as a narrative device that links five stories taking place simultaneously in the course of one night together. What *Nachtgestalten* shares with *Short Cuts* is that both films use multiple narratives to paint a specific social milieu. In a grand design of complex cross-cutting between multiple plot lines, Altman constructs a panorama of America's middle class and the emptiness that afflicts their lives. In a similar fashion, Dresen interweaves three main plot lines, all of which revolve around those on society's margins. Though the film is set in Berlin, Dresen was not specifically interested in Germany's new capital as such, but rather in the lives of underdogs and outcasts in any big city – from the perspective of rats, as he put it (Mund 1999).

This multi-plot film takes place during the course of one night, not just any night, but the night when the Pope is visiting Berlin. Plot strand number one centres on Hanna and Viktor, a homeless couple. Normally they sleep rough in the wet and cold, but since Hanna has been given a

19 Michael Gwisdek (Peschke) and Ricardo Valentin (Feliz) in *Nachtgestalten* (Night Shapes)

hundred Marks by a kind stranger they embark on an odyssey to find a cheap hotel room where they can enjoy a few moments of warmth and intimacy. Plot strand two features Jochen, a naïve and good-hearted farmer who has come to Berlin for a night of adventure, and Patty, a child prostitute and heroin addict. Jochen pays her for an entire night and treats Patty like a romantic date rather than a prostitute, while she is just after her next fix. Plot strand three traces the paths through the night of Peschke, a middle-aged middle manager, and Feliz, a young asylum seeker from Angola. Their paths cross at Berlin-Tegel airport, where Peschke at first wrongly suspects Feliz of having stolen his wallet but then takes the boy under his wing for the night, until contact with Feliz's relatives has been established.

As in *Short Cuts* the dramaturgy of coincidence provides a link between the multiple plots. In the case of Altman's film it is a minor earthquake that shakes up the lives of the several protagonists of LA. In *Nachtgestalten* at some stage or other during the course of the night, at least one member of these three odd couples uses the same taxi, ends up in a police station, runs into the same group of punks, or is given a hundred Mark note. More significantly, they all listen to fragments of the Pope's speech as they zap between the television channels. As the Pope addresses an audience of thousands, using rather hackneyed phrases about the Almighty's power to forgive, the incongruity between the formulaic speech of this figurehead of the Catholic Church and the miserable lives depicted in the three stories at first creates a sense of bitter sarcasm. A heroin-addicted child prostitute, a homeless couple expecting a baby without the prospect of ever setting up a home, a small boy separated from his family in Africa and seeking asylum in a country whose language he does not speak – surely these sad creatures of the night have been forgotten by God. But on closer inspection we realise that each and every one of them is touched by divine mercy which momentarily lights up the all-encompassing darkness around them (see Dresen and Nagy 2002).

For Hanna God's mercy comes in the shape of a hundred Mark note given to her by a stranger. It opens up the prospect of a warm bed and some moments of intimacy with Viktor during which she can shed her rough protective skin and abrasiveness and be tender instead. Patty, the darkest figure of all, is capable of an act of mercy when she puts back the hundred Mark note into Jochen's wallet. Admittedly, she steals 400 DM from her unsuspecting client, but still, she sacrifices a hundred Marks and has to go on the game again. Peschke, the lonely underdog, rediscovers his human side when Feliz embraces him and he, much to his surprise, is capable of reciprocating this gesture, clumsily and hesitantly, for he is clearly unaccustomed to such closeness and affection.

In all three instances the experience of a glimmer of mercy is very limited. Fundamentally, the characters' lives will not change, but even those characters who appear to be irredeemably lost have a spiritual experience that instils them – and the audience – with a sense of hope. Andreas Dresen summarises the controlling idea and spiritual message of *Nachtgestalten* as follows:

> Über allem, was man vielleicht kritisiert an der Gesellschaft, oder was einem mißfällt, schwingt immer die Hoffnung, daß es im Menschen etwas gibt, was unzerstörbar ist. Ein Punkt von Würde, ein Punkt von moralischer Integrität. . . . Selbst wenn es ihnen noch so dreckig geht, daß sie in ihrem Kern etwas haben, was noch nicht kaputt ist und was es zu bewahren gilt. (Dresen and Berghahn 2002)

> (Beyond everything that one criticises or rejects about society, there is always a sense of hope that something exists in every human being that is indestructible. A certain dignity, a certain moral integrity. . . . Even when things are going really badly for them, there is something inside them that will not break, something that is worth preserving.)

The visual equivalent of the film's controlling idea is created by an evocative colour scheme: muted, washed-out colours predominate in the drab and gloomy world inhabited by those night shapes. But each of the three stories is lit up, as it were, by a bright red object that is arguably the objective correlative of this glimmer of mercy. Hanna wears a crimson-coloured coat; Feliz wears a red jacket and red underpants; and Jochen buys a red rose for Patty. One of the punks who meander through the night, stealing first Jochen's bag and then Peschke's car, has bright red hair. Again, the colour red is associated with an act of grace for, significantly, it is this red-haired punk girl who picks up Hanna from the middle of the wet road after she has been beaten up by Viktor in the heat of an argument.

Nachtgestalten proved popular with critics and audiences alike. At the Berlinale in 1999, the former DEFA-actor/director Michael Gwisdek was awarded the Silver Bear for Best Actor on account of his well-observed tragicomic performance as Peschke. Subsequently, numerous other prizes were bestowed upon Dresen's film.[15] Critics praised *Nachtgestalten* as the film that marked the return of social concerns to the German screen, a theme that had been abandoned since the demise of the New German Cinema, and a welcome relief from the preponderance of lightweight comedies (Seeßlen 1999). Though some tried hard to find traces of DEFA didacticism in *Nachtgestalten* (Kühn 1999b), the majority of critics placed Dresen's feature film in a diverse spectrum of traditions of international cinema. This suggests that Dresen is already well on his way to casting off the label 'East German director', while at the same time bringing something to contemporary German cinema that is distinctly East German, or more precisely, East European and that critics refer to as 'humanistischer Realismus' (humanistic realism) (Seeßlen 1999). It is a cinema of social concern imbued with a utopian vision.

Sonnenallee (Sun Alley, Leander Haußmann, 1999): nostalgia for the ex-GDR?

The premiere of *Sonnenallee* on 7 October 1999 was well timed: it coincided with what would have been the fiftieth anniversary of the GDR. In the spirit of this occasion, this retro-style satirical take on life in the GDR during the 1970s is a feel-good movie which essentially asserts that even when living right next to the Wall you could have the time of your life.

The release of *Sonnenallee* was timely in yet another sense: ten years after the fall of the Wall, reunification euphoria had definitely subsided.

More importantly, the attitude of East Germans towards their past underwent a dramatic change. After the initial embrace of all things Western, they had become wary of 'their experience of living in the GDR ... being elided from the German historical record' (Cooke 2003: 160) and of losing their Eastern identity. They were keen to move away from a tainted memory of the past and the stigma of the 'Stasi state' which has dominated the public debate about the former GDR. As memories of the old GDR were becoming somewhat blurred, 'magnifying the achievements while forgetting its repression' (Jarausch 1997: 19), a wave of *Ostalgie* swept across the new federal states. East German brands enjoyed revived popularity; websites devoted to GDR memorabilia, Honecker, Trabis and the GDR's national anthem mushroomed on the internet; East Berlin nightclubs capitalised on this kind of GDR-revival by staging old-time sing-alongs and employing staff dressed in FDJ and border guard uniforms, or even Honecker lookalikes (Naugthon 2000: 20). More recently, the *Ostalgie* phenomenon has become a major media event, with *Ostalgie* shows featuring prominently on German television and making headlines in the press. Unmistakably, the time has come to look back at everyday life in the GDR through a rose-tinted camera lens.

Just a month after *Sonnenallee*, Sebastian Peterson's comedy *Helden wie wir* (Heroes Like Us), based on Thomas Brussig's best-selling reunification novel (1995), premiered on 9 November 1999, celebrating the tenth anniversary of the fall of the Berlin Wall. What both films have in common, apart from being based on screenplays written or co-written by Brussig,[16] is that they are feel-good movies about the now defunct socialist state. Audience demand for such reconciliatory retro-comedies continues, as the box-office success of *Good Bye Lenin!* proves. All three films are grotesque satires about everyday life in the GDR conveyed from the vantage point of adolescents.

This vantage point is of particular significance in explaining the reconciliatory stance of these films. As Micha, the protagonist and narrator of *Sonnenallee*, explains in a voice-over at the end of the film, 'Es war einmal ein Land und ich habe dort gelebt. Wenn man mich fragt, wie es war? Es war die schönste Zeit meines Lebens, denn ich war jung und verliebt' (Once upon a time there was a country and I lived there. If you ask me what it was like, I would reply that I had the time of my life, for I was young and in love). The conflation of memories of the GDR with memories of the experience of first love and youth legitimise a nostalgic idealisation of the GDR, which ultimately paves the way for a normalisation of the GDR's totalitarian legacy. In other respects, too, *Sonnenallee* promotes the project of normalisation.

The film tells the story of a group of adolescents who live at the shorter end of the Sonnenallee, a five-kilometre-long street that stretches from the West Berlin suburb of Kreuzberg to Treptow in the East and that was, until 1989, divided by the Wall. Micha, the film's protagonist and narrator, and his friends do what teenagers all over the world do: they fall in love, have their first sexual encounters, experiment with drugs and try to impress their friends by wearing the hippest clothes and listening to the coolest pop music. What sets the lives of these East Berlin teenagers apart from their peers in the West is the economy of shortage and the all-pervasive authority of the state.

Both aspects are at the centre of the film's satire: much-coveted Western consumer goods such as a Rolling Stones album are only available on the black market, where the names of Western pop stars are whispered as if they were the code words of a conspiracy. Since recreational drugs are unavailable, these kids make do with a herbal asthma remedy mixed with the GDR variety of Coca-Cola to get high. Anything that is desirable must have a Western feel to it. Hence Miriam, the girl on whom Micha has a crush, looks like a living Barbie doll, whereas Sabrina, Mario's girlfriend, dresses in existentialist black to signal her subversive intellectual allegiance to Sartre's philosophy.

Unlike in Western teenage movies, where the parents are the chief antagonists of youthful rebellion, in *Sonnenallee* it is invariably the state. Yet in this placatory comedy even the border guards, the district policeman and the presumed-Stasi neighbour have a human touch that makes these henchmen of a repressive regime appear entirely harmless. The policeman, played by the popular West German actor Detlev Buck, is presented as a sympathetic figure who shares the teenagers' enthusiasm for forbidden pop music. The passport and visa controller is so blinded by his unflinching belief in the superiority of the GDR that it is almost touching: he even considers the GDR-made Minetta, a plastic radio with awful sound quality, superior to a confiscated Japanese hi-fi system. He also mistakes Micha's uncle, who ensures a steady supply of West German consumer goods to the family, as a great supporter of socialism on account of his frequent visits. And the neighbour whom Micha's family suspects to be working for the Stasi turns out to be a harmless undertaker who keeps his profession a secret because death was a taboo in the GDR.

But is this grotesque satire an appropriate reassessment of life under communism? Is it not, rather, unethical to use comedy to deflect from the inhumanity of the GDR's totalitarian system? The latter argument is an objection that perhaps only Germans can raise in response to a

20 Nostalgic memories of the East: *Sonnenallee* (Sun Alley) with Detlev Buck, Patrick Güldenberg, Alexander Scheer and Alexander Beyer

comedy. Several film critics have asserted that the GDR was still no laughing matter (Bisky 2000; Decker 2000), while 'Help e.V.', an organisation that represents the interests of the victims of the Wall, even wanted to take Haußmann to court for making light of their suffering in this comedy. By law they might even have had a case (Wolle 2000), but they could also have been accused of deliberately misunderstanding the film's generic conventions which are writ large all over.

This is not a docu-drama that aspires to historical authenticity. On the contrary, *Sonnenallee* is a self-conscious fictionalisation of the GDR that abounds in intertextual references to its fictional status. First and foremost, it alludes to the DEFA tradition, notably DEFA's cult film per se, *Die Legende von Paul und Paula* (The Legend of Paul and Paula, Heiner Carow, 1973). When Mischa runs across the street to place his life – in the form of his forged diaries – at Miriam's feet, we hear the most memorable song from this 1970s movie, 'Geh zu ihr und laß Deinen Drachen steigen' (Go and see her and let your kite fly high) by the popular East German band 'Die Puhdies' (see Chapter 5). Rushing up the stairs, he encounters Paul (here also played by Winfried Glatzleder) who asks him whether he needs an axe. This is a reference to the famous scene from *Die Legende von Paul und Paula* in which Paul smashes down Paula's front door after she has refused to ever see him again. This is not the only homage paid to DEFA's cinematic tradition. *Sonnenallee* also recreates the artificial Orwo-Color-look, a distinctive feature of DEFA colour films, many of which were made with Orwo-Color film stock, the GDR-brand that was a bestseller across the Eastern Bloc.[17] Colour, as the film's final sequence in which colour fades to black and white suggests, stands for an embellished fictional reality that has little in common with the greyness typically associated with life under socialism. That only prettification through the colourful medium of film can transfigure the drabness of real life is further underscored by Nina Hagen's song 'Du hast den Farbfilm vergessen' (You forgot the colour film) which accompanies the fade from colour to hues of grey at the end.

The film's self-conscious references to the DEFA tradition are further emphasised by the fact that no attempt is made to conceal the studio look. Except for a few on-location scenes next to the Berliner Dom, *Sonnenallee* was shot at the Babelsberg Studio lot, where the shorter end of the Sonnenallee, complete with twenty-six facades, the Wall and border fortifications, was reconstructed on an open-air set of 7,000 square metres that cost the Studio some three million DM.

As if these multiple references to the fictional status of this nostalgic East Side Story were still not sufficient, Brussig and Haußman incorporate a meta-narrative level in the film, in which Micha recasts his biography in a series of diaries, which he rapidly writes when Miriam unexpectedly expresses an interest in his past. In order to impress Miriam, he reinvents his uneventful existence, creating instead a flattering new identity for himself as a dissident and courageous founder of an active resistance group. Micha's aforementioned voice-over at the end of *Sonnenallee* suggests that the entire film is just as embellished an account of the ex-GDR as is the inauthentic account of his life in his diaries.

To ignore the rich intertexuality and irony with which this fairy tale about the GDR is told is to deliberately misunderstand the film. *Sonnenallee* does not purport to give an authentic picture of life in the German Democratic Republic during the 1970s. Instead it projects a nostalgic fantasy that is in equal measure a tribute to a romanticised notion of youth, as it is a reconciliatory offer to East Germans to make peace with their problematic past and thus to regain a positive identification with their part of German history.

The film's feel-good factor is created to a large extent by the seventies music soundtrack and the retro fashion and design. As Paul Cooke notes in his insightful analysis of *Sonnenallee*, the 'nostalgic revisitation' of the 1970s 'which is currently en vogue' in both East and West German youth culture ensured the film's appeal to an all-German audience (Cooke 2003: 163). To an East German audience the affectionate portrayal of such highlights of GDR-made design as the 'mufta', a multifunctional table that would fit into the smallest living room, or a moped by the name of Swallow, and the ubiquitous FDJ uniforms evokes a nostalgic déjà vu experience. Since Brussig and Haußmann come from the East, there is nothing patronising in this slightly grotesque depiction of life on the other side of the Wall. On the contrary, in the film's implicit suggestion that West German teenagers may well have had all the pop music that money could buy but that East German teenagers certainly had a lot more fun, there is even an element of one-upmanship. The film's penultimate scene shows the entire cast and a crowd of extras, including an Erich Honecker lookalike, dancing in the street to the pop song *The Letter* by the American band the Box Tops. Sweet memories of life in the GDR; history as one big party? It would be wrong to interpret this tongue-in-cheek depiction of life behind the Wall as a dangerous form of revisionism. Instead it is the attempt to counteract the process of historical elision and the devaluation of their life experiences that has been lamented by many East Germans ever since unification.

For inspiration, Brussig and Haußman referred to Woody Allen's *Radio Days* (1987) and Peter Bogdanovich's *The Last Picture Show* (1971). Critics have compared *Sonnenallee* to George Lucas' frequently imitated teen movie *American Graffiti* (1973) which, like Bogdanovich's film, nostalgically recalls the sights and sounds associated with American teenage culture in the 1950s and 1960s. Undeniably, American film culture had some impact on post-Wall cinema in the East, but in many respects *Sonnenallee* has even more in common with the Hungarian box-office hit of 1997, *Dollybirds* (Péter Tímár). This 'stylish "retro" musical set in the early 1960s' creates a new and appealing image of a decade that was 'traditionally portrayed as an overtly bleak period (the years after the failed revolution attempt of 1956, which resulted in the Soviet invasion)'. Like *Sonnenallee*, *Dollybirds* plays down the problematic politics by 'reducing references to repressive politics to parody' (Iordanova 2003: 156).

What sets *Sonnenallee* apart from less successful features made in the East after the *Wende* is not just its tongue-in-cheek approach to the GDR's past, but also some fortuitous circumstances in its creation. It was made on the relatively big budget of DM 7 million, twice the average budget of most East German films. It enjoyed considerable pre-release publicity on account of the involvement of the best-selling novelist Brussig. It was co-produced by the East and West German production companies, Ö-Film, Boje Buck and SAT 1 television. Boje Buck also has a distribution arm, Delphi, based in West Berlin, and is co-owned by Detlev Buck, a well-known West German actor and director. The fact that *Sonnenallee* straddled the East–West production and distribution divide certainly contributed to its success. Initially released with 107 copies, a few weeks later nearly 250 prints were in circulation. Though roughly two-thirds of the 2.6 million viewers were based in the new federal states and Berlin (information courtesy of Delphi Filmverleih) it also proved extremely popular in the old federal states. To date *Sonnenallee* is the most profitable Eastern production since unification, and on par with such West German box-office hits as *Wir können auch anders* (2.8 million German viewers) or *Lola rennt* (Run Lola Run, 1999; 2.2 million German viewers). Though the international festival circuit took Haußmann as far as Hollywood and Korea, finding commercial distributors across the Atlantic proved difficult. Yet Haußmann was not unduly concerned about the lack of international resonance of his film. Seeking success abroad, he remarked, was likely to jeopardise one's sense of identity and, in any event, the international success of German films in the past had always been the result of their engagement with specifically German themes. According to Haußmann, the prime target audience of *Sonnenallee* were Germans in the East and West, some eighty million inhabitants, quite a sizeable audience in his view (Haußmann and Amann 2000). In fact, with *Sonnenallee* he wanted to make a film that would bring the still estranged compatriots together through the simple realisation 'So'ne Parties hatten wir auch' (Haußmann, Schaper, and Schulz Ojala, 1999) (We too had parties like that).

One German nation, two German film cultures?

One of the most remarkable aspects of the cinematic representation of the new Germany is how – at least during the first decade after unification – East and West Germans mutually ignored each other. If West Germans are largely absent in films originating in the East, East Germans are equally absent in the majority of films made in the West, *Good Bye Lenin!* being the notable exception and possibly signalling the emergence of a unified German film culture. However, until the new millennium West German filmmakers by and large paid little attention to the changes brought about by unification, presumably because unification had relatively little impact on the old federal states. This also explains why films that do not transcend the post-unification drabness are disregarded by audiences in the West, who see no reason to be burdened with problems that are not their own.

From an Eastern perspective, by contrast, the rapid transformations following the fall of the Wall have been an important theme. Surprisingly and despite the fact that many East Germans felt antagonistic towards and inferior to their Western compatriots, who managed the process of unification in such a way that it has been rightly compared to Western colonisation of the East, these films do not vilify West Germans. While in the early post-Wall films anger and resentment are voiced against the GDR's paternalistic state that suppressed its children and abused its authority, films made at a time when the imbalance of power between the East and West had already become apparent did not in a similar vein put the blame on their Western compatriots, who literally and symbolically featured as the new bosses in their lives. Unemployment, de-industrialised wastelands and desolate, deserted communities are presented as the ubiquitous scars of the capitalist transformation of the East in these films. However, West Germans hardly ever appear as the originators of these socio-economic problems. They remain the depersonalised forces of capitalism and radical upheaval, yet as characters they are remarkably absent in East German post-Wall films. The very notion of an East–West German friendship or love relationship appears to be unthinkable in films made by Eastern directors, whereas in a small number of films made in the old federal states such a rapprochement between East and West is at least conceivable, but rarely a prominent concern.[18] Ultimately, it is these personal bonds that will have to back up the monumental systems transfer in the political and socio-economic sphere in order for unification to achieve its ultimate purpose.

What contribution then do the post-Wall films surveyed here make to the development of a unified German film culture? Though clearly none of these films could have been made in the days of DEFA because they fly in the face of the doctrine of Socialist Realism and broach taboos that would have provoked the censors, they are indebted to DEFA's tradition of social realism. Like DEFA's *Gegenwartsfilme*, East German films of the nineties are socially committed films that are driven by a strong humanist and utopian impulse. Unlike the 'cinema of consensus' that has been identified as the dominant strand of West German film culture during the 1990s (Rentschler 2000), the films discussed here are based on the premise that film has to play a social function. Of course, it was precisely this premise which was at the core of socialist film art in the German Democratic Republic. But it was also at the root of the socially committed *Autorenfilm* in the Federal Republic during the 1960s and 1970s. New German Cinema was in many respects a counter-cinema that critically examined the social ills of contemporary West German society. When a new generation of West German filmmakers abandoned this tradition in favour of socially conformist comedies during the 1990s, East German filmmakers entered into an all-German film culture which they enriched through a specifically Eastern variety of a cinema of social concern.

Sadly, these critical social realist films made in the East have struggled to find receptive audiences, in particular in the old federal states. Yet, in order to break even or achieve moderate commercial success, they have to capture the imagination of viewers in the old and the new federal states. Overcoming this still persistent East–West divide has been a major challenge for productions originating in the new federal states, not least because distributors have been reluctant to promote films with intrinsically East German themes. Or, as the moderate success of Western-produced unification films such as *Die Unberührbare* (starring Hannelore Elsner, a popular West German television star) and *Das Versprechen* (made by Margarethe von Trotta, a well-known West German director) suggests, they only relate to a Western point of view. Even so, the box-office figures of these two films (178,515 and 200,567 respectively, information courtesy of VdF) do not stand up to the success of post-Wall comedies, notably *Wir können auch anders*, *Sonnenallee* and *Good Bye Lenin!* Ironically for a people stereotyped as having no sense of humour, the split screen has at last been sutured with humour.

By far the greatest commonality of taste, however, exists in the audiences' predilection for Hollywood mainstream cinema, which has established itself as the dominant film culture in Eastern Germany, and indeed Eastern Europe, ever since the Iron Curtain fell and communist governments were no longer in a position to protect their citizens and indigenous film cultures from the unmitigated impact of American cinema. In hindsight, it thus seems as if the East German film industry has paid a high price for gaining freedom from state control, being now afflicted by the same problem from which the West German suffers – the insurmountable dominance of Hollywood. This has so far emerged as the strongest unifying force between the still disparate East and West German film cultures.

Notes

1 This chapter focuses on the privatisation of the Babelsberg-based feature film studio. For a detailed account of the privatisation or dissolution of the other studios and facilities belonging to the DEFA complex see Otto (1993). The State Filmarchive was integrated into the Federal Archive (Bundesarchiv). The privatisation of DEFA's film distribution arm, Progress, only occurred in 1997.

2 Of DEFA's roughly 3,500 employees 2,400 were working in the feature film studio (see Chapter 1). By the time of the take-over staffing levels were already reduced to 750 employees.

3 After 1992 the studio was renamed DEFA Studio Babelsberg GmbH, but the reference to DEFA was frequently omitted and eventually, on 9 August 1994, the name DEFA was eliminated from the register of companies. A distinction is made between Media City Babelsberg, which comprises 120 companies with approximately 3,200 employees, and Studio Babelsberg Motion Pictures GmbH, the film production studio within the Media City.

4 However, in 1994 the studio's Executive Director announced that only one-third of the DEFA studio would be maintained for film production while the rest would be put to other uses (Naughton 2002: 56). By 1997 only 350 ex-DEFA employees were still on the payroll.

5 Most middle-sized towns had such film clubs, which were attached to high-schools, universities, enterprises and cultural meeting centres.

6 Figures for 1998–2000 indicate that on average cinema attendance is now almost the same for East and West Germans, namely 1.84 and 1.86 visits per year respectively (Roth 2001: 54), compared with a European average of 1.6 visits per year.

7 Even before unification, Hollywood and West German productions proved far more popular with East German audiences than DEFA or East European and Soviet films. Thus, the top ten films, which accounted for just 7 per cent of all new releases, attracted 50 per cent of all cinema goers! This seems to suggest that a film policy that privileged socialist film culture was not particularly effective (Wiedemann 1991: 86).

8 The feature film studio achieved an annual production volume of 98 million Mark, of which 63 million Mark was generated by productions commissioned by East German television.

9 The about-turn of West German film production in the eighties was also the result of fundamental changes in the film subsidy system. The soft culture-orientated film subsidy was replaced by film funding that prioritised commercial imperatives. Increased co-operation with private television channels, which have become major investors in German film production, has further skewed the agenda from culture to commerce; see Finney (1996: 114–38); Meurer (2000: 72–88); and (Storm 2000).

10 *Good Bye Lenin!* (2003), made by a West German director-scriptwriter team, is the most notable exception. Alternatively, the film's success might indicate that the pattern of the 1990s is beginning to change.

11 For a concise survey of immigrant filmmakers in Germany see Götürk 2002. Mention should also be made of two films, *Gorilla Bathes at Noon* (Dusan Makavejev, 1993) and *Weltmeister* (World Champion, Zoran Solomun, 1994) made by Yugoslav directors now working in Germany. Both films reflect the impact of unification and the subsequent withdrawal of Soviet troops from East Germany on the lives of Russian soldiers and their families.

12 The best-known examples of chernukha films are Petr Todorovsky's *Interdevochka* (Intergirl, 1989) and Vasili Pichul's *Malen'kaya Vera* (Little Vera, 1988). In Polish cinema, the hard-hitting action movies of the 'Young Wolves' set a similar trend. In the German context, a film that comes closest to this trend is *Verhängnis* (Fate, 1994) by the West German director Fred Kelemann.

13 After his graduation film *Leb wohl, Joseph* (Farewell, Joseph, 1989) and several prize-winning but commercially less successful films, Kleinert has been working predominantly for television. For a detailed account of Kleinert's oeuvre see Decker (2001).

14 Dresen's graduation film *So schnell es geht nach Istanbul* (As Quickly as Possible to Istanbul, 1989) was followed by *Stilles Land* (Quiet Country, 1992), a subtle comedy that captures the historic moment when the Wall came down from the periphery of a provincial town. Dresen has also made several films for television, including *Die Polizistin* (The Policewoman, 1999), which was later released in cinemas, and a number of documentaries. His most recent feature film, *Halbe Treppe* (Grill Point, 2002) was awarded the Silver Bear and Special Jury Award at the Berlinale 2002 and attracted 300,000 viewers within the first nine weeks of its cinematic release. For a comprehensive discussion of Dresen's oeuvre see Decker (2001).

15 *Nachtgestalten* was awarded the German Critics Award in Silver and the Pilar Miró Award for Best Director in Valladolid (Spain). With 178,533 viewers, it was one of the top one hundred German films of the year 2000 (www.ffa.de). Abroad it was part of the international festival circuit and was commercially released in South American and Scandinvian countries and in Spain.

16 *Sonnenallee* was co-scripted by Haußmann, who like Brussig has firsthand experience of what it was like to be a teenager in the GDR during the 1970s. Brussig studied dramaturgy at the Babelsberg Film and Television Academy and went on to write novels. Haußmann went to drama school and worked as an actor, theatre director and Director General (*Intendant*) of the Bochum theatre before directing *Sonnenallee*. His most recent film, *Herr Lehmann* (Mr Lehmann, 2003), is another humorous take on unification.

17 Orwo, short for Original Wolfen, is an East German brand of colour and
    black and white film stock that was created in 1964. Originally, the German
    company Agfa had manufactured film at Wolfen but in the early sixties
    it reserved the brand name for films produced in West Germany. From 1964
    on most DEFA films were made with Orwo, while a few were made with
    Eastmancolor (information courtesy of Ralf Schenk). *Sonnenallee* is actually
    shot on Kodak film.
18 Carow's *Verfehlung*, ostensibly the exception to the rule, takes place before
    unification. Hence the antagonist is the GDR's repressive state that makes
    love across the Wall impossible. In West German post-Wall films love rela-
    tionships between East and West Germans are more common: in *Berlin is
    in Germany* the protagonist's ex-wife lives with a new West German part-
    ner; in *Liebe auf den ersten Blick* (Love at First Sight, Ludwig Thome, 1991),
    a West Berlin futurologist and single mother falls in love with an East Berlin
    archaeologist and single father and forms a big, happy family; in *Good Bye
    Lenin!* Alex's sister, Ariane, dates and eventually starts a family with a young
    man from West Berlin.

References

Agde, Günter (ed.) (2000) [1991], *Kahlschlag: Das 11. Plenum des ZK der SED 1965. Studien und Dokumente*, Berlin, Aufbau Taschenbuch Verlag.

Allan, Seán (1999), 'DEFA: an historical overview', in Seán Allan and John Sandford (eds), *DEFA: East German Cinema, 1946–1992*, New York and Oxford, Berghahn Books, pp. 1–21.

Allan, Seán and John Sandford (eds) (1999), *DEFA: East German Cinema, 1946–1992*, New York and Oxford, Berghahn Books.

Anderson, Benedict (1983), *Imagined Communities: Reflections on the Origins and Spread of Nationalism*, London, Verso.

Attwood, Lynne (ed.) (1993), *Red Women on the Silver Screen: Soviet Women and Cinema from the Beginning to the End of the Communist Era*, London, Pandora Press.

Aurich, Rolf (1991), 'Geteilter Himmel ohne Sterne', in Helga Belach and Wolfgang Jacobsen (eds), *Kalter Krieg: 60 Filme aus Ost und West*, Berlin, Stiftung Deutsche Kinemathek, pp. 18–44.

Austin, Guy (1996), *Contemporary French Cinema*, Manchester, Manchester University Press.

Axen, Hermann (1953a), 'Über die Fragen der fortschrittlichen deutschen Filmkunst', in *Für den Aufschwung der fortschrittlichen deutschen Filmkunst*, Berlin, Dietz Verlag, pp. 15–46.

Axen, Hermann (1953b), 'Schlußwort', in *Für den Aufschwung der fortschrittlichen deutschen Filmkunst*, Berlin, Dietz Verlag, pp. 159–66.

BArch/DR117/A/240 (1965), DEFA Betriebsakten, 'Entwicklungsstand, Probleme, sowie Hauptaufgaben des Film- und Lichtspielwesens der DDR bis zum Jahre 1970'.

BArch SAPMO DY30/IV/A2/9.06/124, Bestand SED, ZK Abteilung Kultur (1965), 'Zwei Standpunkte in der Beurteilung des Filmes *Das Kaninchen bin ich*', 15 October 1965.

BArch Film (1966), HV Film 52, 'Argumentation zum Film *Spur der Steine*', 4 July, pp. 1–9.

BArch Film (1969), HV Film 42 A/B, 'Stellungnahme zu *Die Russen kommen*', 13 January.

BArch Film (1980–83), HV Film '*Jadup und Boel*', 3 and 3B.

Bathrick, David (1995), *The Powers of Speech: The Politics of Culture in the GDR*, Lincoln, Nebraska and London, University of Nebraska Press.

Bathrick, David (1998), 'From UFA to DEFA: past as present in early GDR films', in Jost Hermand and Marc Silberman (eds), *Contentious Memories: Looking Back at the GDR*, German Life and Civilization, vol. 24, New York and Washington, DC, Lang, pp. 169–88.

Becker, Jurek (1983), 'Resistance in Jakob der Lügner', *Seminar*, 19, pp. 269–73.

Becker, Jurek (1997) [1969], *Jakob der Lügner*, Frankfurt/Main, Suhrkamp Taschenbuch Verlag.

Bergfelder, Tim (2002), 'Popular cinema: introduction', in Tim Bergfelder, Erica Carter and Deniz Götürk (eds), *The German Cinema Book*, London, BFI Publishing, pp. 15–17.

Berghahn, Daniela (1999a), 'The re-evaluation of Goethe and the classical tradition in the films of Egon Günther and Siegfried Kühn', in Seán Allan and John Sandford, *DEFA: East German Cinema, 1946–1992*, Oxford and New York, Berghahn Books, pp. 222–44.

Berghahn, Daniela (1999b), 'Censorship in GDR cinema: the case of *Spur der Steine*', in Steve Giles and Peter Graves (eds), *From Classical Shades to Vickers Victorious: Shifting Perspectives in British German Studies*, Bern, Berlin and Frankfurt/Main, Peter Lang, pp. 183–98.

Berghahn, Daniela (2000), 'The forbidden films: film censorship in the wake of the Eleventh Plenum', in Diana Holmes and Alison Smith (eds), *100 Years of European Cinema: Entertainment or Ideology?*, Manchester, Manchester University Press, pp. 40–51.

Berghahn, Daniela (2002), 'Liars and traitors: unheroic resistance in antifascist DEFA films', in Daniela Berghahn and Alan Bance (eds), *Millennial Essays on Film and Other German Studies*, Oxford, Bern and Berlin, Peter Lang, pp. 23–39.

Bertaux, Pierre (1978a), *Friedrich Hölderlin*, Frankfurt/Main, Suhrkamp.

Bertaux, Pierre (1978b), 'Hölderlin geisteskrank?', *Sinn und Form*, 6, pp. 1107–128.

Beyer, Frank (1974), 'Traum vom besseren Leben: Zum Film *Jakob der Lügner*', *Neues Deutschland*, 17 December.

Beyer, Frank (2002), *Wenn der Wind sich dreht. Meine Filme, mein Leben*, Munich, List Taschenbuch.

Bisky, Jens (2000), 'Tagebuch. Beleidigend', *Berliner Zeitung*, 30 January.

Blunk, Harry (1984), *Die DDR in ihren Spielfilmen. Reproduktion und Konzeption der DDR-Gesellschaft im neueren DEFA-Gegenwartsspielfilm*, Munich, Profil-Verlag.

Blunk, Harry (1987), 'Bemerkungen zur "Erbe"-Aneignung im Spiegel des DEFA-Spielfilms', *Deutsche Studien*, 25:98, pp. 155–68.

Bowlby, Chris (2002), 'The Singing, Ringing Tree', BBC Radio Four, 28 December.

Brandlmeier, Thomas (1989), 'Von Hitler zu Adenauer: Deutsche Trümmerfilme', in Hilmar Hoffman and Walter Schobert (eds), Zwischen Gestern und Morgen: Westdeutscher Nachkriegsfilm 1946–1962, Frankfurt/Main, Deutsches Filmmuseum, pp. 33–61.

Bredel, Willi (1978) [1937], Dein unbekannter Bruder, Berlin and Weimar, Aufbau Verlag.

Bruk, Franz (1966), VEB DEFA Studio für Spielfilme: Einschätzung zum Film Spur der Steine, 16 May 1966, BArch Film, HV Film 52.

Bruyn, Günther de (1991), 'On the German cultural nation', New German Critique, 52, pp. 60–5.

Buchka, Peter (1987), 'Braver Hölderlin', Süddeutsche Zeitung, 10 Septebember.

Budde, Harald (1982), 'Die Leiden einer Frau: DDR-Film Das Fahrrad', Frankfurter Allgemeine Zeitung, 11 October.

Bulgakova, Oksana (1993), 'The hydra of the Soviet cinema: the metamorphoses of the Soviet film heroine', in Lynne Attwood (ed.), Red Women on the Silver Screen: Soviet Women and Cinema from the Beginning to the End of the Communist Era, London, Pandora Press, pp. 149–74.

Byg, Barton (1992a), 'Generational conflict and historical continuity in GDR film', in Bruce A. Murray and Christopher J. Wickham (eds), Framing the Past: The Historiography of German Cinema and Television, Carbondale and Edwardsville, Southern Illinois University Press, pp. 197–219.

Byg, Barton (1992b), 'Geschichte, Trauer und weibliche Identität im Film: Hiroshima mon amour und Der geteilte Himmel', in Ute Brandes (ed.), Zwischen gestern und morgen. Schriftstellerinnen der DDR aus amerikanischer Sicht, Berlin, Peter Lang, pp. 95–112.

Byg, Barton (1995), 'German unification and the cinema of the former German Democratic Republic', Michigan German Studies (special issue: Gegenwartsbewältigung: The GDR after the Wende) 21, pp. 150–68.

Byg, Barton (1997a), 'Nazism as femme fatale: recuperations of masculinity in postwar Berlin', in Patricia Herminghouse and Magda Mueller (eds), Gender and Germanness: Cultural Productions of Nation, Providence and Oxford, Berghahn Books, pp. 176–88.

Byg, Barton (1997b), 'Parameters for institutional and thematic integration of filmmakers from the former GDR', in Marc Silberman (ed.), What Remains? East German Culture and the Postwar Public, American Institute for Contemporary German Studies, 2, pp. 64–74.

Byg, Barton (1999), 'DEFA and the traditions of international cinema', in Seán Allan and John Sandford (eds), DEFA: East German Cinema, 1946–1992, New York and Oxford, Berghahn Books, pp. 22–41.

Byg, Barton (2002), 'Introduction: reassessing DEFA today', in Barton Byg and Betheny Moore (eds), Moving Images of East Germany: Past and Future of DEFA Film, Washington, DC, American Institute for Contemporary German Studies, pp. 1–23.

Byg, Barton and Betheny Moore (eds) (2002), *Moving Images of East Germany: Past and Future of DEFA Film*, Washington, DC, American Institute for Contemporary German Studies.

Carter, Erica (1997), 'Culture, history and national identity in the two Germanys since 1945', in Mary Fulbrook (ed.), *German History since 1800*, London and New York, Arnold, pp. 432–53.

Carter, Erica (2000), 'Sweeping up the past: gender and history in the post-war German "rubble film"', in Ulrike Sieglohr (ed.), *Heroines without Heroes: Reconstructing Female and National Identities in European Cinema, 1945–51*, London and New York, Cassell, pp. 91–112.

Cooke, Paul (2003), 'Performing *Ostalgie* in Leander Haußmann's *Sonnenallee* (1999)', *German Life and Letters*, 56:2, pp. 156–67.

Corrigan, Timothy (1994, 2nd edn), *New German Film: The Displaced Image*, Bloomington and Indianapolis, Indiana University Press.

Coulson, Anthony S. (1999), 'Paths of discovery: the films of Konrad Wolf', in Seán Allan and John Sandford (eds), *DEFA: East German Cinema, 1946–1992*, New York and Oxford, Berghahn Books, pp. 164–82.

Coury, David N. (1997), 'From aesthetics to commercialism: narration and the new German comedy', *Seminar*, 33:4, pp. 356–73.

Dahlke, Günther (1964), 'Hauptreferat', in Deutsche Akademie der Künste (ed.), *Probleme des sozialistischen Realismus in der darstellenden Kunst behandelt am Beispiel des DEFA-Films 'Der geteilte Himmel'. Referat und Diskussionsbeiträge der II. Plenartagung der Deutschen Akademie der Künste zu Berlin vom 30. Juni 1964*, Berlin, Henschel Verlag, pp. 3–22.

Dalichow, Bärbel (1992), 'Weh Dir, daß Du ein Enkel bist', in *Beiträge zur Film- und Fernsehwissenschaft: Der DEFA-Spielfilm der 80er Jahre – Chancen für die 90er?*, 44, pp. 16–44.

Dalichow, Bärbel (1994), 'Das letzte Kapitel 1989 bis 1993', in Ralf Schenk (ed.), *Das zweite Leben der Filmstadt Babelsberg: DEFA Spielfilme 1946–1992*, Berlin, Henschel Verlag, pp. 328–53.

Damm, Sigrid (2001) [1998], *Christiane und Goethe: Eine Recherche*, Frankfurt/Main and Leipzig, Insel Taschenbuch.

Danyel, Jürgen (1992), 'Vom schwierigen Umgang mit der Schuld: Die Deutschen in der DDR und der Nationalsozialismus', *Zeitschrift für Geschichtswissenschaft*, 10, pp. 915–28.

Danyel, Jürgen (1993), 'Die geteilte Vergangenheit. Gesellschaftliche Ausgangslagen und politische Dispositionen für den Umgang mit Nationalsozialismus und Widerstand in beiden deutschen Staaten nach 1949', in Jürgen Kocka (ed.), *Historische DDR-Forschung: Aufsätze und Studien*, Berlin, Akademie Verlag, pp. 129–47.

Dau, Rudolf, Horst Haase and K. Kliche (1984), 'Zur Aneignung des kulturellen Erbes in der DDR', *Weimarer Beiträge*, 30:9, pp. 1413–22.

'DDR-Film: Personenkult mit Popanz Goethe' (1975), *Der Spiegel*, 45, 3 November, pp. 172–3.

Decker, Kerstin (2000), 'Hart an der Grenze. Die Autoren des Films *Sonnenallee* stellen sich der Kritik der DDR-Opfer', *Der Tagesspiegel*, 1 April.

Decker, Kerstin (2001), 'Neben der Zeit. Die Filme von Andreas Dresen und Andreas Kleinert', in Ralf Schenk and Erika Richter (eds), *Apropos: Film 2001. Das Jahrbuch der DEFA-Stiftung*, Berlin, Verlag Das Neue Berlin, pp. 328–43.

DEFA-Außenhandel (1981), 'Stellungnahme zum Film *Das Fahrrad*', BArch Film, HV Film, 245+C, 22 September 1981.

DEFA Betriebsakten (1965), BArch/DR117/A/240, DEFA Betriebsakten, June.

Demokratischer Frauenbund Deutschlands (1952), '*Frauenschicksale* wird diskutiert', *Neues Deutschland*, 29 August.

Deutsches Filminstitut Frankfurt/Main (ed.) (2001), *Cinematographie des Holocaust. Die Vergangenheit in der Gegenwart: Konfrontationen mit den Folgen des Holocaust im deutschen Nachkriegsfilm*, Munich, edition text + kritik.

Diller, Helmut and Daniela Berghahn (2002), tape-recorded interview, Berlin, 19 July.

Drawe, Christel (ed.) (1996), *So viele Träume: DEFA-Film-Kritiken aus drei Jahrzehnten von Heinz Kersten*, Berlin, Vistas.

Dresen, Andreas and Elisabeth Nagy (2000), 'Interview mit Andreas Dresen, Regisseur von *Nachtgestalten*', www.queer-view.com/01400er/1406nachtgestalten/interview1406 dresen_ 10 January.

Dresen, Andreas and Daniela Berghahn (2002), tape-recorded interview, Potsdam 19 July.

Dudow, Slatan (1952), 'Zur Diskussion über den Film *Frauenschicksale*', *Neues Deutschland*, 21 November.

Dyer, Richard and Ginette Vincendeau (1992), *Popular European Cinema*, London and New York, Routledge.

Eckert, Detlef (1991), 'Die Volkswirtschaft der DDR im Spannungsfeld der Reformen', in Günter Agde (ed.), *Kahlschlag: Das 11. Plenum des ZK der SED 1965. Studien und Dokumente*, Berlin, Aufbau Taschenbuch Verlag, pp. 20–31 [not reprinted in 2nd edn of Agde 2000].

Edgar, Andrew and Peter Sedgwick (1999), *Key Concepts in Cultural Theory*, London and New York, Routledge.

Elsaesser, Thomas (1989), *New German Cinema: A History*, New Brunswick, NJ, Rutgers University Press.

Elsaesser, Thomas (1996), *Fassbinder's Germany: History, Identity, Subject*, Amsterdam, Amsterdam University Press.

Elsaesser, Thomas and Michael Wedel (eds) (1999), *The BFI Companion to German Cinema*, London, BFI Publishing.

Elsaesser, Thomas and Michael Wedel (2001), 'Defining DEFA's historical imaginary: the films of Konrad Wolf', *New German Critique* (special issue on East German cinema) 82, pp. 3–24.

Emmerich, Wolfgang (1980), *Heinrich Mann 'Der Untertan'*, Munich, Wilhelm Fink Verlag.

Emmerich, Wolfgang (1996), *Kleine Literaturgeschichte der DDR*, Leipzig, Kiepenheuer.

Engel, Christine (ed.) (1999), *Geschichte des sowjetischen und russischen Films*, Stuttgart and Weimar, Metzler.

Engler, Wolfgang (2000), 'Strafgericht über die Moderne. Das 11. Plenum im historischen Rückblick', in Günter Agde (ed.), *Kahlschlag: Das 11. Plenum des ZK der SED 1965. Studien und Dokumente*, Berlin, Aufbau Taschenbuch Verlag, pp. 16–36.

Faraday, George (2000), *Revolt of the Filmmakers: The Struggle of Artistic Autonomy and the Fall of the Soviet Film Industry*, University Park, PA, Pennsylvania State University Press.

Farrelly, Daniel J. (1998), *Goethe in East Germany, 1949–1989. Toward a History of Goethe Reception in the GDR*, Columbia, SC, Camden House.

Fehervary, Helen (1977), *Hölderlin and the Left: The Search for a Dialectic of Art and Life*, Heidelberg: Carl Winter Universitätsverlag.

Fehrenbach, Heide (1995), *Cinema in Democratizing Germany: Reconstructing National Identity after Hitler*, Chapel Hill and London, University of North Carolina Press.

Feinstein, Joshua (1999), 'Constructing the mythic present in the East German cinema: Frank Beyer's *Spur der Steine* and the 11th Plenum of 1965', *Central European History*, 32:2, pp. 203–20.

Feinstein, Joshua (2002), *The Triumph of the Ordinary: Depictions of Daily Life in the East German Cinema 1945–1989*, Chapel Hill and London, The University of North Carolina Press.

Fellmer, Claudia (2002), *Stars in East German Cinema*, unpublished PhD dissertation, University of Southampton.

Finney, Angus (1996), *The State of European Cinema: A New Dose of Reality*, London, Cassell.

Fisher, Jaimey (2001), 'Who's watching the rubble-kids? Youth, pedagogy, and politics in early DEFA films', *New German Critique*, 82, pp. 91–125.

Flockton, Chris, Eva Kolinsky and Rosalind Pritchard (2000), 'The New Germany in the East: an introduction', in Chris Flockton, Eva Kolinsky and Rosalind Pritchard (eds), *The New Germany in the East: Policy Agendas and Social Developments since Unification*, London and Portland, OR, Frank Cass, pp. 1–23.

Fox, Thomas C. (1999), *Stated Memory: East Germany and the Holocaust*, Rochester, NY, Camden House.

Frieden, Sandra, Richard W. McCormick, *et al.* (eds) (1993), *Gender and German Cinema: Feminist Interventions*, 2 vols, Providence and Oxford, Berg.

Führmann, Martha (1953), Speech given at the conference of the Central Committee of the SED, 17–18 September 1952 [no title], in *Für den Aufschwung der fortschrittlichen deutschen Filmkunst*, Berlin, Dietz Verlag, pp. 134–8.

Frýdlová, Pavla (1996), *Frauenfilme in Osteuropa: Eine Studie über Filmregisseurinnen in den Kinematographien der ehemaligen sozialistischen Länder*, Berlin, Trafo Verlag.

Fulbrook, Mary (1992), *The Divided Nation: A History of Germany 1918–1990*, Oxford and New York, Oxford University Press.

Fulbrook, Mary (1995), *Anatomy of a Dictatorship: Inside the GDR 1949–1989*, Oxford and New York, Oxford University Press.

Fulbrook Mary (1999), *German National Identity after the Holocaust*, Cambridge, Polity Press.

Garrett, Greg (2001), 'Film', in Derek Jones (ed.), *Censorship: A World Encyclopedia*, London and Chicago, Fitzroy Dearborn, pp. 797–812.

Gehler, Fred (1982), 'Nichts mehr sagen, nichts mehr fragen? Gespräch mit Ulrich Weiß', *Sonntag*, p. 22.

Geiss, Axel (1997), *Repression und Freiheit: DEFA-Regisseure zwischen Fremd- und Selbstbestimmung*, Potsdam, Brandenburgische Zentrale für politische Bildung.

Gemünden, Gerd (1998), 'Between Karl May and Karl Marx: The DEFA "Indianerfilme" (1965–85)', *Film History*, 10, pp. 399–407.

Gerhard, Ute (1994), 'Die staatlich institutionalisierte "Lösung" der Frauenfrage. Zur Geschichte der Geschlechterverhältnisse in der DDR', in Hartmut Kaelble, Jürgen Kocka and Hartmut Zwahr (eds), *Sozialgeschichte der DDR*, Stuttgart, Klett-Cotta, pp. 383–403.

Gilman, Sander (2000), 'Is life beautiful? Can the Shoah be funny? Some thoughts on recent and older films', *Critical Inquiry*, 26:2, pp. 279–308.

Götürk, Deniz (2002), 'Beyond paternalism: Turkish German traffic in cinema', in Tim Bergfelder, Erica Carter and Deniz Götürk (2002) (eds), *The German Cinema Book*, London, BFI Publishing, pp. 248–56.

Goulding, Daniel J. (ed.) (1989), *Post-New Wave Cinema in the Soviet Union and Eastern Europe*, Bloomington, Indiana University Press.

Gräf, Christel (2001), 'Waren Ostfrauen wirklich anders? Zur Darstellung von Frauen im DEFA-Gegenwartsfilm', in Raimund Fritz (ed.), *Der geteilte Himmel: Höhepunkte des DEFA-Kinos 1946–1992*, vol. 2, Essays und Filmografie, Vienna, Filmarchiv Austria, pp. 107–18.

Graffy, Julian (2001), 'Russia: the shelf. Censorship of Soviet films under Brezhnev', in Derek Jones (ed.), *Censorship: A World Encyclopedia*, London and Chicago, Fitzroy Dearborn, pp. 2118–19.

Greffrath, Bettina (1995), *Gesellschaftsbilder der Nachkriegszeit: Deutsche Spielfilme 1945–1949*, Pfaffenweiler, Centaurus-Verlagsgesellschaft.

Grimm, Reinhold and Jost Hermand (eds) (1971), *Die Klassik-Legende. Second Wisconsin Workshop*, Frankfurt/Main, Athenäum Verlag.

Grisko, Michael (2002), 'Zwischen Sozialphilosophie und Actionfilm. Grenzen und Möglichkeiten des Science-fiction-Genres bei der DEFA', in Ralf Schenk and Erika Richter (eds), *Apropos: Film 2002. Das Jahrbuch der DEFA-Stiftung*, Berlin, Verlag Das Neue Berlin, pp. 108–20.

Grote, Heinz (1979), 'Holocaust', *Film und Fernsehen*, 3, p. 2.

Günther, Egon (1990), 'Fragen an Egon Günther nach der Vorführung von *Wenn Du groß bist, lieber Adam*, 6. 2. 1990', Internationales Forum des Jungen Films 1990, 40. Internationale Filmfestspiele Berlin, Info Sheet No. 22.

Günther, Egon and Helga Schütz (1965), *Wenn Du groß bist, lieber Adam* [film script, version 10 July], Potsdam-Babelsberg, VEB DEFA Studio für Spielfilme.

Günther, Egon and Michael Hanisch (1993), 'Warum sind Sie so zornig, Herr Günther?', *Neue Zeit*, 23 December.

Günther, Egon and Ralf Schenk (2000), 'Die verzauberte Welt. Nachdenken über Film und Politik', in Ralf Schenk and Erika Richter (eds), *Apropos: Film 2000. Das Jahrbuch der DEFA-Stiftung*, Berlin, Verlag Das Neue Berlin, pp. 50–75.

Günther, Egon and Daniela Berghahn (2002), tape-recorded interview, Groß-Glienicke, 31 July.

Haase, Jürgen (2002), 'Spur der Filme: Der Progress Film-Verleih und das DEFA-Erbe', in Ralf Schenk and Erika Richter (eds), *Apropos Film 2002: Das Jahrbuch der DEFA-Stiftung*, Berlin, Bertz, pp. 310–15.

Hager, Kurt (1965), 'Protokoll der 11. Tagung des Zentralkomitees 15.–18. Dezember 1965. Rede von Kurt Hager, Mitglied des Politbüros', BArch SAPMO, DY30/2/1/338/JIV 2/1-126 No. 2051, pp. 61–4.

Hake, Sabine (2002), *German National Cinema*, London and New York, Routledge.

Hall, Patrik (1997), 'Nationalism and historicity', *Nations and Nationalism* 3:1, pp. 3–23.

Hames, Peter (2000), '*The Good Soldier Švejk* and after: the comic tradition in Czech film', in Diana Holmes and Alison Smith (eds), *100 Years of European Cinema: Entertainment or Ideology?*, Manchester, Manchester University Press, pp. 64–75.

Hames, Peter (2001), 'Czechoslovakia: film', in Derek Jones (ed.), *Censorship: A World Encyclopedia*, London and Chicago, Fitzroy Dearborn, pp. 635–7.

Hanisch, Michael (2001), 'Nachrichten aus einem Land ohne Schurken oder In Diktaturen hat der Krimi nicht viel zu melden', in Ralf Schenk and Erika Richter (eds), *Apropos: Film 2001. Das Jahrbuch der DEFA Stiftung*, Berlin, Verlag Das Neue Berlin, pp. 194–222.

Hansen, Eric (1995), '*Burning Life*', *Variety* 7, 20 March, p. 51.

Haupt, Jürgen (1980), *Heinrich Mann*, Stuttgart, Metzlersche Verlagsbuchhandlung.

Haußmann, Leander (2003), 'Es kam dicke genug', *Der Spiegel*, 37, pp. 220–1.

Haußmann, Leander, Rüdiger Schaper and Jan Schulz Ojala (1999), 'Der Osten war eine Orgie', *Der Tagesspiegel*, 9 October.

Haußmann, Leander and Johannes Amann (2000), 'Im Kino entscheidet der Zuschauer', *Der Tagesspiegel*, 7 December.

Hayward, Susan (1993), *French National Cinema*, London and New York, Routledge.

Hayward, Susan (2000), 'Framing national cinemas', in Mette Hjort and Scott MacKenzie (eds), *Cinema and Nation*, London and New York, Routledge, pp. 88–102.

Heimann, Thomas (1994), *DEFA, Künstler und SED-Kulturpolitik*, Berlin, Vistas.

Hennings, Dirk (1993), 'Im Lauf der Zeit – die Entwicklung der Kinolandschaft in den neuen Ländern', *Film und Fernsehen*, 4, pp. 4–7.

Herden, Werner (1977), *Geist und Macht: Heinrich Manns Weg an die Seite der Arbeiterklasse*, Berlin and Weimar, Aufbau Verlag.

Herlinghaus, Ruth (1980), 'Wie lebendig ist Geschichte? Kurt Maetzig, Konrad Wolf, Lothar Warnecke und Ruth Herlinghaus im Gespräch (1)', *Film und Fernsehen*, 1, pp. 3–8.

Herminghouse, Patricia (1981), 'Die Wiederentdeckung der Romantik: Zur Funktion der Dichterfiguren in der neueren DDR-Literatur', in Jos Hoogeveen and Gerd Labroisse (eds), *DDR-Roman in der Literaturgesellschaft*, Amsterdam, Rodopi, pp. 217–48.

Herminghouse, Patricia (1983), 'Trends in literary reception: coming to terms with classicism. Goethe in GDR literature of the 1970s', *German Quarterly*, pp. 273–84.

Higson, Andrew (1989), 'The concept of national cinema', *Screen* 30:4, pp. 36–46.

Higson, Andrew (1993), 'Re-presenting the national past: nostalgia and pastiche in the heritage film', in Lester Friedman (ed.), *British Cinema and Thatcherism: Fires Were Started*, London, UCL Press, pp. 109–29.

Higson, Andrew (1995), *Waving the Flag: Constructing a National Cinema in Britain*, Oxford, Oxford University Press.

Higson, Andrew (2000), 'The limiting imagination of national cinema', in Mette Hjort and Scott MacKenzie (eds), *Cinema and Nation*, London and New York, Routledge, pp. 63–74.

Hjort, Mette (2000), 'Themes of nation', in Mette Hjort and Scott MacKenzie (eds), *Cinema and Nation*, London and New York, Routledge, pp. 103–17.

Hochmuth, Dietmar (1994), 'DEFA NOVA – nach wie vor?', in Freunde der Deutschen Kinemathek e. V. (eds), *DEFA NOVA – nach wie vor? Versuch einer Spurensicherung, Kinemathek 82*, pp. 4–7.

Honecker, Erich (1965), 'Protokoll der 11. Tagung des Zentralkomitees 15–18. Dezember 1965. Rede von Genosse Honecker' ['Ein sauberer Staat mit unverrückbaren Maßstäben']. BArch SAPMO, DY30/2/1/338/JIV 2/1-126 No. 2051. (Extracts are reprinted in Agde 2000: 238–51.)

Iordanova, Dina (2003), *Cinema of the Other Europe: The Industry and Artistry of East Central European Film*, London and New York, Wallflower Press.

Jacobsen, Wolfgang, Anton Kaes and Hans Helmut Prinzler (eds) (1993), *Geschichte des deutschen Films*, Stuttgart and Weimar, Metzler.

Jäger, Manfred (1995), *Kultur und Politik in der DDR 1945–1990*, Köln, Verlag Wissenschaft und Politik.

Jahrow, Franz (1966), 'Stellungnahme zu *Berlin um die Ecke*. Abt. Filmproduk-
tion', BArch, DR117 A/0047 (reprinted in *Film und Fernsehen*, 1–2 (1996),
pp. 30–1.)

Jansen, Peter W. and Wolfram Schütte (eds) (1977), *Film in der DDR*, Munich
and Vienna, Carl Hanser Verlag.

Jarausch, Konrad H. (1991), 'The failure of East German antifascism: some ironies
of history as politics', *German Studies Review*, 14:1, pp. 85–102.

Jarausch, Konrad H. (1997). 'Reshaping German identities: reflections on the
post-unification debate', in Konrad H. Jarausch (ed.), *After Unity: Reconfiguring German Identities*, Providence and Oxford, Berghahn Books, pp. 1–23.

Johnson, Vida (1997), 'Russia after the Thaw', in Geoffrey Nowell-Smith, *The
Oxford History of World Cinema*, Oxford, Oxford University Press, pp. 640–51.

Joho, Wolfgang (1957), 'Ein mahnendes Schicksal', *Sonntag*, 9 June.

Jordan, Günter and Ralf Schenk (eds) (2000), *Schwarzweiß und Farbe: DEFA
Dokumentarfilme 1946–1992*, Berlin, Jovis.

Judt, Matthias (ed.) (1998), *DDR-Geschichte in Dokumenten: Beschlüsse, Berichte,
interne Materialien und Alltagszeugnisse*, Bonn, Bundeszentrale für politische
Bildung.

Jung, Fernand (1997), '"Wir alle lieben Paula, aber uns liegt an Paul".
Zur Rezeption des Spielfilms "*Die Legende von Paul und Paula*"', in
Bundeszentrale für politische Bildung (ed.), *Frauenbilder in den DDR-
Medien*, Bonn, Bundeszentrale für politische Bildung, pp. 41–55.

Jung, Thomas (1998), 'Nicht-Darstellung und Selbst-Darstellung: Der Umgang
mit der "Judenfrage" in der SBZ und der frühen DDR und dessen
Niederschlag in Literatur und Film', *Monatshefte*, 90:1, pp. 49–70.

Kaes, Anton (1992), *From Hitler to Heimat: The Return of History as Film*,
Cambridge, MA and London, Harvard University Press.

Kannapin, Detlef (1997), *Antifaschismus im Film der DDR: DEFA-Spielfilme
1945–1955/56*, Köln, PapyRossa Hochschulschriften.

Kannapin, Detlef (2000), 'Gibt es eine spezifische DEFA Ästhetik?', in Ralf
Schenk and Erika Richter (eds), *Apropos: Film 2000. Das Jahrbuch der DEFA
Stiftung*, Berlin, Verlag Das Neue Berlin, pp. 142–64.

Karl, Günther (1964), 'Filmexperiment – im Streitgespräch: Eine Betrachtung
zum Film *Der geteilte Himmel*', *Neues Deutschland*, 5 September.

Kasten, Ullrich and Fred Gehler (1997), 'Rückkehr aus großer Entfernung. Das
Kino des Egon Günther' (television documentary, ORB).

Kattago, Shiobhan (2001), *Ambiguous Memory: The Nazi Past and German
National Identity*, Westport and London, Praeger.

Kenez, Peter (1997), 'Soviet film under Stalin', in Geoffrey Nowell-Smith (ed.),
The Oxford History of World Cinema, Oxford, Oxford University Press,
pp. 389–98.

Kenez, Peter (2001), *Cinema and Soviet Society: From the Revolution to the
Death of Stalin*, London and New York, I. B. Tauris.

Kersten, Heinz (1982), 'Eigene Sicht vom *Fahrrad*: Ein DEFA-Film und Babelsberger Nachwuchsprobleme', *Frankfurter Rundschau*, 16 November.

Kersten, Heinz (1985), 'Halber Hölderlin', *Frankfurter Rundschau*, 6 August.

Kersten, Heinz (1996), '*Dein unbekannter Bruder*', in Christel Drawer (ed.), *So viele Träume: DEFA-Film-Kritiken aus drei Jahrzehnten von Heinz Kersten*, Berlin, Vistas, pp. 194–6.

Kessler, Mario (1993), 'Zwischen Repression und Toleranz: Die SED-Politik und die Juden (1949–1967)', in Jürgen Kocka (ed.), *Historische DDR-Forschung: Aufsätze und Studien*, Berlin, Akademie Verlag, pp. 149–67.

Klaus, Udo (1957), '. . . doch alle Fragen bleiben offen', *Die Weltbühne*, 10 September, pp. 889–91.

Kleinert, Andreas and Joachim Stargard (1991), 'Psychogramme der Veränderung', *Film und Fernsehen*, 1, pp. 32–3.

Kleinert, Andreas and Erika Richter (1996), 'Anarchie und Menschlichkeit. Mit Andreas Kleinert sprach Erika Richter über seinen Film *Neben der Zeit*', *Film und Fernsehen*, 5:6, pp. 52–5.

Klingsporn, Johannes (1991), 'Zur Lage der deutschen Kinowirtschaft', *Media Perspektiven* 12, pp. 794–805.

Klunker, Heinz (1977), 'Expeditionen in den Alltag. Nach Ulbricht: DDR-Filme einer DDR-Generation', in Peter W. Jansen and Wolfgang Schütte (eds), *Film in der DDR*, Munich, Hanser, pp. 135–66.

Knietzsch, Horst (1973), '*Die Legende von Paul und Paula*. Ein Film von Ulrich Plenzdorf und Heiner Carow', *Neues Deutschland*, 31 March.

Knietzsch, Horst (1982), 'Mißlungen. Kino-Premiere: *Das Fahrrad*', *Neues Deutschland*, 29 July.

Knietzsch, Horst (1985), 'Versuch über einen bedeutenden Dichter. *Hälfte des Lebens*, ein DEFA-Film um Friedrich Hölderlin hatte Premiere', *Neues Deutschland*, 19 April.

Knoll, Manfred (1959), '*Kabale und Liebe*. Ein meisterhafter Klassiker-Film Martin Hellbergs', *Junge Welt* (Berlin), 25 December 1959.

Koch, Gertrud (1993), 'On the disappearance of the dead among the living: the Holocaust and the confusion of identities in the films of Konrad Wolf', *New German Critique*, 60, pp. 57–75.

Koepnick, Lutz (2002), 'Reframing the past: heritage cinema and Holocaust in the 1990s', *New German Critique*, 87, pp. 47–82.

Kohlhaase, Wolfgang (1977), [Untitled speech], in Hermann Herlinghaus, Verband der Film- und Fernsehschaffenden (eds), *Dritter Kongreß des Verbandes der Film- und Fernsehschaffenden der Deutschen Demokratischen Republik, 3.–5. May 1977 in Berlin*, part I, Berlin, pp. 54–7.

Kohlhaase, Wolfgang (1990), 'Es ging, in der damaligen Diktion, um den Schutz des Landes vor dem Unverstand der Filmemacher. Gespräch mit Wolfgang Kohlhaase. 29. Januar 1990', 20. Internationales Forum des Jungen Films Berlin, 40. Internationale Filmfestspiele Berlin, Info Sheet No. 18.

Kolinsky, Eva (1993), *Women in Contemporary Germany: Life, Work and Politics*, Providence and Oxford, Berg.

König, Ingelore, Dieter Wiedemann and Lothar Wolf (eds) (1995), *Zwischen Bluejeans und Blauhemden: Jugendfilm in Ost und West*, Berlin, Henschel Verlag.

König, Ingelore, Dieter Wiedemann and Lothar Wolf (eds) (1996), *Zwischen Marx und Muck: DEFA-Filme für Kinder*, Berlin, Henschel Verlag.

Kosta, Barbara (1994), *Recasting Autobiography: Women's Counterfictions in Contemporary German Literature and Film*, Ithaca and London, Cornell University Press.

Kreimeier, Klaus (1999), *The Ufa Story: A History of Germany's Greatest Film Company, 1918–1945*, translated by Robert and Rita Kimber, Berkeley and Los Angeles, University of California Press.

Kühn, Heike (1999a), 'Die Triebe des Dichters: Wir wollen auch vom Goethe-Jahr profitieren: Egon Günthers Film *Die Braut*', *Frankfurter Rundschau*, 28 May.

Kühn, Heike (1999b), 'Kein Loch im Häkelmuster, Im Papst-Stau: Andreas Dresens Film *Nachtgestalten*', *Frankfurter Allgemeine Zeitung*, 14 August.

Kuhlbrodt, Dietrich (1991), 'Im Zug nach Westen', in Helga Belach and Wolfgang Jacobsen (eds), *Kalter Krieg: 60 Filme aus Ost und West*, Berlin, Stiftung Deutsche Kinemathek, pp. 106–20.

Lemke, Udo and Peter Welz (1993), 'Ausbruch junger Frauen – gegen das Establishment', *Sächsische Zeitung*, 28 December.

Leistner, Bernd (1977), 'Zum Goethe-Bezug in der neueren DDR-Literatur', *Weimarer Beiträge*, 23:5, pp. 86–120.

Lewis, Alison (2002), 'En-gendering remembrance: memory, gender and informers for the Stasi', *New German Critique*, 86, pp. 103–34.

Liehm, Mira and Antonín Liehm (1977), *The Most Important Art: Soviet and East European Film after 1945*, Berkeley, University of California Press.

Linville, Susan E. (1998), *Feminism, Film, Fascism: Women's Auto/Biographical Film in Postwar Germany*, Austin, University of Texas Press.

Loiperdinger, Martin (2002), 'State, legislation, censorship and funding', in Tim Bergfelder, Erica Carter and Deniz Götürk (eds), *The German Cinema Book*, London, BFI Publishing, pp. 148–57.

Ludin, Malte (1996), *Wolfgang Staudte*, Reinbek, Rowohlt.

Mäde, Hans Dieter (1984), 'Stellungnahme zu *Hälfte des Lebens*', BArch Film, HV Film 107 and 107B.

Maetzig, Kurt (1966), 'Der Künstler steht nicht außerhalb des Kampfes', *Neues Deutschland*, 5 January.

Maetzig, Kurt (1990), 'Es war, als wenn ein Damoklesschwert auf die gesamte Kultur unseres Landes herunterfiel', 20. Interntationales Forum des Jungen Films Berlin 1990, 40. Internationale Filmfestspiele Berlin, Info Sheet No. 16.

Mandelkow, Karl Robert (1977), 'Wandlungen des Klassikbildes in Deutschland im Lichte gegenwärtiger Klassikkritik', in Karl Otto Conrady (ed.), *Deutsche Literatur zur Zeit der Klassik*, Suttgart, Reclam, pp. 423–39.

Mandelkow, Karl Robert (1983), 'Die literarische und kulturpolitische Bedeutung des Erbes', in Hans-Jürgen Schmitt (ed.), *Die Literatur der DDR*, vol. 11 *Hansers Sozialgeschichte der deutschen Literatur*, Munich and Vienna, Hanser, pp. 78–119.

Mann, Heinrich (1963), *Briefe an Karl Lemke 1917–1949*, Berlin, Aufbau Verlag.

Mann, Heinrich (1984), *Man of Straw*, Harmondsworth, Penguin.

Mann, Heinrich (1993) [1918], *Der Untertan*, Munich, Deutscher Taschenbuch Verlag.

Mann, Thomas (1960), *Gesammelte Werke*, 13 vols, Frankfurt/Main, S. Fischer.

Mann, Thomas (1995) [1939], *Lotte in Weimar*, Frankfurt/Main, Fischer Verlag.

Martenstein, Harald (1999), 'Berlin, wie kein Papst es kennt', *Der Tagesspiegel*, 15 February.

Mattusek, Matthias (1990), 'Honeckers Hollywood', *Der Spiegel*, 12, pp. 258–65.

McCarthy, Todd (1999), '*Jakob the Liar*', *Variety*, 13–19 September, p. 51.

McCormick, Richard (1991), *Politics of the Self: Feminism and the Postmodern in West German Literature and Film*, Princeton, NJ, Princeton University Press.

Menter, Leo (1951), 'Der Fluch des Untertans', *Die Weltbühne*, 36, pp. 1194–7.

Merkel, Ina (1994), 'Leitbilder und Lebensweisen von Frauen in der DDR', in Hartmut Kaelble, Jürgen Kocka and Hartmut Zwahr (eds), *Sozialgeschichte der DDR*, Stuttgart, Klett-Cotta, pp. 359–82.

Meurer, Hans Joachim (2000), *Cinema and National Identity in a Divided Germany 1979–1989: The Split Screen*, Lewiston, Queenston and Lampeter, The Edwin Mellen Press.

Miltschitzky, Elisabeth (1998), *Hölderlin – ein traumatisierter Dichter als Filmheld*, Marburg, Tectum Verlag.

Monk, Claire (2002), 'The British heritage-film debate revisited', in Claire Monk and Amy Sargeant (eds), *British Historical Cinema*, London and New York, Routledge, pp. 176–98.

Mückenberger, Christiane (1990), *Prädikat: Besonders schädlich*, Berlin, Henschel Verlag.

Mückenberger, Christiane (1999), 'The anti-fascist past in DEFA films', in Seán Allan and John Sandford (eds), *DEFA: East German Cinema, 1946–1992*, New York and Oxford, Berghahn Books, pp. 58–76.

Mückenberger, Christiane and Günter Jordan (1994), '*Sie sehen selbst, Sie hören selbst . . .': Die DEFA von ihren Anfängen bis 1949*, Marburg, Hitzeroth.

Mückenberger, Jochen (1965), 'Stellungnahme zu *Das Kaninchen bin ich*', BArch Film, HV Film 50.

Müller, Hermann (1951), '*Der Untertan*. Wolfgang Staudtes Film warnt vor Militarismus und Nationalismus', *Neues Deutschland*, 2 September.

Mund, Martin (1999), 'Berlin aus der Rattenperspektive. *Nachtgestalten* von Andreas Dresen', *Neues Deutschland*, 12 August.

Münkler, Herfried (1998), 'Antifaschismus und antifaschistischer Widerstand als politischer Gründungsmythos der DDR', *Aus Politik und Zeitgeschichte*, 45, pp. 16–29.

Naughton, Leonie (2002), *That Was the Wild East: Film Culture, Unification, and the 'New' Germany*, Ann Arbor, University of Michigan Press.

Navailh, Françoise (1992), 'The image of women in contemporary Soviet cinema', in Anna Lawton (ed.), *The Red Screen: Politics, Society, Art in Soviet Cinema*, London and New York, Routledge, pp. 211–30.

Netzeband, Günter (1990), 'Der Winter ist kalt: Der Aufbruch nach Stalins Tod und die Verbote von Filmen in den 60er Jahren', *Film und Fernsehen*, 8, pp. 44–8.

Niven, Bill (2002), *Facing the Past: United Germany and the Legacy of the Third Reich*, London and New York, Routledge.

O'Doherty, Paul (1997), 'Fiddler in the Ghetto: the film of Jurek Becker's novel *Jakob der Lügner*', in Jeff Morrison and Florian Krobb (eds), *Text into Image: Image into Text*, Amsterdam, Atlanta, GA, Rodopi, pp. 307–17.

Orbanz, Eva (ed.) (1977), *Wolfgang Staudte*, Berlin, Verlag Volker Spiess.

Osang, Alexander (2003), 'Zu Gast im Party-Staat', *Der Spiegel*, 37, pp. 212–22.

Otto, Hans-Rainer (1993), 'DEFA ade: Abwicklung eines Filmlandes', in Gesellschaft zum Schutz von Bürgerrecht und Menschenwürde e. V. (ed.), *Unfrieden in Deutschland. Wissenschaft und Kultur im Beitrittsgebiet*, Weissbuch, vol. 2, Berlin, Kolog Verlag, pp. 284–9.

Otto, Hans-Rainer (2001), 'Kinoalltag und Kinokultur in der DDR', in Raimund Fritz (ed.), *Der geteilte Himmel: Höhepunkte des DEFA-Kinos 1946–1992*, vol. 2, Vienna, Filmarchiv Austria, pp. 173–84.

Otto, Hans-Rainer and Daniela Berghahn (2002), tape-recorded interview, Berlin, 31 July.

Pehnert, Horst and Daniela Berghahn (2002), tape-recorded interview, Zeuthen, 17 July.

Pflaum, Hans Günther and Hans Helmut Prinzler (1992), *Film in der Bundesrepublik Deutschland*, Bonn, Inter Nationes.

Pflügl, Helmut and Raimund Fritz (eds) (2001), *Der geteilte Himmel: Höhepunkte des DEFA-Kinos 1946–1992*, 2 vols, Vienna, Filmarchiv Austria.

Pommer, Elisabeth (1999), *Kinobesuch im Lebenslauf: Eine historische und medienbiographische Studie*, Konstanz, UVK Medien.

Quett, E. (1986), *Filmografie der künstlerisch-technischen und ökonomischen Daten. DEFA-Kinospielfilme*, vols 1–4, Potsdam-Babelsberg, VEB DEFA-Studio für Spielfilme.

Ramseger, Georg (1951), 'An den Rockschößen der Macht', *Die Welt* (Berlin), 11 March.

Rauhaut, Michael (1991), 'DDR-Beatmusik zwischen Engagement und Repression', in Günter Agde (ed.), *Kahlschlag: Das 11. Plenum des ZK der SED 1965. Studien und Dokumente*, Berlin, Aufbau Taschenbuch Verlag, pp. 52–63.

Rehan, Rosemarie (1985), 'Die unterschiedlichen Gesichter des Friedrich Hölderlin', *Film und Fernsehen*, 6, pp. 10–12.

Reichelt, Klaus (1983), '*Das Fahrrad*', BArch Film, HV Film 245+C.

Reimer, Robert C. and Carol J. Reimer (1992), *Nazi-Retro Film: How German Narrative Cinema Remembers the Past*, New York, Twayne.

Rentschler, Eric (ed.) (1986), *German Film and Literature: Adaptations and Transformations*, New York and London, Methuen.

Rentschler, Eric (1987), 'Germany: the past that would not go away', in William Luht (ed.), *World Cinema since 1945*, New York, Ungar, pp. 208–51.

Rentschler, Eric (1996), *The Ministry of Illusion: Nazi Cinema and Its Afterlife*, Cambridge, MA and London, Harvard University Press.

Rentschler, Eric (2000), 'From New German Cinema to the post-Wall cinema of consensus', in Mette Hjort and Scott MacKenzie (eds), *Cinema and Nation*, London and New York, Routledge, pp. 260–77.

Richter, Erika (1994), 'Zwischen Mauerbau und Kahlschlag. 1961 bis 1965', in Ralf Schenk (ed.), *Das zweite Leben der Filmstadt Babelsberg: DEFA Spielfilme 1946–1992*, Berlin: Henschel, pp. 158–211.

Richter, Erika (2001), 'Die Verbotsfilme der DEFA', in Fritz Raimund (ed.), *Der geteilte Himmel: Höhepunkte des DEFA-Kinos 1946–1992*, vol. 2, Vienna, Film Archiv Austria, pp. 49–62.

Rinke, Andrea (2001), *From Models to Rebels and Misfits: Images of Women in DEFA 'Gegenwartsfilme' 1972–1982*, unpublished PhD dissertation, University of Reading.

Roberts, Shari (1997), 'Western meets Eastwood: genre and gender on the road', in Steven Cohan and Ina Rae Hark (eds), *The Road Movie Book*, London and New York, Routledge, pp. 45–69.

Roos, Hans-Dieter (1964), '*Der geteilte Himmel*: Konrad Wolf zeigt DEFA-Film in München', *Süddeutsche Zeitung*, 1 November.

Rosen, Philip (1984), 'History, textuality, nation: Kracauer, Burch, and some problems in the study of national cinemas', *Iris*, 2, pp. 69–84.

Rostin, Gerhard (1952), 'Die Filmkritik: *Frauenschicksale*', *Neue Filmwelt*, 7, pp. 18–19.

Roth, Markus (ed.) (2001), *Filmstatistisches Jahrbuch 2001*, Baden-Baden, Nomos Verlagsgesellschaft.

Rother, Hans-Jörg (1973), 'Konstruktion eines Irrtums', *Forum*, 7, 1 April.

Rother, Hans-Jörg (1996), 'Georg, wo ist dein Bruder Sergej? Das Tragische kann nur grotesk sein: Andreas Kleinerts Film *Neben der Zeit*', *Frankfurter Allgemeine Zeitung*, 1 October.

Rother, Hans-Jörg (1999), 'Das Spiel ist aus. *Wege in die Nacht* von Andreas Kleinert', *Film und Fernsehen*, 3:4, pp. 8–9.

Sander, Helke and R. Schlesier (1974), '*Die Legende von Paul und Paula*: eine frauenverachtende Schnulze aus der DDR', *frauen und film*, 2, 8–47.

Sandford, John (1981), *The New German Cinema*, London, Eyre Methuen.

Sandford, John (1989), 'The "Literaturverfilmungswelle"', in Keith Bullivant (ed.), *After the Death of Literature: West German Writing of the 1970s*, Oxford and New York, Berg, pp. 155–75.

Sandford, John (1995), 'The German media', in Derek Lewis and John R. P. McKenzie (eds), *The New Germany. Social, Political and Cultural Challenges of Unification*, Exeter, Exeter University Press, pp. 199–219.

Santner, Eric (1990), *Stranded Objects: Mourning, Memory, and Film in Postwar Germany*, Ithaca and London, Cornell University Press.

Schayan, Janet (2001), 'Film City Babelsberg', *Deutschland*, 4, pp. 43–7.

Schenk, Ralf (1981), '*Dein unbekannter Bruder*', BArch Film, HV Film 248B, pp. 1–20.

Schenk, Ralf (1993), 'Nicht nur "Honeckers Hollywood". Die Geschichte des DEFA-Spielfilmstudios', *Film und TV-Kameramann*, 5, pp. 78–88.

Schenk, Ralf (1994a), 'Mitten im Kalten Krieg: 1950 bis 1960', in Ralf Schenk (ed.), *Das zweite Leben der Filmstadt Babelsberg: DEFA Spielfilme 1946–1992*, Berlin, Henschel Verlag, pp. 50–157.

Schenk, Ralf (ed.) (1994b), *Das zweite Leben der Filmstadt Babelsberg: DEFA Spielfilme 1946–1992*, Berlin, Henschel Verlag.

Schenk, Ralf (ed.) (1995), 'Dokumente', *Regie: Frank Beyer*, Berlin, Edition Hentrich, pp. 107–52.

Schenk, Ralf (1996a), 'Der weite Weg ins neue Vaterland: Ostdeutsche Kinoregisseure nach dem Ende der DEFA (1)', *Film-Dienst*, 11, pp. 8–11.

Schenk, Ralf (1996b), 'Der weite Weg ins neue Vaterland: Ostdeutsche Kinoregisseure nach dem Ende der DEFA (2)', *Film-Dienst*, 12, pp. 12–15.

Schenk, Ralf and Frank Beyer (1995), 'Damit lebe ich bis heute. Frank Beyer im Gespräch mit Ralf Schenk', in Ralf Schenk (ed.), *Regie: Frank Beyer*, Berlin, Edition Hentrich, pp. 8–105.

Schenk, Ralf and Ullrich Kasten (1994), *DEFA zwischen Utopie und Wirklichkeit*, television documentary, MDR.

Schenk, Ralf and Erika Richter (eds) (2000), *apropos: Film 2000. Das Jahrbuch der DEFA-Stiftung*, Berlin, Verlag das Neue Berlin.

Schenk, Ralf and Erika Richter (eds) (2001), *apropos: Film 2001. Das Jahrbuch der DEFA-Stiftung*, Berlin, Verlag das Neue Berlin.

Schenk, Ralf and Erika Richter (eds) (2002), *apropos: Film 2002. Das Jahrbuch der DEFA-Stiftung*, Berlin, Bertz.

Schieber, Elke (1994), 'Anfang vom Ende oder Kontinuität des Argwohns. 1980–1989', in Ralf Schenk (ed.), *Das zweite Leben der Filmstadt Babelsberg: DEFA Spielfilme 1946–1992*, Berlin, Henschel, pp. 264–327.

Schieber, Elke and Daniela Berghahn (2002), tape-recorded interview, Potsdam, 18 July.

Schittly, Dagmar (2002), *Zwischen Regie und Regime: Die Filmpolitik der SED im Spiegel der DEFA-Produtionen*, Berlin, Ch. Links Verlag.

Schlenker, Wolfram (1977), *Das 'kulturelle Erbe' in der DDR: Gesellschaftliche Entwicklungen und Kulturpolitik 1945–1965*, Stuttgart, Metzler.

Schmidt, Evelyn (1993), 'Na und?', in Dietmar Hochmuth (ed.), *DEFA NOVA – nach wie vor?*, Berlin, Freunde der Deutschen Kinemathek e. V., pp. 131–4.

Schnurre, Wolfdietrich (1946), [untitled film review including review of *Die Mörder sind unter uns*] *Deutsche Film-Rundschau*, 5 November, in Stiftung Deutsche Kineamathek (eds) (1990), *In jenen Tagen: Filme der frühen Nachkriegszeit*, Berlin, Museum Deutsche Kinemathek, p. 12.

Schreiter, Herfried (1973), 'Was dieser Liebe fehlt', *Forum* 7, 1 April.

Schüler, Klaus, (1974), 'Unzerstörbar die Würde des Menschen: *Jakob der Lügner*, ein Film von Frank Beyer', *Neues Deutschland*, 25 December.

Schulz, Günter (2001), 'Die DEFA (Deutsche Film Aktiengesellschaft) 1946–1990: Fakten und Daten', in Raimund Fritz (ed.), *Der geteilte Himmel: Höhepunkte des DEFA-Kinos 1946–1992*, vol. 2, Vienna, Filmarchiv Austria, pp. 185–97.

Sebe, Günther (1982), 'Fahrrad-Diebe?', *Berliner Zeitung*, 24 July.

Seeßlen, Georg (1999), 'Außen. Nacht. Andreas Dresens *Nachtgestalten* machen Hoffnung auf ein anderes deutsches Kino', *Die Zeit*, p. 33.

Seeßlen, Georg (2000), 'Faschismus, Krieg und Holocaust im deutschen Nachkriegsfilm', in Ralf Schenk and Erika Richter (eds), *apropos: Film 2000. Das Jahrbuch der DEFA-Stiftung*, Berlin, Verlag das Neue Berlin, pp. 254–88.

Seidel, Hans-Dieter (1975), 'Kein Wunder. Thomas Manns *Lotte in Weimar* als Film aus der DDR', *Stuttgarter Zeitung*, 24 December.

Shandley, Robert A. (2001), *Rubble Films: German Cinema in the Shadow of the Third Reich*, Philadelphia, Temple University Press.

Silberman, Marc (1986), '*Semper fidelis*: Staudte's *The Subject* (1951)', in Eric Rentschler (ed.), *German Film and Literature: Adaptations and Transformations*, New York and London, Methuen, pp. 146–60.

Silberman, Marc (1995), *German Cinema: Texts in Context*, Detroit, Wayne State University Press.

Silberman, Marc (1996), 'What is German in German cinema?', *Film History* 8, pp. 297–315.

Silberman, Marc (1997), 'Problematizing the "socialist public sphere": concepts and consequences', in Marc Silberman (ed.), *What Remains? East German Culture and the Postwar Public*, American Institute for Contemporary German Studies, 2, pp. 1–37.

Soldovieri, Stephan (1998a), *Negotiating Censorship: GDR Film at the Juncture of 1965/66*, unpublished PhD dissertation, University of Wisconsin-Madison.

Soldovieri, Stephan (1998b), 'Socialists in outer space: East German film's Venusian adventure', *Film History* 10, pp. 382–98.

Spangenberg, F. (1984), 'Einschätzung des DEFA-Spielfilms *Hälfte des Lebens* zur staatlichen Zulassung am 7. 12. 1984', 6 December, BArch Film, HV Film 107.

Spoden, Madina (1990), 'Lissy (1957): Gedanken beim neuerlichen Sehen', *Beiträge zur Film- und Fernsehwissenschaft*, 31:39, pp. 27–33.

Stishova, Elena (1993), 'The mythologization of Soviet woman: *The Commissar* and other cases', in Lynne Attwood (ed.), *Red Women on the Silver Screen: Soviet Women and Cinema from the Beginning to the End of the Communist Era*, London, Pandora Press, pp. 175–85.

Stolze, Raymund (1982), 'Fragen zu einem neuen DEFA-Film. *Dein unbekannter Bruder* bleibt unter dem Anspruch der literarischen Vorlage Willi Bredels', *Junge Welt*, 14 May.

Storm, Sebastian (2000), *Strukturen der Filmfinanzierung in Deutschland*, Potsdam, Verlag für Berlin-Brandenburg.

Stott, Rosemary (2000), 'Entertained by the class enemy: cinema programming policy in the German Democratic Republic', in Diana Holmes and Alison Smith (eds), *100 Years of European Cinema: Entertainment or Ideology?*, Manchester, Manchester University Press, pp. 27–39.

Stott, Rosemary (2002), 'Continuity and change in GDR cinema programming policy 1979–1989: the case of the American science fiction import', *German Life and Letters*, 55:1, pp. 91–9.

Strauß, Annette (1996), *Frauen im deutschen Film*, Frankfurt/Main, Peter Lang.

Sturken, Marita (2000), *Thelma & Louise*, London, BFI Publishing.

Sylvester, Regine (1992), *The Forbidden Films*, Munich, Goethe Institute.

Sylvester, Regine and Hans Lohmann (eds) (1973), *Die Legende von Paul und Paula im Gespräch*, Potsdam, VEB DEFA Studio für Spielfilme [unpublished manuscript].

Taylor, Richard (1998, 2nd edn), *Film Propaganda: Soviet Russia and Nazi Germany*, London and New York, I. B. Tauris.

Taylor, Richard (2000), 'But eastward, look, the land is brighter: towards a topography of utopia in the Stalinist musical', in Diana Holmes and Alison Smith (eds), *100 Years of European Cinema: Entertainment or Ideology?*, Manchester: Manchester University Press, pp. 11–26.

Taylor, Richard, Nancy Wood, Julian Graffy and Dina Iordanova (2000), *The BFI Companion to Eastern European and Russian Cinema*, London, BFI Publishing.

Traube, Rolf (1966), 'Deutsches Schicksal: *Der geteilte Himmel*', *Deutsche Volkszeitung Düsseldorf*, 20 May.

Tumpener, Katie (2002), 'DEFA: Moving Germany into Eastern Europe', in Barton Byg and Betheny Moore (eds), *Moving Images of East Germany: Past and Future of DEFA Film*, Washington, DC, American Institute for Contemporary German Studies, pp. 85–104.

Turovskaya, Maya [aka Maja Turowskaja] (1992), 'Das jüdische Thema im sowjetischen Film der Stalin-Zeit', in Erika Gregor, Ulrich Gregor and Helma

Schleif (eds), *Jüdische Lebenswelten im Film*, Berlin, Freunde der Deutschen Kinemathek, pp. 287–9.

Turovskaya, Maya (1993a), 'Woman and the "woman question" in the USSR', in Lynne Attwood (ed.), *Red Women on the Silver Screen: Soviet Women and Cinema from the Beginning to the End of the Communist Era*, London, Pandora Press, pp. 133–40.

Turovskaya, Maya (1993b), 'Women's cinema in the USSR', in Lynne Attwood (ed.), *Red Women on the Silver Screen: Soviet Women and Cinema from the Beginning to the End of the Communist Era*, London, Pandora Press, pp. 141–8.

Ulbricht, Walter (1966), 'Brief des Genossen Walter Ulbricht an Genossen Prof. Kurt Maetzig', *Neues Deutschland*, 23 January.

Vater, Hubert (1981), 'Was ich mir von unseren Filmemachern wünsche', *Neues Deutschland*, 17 November.

Vincendeau, Ginette (ed.) (1995), *Encyclopedia of European Cinema*, London, BFI Publishing.

Vincendeau, Ginette (ed.) (2001), *Film/Literature/Heritage: A Sight and Sound Reader*, London, BFI Publishing.

Voigt, Jutta (1982), '*Dein unbekannter Bruder*', *Sonntag*, 22.

Wackwitz, Stephan (1997), *Friedrich Hölderlin*, Stuttgart, Metzler.

Walker, John Albert (1993), *Art and Artists on Screen*, Manchester, Manchester University Press.

Walsh, Michael (1996), 'National cinema, national imaginary', *Film History*, 8, pp. 5–17.

Wehrstedt, Norbert (1996), 'Indianerwestern made in GDR', in Ingelore König, Dieter Wiedemann and Lother Wolf (eds), *Zwischen Marx und Muck: DEFA-Filme für Kinder*, Berlin, Henschel Verlag, pp. 55–69.

Wehrstedt, Norbert (2001), 'Das Genre-Kino der DEFA', in Raimund Fritz (ed.), *Der geteilte Himmel: Höhepunkte des DEFA-Kinos 1946–1992*, Vienna, Filmarchiv Austria, pp. 91–106.

Weishaupt, Georg (1993), 'Immobilienprofis wollen Filmstadtgelände vergolden', *Handelsblatt*, 13 January.

Welsh, Helga A., Andreas Pickel and Dorothy Rosenberg (1997), 'East and West German identities: united and divided?', in Konrad H. Jarausch (ed.), *After Unity: Reconfiguring German Identities*, Providence and Oxford, Berghahn Books, pp. 103–36.

Wengierek, Reingard (1999), 'An der neuen Freiheit verreckt. Andreas Kleinerts Psychogramm einer verschwundenen Gesellschaft: *Wege in die Nacht*', *Die Welt*, 25 November.

Wenk, Karin (1997), 'Filmleuten wird die Tür gewiesen: Massenentlassungen im Studio Babelsberg sollen rote Zahlen tilgen', *Medium* 1, p. 20.

Wiedemann, Dieter (1991), 'Wo bleiben die Kinobesucher? Daten und Hypothesen zum Kinobesuch in der neuen deutschen Republik', in *Medien der Ex-DDR in der Wende*, Berlin, Vistas, pp. 81–99.

Wiedemann, Dieter (1996), 'Der DEFA-Kinderfilm – zwischen pädagogischem Auftrag und künstlerischem Anliegen', in Ingelore König, Dieter Wiedemann and Lothar Wolf (eds), *Zwischen Marx und Muck: DEFA-Filme für Kinder*, Berlin, Henschel Verlag, pp. 21–31.

Wiegand, Wilfried (1999), 'Ein Mann sieht rot. Filmfestspiele Cannes: Andreas Kleinerts *Wege in die Nacht* zum Auftakt der "Quinzaine" ', *Frankfurter Allgemeine Zeitung*, 15 May.

Wischnewski, Klaus (2000), 'Die zornigen jungen Männer von Babelsberg', in Günter Agde (ed.), *Kahlschlag: Das 11. Plenum des ZK der SED 1965. Studien und Dokumente*. Berlin, Aufbau Taschenbuch Verlag, pp. 355–71.

Witt, Günter (1965), 'Tagungen des Zentralkomitees: Protokoll der 11. Tagung des Zentralkomitees 15.–18. Dezember 1965', BArch SAPMO, DY30 IV/2/338. JIV 2/1-126 No. 2051.I. pp. 23–6.

Wittfoth, Antje (1987), *Dein unbekannter Bruder in der antifaschistischen Traditionslinie des DEFA-Spielfilms*, unpublished thesis, Hochschule für Film und Fernsehen der DDR Konrad Wolf, Potsdam-Babelsberg.

Wolf, Christa (1973) [1963], *Der geteilte Himmel*, Munich, Deutscher Taschenbuch Verlag.

Wolf, Christa, Gerhard Wolf, Konrad Wolf, Willi Brückner and Kurt Barthel (1963), *Der geteilte Himmel*, Potsdam-Babelsberg, VEB DEFA Studio für Spielfilme.

Wolf, Dieter (2000), *Gruppe Babelsberg: Unsere nicht gedrehten Filme*, Berlin, Verlag das Neue Berlin.

Wolf, Konrad (1964), 'Diskussionsbeitrag', in Deutsche Akademie der Künste (ed.), *Probleme des sozialistischen Realismus in der darstellenden Kunst behandelt am Beispiel des DEFA-Films Der geteilte Himmel. Referat und Diskussionsbeiträge der II. Plenartagung der Deutschen Akademie der Künste zu Berlin vom 30. Juni 1964*, Berlin, Henschel Verlag, pp. 55–61.

Wolf, Konrad and Ulrich Gregor (1966), 'Konrad Wolf, interview by Ulrich Gregor', in Ulrich Gregor (ed.), *Wie sie filmen*, Gütersloh, Sigbert Mohn Verlag, pp. 309–38.

Wolff, Franca (1999), 'Das dritte Leben der Filmstadt Babelsberg', in Jürgen Wilke (ed.), *Massenmedien und Zeitgeschichte*, Konstanz, UVK, pp. 594–605.

Wolle, Stefan (2000), 'Schatten in der Sonnenallee', *Die Welt*, 11 February.

www.defa-stiftung.de
www.ffa.de
www.goethe.de
www.icestorm.de
www.icestorm-video.com
www.progress-film.de
www.umass.edu/defa

Index